Writing for the Mass Media

Fifth Edition

James Glen Stovall
University of Alabama

Allyn and Bacon
Boston • London • Toronto • Sydney • Tokyo • Singapore

This book is dedicated to
MARTHA ELIZABETH STOVALL
1914-1982
who loved books and taught others to do the same.

Between the time Website information is gathered and
then published, it is not unusual for some sites to have
closed. Also, the transcription of URLs can result in unin-
tended typographical errors. The publisher would appreciate notification where these occur so that they may be
corrected in subsequent editions. Thank you.

Cont[ents]

Contents

Preface

Writing is one thing; writing about writing is another. Like most people, I cannot remember the first word or the first sentence that I wrote. (I am reasonably sure they were not momentous.) I can remember always being encouraged to write, however, by parents and teachers who knew the importance of writing.

I have always enjoyed and admired good writing, and I continue to be in awe of it. How Mark Twain could have created such a wonderful and timeless story as The Adventures of Tom Sawyer, how Henry David Thoreau could distill his thoughts into the crisp and biting prose of Walden, or how Red Smith could have turned out high-quality material for his sports column day after day—all of this is continually amazing to me. I frankly admit, I don't know how they did it.

And yet, here I am writing about writing. Why should I be doing this? At least three reasons occur to me immediately. I am fascinated by the process of writing. I write about it so I can understand it better. For me, it is a process of self-education. I hope that some of the insights I have discovered will rub off on those who read this book.

I am convinced that while great writing might be a gift to a chosen few, good writing is well within the reach of the rest of us. There are things we can do to improve our writing.

I care about the language and the way it is used. Those of us fortunate enough to have English as a native language have been given a mighty tool with which to work. It is powerful and dynamic. An underlying purpose of this book is to encourage the intelligent and respectful use of this tool.

This book is the product of many people, some of whom were listed in the first three editions. For this edition, I particularly want to thank David Davies, who generously contributed many of his exercises and ideas, and Matt Bunker, who wrote the chapter on media and the law despite a very short deadline.

Renée Bangs edited and proofread the final manuscript of this edition with much diligence and intelligence. She also created the index. Her suggestions proved very helpful, and her work has done much to improve this book. I am very grateful for her efforts.

Those who conducted a review of the third edition and gave me many helpful suggestions were Hong Cheng of Bradley University and John Palen of Central Michigan University.

I also want to thank Pam Doyle, who offered some extremely helpful suggestions on the Writing for Broadcast chapter for the third edition, and I continue to use those ideas; and Mark Arnold, who uses the book and has a unique perspective on what belongs in it.

My colleagues on the faculty of the Department of Journalism at the University of Alabama, especially Ed Mullins and David Sloan, have always supported me in the efforts that I have put into this book.

My wife, Sally, remains my chief critic and proofreader and always a source of encouragement. My son, Jefferson, as I write this, is a college sophomore making his own contributions to the world of writing.

This book, like the previous editions, is dedicated to my mother, Martha Elizabeth Stovall, who was my first editor.

James Glen Stovall

James Glen Stovall teaches journalism at the University of Alabama where he has been a faculty member since 1978. He received his Ph.D. from the University of Tennessee and is a former reporter and editor for several newspapers, including the *Chicago Tribune*. He also has more than five years of public relations experience. He is the author of a number of books, including *Infographics: A Journalist's Guide*, published by Allyn and Bacon in 1997.

1

Sit down & write

I have sworn upon the altar of God, eternal hostility against every form of tyranny over the mind of man. (1800)

Equal and exact justice to all men, of whatever state or persuasion, religious or political; peace, commerce, and honest friendship with all nations, entangling alliance with none. . . . Freedom of religion; freedom of the press, and freedom of person under the protection of the habeas corpus, and trial by juries impartially selected. These principles form the bright constellation which has gone before us and guided our steps through an age of revolution and reformation. (1801)

Enlighten the people generally and tyranny and oppressions of the body and mind will vanish like evil spirits at the dawn of day. (1816)

Thomas Jefferson

Introduction

Ideas carry a society forward. The ideas of freedom, independence, individualism, religion and social order first existed in the minds of men and women but are crystallized for us by great writers and thinkers such as Thomas Jefferson.

The written word is one of the most powerful forces available to humans. It has the ability to carry ideas and information, to entertain and distract, and to change the lives of individuals and nations. The person who wants to write rarely realizes the power contained in writing. Yet it is there — and available to those who have the information and ideas and who are clever and hardworking enough to learn to write well.

How do you write well?

That question defies a quick, simple answer. Yet all of us have had to consider it. We began that consideration at least by the time we were in the second grade when our teachers made us write in paragraphs. By the fourth grade, we were learning the rules of grammar and punctuation, wondering what in the world these had to do with good writing. (A lot, as it turns out, although we may be reluctant to admit it.) Outside the classroom, we were writing in our diaries or writing thank you letters to relatives or notes to friends.

At some point, we learned that whatever else writing is — fun, exciting, rewarding — it is not easy. Writing is hard work. As Red Smith, a sports writer for the New York Times, once put it, "There's nothing to writing. All you do is sit down at a typewriter and open a vein."

Smith's point is not just that writing is hard but that it requires us to give of ourselves. Writing demands total commitment, even if it is just for a few minutes. We can think of nothing else, and do nothing else, when we are writing. The first step to good writing is recognizing this essential point.

But the question still remains. How do you gather together the words that will convey the information, ideas, or feelings you want to give to the reader? How do you write well?

What is good writing?

Good writing, especially good writing for the mass media, is clear, concise, simple, and to-the-point. It transmits information, ideas and feelings to the reader clearly but without overstatement. Good writing is writing that outlines pictures of ideas that readers can fill in with their imagination.

Good writing is efficient. It uses only the minimum number of words to make its point. It doesn't waste the reader's time.

Good writing is precise. Good writers use words for their exact meaning; they do not throw words around carelessly.

Good writing is clear. It leaves no doubt or confusion in the reader's mind about its meaning.

Good writing is modest. It does not draw attention to itself. Good writing does not try to show off the intelligence of the writer. It lets the content speak for itself, and it allows readers to receive messages directly. Writing should not get in the way of what people need and want to read.

So, how do you do it? How do you write well?

The answer to these questions begins with proper preparation.

Getting ready to write

Those who would write for the mass media must understand the implications of what they do. Part of the pre-writing process is developing a sense of what it means to communicate with a mass audience. Writers should understand that they are no longer writing for individuals (an essay for an English teacher, an e-mail to a friend) but for a larger audience.

Nor are they writing for themselves. Much of the writing done in K-12 education is justified as a means of self expression for students. This kind of writing is a valuable exercise, but in the mass media environment there is relatively little room for self expression. Audiences are interested in the information and ideas that a writer presents, not in how the writer feels or in what the writer thinks. This fact drives the spare, unadorned style of writing that the media demand.

Following closely on this lack of self expression is that in most media environments, writing is a collaborative effort. That is, writers expect to be edited. Their work is not completely their own. Someone else has the power to alter and, we hope, improve it. The editing process is inseparable from the process of writing for the mass media.

Both within their own psyches and their working environments, writers for the mass

Figure 1-1

Mark Twain on using simple words

I never write "metropolis" for seven cents because I can get the same price for "city." I never write "policeman" because I can get the same money for "cop."

media need to develop an active sense of integrity about what they do. This sense of integrity acts as a regulator for their behavior, making them unwilling to accept inaccuracies or imprecision and unable to live with less than a very high standard of personal and intellectual honesty. They must understand and assimilate the ethical standards of their profession.

Would be writers for the mass media should understand enough about the process of writing to know that they can always improve, that they can always do better. They must view their craft with a dose of humility. Every writer, no matter how experienced or talented, begins with a blank page or an empty computer screen. The writer must put the words there, and no amount of experience or talent guarantees success. A good writer should always be willing to do whatever it takes to improve in the craft.

Finally, the would-be writer must do four things:

Know the tools of the trade. Just as a good carpenter knows hammers and nails, good writers must also know and understand the tools with which they work. For writers, a knowledge of the rules of grammar and spelling is mandatory. (Not all writers have to be great spellers, but they should know the rules, and they should always work with a dictionary close at hand.) Writers must know the precise meanings of words and how to use words precisely; although they do not have to use every word they know, having a variety available gives the writer extra tools to use if needed. (Most of us have a vocabulary of about 5,000 to 6,000 words; one scholar estimated that William Shakespeare knew about 30,000 words.)

Writers must not only know the language, but they must understand and be genuinely interested in it. The written word is a powerful instrument with which the lives of many people can be affected. Writers who do not understand this fact do not know what they are dealing with and will not be able to use the language effectively. Writers should also be caretakers of the language, unwilling to see English misused and abused.

Today's writers must also be computer-literate. They should understand the commands and details of a word processing program, the ways to change and move text, and the proper use of spelling checkers and other utility programs. Writing for the mass media today demands that writers use their time and equipment efficiently.

Know your subject. Writers must have a clear idea to guide them in their writing. If you do not understand thoroughly what you are writing about, your readers will not understand what you have written. Beginning writers frequently have trouble with this most basic requirement of good writing. They sometimes believe that they can "write" their way through a subject, that just getting the words down is enough. Even experienced media professionals sometimes fail to understand their topics. For example, some journalists try to write about events without properly researching the background or checking with enough sources. Some advertising copywriters try to compose ads without understanding the product or the audience to whom the ad is directed. In both cases, the writing misses the mark. It is often confusing and inefficient.

If you are writing about something you do not understand, stop writing and find out what you need to know. Ask questions of people who do know. Look things up. Or just think the subject through more thoroughly. Writing without understanding or without having your subject firmly in your own mind is like writing with a broken pencil.

Write it down. This may be the most basic point of all: You cannot be a writer unless you put words on paper or on a computer screen. People can think, talk, and agonize all night about what they would like to write. They can read and discuss; they can do research and even make notes. But no one is a writer until ideas become words, and sentences become paragraphs. At some point, the writer must sit down and write.

Writing is very hard work for most people, and few have the tenacity to stick with it. Anthony Trollope, a nineteenth-century English novelist, would begin writing at 5:30 a.m. He would write for two and a half hours, producing at least 250 words every fifteen minutes. Trollope responded to the demands of writing with a strict routine. So did Isaac Asimov, a man who wrote books on subjects ranging from Shakespeare to the Bible to science fiction. Asimov would wake up every morning at 6 a.m. and be at his typewriter writing by 7:30 a.m. He would then work until 10 p.m. He wrote more than 500 books in his lifetime.

Writing is physically difficult because it demands maintaining a stationary position and concentrating for a long time. Writing is mentally difficult because of the effort it takes to know a subject well enough and to think clearly enough to put it down on paper.

In addition, writing involves some risk. We can never be certain that we will be successful in our writing. Something happens to our beautiful thoughts when we try to confine them to complete sentences, and what happens is not always good. Writers must take the chance of failure.

Writers for the mass media have an advantage in overcoming this tendency. Their job is to write, and their circumstances force them to write. They must meet deadlines, often on a daily basis. Working effectively in the mass media environment often requires more discipline than that required of the casual or occasional writer.

Rewrite what you have written. Writing is such hard work that most of us want to do it and forget it. That's natural, but good writers don't give in to this tendency. Good writers have the discipline to reread, edit, and rewrite.

Rewriting requires that a writer reread critically. Writers cannot go through this process patting themselves on the back for all the fine phrases they have produced. Writers must constantly ask if the writing can be clearer, more precise, and more readable. And writers should have the courage to say, "This isn't what I wanted to say," or even, "This isn't very good."

Writers for the mass media often work in circumstances that dictate that someone else read what they have written and make judgments about it. Having another person read what you have written and then give you an honest evaluation of it usually makes for better writing. But writers for the mass media are also at a disadvantage because their deadline pressures often prevent thorough rereading and rewriting.

Figure 1-2

Rewriting and editing

An early draft of text from Chapter 1 is at the right. Note how the editing process changed and improved the final copy.

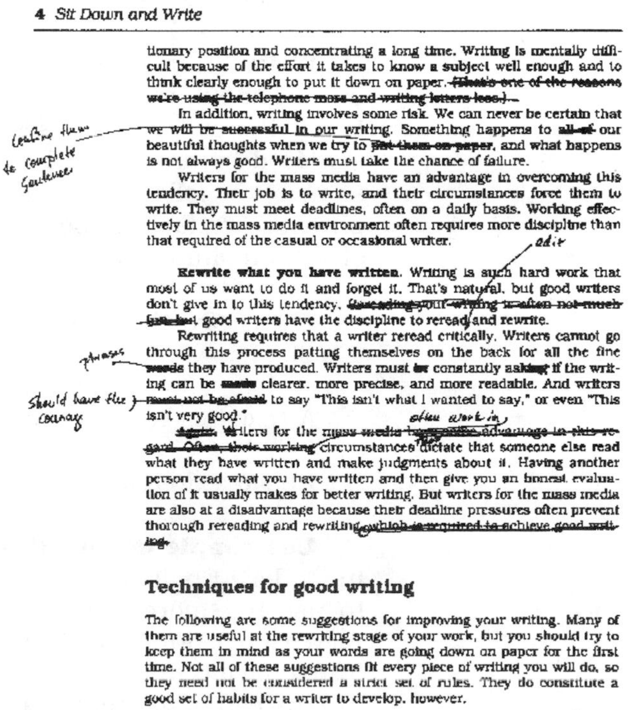

Figure 1-3

Isaac Asimov on writing

I try only to write clearly, and I have the very good fortune to think clearly so that the writing comes out as I think, in satisfactory shape.

Techniques for good writing

The following are some suggestions for improving your writing. Many of them are useful at the rewriting stage of your work, but you should try to keep them in mind as your words are going down on paper or on the computer screen for the first time. Not all of these suggestions fit every piece of writing you will do, so they need not be considered a strict set of rules. They do constitute a good set of habits for a writer to develop, however.

Write simply. This is a thought you'll see repeatedly in this book. The key to clarity is simplicity. A clear, simple writing style is not the exclusive possession of a few gifted writers. It can be achieved by students who are just beginning a writing career if some of the following suggestions are kept in mind. The following phrases are famous because they convey powerful messages in clear and simple language:

These are the times that try men's souls. (Thomas Paine, 1776)

A rose is a rose is a rose is a rose. (Gertrude Stein, 1913)

I have a dream. (Martin Luther King Jr., 1963)

Use simple words. "It is a general truth," Henry Fowler wrote in Modern English Usage, "that short words are not only handier to use but more powerful in effect; extra syllables reduce, not increase, vigour." Fowler was talking about the modern tendency to use facilitate instead of ease, numerous instead of many, utilize instead of use, etc. Many people try to use big or complicated words, thinking it will impress the reader. It doesn't; it has the opposite effect. Benjamin Franklin once wrote, "To write clearly, not only the most expressive, but the plainest words should be chosen."

Use simple sentences. Not every sentence you write should be in the simple sentence format (subject-predicate or subject-verb-object), but the simple sentence is a good tool for cleaning up muddy writing. For example, take the following sentence (which appeared in a large daily newspaper): "She was shot through the right lung after confronting a woman married to her ex-husband inside the Food World store on Bankhead Highway shortly before 1 p.m." The confusion could be lessened by breaking this one sentence into three simple sentences: "She was in the Food World store on Bankhead Highway shortly before 1 p.m. She confronted a woman married to her ex-husband. She was shot through the right lung."

Don't use one word more than is necessary. Almost every writer uses too many words on occasion. Even the best writers need to be edited. Go back a couple of paragraphs and look at the Fowler quote; it has at least two unnecessary words. Writers should use the minimum number of words necessary to express their ideas and information.

Simple, straightforward prose is mandatory for writing for the mass media. It has no substitute, and its absence will not be excused by readers or listeners.

A first cousin to simplicity is brevity. Writers should never use one more word than is necessary in their writing. They should be on the lookout for words, phrases, and sentences that do not add substantially to the content of what they are writing. They should also guard against those fancy phrases that draw attention to the writing and the writer — and take away from the content.

Eliminate jargon, clichés, and "bureaucratese." Jargon is the technical language that is used in specialized fields or among a small group of people. Scientists, sportswriters, and even students have their own jargon. Good writers, especially those for the mass media, should use words and phrases commonly understood by most people. It makes no sense to cut people off from receiving your ideas by using language that they cannot understand.

Clichés are overused words and phrases. They are phrases that have ceased to be meaningful and have become trite and tiresome. For example, "dire straits," "he's got his act together," "it's a small world," "par for the course," "you don't want to go there" and "vast wasteland" have been used so much that they have lost their original luster. All of us have our favorite clichés; the trick is not to use them.

Bureaucratese is a general name for a serious misuse of the language. In order to make themselves or what they write sound more important, many people try to lather their writing with unnecessary and imprecise phrasing. A speechwriter once handed President Franklin Roosevelt a draft of a speech with the following sentence: "We are endeavoring to construct a more inclusive society." Roosevelt changed it to say: "We are going to make a country in which no one is left out." Roosevelt's simple words carry far more weight than those of his speechwriter.

Once, a football coach at a major state university was on a recruiting trip and heard over the radio that he had been fired. The next day, the athletic director at the school issued the following statement: "I regret the premature publication of the decision before appropriate notification could be made to all parties involved." The athletic director would not have sounded like such a fool if he had simply said, "I'm sorry we didn't get to tell him before the story got out."

Use familiar words rather than unfamiliar words or foreign phrases. William F. Buckley, the conservative newspaper columnist, tries to include at least one or two words that will send his readers scurrying to a dictionary. Readers expect this of Buckley and seem to accept it. Buckley is the exception, however. There are times when a writer must use a word that is not known by all of a mass audience, but those times are rare. Writers should not try to educate the masses by introducing them to new words. Such writing slows the reader down; it makes the reader think about the writing rather than the content; and it eventually drives the reader away.

Foreign phrases often have the same effect. They add little to the content and are often irritating to the reader. At times they may even be insulting, particularly when the writer does not bother to translate them.

Vary sentence type and length. There are four kinds of sentence structures: simple, complex, compound, and compound-complex. Using only one kind of sentence is boring. A good variety of types and lengths of sentences gives pace to writing. It allows the reader's mind to "breathe," to take in ideas and information in small doses.

Such variation also helps the writer. Writers often get so involved in what they are writing that they have trouble expressing their ideas clearly. They try to pack too much into one sentence or one paragraph. Breaking down complex and compound sentences into simple sentences, and then putting these sentences back into a variety of forms, often promotes clarity in writing.

One thing writers should not overuse is the inverted sentence. A good example of this kind of sentence is the previous sentence—and this sentence. The inverted sentence is not a good idea in writing for the mass media. Writers want to get ideas and information to readers quickly and efficiently.

Nouns and verbs are the strongest words in the language. Sentences should be built around nouns and verbs; adjectives and adverbs, when they are used, should support the nouns and verbs. Relying on adjectives and adverbs, particularly in writing for the mass media, is a mistake.

Verbs are the most important words that a writer will use. A good verb denotes action; a better verb denotes action and description. While adjectives and adverbs modify (that is, they limit), verbs expand the writing. They get the reader involved in the writing as no other part of speech does.

A good writer pays close attention to the verbs that he or she uses.

Transitions tie together what you have written. Readers should be able to read through a piece of writing without stops or surprises. Introducing a new idea or piece of information without adequately tying it to other parts of a story is one way to stop a reader cold.

Writing for the mass media

Good writing can go anywhere. The good English theme has much in common with the good news story or the good letter to Mom or the informative label on a bottle of aspirin. All of these pieces of writing have different purposes and different audiences, and they express different ideas. But good writing is good writing.

Writing for the mass media differs from other forms of writing in several aspects:

Subject matter. Writers for the mass media must take on a wide variety of subjects, including news stories, feature stories, advertisements, letters, editorials, and so on.

Purpose. Writing for the mass media has three major purposes: to inform, entertain, and persuade.

Audience. Mass media writing is often directed to a wide audience, and this fact dictates not only the subject matter but the way in which something is written.

Circumstances of the writing. Writing for the mass media often takes place in the presence of others who are doing the same thing. The writing is frequently done under deadline pressure, and many times several people will have a hand in writing and editing a particular item for the mass media.

Becoming a professional

Much of what has been discussed in this chapter has revolved around the qualities and skills necessary to be a professional writer. Those who want to make a career of writing in a media environment have to develop these personal and professional qualities and must hone their skills.

One quality that we have not discussed yet is versatility. Rarely do media professionals stay with their first job. Even more rarely does their career involve just one type of writing. Most professionals will have a variety of jobs throughout their career, and they will be called upon to write in various forms and structures.

Developing a professional agility will be a valuable asset to anyone pursuing a writing career.

This book, in fact, is based on the assumption that all writers need to learn a variety of forms to survive in the mass media. Here students will learn some of the basic principles of good writing — techniques that we have already reviewed in this chapter. Students will read about the importance of using standard English well and the vital role that a stylebook plays in their daily work. They will also be introduced to some of the basic forms of writing.

One of the most important is the inverted pyramid structure of news writing. This structure demands that information be presented in order of its importance rather than in chronological order. The writing must also conform to certain journalistic conventions, such as attribution and proper identification of persons mentioned in the story.

Broadcast writing — writing that is written to be read aloud and hear — demands a different structure, dramatic unity, that emphasizes simplicity and efficiency.

Writing advertising copy requires that writers have a facility with the language so they can use information for persuasive effects.

Writing for public relations calls for wide versatility on the part of practitioners. In most public relations jobs, writers must use the inverted pyramid, good letter writing structures, and broadcast and advertising techniques.

Writing for the World Wide Web combines all of these structures, techniques, and forms. Still, there is a type of writing on the Web that is almost peculiarly its own. That type of writing has its base in a concept called hypertext. Prose writing is linear — that is, you begin at the beginning and read through to the end. Hypertext is non-linear. The text is broken into bits and structured so that a reader can begin at any number of points and decide which sequence suits his or her purposes. These bits of writing should relate to the whole, but they also need to stand by themselves within the context of the entire article or web site. They are generally hierarchical; that is, they go from the general to the specific. But because the Web offers readers the opportunity to move quickly from one item to another, the writer must also look for opportunities to "link" parts of the writing with other parts to make it easier for the reader to move around. This means the writer needs to anticipate how the reader might navigate within a Web site.

Another demand on writers using the hypertext structure is the ability to write headlines, subheads, and summaries. Writing headlines and subheads for the Web is far less restrictive than writing them for newspapers or magazines in terms of making them fit into a certain space. Web writers are likely to have many more options and fewer typographical rules than the headline writer for newspapers. But their abilities to summarize, whether in headline, subhead or summary form, will be severely tested, just as they are in traditional media. Summaries demand precise and concise use of the language. They also demand that the writer understand the material being summarized so well that he

Figure 1-4

Leonardo da Vinci's journal

Leonardo da Vinci could observe, write and draw, and he integrated these talents into his journal entries. He was not bound by column rules or other restrictions of the printing press.

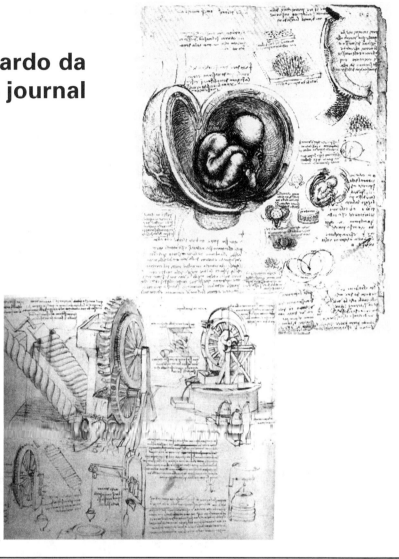

or she can do it accurately. Summarizing is a skill that is essential to the web writer. (All of these and other concepts of writing for the Web will be covered in Chapter 6.)

Text and images

The advent of the World Wide Web has highlighted another phenomenon that writers should understand: the integration of graphics and text. The best publications, broadcasts, and Web sites are built around strong graphic as well as textual elements. Graphics are a vital part of mass communication, and people who are involved in any mass medium must be fluent in the use of both graphics and text.

The integration of graphics and text is an interesting phenomenon because it simulates in some ways written communication before the printing press was invented around 1455. Writers often wrote freely using both graphics and text to transmit their ideas and information. Leonardo da Vinci, one of the greatest intellects and most talented people in the history of western civilization, used both text and drawings for his scientific journals. Many of his writings were texts that were built around a variety of pictures.

The advent of the printing press signaled a more distinct delineation of graphics from text. For the printing press, the emphasis was on text. Type could be handled easily and quickly on the press; that was the basis of its profound impact on human beings. But graphics and illustrations were left behind. The press could certainly handle such items, but they were a lot more trouble to produce than simple type.

The development of the technology to produce graphics lagged far behind, and it was not until the late 19th century that it began to catch up. During the last half of the 19th century, publishers developed techniques that could get illustration into print along with type. The half-toning process that allows pictures to be printed was also part of this technological development.

Still, graphics were not fully integrated with text. Possibly this was due to the legacy of 400 years of printing text. By necessity, text was important in the printing press. Graphics were extra, not as important. We still live with that legacy today. Almost every non-fiction book that you buy will contain pictures, but those pictures are grouped onto a few pages in the middle of the book. Technically, there is no reason why this should happen. A picture could be placed in a part of the book where the text refers to it. But our habit of separating text and graphics lives on.

By the latter quarter of the 20th century, news publications were beginning to see the value of graphics and illustrations in presenting content to the reader. Graphics could say what text could not, and they could show what pictures could not. Newspapers such as the Chicago Tribune made major investments in producing good graphics and integrating them with text material. The explosion of USA Today onto the world of journalism in 1982 took the use of graphics for journalistic purposes to a new level. Journalists began learning the uses and conventions of presenting data in a graphic format (see Chapter 5 for a full discussion of this subject), and they quickly began to see the value of graphics in presenting information quickly and efficiently.

Figure 1-5

19th century illustration

Harper's Magazine, shown above, was typical of the way illustration was integrated with text for a mass readership publication in the late 19th century.

The World Wide Web, ironically, brings us one step closer to the techniques of the 15th century writer, who used both text and graphics in a sometimes seamless way. Leonardo da Vinci's wide range of talents — and his willingness to make full use of them — gives us a fitting metaphor for meeting the challenges of communicating in the 21st century. Today's writer will have to know more than just how to communicate with text. The writer will need to know the conventions and uses of graphic forms and must constantly be on the alert for better ways to present information and ideas. The writer of the 21st century must have a wide range of understanding about how to communicate and how to use the tools — all of the tools — of communication.

And finally . . .

With the proper study and practice, anyone can become a better writer. Writing is not simply an inherent talent that some people have and others do not. There are steps that each of us can take to improve our writing, and this book will examine some of those steps and help you put them into practice.

Writing is a process. That is, the rules, techniques, and suggestions in this book must be mixed in with the individual's style, thoughts, and methods, and with the subject and form of the writing. They all should work together to produce writing that is good. The suggestions made in this book about achieving good writing are meant to help this process work.

Writing requires discipline. Most people give up writing as soon as they can because it is such hard work. It is physically, mentally, and emotionally demanding. The person who commits to writing must marshal all of his or her resources for the task.

Writing is building. Good writing doesn't happen all at once. It is formed, word by word, sentence by sentence, thought by thought. The writing process is often slow, tedious, and frustrating. But the product of this process-good writing-is well worth the effort.

Finally, reading about good writing is only the first step to learning about good writing. Reading good writing is the next step. If you are interested in learning to write well, in any form, you should read as much as possible-newspapers, magazines, books, and anything else you can get your hands on. Then there is the writing itself. This chapter tells you to "sit down and write." That is the only way to become a good writer.

Points for consideration and discussion

1. The author makes several strong points about what is and is not good writing. Did you find anything surprising or unusual about them? Do you agree with what he says about good writing?

2. Many teachers and philosophers believe the following: "Writing is thinking." How do you react to this statement?

3. Do you think that writing is becoming more visual, as the author asserts? Look at the pages from the journal of Leonard da Vinci on page 11. One of these pages is some notes he made about the engineering of water-lifting equipment. With the advent of the Internet, are we about to embark on an age of writing that looks like this?

4. Look up a passage from a book that you have read recently. What characteristics of good writing discussed in this chapter are exemplified in that passage? What characteristics of good writing are not present?

5. In the passage that you selected, make a list of the verbs. How many of them are linking verbs ("to be" verbs, such as is, was, were, etc.)? How many of them are active verbs? How many are passive?

6. The author says, "Good writing is good writing," no matter what form it's in. What does he mean by that? Do you agree?

Further reading

Brian S. Brooks, James L. Pinson, Jean Gaddy-Wilson, Working with Words. New York: Bedford/St. Martin's Press, 4th ed., 1999.

Kristie Bunton, Thomas B. Connery, Stacey F. Kanihan, Mark Neuzil, David Nimmer, Writing Across the Media, Boston/New York: Bedford/St. Martin's, 1999.

H. W. Fowler, A Dictionary of Modern English Usage, (second edition, revised by Sir Ernest Gowers) Oxford: Oxford University Press, 1991.

William Safire and Leonard Safir, Good Advice on Writing: Writers Past and Present on How to Write Well, New York: Simon and Schuster, 1992.

William K. Zinsser. On Writing Well, 6th ed., New York: HarperCollins, 1998.

Chapter 1   Sit down & write

Exercises

• *The following section contains a variety of beginning writing exercises. You should follow your instructor's directions in completing them.*

Autobiography

Write a 350-word summary of your life. Tell the most important things that have happened to you. Also talk about the things that interest you the most.

Letter to Mom

Write a letter to your mother, father, or some other close relative. The main part of your letter should be about the course that requires this assignment. Include some information about the professor for the course, what the course is about, the procedures for the class, the grading and attendance policies, and anything else you think is important. You will also want to give the name of your lab instructor. The letter should be at least 250 words long.

Describe your neighbor

Describe the person sitting nearest to you. Be specific. Give the reader a lot of details about the person's physical appearance, including hair and eye color, height, shape of the face, the kind of clothes the person is wearing, and so on. Write at least 200 words.

An incident

Write about something that happened to you in the last week. It could be something dramatic, such as being in an automobile accident or meeting a famous person, or something common such as eating a meal or taking a ride on a bus. You should include some dialogue (quoting someone directly) in the description of this incident. Write 250 words.

Action

Describe a person or a group of people doing something. It could be something like a couple of carpenters building a part of a house or your roommate trying to type a paper. Be sure to focus on the physical activity and on how people are doing it. Don't try to describe how the people feel or what they may think about what they are doing. Simply write about what you can see and hear. Write 350 words.

Autobiography-1

Write a 200-word autobiography in the third person (do not use "I," "me," or any other first person pronoun. Also, use only simple sentences.

Here's an example of how it might begin:

John Smith was born on April 15, 1983, in Decatur, Ill. He is the son of Adele and Wayne Smith. John's parents moved to Chicago when he was three years old . . .

Autobiography-2

Write a 300-word autobiography, but confine it to a single aspect of your life. As in the exercise above, write in the third person.

Select the aspect of your life you want to write about. Think about all of the different ways that aspect of your life affects you. Think also about how it began and what it means to you now. Construct your essay around the points that you think are the most important.

In your first sentence, let the reader know immediately what you are writing about, and try to use an active, descriptive verb.

Here's an example:

Playing the piano always lifts the spirits of John Smith . . . .

There is no doubt about what the subject of this essay is.

Biography

Write a 300-word biography of one of your classmates, but as in the previous exercise, confine it to a single aspect of his or her life.

Everything you write in this essay should be accurate, so you will have to talk with that person.

Make sure you spell that person's name correctly and accurately record all of the details you will include in your essay.

Remember that you are writing about only one aspect of that person's life, not a complete biography. Leave out information that does not pertain directly to the specific subject about which you are writing.

As with the previous exercise, let the reader know immediately what your subject is and try to use a strong, active verb in the first sentence.

Instructions–1

Tell step-by-step how to do something. For example, tell how to change the oil in a car, use a tape recorder, or build a fire. Use simple terms and simple sentences so that anyone who can read could understand it. The following is an example of such a set of directions.

In order to drive a nail into a piece of wood, follow the steps below:
1. Be sure the wood is on a solid surface.
2. Check the nail you are using to make sure it is straight; if it is bent, discard it.
3. Hold the pointed end of the nail against the wood with the thumb and the first finger.
Etc.

The activity that you describe should have at least seven steps.

Instructions–2

Describe the procedure for tying a shoelace in 100 or fewer words. You might approach the assignment this way: Write the procedure without regard to how many words you are using. Once you have finished the first draft, edit it to take out as many words as possible but still have it make sense. What does this tell you about the way you write?

Building

Describe the building in which this class is being held. Don't go outside and look at it but describe it from what you remember. Write at least 150 words.

Rewriting

Rewrite the letter below using simpler language. Make sure that you include all of the information contained in the original letter.

Dear Stockholder:

In accordance with company policies and the federal law, this letter is to inform you of the general annual meeting of the stockholders of this company which will be held on the 30th day of March of this year. The place of the meeting will be in the ballroom of the Waldorf Hotel, which is located at 323 Lexington Avenue, in New York. The beginning time of the meeting will be at nine o'clock in the morning on the 30th of March.

The agenda for this meeting includes a number of items and actions of great import to the company and its stockholders. The election of officers for the company's board of directors will take place beginning at approximately half past ten o'clock. This election follows the annual reports on the company's activities and financial position which will be presented by the president of the company and the chairman of the board of directors. Other items on the agenda include discussions of the company's operations in the foreign arena and the possibilities for investments in new areas of technology. Time will also be appropriated for discussions of general concerns of stockholders and for the answering of questions from stockholders directed to the company's officers. It is the sincere wish of the company's board of directors and officers that you will be able to attend this most important and hopefully informative meeting. The input of the company's stockholders is an important part of this company's operation and planning for the future.

Sincerely,
The Company President

2

Basic tools of writing

Introduction

At some point during the last half of the 20th century, the study of grammar and punctuation - and the learning and practice of the rules of the language — fell out of favor in the nation's school systems. Grammar is sometimes difficult and not always very interesting. It came to be symbolized by aging, authoritarian schoolmarms all too willing to whack a terrorized child across the knuckles if a comma was misplaced.

That image obscured for students the deeply interesting subject of the language itself — how it developed, how it is used and how it changes.

More insidious than this bad image, however, is that some educators began to believe that grammar and punctuation were unimportant, or even an hindrance to writing. Students should be free to express themselves, the thinking went, without being bound by rules of grammar and punctuation. To learn these rules was a waste of the student's precious time and to require that they be applied to writing was stifling to a student's emerging creativity.

Artistically, educationally, and practically, this thinking is nonsense.

Writing is impossible in any form unless you know how to use the tools of writing. These tools are all the things a writer can use to present information and ideas — rules of grammar and punctuation, precise meanings for words, and proper spelling. The writer who knows these tools can write with authority. That writer can take on the forms of writing demanded by the mass media.

English is a basic tool of the writer. Like any other worker, the writer must know the tools of the trade — their possibilities as well as their limitations. Knowing when these tools can be properly used is vital. The writer who cannot effectively use the English language is like a carpenter who cannot saw a straight line. The products of such a writer or carpenter will not inspire confidence; nor will they be items people want to purchase.

Unlike the carpenter's hammer or saw, however, the English language is an extremely complex tool. It has many nuances and subtleties. People spend years mastering English. There are many rules for its usage and many arguments about the propriety of some of these rules.

One thing that makes English so complex is its dynamic nature. English is the closest thing the world has to an international language. It is spoken and understood by more than 300 million people in nearly every part of the globe. But no central authority governs its use. Consequently, the language is always changing. New words and expressions come into use as others fade. Old words take on new meanings. English is mixed with other languages. Spelling rules shift with differing usage. Humans are constantly discovering new phenomena needing description in the language. All this makes English a difficult but exciting tool.

Using the language effectively requires knowing the basic rules and conventions. Writers should know thoroughly the eight basic parts of speech (nouns, verbs, adjectives, adverbs, pronouns, conjunctions, interjections, and prepositions), and the basic unit of the English usage (the sentence) and its two parts (subject and predicate). They should not only have an eye for the language, but they should also have an ear for it. Writers should know when things that are technically correct sound wrong. Beyond that, they should be able to recognize — and hear — the confusing phrase, the unclear sentence, and the absence of transition. They must be able to spot the confusion and illogic that are the harbingers of misinformation, inaccuracy, and a failure to communicate. Like the carpenter, the writer should use the language to saw a straight line to the reader.

That straight line is one of the chief goals of the writer for the mass media. The writer who does not use English correctly will annoy the reader and call a publication's credibility into question. A misspelled word will not destroy a publication, and an agreement error will not inspire calls for a repeal of the First Amendment, but too many such mistakes will convince the reader that a publication is not worth his or her time and money.

Grammar

Grammar is a system of rules that defines the use of the language. Because English is complex and widely-used, its grammar rules are involved, complex, sometimes contradictory, and ever-changing. Yet all of us manage to learn some form of grammar, and we tend to use the language with a consistency that conforms to the rules that we have learned.

English is too dynamic a language to say that the rules of grammar are absolute. The best we can say is that grammar rules are commonly accepted or that they are imposed — with varying degrees of effectiveness — by some authority such as an English teacher or a grammar book.

Many writers for the mass media take an active interest in the rules of grammar and language usage. They often join in debates about how a word should be spelled or which syntax is proper. So they should. Writers need to have an interest in the language and how it is used. But that interest should be secondary to the more important goal of using the language so that it will convey the information and ideas that a writer must convey. Grammar, then, is a tool that allows the writer to communicate with an audience.

The purpose of this section is not to explain all grammar rules but to lay the basis for an understanding of how the language is commonly used and to point out some problems that often plague those beginning to write for the mass media. We begin our look at language with one of its basic units, the sentence.

Figure 2-1

Glossary of grammar terms

- **Subject** - A noun or noun substitute about which something is asserted or asked in the predicate.
  John is a good student.
  They were happy to hear the news.

- **Verb** - Denotes action, occurrence, or existence.
  Run, jump, did, is, were, etc.

- **Verbals:**
  Gerund - A verbal that ends in -ing and functions as a noun.
  Borrowing money is a mistake.
  Drinking before driving is dangerous.
  Participle - A verb form that may function as part of a verb phrase (was laughing, had finished) or as a modifier (a finished product; the players, laughing at their mistakes.....)
  Infinitive - Verbal used primarily as a noun, usually in present tense and usually preceded by the word to.
  Hal wanted to *open* the present.
  She failed to *stop* on time.

- **Pronoun** - Takes the place of nouns. (he, she, it, we, they, etc.)

- **Relative pronoun** - Refers to a noun elsewhere in the sentence.

Leslie is the *one* who likes to bowl.
The board delayed *its* vote.

- **Antecedent** - A word or word group a pronoun refers to.
  Like their trainers, animals can be polite or rude.
  Reversing its earlier position, the board approved the project.

- **Agreement** - Correspondence in number or person of a subject and verb.
  (In easy tasks, boys ask, the woman did it herself, the man did it himself)

- **Clause** - A sequence of related words within a sentence.
  Essential or restrictive clause - Limits the word referred to by imposing conditions.
  Every drug *condemned by doctors* should be removed from the market.
  All children *under 12 years of age* eat free.
  Non-essential or non-restrictive clause - Not necessary to the meaning of the sentence, can be omitted.
  My best friend, *John*, understands me.
  The teacher, *Mrs. Smith*, gave extra credit.
  Independent clause - A clause which can stand alone in its meaning. An independent clause often functions as the

main clause in the sentence.
I want to go to Tut's Place because I am getting hungry.
Dependent clause - A clause which serves as an adverb, an adjective or a noun in the sentence. A dependent clause cannot stand alone and maintain its full meaning.
I want to go to Tut's Place *because I am getting hungry.*

- **Inverted sentence** - One in which the usual or expected word order is changed.
  At the head of the class stands the professor.

- **Coordinating conjunction** - One of the seven connectives used to connect and relate words and word groups of equal grammatical rank *(and, but, for, or, nor, so, yet).*

- **Modifier** - A word or word group that describes, limits, or modifies another.
  The blue sky ...
  He studied vigorously ...
  The doorway at the bottom of the stairs ...

- **Parallelism** - Using grammatically equal and corresponding words or word groups together in a sentence or paragraph.
  Wrong: She like running, cooking and to swim.
  Correct: She likes running, cooking and swimming.

Sentences. A sentence is a group of words that contain a subject and a verb, and express a complete thought. "John ran to the store" is a complete sentence; it has a subject, John, and a verb, ran, and it expresses a complete thought. "After the rain stopped" is not a complete sentence; it does have a subject and a verb, but it does not express a complete thought. A phrase like "after the rain stopped" is called a dependent clause; it contains a subject and a verb but cannot stand alone. "John ran to the store" is an independent clause.

Structurally, there are four kinds of sentences: simple, complex, compound, and compound-complex. A simple sentence is one that has an independent clause and no dependent clauses, such as:

John ran to the store.

A complex sentence is one which has an independent clause and a dependent clause.

This is a complex sentence because it contains one of each kind of clause. A compound sentence is a sentence that contains two independent clauses, and these clauses should be separated by a comma and a coordinating conjunction.

John ran to the store, but he walked back.

| Independent clause | | Independent clause |

Comma and
coordinating conjunction

The sentence above is a compound sentence because it contains two independent clauses; they are separated by a comma and the coordinating conjunction "but." Another common coordinating conjunction is "and." Sometimes a semicolon substitutes for the conjunction.

A compound-complex sentence is a sentence that contains two independent clauses and a dependent clause. The independent clauses should be separated by a comma and a coordinating conjunction, such as in the following sentence:

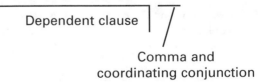

Here's a tip for recognizing the four different kinds of sentences. Look for the comma and coordinating conjunction. If a sentence does not have these two elements together, it is either a simple or a complex sentence. Then you need to look for a dependent clause. If there is one, it is a complex sentence; if not, it is a simple sentence. If the sentence does have a comma and coordinating conjunction together, it is either a compound or a compound-complex sentence. Again you need to look for the dependent clause. If it is there, the sentence is compound-complex; if it is not there, the sentence is a compound sentence.

In addition to the structural classification, sentences may also be classified by their content as declarative, interrogative, imperative, and exclamatory. A declarative sentence is one which makes a statement. This is the most common type of sentence. An interrogative sentence is one which asks a question, and it is usually ended by a question mark (?). An imperative sentence is a command; it is usually ended by a period, but it may also end with an exclamation mark (!). An exclamatory sentence expresses some strong emotion (excitement, joy, fear, etc.) and usually ends with an exclamation mark.

Sentence fragments. Earlier we referred to sentences as groups of words that express a complete thought. Sometimes, someone will write a group of words which does not express a complete thought. That is a sentence fragment. There are some situations in writing where using a sentence fragment may be appropriate. Generally writers for the mass media should write in complete sentences.

Parts of speech. English contains eight parts of speech: nouns, pronouns, adjectives, adverbs, verbs, conjunctions, prepositions, and interjections. You should be able to recognize any of those in any sentence.

Nouns are the names of objects or concepts.

Pronouns are substitutes for nouns, and they are among the most confusing parts of speech. There are two ways of looking at pronouns. One way is to decide what "person" they refer to; they may be first-, second-, or third-person pronouns. Another way of looking at pronouns is examining a pronoun's case: subjective, objective, or possessive. Subjective case means that the pronoun can be used as the subject of a sentence; objective case means that it can be used as the object of a verb or a preposition; possessive case means that the pronoun is used as a modifier for a noun and indicates possession.

Adjectives modify nouns; that is, they give some description to the noun or define it in some way.

Adverbs modify verbs, but they may also modify adjectives or other adverbs. Many adverbs end in -ly.

Verbs express action or state of being. We usually refer to verbs as being in a particular tense — or the time of the action. There are three basic tenses: past, present, and future. You should be able to recognize the tense of any verb in any sentence.

Conjunctions connect words, phrases, and clauses together. The most commonly used conjunctions are and, but, so, or, and nor.

Figure 2-2

Ernest Hemingway on punctuation

My attitude toward punctuation is that it ought to be as conventional as possible. The game of golf would lose a good deal if croquet mallets and billiard cues were allowed on the putting green. You ought to be able to show that you can do it a good deal better than anyone else with the regular tools before you have license to bring in your own improvements.

Prepositions are words which go with nouns or pronouns to modify other nouns, pronouns, or verbs. Some common prepositions are in, at, from, to, on, and with.

Interjections are words that express strong emotion (wow!). When they are inserted into sentences, they should be set off by commas.

Most of the time, most people use the language correctly. That includes students who are learning to write for the mass media. However, there are some areas of grammar that continue to give students problems. A few of these are discussed in the following sections.

Agreement. Agreement refers to singular or plural references. A singular subject takes a singular verb; plural subjects take plural verbs. In the sentence "The clock strikes on the hour," the subject is clock. A singular noun, clock, takes the singular verb, strikes. However, if the sentence were "The clocks strike on the hour," the plural subject, clocks, would take the plural verb, strike. All that is fairly simple, but what about a sentence like this: "The consent of both sets of parents are needed for a juvenile marriage." The subject and verb in this sentence are not in agreement. Consent is the subject, not sets or parents. Consequently, the verb should be is, not are.

Agreement is also a problem when you are using pronouns to refer to nouns. These nouns are called antecedents, and pronouns should always agree with their antecedents. In the sentence "The boys believed they could win," the antecedent boys agrees in number with the pronoun they. Often, however, the following mistake is made: "The team believed they could win." The antecedent team is a singular noun, and its pronoun should also be singular. The sentence should read, "The team believed it could win."

Active and passive voice. One of the most important grammatical tools that writers for the mass media should learn is recognition of the active and passive voice. Active and passive voice refer to the way in which verbs are used. If a verb is used in the active voice, the emphasis is on the subject as the doer or perpetrator of the action. Passive voice throws the action onto the object and often obscures the perpetrator of the action. It is formed by putting a helping verb such as "is" or "was" in front of the past tense of the verb. Look at the following examples:

Active: John throws the ball.
Passive: The ball is thrown by John.

Active: The president sent the legislation to Congress.
Passive: The legislation was sent to Congress by the president.

Active: The governor decided to veto the bill.
Passive: It was decided by the governor to veto the bill.

Generally, writers for the mass media try to use the active rather than the passive voice. The active voice is more direct and livelier. It is less cumbersome than the passive voice and gets the reader into the action of the words more quickly. When you edit your writing and find that you have written in the passive voice, you should ask, "Would this sentence be better if the verb were in the active voice?" Very often the answer will be yes.

Sometimes the answer will be no. When changing passive voice to active voice puts the wrong emphasis on the sentence, the passive voice should be used. Consider the following sentence, "The victims were rushed to a hospital by an ambulance." If we practiced strict adherence to the active voice, we would change that sentence to read, "An ambulance rushed the victims to a hospital." The important part of that sentence is the victims, not the ambulance. So, the use of the passive voice can occasionally be justified.

Take a look at the third set of examples above. In the passive voice sentence, the indefinite pronoun it is used with the passive voice verb. This usage is particularly insidious because it obscures those responsible for an action. This construction, it with a passive voice verb, is not acceptable in writing for the mass media.

Dangling participles. A participial phrase at the beginning of a sentence should modify the sentence's subject and should be separated from it by a comma. One would not write, "After driving from Georgia to Texas, Tom's car finally gave out." The car didn't drive to Texas; it was driven. We must assume from this sentence that it was Tom who did the driving.

Appositive phrases and commas. Appositive phrases follow a noun and rename it. Such phrases are set off by commas in almost all cases. For example, in the sentence "Billy Braun, Tech's newest football star, was admitted to a local hospital yesterday," the phrase "Tech's newest football star" is the appositive to "Billy Braun." It is important to remember to put a second comma at the end of the appositive. This is easy to overlook if the appositive is extremely long. For example, the sentence "Job Thompson, the newly named Will Marcum State Junior College president who succeeded Byron Wilson has accepted the presidency of the Association of Junior College Administrators," needs a comma after Wilson.

That and which. One of the jobs of these two pronouns is to introduce dependent clauses. The trick is knowing which one to use. "Which" introduces non-essential clauses — clauses that are not necessary to the meaning of the sentence. In the sentence, "John wrecked his car, which he bought only last month," the clause "which he bought only last month" is not essential to the meaning of the sentence. "John wrecked his car" could stand alone as an understandable sentence. Non-essential clauses are usually set off from the rest of the sentence by commas.

That introduces an essential clause, one necessary to gain a proper understanding of the sentence. In the sentence, "Jane wanted the kind of computer that she had always used," the clause "that she had always used" is essential to understanding the sentence. The sentence would not make sense without it. Essential clauses are not set off by commas. When you are editing your copy, find all of the instances where you used which and determine whether or not you used it properly.

Punctuation

Commas (,), semicolons (;), periods (.), apostrophes (') and colons (:) are among the most common forms of punctuation.

The **comma** is a mere blip on a page of type. No other punctuation mark, however, gives students more problems, raises so many questions among writers, and causes so much controversy among grammarians. Consequently, we need to give some added attention to the comma.

The comma is an extremely useful tool, and that is part of its problem. It is so useful that its uses are hard to prescribe.

For example, Harbrace College Handbook says that a comma should be used to separate items in a series, such as "red, white, and blue," including a comma before the conjunction (in this case, before and). Newspaper editors are afraid of using too many commas, so they have set up some rules against their use. Thus, the Associated Press (AP) Stylebook advises writers: "Use commas to separate elements in a series, but do not put a comma before the conjunction in a simple series." Using this rule, the example becomes "red, white and blue."

James J. Kilpatrick, the newspaper columnist and commentator on grammar and usage, has advocated abolishing most rules for using commas, saying that there are too many exceptions for each of the rules to make them useful. A comma, he says, should simply be used whenever a pause is needed. That may be an adequate philosophy for the experienced writer, but for the student just learning the rules, the relevant questions are "When should I use a comma?" and "When is it wrong to use a comma?"

Webster's Seventh Collegiate Dictionary, in its grammar section, gives three general instances for using commas:

Commas used to set off items. These are commas used to set off parenthetical or independent words ("Inside, the building was dark and lonely. Nevertheless, the boys entered."); appositions and modifiers ("The man, who was nearly seven feet tall, was arrested. His reaction, silent and calm, was a surprise."); and transitional words ("On the other hand, the brothers held differing views.").

Commas used to separate items. These commas separate introductory clauses or phrases from other parts of the sentence ("After driving all night, they were exhausted."); items in a series ("The flag is red, white and blue"-if we use AP style); and parts of a compound sentence ("The sky is blue, and the grass is green.").

Commas used arbitrarily. Some instances in writing simply demand commas, such as large figures (28,000), dates, addresses, and inverted names (Smith, John C.).

Students trying to learn when to use commas should remember what the AP Stylebook has to say about punctuation in general: "Think of it (punctuation) as a courtesy to your readers, designed to help them understand a story." The comma that helps the reader is correctly placed.

Semicolons are used to separate independent clauses in the same sentence (see above) and to separate long items in a series ("Attending the dinner were John Smith, mayor of Tuscaloosa; Mary Johnson, president of the League of Women Voters; Joe Jones, vice-president of Jones Steel, Inc.; and Rhonda Jackson, head of the Committee for Better Government").

Colons are often used to link the latter part of a sentence to some previous part. For example: "The flag contains the following colors: red, white, and blue."

The **period** is most often used to end sentences, but it has other uses, such as ending abbreviations (Mr.). The question mark is used to end interrogative sentences, and the exclamation point ends sentences and expressions of excitement.

After the comma, the proper use of its cousin, the **apostrophe**, probably gives students more problems than any other form of punctuation. The apostrophe can be used in a number of ways. First, we use apostrophes to form possessives, as in "Mary's hat"

Figure 2-3

Punctuation and meaning

These five sets of words are the same and in the same order. Yet they have vastly different meanings because of the punctuation that is used.

God save the Queen.

God, save the Queen.

God save the Queen?

God save the Queen!

God. Save the Queen.

and "Tom's book." If a word ends in s or the plural of the noun is formed by adding s, the apostrophe generally goes after the final s, and no other letter is needed. For example, the possessive of the word hostess is hostess'. The plural possessive of the word team is teams'.

Even professionals have problems when the word it and an apostrophe come together. Is it its, it's, or its'? Here are some rules worth memorizing. Its (without the apostrophe) is the possessive of the pronoun it, as in "its final score." It's (with the apostrophe) is a contraction meaning it is, as in "it's hard to tell." Its' makes no sense because it has no plural form.

Comma splices and run-on sentences. When two independent clauses are connected, they must be connected by two things: a comma and a conjunction. When two clauses are connected only by a comma, that is called a comma splice or a run-on sentence. For example, "The team won its final game, now they are the champs" is a comma splice or run-on sentence. The reader needs a conjunction to help separate the two sentences. Just as incorrect is the compound sentence with no comma before the conjunction: "The team won its final game and now they are the champs."

Commas between subject and verbs. Commas should be used to separate phrases and other elements in a sentence, but they should not be used solely to separate a subject from its verb. You would not write, "The boy, sat on the bench," but neither should you write, "The moment the train comes in, is when we will see her" or "Having no money, is a difficult thing."

Spelling

We are living in an age of spelling rules. It was not always so. Centuries ago, when English was evolving as a written language, there were practically no rules of spelling. Writers spelled the way they thought words sounded, and that accounted for some wildly differing ways in which some words were spelled. As certain spellings were used more and more, they became generally accepted, although not universally so. By the eighteenth century, when the fathers of our modern dictionaries began their work, they not only had to decide among diverse spellings for words, but they also had to contend with generally accepted spellings that might not be the best or most efficient.

Since that time, movements to simplify the spelling of certain words have sprung up. These movements have targeted words that end in a silent e, such as give, live, have, and bake, and other such silent combinations, such as "-ough" (for example, thought should become thot, and through should become thru).

Despite the efforts of many people during the last two centuries, spelling changes have occurred very slowly. People learn to spell most of the words they use before they are ten years old, and they are not comfortable in changing what they have learned. It is not up to those in the mass media to lead the fight for more simplified spellings. (Several years ago a number of newspaper editors ran into some trouble on this very point. Thinking that the spelling of a number of words was clumsy and confusing , these editors arbitrarily changed the way these words were spelled in their newspapers. Through became thru, thorough became thoro, and employee turned into employe. Reader acceptance of these changes was less than complete, and many editors had to beat a hasty retreat.) Rather, people in the mass media should make sure that what they write conforms to the generally accepted rules of spelling and that the spellings they use do not distract or surprise the reader.

Spelling correctly involves three thought processes: applying phonics, memorizing some words, and knowing the rules that usually apply to most words. Writers should know how to do all three. Phonics can be learned, either in early years or later. One must memorize those words that are not spelled phonetically or do not follow spelling rules. However, most words can be spelled

Figure 2-4

Samuel Johnson

JOHNSON AND BOSWELL AT THE MITRE.

Samuel Johnson (on the right of the picture) was an unlikely candidate to be a leading figure in the development of English, and yet he is rated as second only to Shakespeare in his contributions. After nine years of work, Johnson produced the *Dictionary of the English Language* in 1755. It was not the first attempt at compiling, defining, and standardizing the spelling of the words in the English language, but it was to date the most elegant. The dictionary had 43,000 definitions and 114,000 quotations from all of English literature. Johnson's reputation was secured when he met a young Scottish lawyer, James Boswell, who became devoted to him. Boswell had a remarkable memory, and after Johnson died in 1784, Boswell wrote a two-volume biography of him that is still considered one of the greatest biographies in the English language.

correctly without memorization because either rules or phonetics apply to the majority of English words. Some of the rules, with known exceptions, are explained in the following paragraphs.

1. With words of one syllable or words accented on the last syllable that end in a single consonant preceded by a single vowel, the final consonant is doubled before adding ed or a syllable beginning with a vowel-for example, plan, planned; prefer, preferred; wit, witty; hot, hottest; swim, swimming; stop, stopped; bag, baggage; beg, beggar.

There are a few exceptions. One illustrates the impact of the accent on certain syllables. Refer becomes reference, without doubling the r, but the accent also changes away from the final syllable when the suffix is added.

There are other exceptions: words ending in k, v, w, x, and y; benefit, benefited; chagrin, chagrined (even though stress stays on the final syllable of the new word).

2. A final e is usually dropped on addition of a syllable beginning with a vowel: come, coming; guide, guidance; cure, curable; judge, judging; plume, plumage; force, forcible; use, usage. There are exceptions: sale, saleable; mile, mileage; peace, peaceable; dye, dyeing.

3. A final e is usually retained on addition of a syllable begin-

ning with a consonant: use, useless; late, lately; hate, hateful; move, movement; safe, safety; white, whiteness; pale, paleness; shame, shameful. The case of nine, ninety, nineteen, but ninth is an exception. Other exceptions are judge, judgment and argue, argument.

4. Words ending in a double e retain both e's before an added syllable: free, freely; see, seeing; agree, agreement, agreeable.

5. Words ending in a double consonant retain both consonants when one or more syllables are added: ebb, ebbing; enroll; enrollment; full, fullness; dull, dullness; skill, skillful; odd, oddly; will, willful; stiff, stiffness.

6. Compounds of all, well, and full drop one l: always, almost welfare, welcome, fulfill. (This is really a listing of exceptions to rule 5.) Exceptions include fullness and occasions when a word is hyphenated (as with full-fledged).

7. I before e, except after c, or when sounded like a, as in neighbor or weigh; receive, deceive, relieve, believe.

8. A final y preceded by a consonant is usually changed to i with the addition of an ending not beginning with i: army, armies; spy, spies; busy, business. Some exceptions are shy, shyness; pity, piteous (but not pitiful). The ay endings are usually exceptions: for example — play, played.

9. This is really not a rule but just some information about a few tricky words, which must be described as exceedingly difficult. These must be memorized: exceed, proceed, and succeed all end with -ceed, but supersede ends with -sede. All others with this sound end in -cede. These include precede, intercede, secede, concede, accede, and recede.

Rule 9 tells you how to become a very good speller. Memorize the tricky words and the spelling "demons," and if you know both your rules and phonics, you can spell most of the rest.

You will also need to know some of the basic rules for forming plurals. Here are a few:

1. Most plurals for nouns are formed by simply adding s to the root word.

2. Nouns ending with s, z, x, ch or sh usually require an es ending to form the plural.

3. When a word ends with a consonant and then a y, the y is changed to i and an es is added (example: army, armies).

4. When a word ends in a vowel and a y, you can simply add an s for the plural (example: bay, bays).

5. Compound words without hyphens simply take an s on the

Figure 2-5

Spelling reform

Simplifying the way we spell words has been the dream of many prominent people, not just school children. One of the leaders of spelling reform was Robert McCormick, who in the 1930s ordered his newspaper, the Chicago Tribune, to use shortened forms of words such as "tho," "iland," "frate," "thru," and "jaz." These spellings never caught on with the public or with lexicographers, however. In 1975, twenty years after McCormick died, the Tribune reverted to using generally accepted spellings. McCormick was not the only one to try. President Theodore Roosevelt and writer Mark Twain were also advocates of simplified spelling rules.

Robert McCormick
and the Tribune Tower in Chicago

end (cupful, cupfuls), but compound words with a hyphen take the s on the significant word (son-in-law, sons-in-law).

6. The AP Stylebook advises that 's should be used only in forming the plural of single letters (A's, B's) but not figures (1920s, 727s). Never use 's to form the plural of a word that is fully spelled out.

Computer aids

When the widespread use of word processors began in the late 1970s and early 1980s, they were little more than electronic typewriters that allowed writers to store documents and change them with ease. The software for these machines has grown increasingly sophisticated, and now they are becoming full-fledged partners in the writing process. Three major types of software are available to the writer: spelling dictionaries, stylebooks and grammar checkers.

Spelling dictionaries are large lists of words that reside in the computer's memory. In some software programs, they are activated while the document is being written and will check the spelling of words as the document is being created. In other programs, they can be activated whenever the writer wants to use them. They check spelling by matching the words in the document to the words in the list. When a word in the document does not match a word in the dictionary list, it is highlighted for the

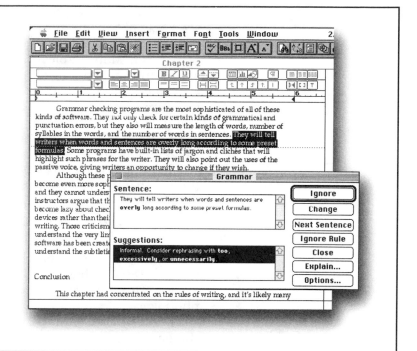

Figure 2-6

Grammar checkers

Grammar checkers are attached to many word processing programs. But these attachments generally will only highlight potential problems. The user still has to make a decision on what changes to make.

writer. Most spelling programs will then offer a set of alternative words for the writer. Writers can also "look up" words while they are writing; they can type a word and then ask the spelling program to check to see if it matches a word in the dictionary list.

The obvious shortcoming of these spelling programs is that they cannot understand the meaning of the words they are matching. Consequently, a writer can use the wrong word, and if it is spelled correctly, the spelling program will not find it. For example, if a writer makes a simple typographical error as in the sentence, "I am coming to you house tonight," the spelling program will not understand that the word you should be your. Because you is spelled correctly and matches a word in its list, it will skip over that error.

Stylebook programs work in much the same way. (Stylebooks and their importance are discussed in the next chapter.) Style guide programs can be installed on a computer, and when a writer has a question about a style rule, he or she can call up the program without leaving the document that is being produced. Some programs will automatically check a document for some style errors, but these checkers have some of the same shortcomings as spelling programs. They cannot catch all of the errors of meaning.

Grammar checking programs are the most sophisticated of all of these kinds of software. They not only check for certain kinds of grammatical and punctuation errors, but they also will measure the length of words, number of syllables in the words, and the number of words in sentences. They will tell writers when words and sentences are overly long according to preset formulas. Some programs have built-in lists of jargon and clichés that will highlight such phrases for the writer. They will also point out the uses of the passive voice, giving writers an opportunity to change it if they wish.

Although these programs have grown in sophistication-and are likely to become even more sophisticated-they cannot find all the errors in a document, and they cannot understand meanings or context. Many professionals and instructors argue that they should not be used at all because they allow writers to become lazy about checking their own work and dependent on these mechanical devices rather than their own knowledge and understanding of what they are writing. Those criticisms and fears are valid. Beginning writers should understand the very limited capacities of all of this software. No piece of software has been created that comes close to the ability of the mind to understand the subtleties and complexities of the English language.

Words, words, words

English works, as any language does, because of a combination of systems that students who seek to use it need to understand. Those systems are lexicon, grammar, semantics and phonology.

Lexicon deals with the words that form the building blocks of the language. As society changes, new words must be created to express those changes. Certain rules govern the formation and development of words. We take words from a variety of sources (from ancient Latin to inner city street talk), but English has developed some rules for using those words. We have prefixes and suffixes, for instance, that allow words to be formed into useful entities. The prefix "anti" lets a word approach the opposite of its accepted meaning; the suffix "ed" can be added to many root verbs to form the past tense. Standard dictionaries that we keep on our desks are the chief source of our knowledge of the rules of lexicon.

Much of this chapter has been devoted to describing the rules of grammar for what we consider standard English. Grammar is the way in which we string words together to describe complex thoughts, ideas or actions. Grammar is also concerned with word order. The English standard order of words in a sentence is subject, verb, predicate. That order is not followed in other languages, however. Because English is widely used, the rules of grammar are studied and evaluated continuously by people who use the language professionally. English is also a democratic language, so that common usage eventually formalizes many of the rules of grammar.

Semantics is concerned with the meanings that users assign to words. What a words symbolizes — or means — can change over time. The history of words and phrases, called etymology, can be a fascinating study, and many scholars spend productive careers doing that. Media professionals should pay particular attention to semantics because much of their work depends on a common understanding of the meanings of words.

Phonology is the system by which the language is spoken. A language has far fewer sounds than words; most English speakers get by with about 40 sounds, or phonemes. Phonology allows a language to develop a standard way of being spoken so we can understand one another. (Some would argue that writing constitutes a fifth system of the language because the rules of writing differ from the phonology rules. Not all experts accept that thinking, however.)

The rules of each of these systems are important because they allow us to have a common application of the language. They are "rules" not so much that they must be enforced but because they represent the common understanding that we all have about the language. If this common understanding did not exist, the efforts of a writer for the mass media to communicate with an audience would be frustrating or useless. That is why the rules are important. That is why the professional must understand, use and study the rules. The rules in each of these systems will undoubtedly change within the lifetime of the writer, but there will also be rules.

Writing with clarity

So far, this chapter has concentrated on the rules of writing, and it is likely many beginning writing students find a lengthy discussion of these rules boring, if not oppressive.

Serious students of writing, however, will remember through all this discussion why we should be concerned about the rules: In writing for the mass media, we are trying to transmit information and ideas to an audience of readers and listeners. Will bad grammar, misspelling, sloppy punctuation, and misuse of words help accomplish that goal? Will these mistakes tell the reader that the content of your communication is accurate and worthwhile — worthy of the audience's time and effort to understand it?

The answer, of course, is no. Good grammar, precise word usage, and correct spelling are a means to an end. That end is communicating with the reader or viewer. Grammar, spelling and usage are merely tools that a writer uses to convey information and ideas.

Writing is not just fitting words and phrases into a form. If it were, a computer would have been invented long ago to accomplish that tedious task. Writing is much more than mastery of grammar and spelling and even more than mastering the information and ideas about which you are writing. Writing is thinking — the mysterious process of the brain, acting in conjunction with the heart and soul — whereby we form and reform our thoughts and try to communicate and make sense of the world.

Points for consideration and discussion

1. What image of grammar and grammarians did you form in grade school or high school? Was it the one the author describes at the beginning of this chapter?

2. The author makes a strong case for knowing the rules of grammar, but some people do not think that this knowledge is very important. They believe that you can write well without knowing these rules. What do you think?

3. The text says that there are some times when a sentence fragment might be appropriate. When would that be?

4. What do you think are the most important rules for using a comma?

5. Explain the difference between its, it's, and its'.

6. Make a list of words that you think should be spelled differently.

7. Make a list of words that you often hear people misusing.

8. What is the rule of grammar, spelling or punctuation that you would most like to abolish?

Further reading

Bill Bryson, The Mother Tongue: English and How it Got that Way. New York: William Morrow and Co., 1990.

R. Thomas Berner, Language Skills for Journalists, 2nd ed., Boston: Houghton Mifflin, 1984.

John C. Hodges and Mary Whitten, Harbrace College Handbook, 13th ed., Ft. Worth, Texas: Harcourt Brace College Publishers, 1999.

Lauren Kessler and Duncan McDonald, When Words Collide, 5th ed., Belmont, CA: Wadsworth, 2000.

Floyd Watkins, William Dillingham, and Edwin Martin, Practical English Handbook, Boston: Houghton Mifflin, 1996.

On the Web: Grammar, spelling, punctuation, and other tools of the writer are certainly not neglected topics on the Internet. Start with the following: On-Line English Grammar, www.edunet.com/english/grammar/index.html. You will be able to find many other similar references.

Chapter 2 Basic tools of writing

Exercises

• *The following section contains a variety of beginning writing exercises. You should follow your instructor's directions in completing them.*

2–1 Writing Skills

The following sentences were taken from newspapers and television broadcasts. Correct the errors you find either by copy-editing or by rewriting the sentences. Underline your corrections. Some of the sentences are correct, and you should write correct in the margin.

1. He is one of the greatest choreographers who has ever lived.

2. The general assumed what was then described as dictorial powers.

3. The couple has two children.

4. Inside the box was a man and a woman.

5. Absent from the meeting were the mayor and two councilmen.

6. Every fireman in the city, 250 in all were called out.

7. A total of 650 Eskimos was examined and tested.

8. Only two in four were urgent cases, a group that included cardiacs, asthmatics and those found unconscious.

9. The chairman stated that response to the committee's activities has convinced him that the money for renovation can be raised.

10. Business administration and journalism courses provide the student with good background for work in public relations.

11. Here comes the famous Kilgore College Rangerettes onto the field to perform at halftime.

12. Leading the United States' show of strength were Arthur Ashe and Clarke Graebner.

13. The investigation revealed that none of the team members were involved in illegal endorsements of sports clothing.

14. "There's two knocked out cold on the floor!" the sportscaster shouted.

15. Every one of us have asked that question sometime in our lives.

2–2 Writing Skills

Do whatever is necessary to correct the following sentences.

1. Their rival forces meanwhile prepared to meet Wednesday to patch up peace.

2. Pasadena California is the site of the Rose Bowl.

3. It was O. J. Simpson (who, whom) the coach praised so highly.

4. The tomb of the pharaoh had (laid, lain) buried in the desert for centuries.

5. I heard the train whistle at the crossing that was going to Denver.

6. She borrowed an egg from a neighbor that was rotten.

7. For a year we almost heard nothing from our former neighbors.

8. There was a canary in a cage that never sang.

9. We hope that you will notify us if you can attend the banquet on the enclosed post card.

10. Come here Mary and help us.

11. I know she (swum, swims) the channel regularly in this weather.

12. The children looked forward to celebrating Christmas for several weeks.

13. After setting foot on the uninhabited island of Europe, off Africa, to direct the filming of the sea turtles, a hurricane whirled across the Indian ocean and hit the island.

14. He ran swiftly the dog in front of him and plunged into the forest.

15. The casings had (tore, torn) (loose, lose) from their bearings.

2–3 Punctuation

In the following sentences, insert the correct punctuation.

1. I subscribe to the New Yorker Harper's Magazine and the Reporter

2. Seven legislators from the southern part of the state changed their votes and with their help the bill was passed.

3. Do you like your steak rare medium or well done?

4. A tape recorder gives very accurate reproduction and it has the great advantage that it can be used at home as well as at the studio.

5. The gun went off and everyone jumped

6. The new cars are certainly more powerful but it is doubtful that they are any safer

7. Light entered the room through cracks in the walls through holes in the roof and through one small window.

8. Hundreds of church bells ringing loudly after years of silence announced the end of the war

9. The book was lying where I left it

10. The advisor who is never in his office makes registration difficult

11. Some years ago I lived in a section of town where almost everyone was a Republican

12. Hearne was still disclaiming with great eloquence but no one in the crowd was listening

13. I bought a large bath towel

14. We were sitting before the fire in the big room at Twins Farms and Lewis had rudely retired behind the newspaper

15. The ranchmen rode with their families into the little town and encouraged their sons to demonstrate their skill with broken horses

2–4 Pronouns and Verbs

In the following sentences, underline the correct pronoun or verb.

1. He is the player (who, whom) probably will play short-stop.

2. Is this the person (who, whom) you want?

3. Each of the three quarterbacks (is, are) good runners.

4. Both Baylor and Arkansas (has, have) won six games and lost two.

5. Either of the two players (are, is) eligible.

6. Each of the members (was, were) in (his, their) seat(s) when the session began.

7. (Who, Whom), then, would the tax hurt?

8. Do you know to (who, whom) that notebook belongs?

9. (Who, Whom) is going with the reporter to get a picture of the crash?

10. He declared that everybody must play (his, their) part.

11. This story is between you and (I, me).

12. No matter how you look at it, it was (I, she, her) (who, whom) they opposed.

13. Bryan is the kind of man (whom, who) always thinks before he acts.

14. This is the only one of the typewriters that (is, are) working.

15. Everyone was on (their, his or her) best behavior.

2–5 Verbs

In the following sentences, underline the correct form of the verb.

1. What (lays, lies) in the future for Alaska?

2. He had been (lain, laid) on a stretcher.

3. "(Lay, Lie) down and be quiet for an hour," he ordered.

4. The six-year-old boy was just (setting, sitting) there in the ruins, trying not to cry.

5. The Ohio State football team (sat, set) back and enjoyed the movie of its game with Michigan.

6. The men worked all night (raising, rising) a monument in spite of the (raising, rising) tide of the river.

7. After lunch she had (laid, lain) down for a nap.

8. The hard tackling by the Georgia Bulldogs had really (began, begun) to tell.

9. Suddenly a cloud of dust (rises, raises) in the west.

10. Had the tight end simply (fell, fallen) on the ball, he would have (catched, caught) it.

11. Spillane (led, lead) you to believe that the butler was the murderer.

12. Chris Gilbert had (proved, proven) to be the outstanding player.

13. He said that he could (loose, lose) his fortune, but he had (chose, chosen) to gamble all he had.

14. The Smiths (use, used) to live in San Francisco.

15. The man was lucky he wasn't (drown, drowned).

2–6 Clauses

In the following sentences, underline the independent clause and circle the subordinate (dependent) clause.

1. They agreed to open negotiations when both sides ceased fire.

2. If he had known, he would never have said that.

3. Since the current was swift, he could not swim to shore.

4. The horse came up to the first jump, when he stumbled and threw Jean off.

5. This is called the cryptozoite stage, after which the plasmodia break out of the liver cells and float about in the blood stream.

6. An especially big wave rolled in, when I finally managed to get my line unsnagged.

7. While walking past the building, the night watchman noticed the door was unlocked.

8. Harkey's injured knee has failed to heal completely; therefore, he may see little action against Notre Dame on Saturday.

9. The Ace Manufacturing Company, where I used to work, went bankrupt.

10. This last semester, if it has done nothing else, has given me confidence in myself.

Write five correct sentences containing independent and subordinate clauses.

1.

2.

3.

4.

5.

2-7 Punctuation

In the following sentences, insert the correct punctuation.

1. Nobody knows the trouble I've seen nobody knows but Jesus. **(This is a line from a Negro spiritual. Punctuate it as if it were in the middle of a paragraph.)**

2. The responsible reporter one who is scrupulously honest will still encounter problems.

3. Abraham Lincoln died on April 15 1865 after being shot while attending a play at Fords Theater.

4. My son was born on Nov 15 1980 It was a Saturday so I didnt get to go to the football game

5. Why do you come over to my place

6. Writing for the mass media takes much skill perserverence and hard work.

7. Wow I couldnt think of any place better to eat myself.

8. According to my professor the world is absolutely positively flat and you should never forget it.

9. Where are the carpenters where are the bricklayers and most of all where are the gardners when we need them the most.

10. I couldnt come to class today Joe said because I had the flu.

11. Joe got a new computer which set his parents back a good bit and hes been dying to tell everybody about it.

12. Help I need somebody the Beatles sang Not just anybody Help I need somebody Help.

2–8 Word Choice

In the following sentences, fill in the blank with one of the words that appears in parentheses.

1. _____ are good reasons why _____ about to sell _____ house. (there, their, they're)

2. _____ not _____ late _____ give the cat milk. (its, it's, to, too)

3. If _____ going home, take _____ books with you. (your, you're)

4. Do you know _____ the _____ is pleasant _____ ? (whether, weather, there, their, they're)

5. They _____ known for a long time that you would _____ gone if you had heard _____ the game in time. (have, of, 've)

6. Where _____ are many opinions, most people feel justifed in holding on to _____ own; and while there are several scientific explanations for stubborness, _____ be few changes unless we can convince men that they ought to be more open-minded. (there, their, they're, there'll)

7. My _____ objection to the _____ of that school is that he is a man of no _____ (principal, principle)

8. Not until _____ will you be able to tell whether you have more _____ you need. (than, then)

9. If _____ strap is _____ , you may _____ your books. (lose, loose, you're, your)

10. Not even in the _____ would I _____ the table before eating _____ (desert, dessert)

11. "_____ going to punch _____ nose?" (whose, who's)

12. We _____ the ruling without protest, although we _____ all those over 45. (except, accept)

13. His speech _____ the audience greatly. (affected, effected)

14. _____ 50,000 people attend the opening game of the World Series. (Over, More than)

15. He was always one to do things _____ .(different, differently)

2–9 Word Choice

In the following sentences, fill in the blank with one of the words that appears in parentheses. The definitions of most of these words can be found in Appendix C.

1. The bomb, which was to _____ havoc on the whole block, killed so many people that their bodies soon began _____. (reek, wreak)

2. The newsmagazine _____ she subscribed to never seemed to tell her all that she needed to know. (that, which)

3. When he put the book down, he decide that he had just read something very _____. (unique, unusual)

4. The _____ of Queen Victoria was a long and prosperous one. (rein, reign)

5. He decided to _____ his bike down to the town square to see if he could _____ the things that he had made. (peddle, pedal)

6. The priest chose not to _____ the cloths that were spread across the _____. (alter, altar)

7. We visited the _____ building, where we saw the state legislature in session. (Capital, capital, Capitol)

8. All of the fraternities on campus came together to form a voting _____ that could not be overcome by the independent students. (block, bloc)

9. He _____ the poor child's way of speaking. (flouted, flaunted)

10. The professor tried her best to make the grading system more _____. (equal, equitable)

11. I did not make it to the movie last night _____ all the homework I had to do. (due to, because of)

12. She was irritated by the _____ tone he used when he said, "And what have you been doing all week long?" (official, officious)

2–10 Brevity

Edit all unnecessary words from the expressions below.

wore a white goatee on his chin

throughout the length and width of the entire nation

was positively identified

appeared to be ill

a dead body was found

in the city of Los Angeles

cost the sum of ten dollars

broke an existing rule

for the month of May

for a short space of time

an old pioneer

the present incumbent

will draw to a close

at the corner of Sixth and Elm streets

for the purpose of shocking

2-11 Wordiness

The sentences below use too many words. Edit them carefully to reduce the number of words, but do not cut out important information. If necessary, rewrite them completely.

1. He was kind of a large man, heavy in weight, and not a very bright guy whose ability to think things through thorougly was pretty limited.

2. The actual photograph was taken by John Smith and showed a room that was littered with paper and other items and furnished with furniture of a cheap quality.

3. Always confused by any kind of mathematical problem, Sally, for no reason that anyone could ever figure out, signed up for one of the hardest and most difficult math courses in the entire curriculum.

4. His past performance in not being able to win people over to his particular point of view certainly indicated to us that he was very likely to do poorly as a political candidate running for mayor.

5. My future plans include enrolling in a college or university where I can study the field of journalism and can improve my natural-born talent for writing.

6. The committee, meeting in executive session with no one else there, made the decision to cease and desist the practice of requiring members of the organization to pay money to attend all of the functions of the organization.

2-12 Wordiness

The sentences below use too many words. Edit them carefully to reduce the number of words, but do not cut out important information. If necessary, rewrite them completely.

1. Owing to the fact that the prerequisite courses had not been taken by John, he was having a great deal of difficulty and had to spend a lot of time figuring out his schedule for the semester that is coming up.

2. There is little consideration given by our professors to the very real problem that our textbooks are often extremely costly and expensive.

3. Alex said that the thing to do if he wanted to improve his writing would be to read as many good books as he could possibly read in the time available to him.

4. Baseball has always been thought of as the national past-time, but for all intents and purposes, football has replaced baseball as the favorite sport for many people across this country.

5. During the period of time that included most of February, Laura stayed cooped up in her room and tried to fight off the effects of a very bad and debilitating cold.

6. Basically, I have a disinclination and a disinterest in helping people who are not willing to do some things such as show up for work on time and put forth the effort that it often takes to succeed in this life.

2-13 Writing problems

Correct any problems that appear in the following sentences.

1. Gilligan was so charmed by the desert aisle he decided to marry the movie star.

2. Like that nice Professor said, we should always study for our exams.

3. The cantaloupe-throwing contest was canceled due to averse weather.

4. Rushing to the sight of the crime, the prosecuting attorney was horrified at the grizzly murder scene.

5. The criminal alluded police by hiding under a Toyota Corolla.

6. Faining illness, the President refused to make the trip to Tulsa.

7. Morgan canceled the funeral service after the dead man turned out to be alive.

8. Less than 100 pumpkins were piled in Smith's car.

9. Hurricane Bubba ravaged the Gulf Coast, causing $10 billion in damages.

10. The dancing troupe refused to buy their tights at wholesale.

11. The restaurant owners upped the price of rutabagas by 100 percent whenever Mark Arnold came to town.

12. The journalist's cannon of ethics prohibits taking gifts from sources.

13. Journalists should be guided by one principle: Always be accurate.

3

Style &
the stylebook

Introduction

When you write about Frisbees, you should capitalize the word. You should avoid using the word "definitely"; it does not add any information to your sentence. The soft drink Dr Pepper does not have a period after the "Dr" in its title. Some words use hyphens (post-mortem), while similar words do not (postgraduate).

How can you know all this? And what does it matter? These are small things, are they not, really unworthy of much consideration?

Maybe to the rest of the world they are small considerations, but to writers for the mass media, the points made in the first paragraph are of enormous importance. Writing accurately, precisely, and consistently is the hallmark of professionalism. Paying attention to the details of writing — and getting those right — means that a writer is likely to be paying attention to facts, context, and meaning. It means the writer is thinking at various levels, understanding that misplaced commas or errors in capitalization can distract the reader from great ideas or important information.

This kind of thinking is the genesis of style.

In media writing, style is the general orientation a writer has toward his or her work. It does not refer to the way a writer, such has Ernest Hemingway or William Faulker, arranges sentences or paragraphs. Rather, it is the conventions and assumptions underlying the writing and the generally accepted rules of writing and usage for a particular medium. This chapter discusses both the conventions and the rules.

The three most important concepts of media writing are accuracy, brevity, and clarity; the most important is accuracy.

Accuracy

The chief goal of any writer for the mass media is accuracy. A writer will spend much energy in "getting it right." That is, the writer will make every reasonable attempt to ensure that everything in the writing is factually correct and that the language and style the writer uses present that information correctly.

Accuracy is important to the writer for a number of reasons. First, our society puts much stock in truth and honesty, and most people in our society have come to expect that the mass media will take reasonable steps to be accurate in the information they present. There is a great tendency for mass audiences to believe what they see and read in the mass media, and this tendency translates into a responsibility that those who work in the mass media must fulfill.

A very practical reason for an emphasis on accuracy is that people will not watch or subscribe to media they believe to be inaccurate. A newspaper, television station, advertising agency, or public relations department that does not tell the truth will not be trusted by the people it is trying to serve and ultimately will not be effective.

The most compelling reason for a strong emphasis on accuracy, however, comes not from the audience but from individuals inside the mass media. Few people, if any, want to be false in what they do or want their life's work to be looked upon as a charade. Consequently, they feel a moral need to do the best they can; in the mass media professions, that means trying to produce accurate information and present it honestly.

How can a writer for the mass media be accurate? What are the steps that will ensure that the information presented in the writing is correct? These next two chapters will discuss practical measures about gathering information and writing news. Thinking about accuracy begins here by making the following observations.

Writers for the mass media should have an open mind. They should be receptive to new ideas and to various points of view. They should listen to those with whom they may disagree as well as agree. They will not put everything they read and hear in their writing, but the more they know, the better judgments they can make about the accuracy of what they write.

Following closely on this characteristic is that writers for the mass media should read widely. Reading, even in the age of video, is still the best way for a person to prepare himself or herself as a writer.

Writers for the mass media should pay attention to the details of what and how they write. The previous chapter discussed the importance of using the language correctly. That discussion continues in this chapter about style. Individually, many of the points made in each of these chapters are small ones, but as a whole, they are important for the writer's effort to achieve accuracy. Accuracy may be thought of as a large building made up of many small bricks. The writer is the bricklayer and must pay attention to each of the bricks as they are put down.

Clarity

Clarity must be one of the chief goals of a writer for the mass media. Facts that are unclear are of little use to the reader. The English language is extremely versatile, but that versatility can lead to confusion when the language is in the hands of amateurs. Writers must be experts in the language and in the proper and clear structuring of a story. Writers must be on constant guard against writing or story structures that could be confusing to the reader.

The pursuit of clarity is a state of mind for the writer. Everything the writer does must promote the clarity of the copy. After a piece of copy is written, a writer must look at it with a fresh mind — one that is unencumbered with too much knowledge of the subject. The writer must, like the reader, approach a story as one who was not there and did not see it happen and who has not talked with anyone about it. This approach is doubly difficult for the writer who has followed one of the first rules of good writing — knowing the subject thoroughly. Writing clearly and editing for clarity demand a rare degree of mental discipline on the part of the writer.

The opposite of clarity is confusion. Confusion can infiltrate a story in many ways, and it is the writer's responsibility to eliminate this confusion. The chief source of confusion is often the writer who does not understand his or her subject. Writers who do not understand their subjects are likely to write a story that other people cannot understand.

Clear writing is an art, but it is also a skill. Expressing thoughts, ideas, and facts in a clear way is one of the most difficult jobs a writer has-even though the product may read as if the clarity were easily accomplished. The mind moves much faster than we can write or even type; thoughts can be easily jumbled, and so can writing. The key to clear writing is understanding the subject. When a writer can express thoughts about a subject in clear terms, then that understanding has been achieved.

The following are some tips for helping writers and editors achieve clarity in their writing:

Keep it simple. Many people believe that they can demonstrate their intelligence by using complex terms (like terminology). Their language, they feel, will show others that they have mastered a difficult subject or that they speak or write with authority. Consequently, they use big words and complex sentences to express the simplest ideas.

The problem with this attitude is that people forget their orig-

Tips on AP style

Abbreviations

- Spell out, do not abbreviate, names of organizations, firms, agencies, universities and colleges, groups, clubs or governmental bodies the first time the name is used. (i.e., on first reference)

- But abbreviate such names on second reference, as here:
  First ref: Civil Aeronautics Board
  Second ref: the board.
  First ref: National Organization for Women
  Second ref: NOW

- DO NOT use an abbreviation or acronym in parentheses after the first reference of a full name. Wrong: The Radical Underwater First United Sailors (RUFUS) meets tonight. Right: The Radical Underwater First United Sailors meets tonight.

- Don't use unfamiliar acronyms. Wrong: RUFUS was formed in 1923.

- In street addresses abbreviate these:
Street	St.	1234 Goober St.
Avenue	Ave.	3506 Loblolly Ave.
Boulevard	Blvd.	80 Crabtree Blvd.

  BUT, the words road, alley, circle, drive, etc. are never abbreviated.

by David Davies

Tips on AP Style

Capitalization

• Capitalize names of holidays, historic events, church feast days, special events, etc., but not seasons:
Mother's Day Labor Day Orientation Week
fall storm autumn leaves winter tomatoes
spring break

• DO NOT capitalize points of the compass in usages like these:
an east wind southern Arkansas
western Canada southeast Forrest County
BUT DO CAPITALIZE points of the compass when part of the name of a recognized geographic area:
Southern California Midwest
the South the West Coast

• Capitalize the proper names of nationalities, peoples, races, and tribes:
Indian Arab Caucasian Afro-American
Hispanic

• Capitalize and place quotation marks around the names of books, plays, poems, songs, lectures or speech titles, hymns, movies, TV programs, etc., when the full name is used.
"The Simpsons" "The Catcher in the Rye"
"Arsenic and Old Lace"
"Star Wars" "Lucy in the Sky With Diamonds".

by David Davies

inal purpose for writing — to communicate ideas. Any writing that draws attention to itself, and thus draws attention away from the content, is ineffective. Writing should be as simple and straightforward as possible. Reporters and editors should use simple terms and sentence structures. They should avoid piling adjectives and phrases on top of one another. They should do this, not in order to talk down to their readers, but to transmit ideas and facts as efficiently as possible.

Avoid all kinds of jargon — even your own. Jargon is specialized language that almost all groups develop. Students, baseball managers, doctors, and gardeners use words that have special meaning for them and no one else. Journalists are not doing their jobs if they simply record jargon, however accurately, and pass it on to the reader. Journalists must be translators. They must understand the jargon of different groups they cover but must be intelligent enough not to use it in their stories. Writers, too, must keep a watch out for the jargon that can slip into stories. Phrases like "viable alternative," "optimum care," and "personnel costs" must be made to mean something by journalists. They cannot simply thrust them on the reader and believe that they have done their job adequately.

Be specific. Journalists must set the stage of the story for their readers. They must make sure that their readers understand what is going on, when it is happening, where it is happening, and how it is taking place. Reporters and editors cannot assume that readers know very much about the stories they write and edit. They cannot get by with telling readers that it was a "large crowd" or a "long line" or a "beautiful landscape." Stories are built on facts — little facts and big facts. Sometimes it is the little facts that will make the difference in whether or not a reader understands a story.

Readers who have not seen what reporters have seen will not know what reporters are talking about. One aspect of this problem occurs with the use of "the," especially by less experienced reporters. For example, a lead paragraph may begin in the following way, "City council approved funds for purchasing the new computer system for the finance department at its meeting

Tuesday night." A reader is likely to ask, "What new computer system?" While covering the story, the reporter kept hearing everyone talk about "the new computer system," so that's what appeared in the story. Writers particularly need to watch for this kind of assumption and to make sure that readers are not left behind by the assumptions a writer makes.

Check the time sequence. Most news stories will not be written in chronological order, but readers should have some idea of the narrative sequence of the events in a story. When the time sequence is not clear, readers may become confused and misunderstand the content of the story.

Transitions. Transitions are necessary for smooth, graceful, and clear writing. Each sentence in a story should logically follow the previous sentence or should relate to it in some way. New information in a story should be connected to information already introduced. Readers who suddenly come upon new information or a new subject in a story without the proper transition will be jolted and confused. The following first paragraphs of a story by a beginning writing student about the high costs of weddings illustrates the point about transitions:

```
     The nervous young man drops to one
knee, blushes and asks that all-impor-
tant question.
     What about all the planning
involved in a wedding, from reserving
the church to choosing the honeymoon
site? June and July are the traditional
months for making the   big decision,
according to Milton Jefferson of the
Sparkling Jewelry Store.
     Jefferson said most engagements
last from seven to 16 months.
     A woman sometimes receives a ring
that has been passed down through her
fiancé's family for generations, or
maybe her boyfriend has bought an estate
ring.
```

The first paragraph assumes that the reader will know what "that all-important question" is. This assumption might be acceptable if the second paragraph followed the lead properly, but it does not. Instead, it plunges the reader into the subject of planning a wedding; the reader has no indication from the lead that this is coming next-and what happened to "that all-important question?"

In a similar manner, the second sentence of the second paragraph introduces yet another new subject to the reader, again without the proper transition. The reader is taken from a question about planning to the traditionally popular months for weddings, with no connection being made between them. In addition, the attribution forces the reader to make another leap. The reader must say, "The man is a jewelry store owner. Jewelry stores sell wedding rings. The jewelry store owner, then, is an authority about when weddings occur."

The third paragraph introduces yet another new subject6565 the length of engagements. Again, the reader is bombarded by one fact after another with no transitions to help them make sense.

The fourth paragraph talks about how prospective brides attain their wedding rings. What has this information got to do with what has been said? The writer has left it to the reader to figure it all out. The writer has said, "My story is about weddings. Therefore, anything I put in my story about weddings is okay."

Good writers need to develop a mental discipline that prevents this shoddy thinking and writing. They must read their own copy with cold and glaring eyes, never assuming that a reader will take the time and effort to "figure out" what the writer has written. (For more on transitions, see Chapter 5, pages 151-154.)

Brevity

"Brevity is the soul of wit," according to Polonius, Shakespeare's ill-fated character in Hamlet. Polonius was, in reality, one of Shakespeare's most verbose personalities. Words came tumbling out of his mouth. He went on and on. He was not only verbose; he was boring. Polonius was one of those people you try to avoid at parties. He talked too much.

Writers can do the same thing. They can use too many words, piling phrase upon phrase and letting the sentences run on far after their thoughts have run out. They put too many words in the way of what really needs to be said.

Writers need to recognize when they are being long-winded. They should remove the well-turned phrase that is unnecessary and eliminate that which has already been stated. The process can go too far, of course. Accuracy and clarity should never be sacrificed for brevity's sake, but brevity should be another major goal of the writer.

The following are some tips for achieving brevity:

Get to the point. What is the story about? What does the story need to tell the reader? A writer needs to be able to answer these questions in the simplest terms possible. This is sometimes the hardest part of writing or editing, but once that is done, the writing or editing job can become much easier.

Watch for redundancies and repetitions. A redundancy uses too many words to express an idea. Redundancies in the language abound: Easter Sunday (Easter is always on Sunday); component parts (parts are components); advance notice (what other kind is there?). Redundancies show a lack of disciplined thinking. They slip into writing unnoticed, but their presence can make the most important stories seem silly.

Repetitions repeat words or phrases more than is necessary for the reader to understand what is meant. Repetition is also an indication that the editor was not concentrating on the story. Sometimes facts need to be repeated for clarity's sake, but this is not often the case.

Cut out unnecessary words. There may be words in a story that simply add nothing to its meaning. These words are hard to pin down, but a sharp-eyed writer can spot them. They are words like really, very, and actually. They are phrase-makers, but they do not tell the reader much.

Finally, when you have run out of things to write about, stop writing.

Journalistic conventions

A strong sense of professionalism has developed in journalism and the mass media during the last 100 years. With this professionalism has come a powerful tradition of conventions in journalistic writing. Like rules of style, these conventions are known to trained writers and used by them to communicate things about their stories to readers. Most readers do not think about what these conventions are when they read the newspaper, hear a news broadcast or read news on a web site. Yet most news consumers expect these conventions to be followed when professionals are making news judgments.

The conventions include both the basic structures of the stories and the individual ordering of facts and even words within sentences that are regularly used in certain types of stories.

Inverted pyramid. The inverted pyramid is the structure most commonly used for the modern American news story for print. For the writer, the inverted pyramid structure means two things. First, information should be presented in the order of its importance, with the most important facts coming at the beginning. Second, a story should be written so that if it needs to be cut, it may be cut from the bottom without loss of essential facts or coherence. The inverted pyramid is certainly not the only acceptable structure for the presentation of news, but its use is so widespread that if it is not used, the facts of a story must dictate the alternate form used by the writer. Chapter 5 will further discuss writing with the inverted structure.

Many in and out of journalism believe that the inverted pyramid structure has lost its usefulness and that journalists should develop and use other structures. One of the objections to the inverted pyramid is the argument that in the age of instant communication through television and other means, the inverted pyramid is no longer necessary for readers of the written word. They are likely to know what the news is because they have seen it or heard it in some other medium.

Another objection to the inverted pyramid is that it restricts

Tips on AP Style

Numbers

- As a general rule, spell out both cardinal and ordinal numbers from one through nine. Use Arabic figures for 10 and above.

  first day   one woman   10 days
  21st year   nine years   50 more

- Use commas in numbers with four or more digits, EXCEPT IN YEARS AND STREET ADDRESSES:

  1,500 eggplants   23,879 students
  7034 Aunt Bea St.   the year 1984

- The words billion and million may be used with round numbers:

  3 million miles $3 million   10 billion years
  $10 billion

- Numbers over a million may be rounded off and expressed this way, including sums of money:

  2.75 million rather than 2,752,123.
  About $2.35 million rather than $2,349,999.

by David Davies

the creativity of the writer. Many writers argue that stories are more readable and even more accurate if they take some other form, particularly a narrative or chronological form.

Because of its emphasis on presenting information from most important to least important, the inverted pyramid structure often prevents writers from putting dramatic endings onto their stories. This characteristic is another reasons why many writers and editors object to its use. They argue that the inverted pyramid washes the drama out of a story.

Despite these objections, the inverted pyramid structure has remained a standard form for news writing. It has even gained strength because of its usefulness in writing for the web (see Chapter 6).

Types of stories. Commonly accepted news values (discussed in the next chapter) make it incumbent upon reporters and editors to cover and give importance to certain types of stories. These kinds of stories are handled so often that a set of standard practices governing how they are written has been established. For instance, the disaster story must always tell early in the story if anyone was killed or injured. Newspapers develop their own styles for handling obituaries, and some even dictate the form in which the standard obituary is written. For instance, the New York Times has a set two-sentence lead for an obituary: "John Smith, a Brooklyn real estate dealer, died at a local hospital yesterday after a short illness. He was 55 years old." Other types of routine stories are those concerning government actions, the courts, crime, holidays, and weather. These stories have standard forms in many newspapers and other publications.

Balance and fairness. One of the basic tenets of American journalism is fairness. Journalists should attempt to give all people involved in a news story a chance to tell their sides of it. If an accusation is made by a news source concerning another person, that person should be given a chance to answer in the same story. Journalists should not take sides in a controversy and should take care not to even appear to take sides.

Writing and editing a balanced story means more than just making sure a controversial situation or issue is covered fairly. In a larger sense, balance means that journalists should understand the relative importance of the events they cover and should not write stories that overplay or underplay that importance. Journalists are often charged with "blowing things out of proportion," and sometimes the charge is a valid one. They should make sure that they are not being used by news sources and being put in a position of creating news rather than letting it occur and then covering it.

The concepts of balance and fairness sometimes come under the name of objectivity, a term you are likely to hear often in the world of the mass media. Objectivity means that a news reporter, editor, and publication could and should report only what they know and can find out. They should be scrupulously "fair" to all sides of a story, although "fair" has many different meanings. In being objective, news people should not inject themselves or their opinions into a report. Objectivity assumes not only that journalists should do all of these things but that they can do them.

Many inside and outside the profession have come to believe that journalists cannot achieve the standards set by objectivity and that attempts to do so actually hurt their performance. Objectivity, they argue, demands that journalists suspend their judgment in ways that would prevent them from fully informing their readers and viewers. Journalists must always decide what stories to cover, whom to use as sources, and what information to include and exclude in their reports. The very fact that these decisions must be made flies in the face of an ideal standard of objectivity.

The impersonal reporter. Closely associated with the concepts of balance and fairness is the concept of the impersonal reporter. Reporters should be invisible in their writing. Reporters should not only set aside their own views and opinions, but they should avoid direct contact with the reader through the use of first-person (I, we, me, our, my, us) or second-person (you, your) pronouns outside of direct quotes.

Reporters and editors inherently state their opinions about the news in deciding what events they write about, how they write about them, and where they place those stories in the paper. No journalist can claim to be a completely unbiased, objective observer and deliverer of information. Yet stating opinions directly and plainly is generally not an acceptable practice. Even for reporters to include themselves with readers is not a good idea. For example, the following lead is not acceptable because of its use of a first-person pronoun: "The Chief Justice of the Supreme Court said yesterday our legal system is in serious trouble." There may be someone reading this story who makes no claim to the United States' legal system, and the reporter should write for that person as well as for all who do.

Journalism in this era is beginning to see cracks in the armor of the impersonal reporter. More personal references are showing up in news stories, and reporters are acknowledging their own involvement in news events. One example of this occurred during the Persian Gulf War in 1991 when Peter Arnett of the Cable News Network was allowed to remain in Iraq and to send live reports from there while American bombers were destroying many parts of the country. Arnett's unique position was part of

Tips on AP Style

Punctuation

- A colon is used in clock time.
  8:15 a.m.   9:15 p.m.   10 a.m. (not 10:00 a.m.)

- General rules for the hyphen: (See hyphen entry in punctuation section at the back of the stylebook for complete guidelines.)
  - The hyphen is used in phrasal adjectives:
  a 7-year-old boy   an off-the-cuff opinion
  a little-known man
  - But the hyphen is not used in sequences in which the adverb has an -ly suffix:
  a gravely ill patient   a relatively weird student
  - In combinations of a number plus a noun of measurement, use a hyphen:
  a 3-inch bug   a 6-foot man   a two-man team
  - A hyphen is always used with the prefix -ex, as in:
  ex-president   ex-chairman

- The comma is omitted before Roman numerals and before Jr. and Sr. in names:
  Adlai Stevenson III   John Elliot Jr.

by David Davies

the story itself, and both he and CNN recognized that in their reporting of the war. Readers and viewers often realize that reporters are involved in the stories they cover, and news organizations feel they should honestly state what that involvement is.

Reliance on official sources. Much of the information printed in the news media comes from what we might call "official" sources. These sources are those who are thought to have expertise on the subject, not those who may merely have opinions about the subject. An example of this reliance might be found in a story about inflation. A journalist writing a story about inflation would probably use information from government reports and the studies and opinions of respected economists and influential politicians. These would be the official sources, and they would have a large amount of credibility with the reader. An "unofficial" source might be a homemaker, who would certainly have an opinion about the effects, causes, and cures of inflation, but who would probably not have information that would be credible in the mass media.

The use of official sources has come under scrutiny and some criticism. Studies of sources used by journalists show that the sources themselves are relatively few in number, thus limiting the range of information and opinion that is presented to the reader. Another objection to the use of official sources is that too few people affected by events are quoted. The example of the inflation story in the previous paragraph is a good example. The unofficial source of the homemaker or the hourly wage earner is often ignored. Finally, media critics object to official sources because they are likely to be white and male. Relatively few women and members of other ethnic and racial groups make it into the realms of official sources.

Attribution and quotes. Journalists should make it clear to readers where information has been obtained. All but the most obvious and commonly known facts in a story should be attributed. Writers should make sure that the attributions are helpful to the reader's understanding of the story and that they do not get in the way of the flow of the story.

A number of journalistic conventions have grown up around the use of indirect and direct quotations. First, except in the rarest instances, all quotes must be attributed. The exception is the case where there is no doubt about the source of the quote. Even then, editors should be careful.

Second, using quotation marks around a word or group of words means that someone has spoken or written those exact words. A writer must not put words inside quotation marks that have not been used by the source. Sometimes a writer is tempted to say, "I know my source said that, but I am sure she meant something else, so I'm going to change the quote to what was meant rather than what was said." This is a dangerous practice at best. In this situation, the best course for the writer is to get in touch with the source and ask about the quote in question. Most of the time, people's exact words will accurately express their meaning.

Finally, should incorrect grammar and slang, profane or offensive language appear in a direct quotation? Most publications have policies in place for the use of profane or offensive language. The question of bad grammar plagues journalists. Journalists have a commitment to accuracy, which dictates that they should use the exact words that their sources use. Quoting someone using bad grammar can make that person appear unnecessarily foolish and can distract from the real meaning of the story. Most professionals believe that if a source is used to being quoted, grammatical mistakes should be included in the statements they make. The grammatical mistakes of those who are not used to talking with journalists should be changed, however. Neither practice should be followed in every instance. Writers and editors should make a decision together when these situations come up.

These conventions are important to observe if journalists are to gain the respect of their readers and colleagues. Conventions should not be looked upon as arbitrary rules that must be followed at the expense of accuracy and clarity. Rather, they are a set of sound practices that are extremely useful to journalists in the process of deciding what to write and how to write it.

Journalistic style

English is an extremely diverse language; it gives the user many ways of saying the same thing. For instance, 8:00, eight o'clock, 8 A.M., eight a.m., and eight in the morning may all correctly refer to the same thing; a reference may be to the president, the U.S. president, the president of the United States, and so on. All of these references are technically correct, but which one should a journalist use? And does it really matter?

The answer to the first question is governed by journalistic style. Style is a special case of English correctness which a publication adopts. It does so in order to promote consistency among its writers and to reduce confusion among its readers. Once a style is adopted, a writer won't have to wonder about the way to refer to such things as time.

Journalistic style may be divided into two types of style: professional conventions and rules of usage. Professional conventions have evolved during years of journalistic endeavor and are now taught through professional training in universities and professional workshops. The rules of usage have been collected into stylebooks published by wire services, news organizations, syndicates, universities, and individual print and broadcast news operations. Some of these stylebooks have had widespread acceptance and influence. Others have remained relatively local and result in unique style rules accepted by reporters and editors working for individual news organizations.

For example, a publication may follow The Associated Press Stylebook and United Press International Stylebook and say that AM and PM should be lowercase with periods: a.m. and p.m. The writer will know that a reference to the president of the United States is always simply "president," lowercased, except when referring to a specific person, such as President Clinton.

Likewise, the reader will not be confused by multiple references to the same item. Unconsciously, the reader will expect the style that the publication uses. Consequently, if the reader is very familiar with a college newspaper and that paper always refers to its own institution as "the University," uppercase, the reader will know what that means.

Similarly, a reporter may follow the usual convention in newspaper writing and write the sequence of time, date, and place of a meeting despite the fact that it may seem more logical to report the date before reporting the time.

Having a logical, consistent style is like fine-tuning a color television. Before the tuning, the colors may be there and the picture may be visible. Eventually, however, the off-colors and the blurry images will play on the viewer's mind so that he or she will become dissatisfied and disinterested. That could cause the viewer to stop watching altogether. In the same way, consistent style harmonizes a publication so that reading it is easier for a reader and offers few distractions from the content.

Beyond that, the question may still remain: Does style really matter? The answer is an emphatic "yes!" Many young writers think of consistent style as a repressive force hampering their creativity. It isn't. Style is not a rigid set of rules established to restrict the creative forces in the writer. Style imposes a discipline in writing that should run through all the activities of a communicator. It implies that the communicator is precise not only with writing but also with facts and with thought. Consistent style is the hallmark of a professional.

Adherence to a consistent style is also important to society. As Thomas W. Lippman writes in the preface to The Washington Post Deskbook on Style, "A newspaper is part of a society's record of itself. Each day's edition lives on in libraries and electronic archives, to be consulted again and again by the scholars and journalists of the future. The newspaper is thus the repository of the language, and we have a responsibility to treat the language with respect. The rules of grammar, punctuation, capitalization, spelling, and usage set down here are our way of trying to meet that responsibility."

Editors are the governors of the style of a publication. It is their job to see that style rules are consistently and reasonably applied. If exceptions are allowed, they should be for specific and logical reasons and should not be at the whim of a writer. Editors and writers should remember that consistent style is one way of telling readers that everything in the publication is certified as accurate.

Stylebooks

Stylebooks are a fact of life for writers for the mass media. Any area of writing, from newspapers to advertising agencies to public relations firms, will require the use of some form of stylebook. Stylebooks deal primarily with three things, the first and foremost being consistency. The main reason for the existence of any stylebook is to promote consistency in writing. To do this, a stylebook establishes the rules of writing for a publication. These are often arbitrary rules, such as using a.m. instead of AM to refer to morning times and spelling certain numbers out while using figures for others. These rules also eliminate inconsistencies in spelling, such as mandating that the Southeast Asia country be spelled Vietnam rather than Viet-Nam. Stylebooks also deal with usage, particularly when dictionaries assign a variety of meanings to a word. A good stylebook will say when a word should be properly and consistently used. Beyond that, a good stylebook helps a writer find the precise words he or she needs.

This chapter refers mostly to The Associated Press Stylebook and Libel Manual because that is the most commonly used reference for writers in the mass media. The first AP stylebook appeared in 1953, growing out of demands from newspaper editors who subscribed to the Associated Press wire service. Many of these editors wanted to make their local copy consistent with the copy they were receiving and running from the AP. Many of these same newspapers also subscribed to the nation's other major wire service, United Press International, and they wanted the wire services to use a consistent style. Consequently, AP and UPI got together and came up with a common stylebook in 1960. These first stylebooks were simply small handbooks that dealt mainly with the rules of writing. During the next decade, newspaper editors saw the need for a book that would also deal with usage, so in 1975 a committee of editors from AP and UPI again cooperated to compile a comprehensive stylebook that would answer many of the questions that arise in newsrooms daily.

Other publications have produced comprehensive stylebooks. Two of the most influential are The New York Times Manual of Style and The Los Angeles Times Stylebook. Each contains many local references and has become the major style reference for writers on those publications. Most publications, however, have small stylebooks that deal with local style questions and preferences and rely on a larger reference, such as The AP Stylebook and Libel Manual, to answer broader questions.

Any publication, even college newspapers and yearbooks, should have its own stylebook because there are always local questions a major reference work will not answer. For instance, how should students be identified? One college newspaper stylebook says that students should be identified by class rank and major, as in "Mary Smith, a junior in journalism"; a stylebook for another student newspaper says that students should be identified by major and hometown, as in "Mary Smith, a journalism major from Midville." Style problems like this one need to be answered by a local stylebook.

Another important style reference is A Manual of Style by the University of Chicago Press. This book is the chief reference for what is known as the "Chicago style," a style used by most book publishers. It contains a number of major differences from the AP Stylebook. For instance, Chicago style mandates that numbers one through one hundred be spelled out, while AP style says that numbers one through nine should be spelled out. Chicago style began as a single proofreader's sheet in 1891 and was first published for those not working with the University of Chicago Press in 1906. Today it is more than 500 pages long and deals extensively with footnotes, referencing, and many other style problems that arise when books are produced.

Still another important style reference is the Style Manual of the U.S. Government Printing Office. This is the style guide for all government publications and is particularly good in dealing with governmental material and foreign languages.

Stylebooks are an important factor in the life of a media professional. They should be adhered to, but with a note of caution. Roy Copperud, author of A Dictionary of Usage and Style, criticizes those who use style rules arbitrarily or who enforce style rules that make no sense. "Meditation and prayer lead to the conviction that the best style is the one which governs least." Style rules should not inhibit creativity or initiative in writing. They should promote readability. Style, as The United Press International Stylebook points out, is the "intangible ingredient that distinguishes outstanding writing from mediocrity."

The Associated Press Stylebook

The Associated Press Stylebook is as much a reference manual today as it is a book of rules for consistent writing. The book has been expanded to explain the differences in words that some are tempted to use interchangeably. It gives valuable information that will help reporters and editors understand a wide variety of topics. It contains lists of weights and measures, military titles and sports terms. The book has references on governmental agencies and prominent companies and private organizations.

The heart of the book is still the rules of writing. The following are some of the AP style rules for problem areas that confront beginning writers:

Capitalization. Unnecessary capitalization, like unnecessary punctuation, should be avoided because it slows reading and makes the sentence look uninviting. Some examples: Main Street, but Main and Market streets; Mayor John Smith, but John Smith, mayor of Jonesville; Steve Barber, executive director of the State Press Association. (Note lowercase title after name, but uppercase for State Press Association, a formal name and therefore a proper noun.)

Abbreviation. The trend is away from alphabet soup in body copy and in headlines, but some abbreviations help conserve space and help to simplify information. For example: West Main Street, but 20 W. Main St. The only titles for which abbreviations are called for (all before the name) are Dr., Gov., Lt. Gov., Mr., Mrs., Rep., the Rev., Sen., and most military ranks. Standing alone, all of these are spelled out and are lowercased. Check the stylebook for others.

Punctuation. Especially helpful are the sections of the stylebook dealing with the comma, hyphen, period, colon and semicolon, dash, ellipsis, restrictive and nonrestrictive elements, apostrophe, and quotation marks.

Numerals. Spell out whole numbers below ten, and use figures for ten and above. This rule applies to numbers used in a series or individually. Don't begin sentences with numerals, as a rule, but if you must, spell them out.

Spelling. In journalism a word has but one spelling. Alternate spellings and variants are incorrect (because of the requirement of style consistency). Make it adviser, not advisor; employee, not employe; totaled, not totalled; traveled, not travelled; kidnapped, not kidnaped; judgment, not judgement; television, not TV, when used as a noun; under way, not underway; percent, not per cent; afterward, toward, upward, forward (no 's); vs., not versus or vs; vice president, not vice-president. Check the stylebook or a dictionary for others.

Usage. Comprise means to contain, not to make up. "The region comprises five states," not "five states comprise the region" and not "the region is comprised of five states." Affect means to influence, not to carry out. Effect means a result when it's a noun and means to carry out when it's a verb. Controller and comptroller are both pronounced "controller" and mean virtually the same thing, though comptroller is generally the more accurate word for denoting government financial officers, and controller is better for denoting business financial officers. Hopefully does not mean it is hoped, we hope, maybe, or perhaps -it means in a hopeful manner: "Hopefully, editors will study the English language" is not an acceptable usage of the word.

Ages. Use numerals always: a 2-month-old baby; he was 80; the youth, 18, and the girl, 6, were rescued.

Dates. Feb. 6 (current calendar year); in February 1978 (no comma); last February.

Dimensions. He is 5 feet 9 inches tall; the 5-foot 9-inch woman; a 7-footer; the car left a skid mark 8 inches wide and 17 feet long; the rug is 10 by 12. The storm brought 1 1/2 inches of rain (spell out fractions less than one).

Language sensitivity

Writers must understand that language has the ability to offend and demean. Readers and viewers of the mass media are a broad and diverse group, and those who would communicate with them should be aware of the language sensitivities of some of the people within that group. While some people have gone to extremes in identifying supposedly offensive language, there are terms and attitudes in writing that should legitimately be questioned and changed. The current state of public discourse demands it.

Writers have not always paid attention to such sensitivities. Phrases such as "all men are created equal" and "these are the times that try men's souls" drew no criticism for their inherent sexism when they were first published, largely because women were not allowed to be a major part of the public debate. We may accept those phrases now because we understand the context in which they were written, but we would not approve of them if they were written in our age.

Media writers should examine their work closely to make sure that they have treated people fairly and equitably, that they have not lapsed into easy or commonly accepted stereotypes, that they have not used phrases or descriptions that demean, and that they have included everyone in their articles who is germane to the subject. The following are a few areas in which writers should take special care:

Sexist pronouns. It is no longer acceptable to use the pronoun he when the referent may be a man or woman. "A student should always do his homework" should be "A student should always do his or her homework." In some instances, rewriting the sentence using plurals is easier: "Students should always do their homework." Sometimes a sentence can be rewritten so that it does not require any pronoun. "Students should always do homework that is assigned."

Titles. Many titles that had sexist connotations, such as "mailman" and "fireman" are being phased out of the language, becoming "mail carrier" and "firefighter." (In these two cases, not only are the terms gender neutral, but they are much more descriptive.) Writers need to be aware, however, that some gender-based titles are still common, and they should look for more acceptable alternatives.

Descriptions. "All people are described equal." That awkward take-off on the Thomas Jefferson phase should be an abiding principle of the modern writer for the mass media. One of the classic areas in which this has not been done has been references to women's appearance and attire. Sometimes such references are important to an article, but often they are not. They are included gratuitously and as such are offensive.

Racial descriptions and references may not be necessary. Richard Arrington was the mayor of Birmingham, Alabama. To describe him as "Richard Arrington, the black mayor of Birmingham" is not necessary unless it is important to the understanding of a story to know his race. The test here is to ask the questions, "What if Richard Arrington were white? Would it be important to know that?"

Stereotypes. Our society abounds in stereotypes, and not all are based on race. We describe women who stay at home as women who "don't work." We refer to a "Jewish mother" as someone with certain hectoring characteristics, not remembering that not all Jewish women who have children have those characteristics. We write about "southern bigots," forgetting that bigots can live anywhere in the country. An older woman who has never married is called a "spinster," when she may never have spun anything in her life. We should constantly question these blanket references and phrases-and more importantly, our attitudes that give rise to these descriptions.

Illness and disability. American society is taking some steps, by private initiative as well as by law, to open itself to people who have various handicaps, disabilities, or limitations. One of the things that Americans should learn as this happens is that identifying people by these limitations is in itself unfair and inaccurate. To say that a person "has a handicap" is different from

Tips on AP Style

Time

- Time in newspaper usage is always a.m. or p.m. Don't use tonight with p.m. or this morning with a.m., because it is redundant. Don't use the terms yesterday and tomorrow to describe when an event occurred. It is OK, however, to say today.

- In describing when an event happens, use the day of the week if the event occurs in the last week or the next week. BUT, use the calendar date if the event is longer than a week ago or farther than a week off.

- Generally, it's more readable to put the time, then the date, when an event will occur:
  RIGHT: The train arrives at 3 p.m. Jan. 3.
  WRONG: The train arrives on Jan. 3 at 3 p.m.

- Never put both the day of the week and the date that an event will occur:
  RIGHT: The fireman's ball will be on Jan. 3.
  WRONG: The fireman's ball will be on Monday, Jan. 3.

- CORRECT: It's 7 p.m.
  INCORRECT: It's 7:00 p.m.

by David Davies

saying that a person is "handicapped." The way in which these limitations are referred to can also be disabling. For instance, to describe someone as a "reformed alcoholic" is neither complimentary nor benign; "reformed" implies that the person did something wrong and now the problem is solved. A person who is an alcoholic but who no longer drinks is "recovering." To say that someone has a "defect," such as a "birth defect," is to demean by implication (i.e., the person is defective). It would be better to say a person "was born with a hearing loss."

These are just a few of the areas in which writers need to maintain great sensitivity and to continue close examination of their work. Constantly questioning what you have written and making reasonable changes is not just the mark of a good writer; it is a sign of an intelligent and sensitive person.

Conclusion

This chapter attempts to introduce you to the concept of style and what it means to those who work in the mass media. Conforming to the rules and conventions of the medium in which you are working is the mark of a true professional. Strict adherence to the details of style shows that you care about what you write.

Points for consideration and discussion

1. How has this chapter changed your thinking about the meaning of "style" and its use in writing for the mass media?

2. What are some of the reasons why there is such a strong emphasis on accuracy in writing for the mass media? How does adherence to a consistent style contribute to goal of accuracy for a journalist?

3. Find a piece of writing in which you think that writer used big words instead of simple ones. Rewrite it using the simpler language. Now compare the two pieces of writing. Which is better?

4. Some people say that a consistent style restricts creativity, while others say it enhances creativity. What are the arguments on both sides of this question?

5. The concept of objectivity is a controversial one in the field of journalism. Why do you think it causes so much controversy?

Further reading

The Associated Press Stylebook and Libel Manual. 6th ed., New York: The Associated Press, 1996.

Theodore Bernstein, The Careful Writer, A Modern Guide to English Usage. New York: Atheneum, 1973.

Theodore Bernstein, Watch Your Language. Great Neck, NY: Channel Press, 1958.

Roy Copperud, A Dictionary of Usage and Style. New York: Avenel Books, 1982.

Thomas W. Lippman, The Washington Post Deskbook on Style. New York: McGraw Hill, 1989.

A Manual of Style. 14th ed, Chicago: University of Chicago Press, 1993.

The New York Times Manual of Style and Usage. Allan M. Siegal and William G. Connolly, New York: Times Books, 1999.

Lawrence C. Soley. The News Shapers: The Sources Who Explain the News. New York: Praeger, 1992.

William Strunk and E.B. White. The Elements of Style. 4th ed. Boston: Allyn and Bacon, 1999.

U.S. Government Printing Office Style Manual. Rev. Ed. Washington, DC: Government Printing Office, 1993.

On the Web: Check out The Curmudgeon's Stylebook, at a place called The Slot: A Spot for Copy Editors, www.theslot.com, or Webmaster Writing Resources at www.cio.com.

Chapter 3 Style & the stylebook

Exercises

• *The following section contains a variety of style exercises. You should follow your instructor's directions in completing them.*

3–1 Using the stylebook

1. He was charged with trafficing in drugs.

2. The Rev. Billy Grahm said God was alive and His will would triumph.

3. The flag, which Francis Scott Key saw, has been preserved.

4. life-like, outfielder, inter- racial, IOU's (plural)

5. Pianoes, nation-wide, P.T.A., Viet-nam War

6. The train will arrive at twelve noon on Tues.

7. The US Census Bureau defines the south as a seventeen state region.

8. The judge ruled that because of his oral skills he had entered into a verbal contract.

9. She had an afternoon snack of some Oreo cookies and Coke.

10. harrass, accomodate, weird, likeable

11. Circle the correct form:

    Donut, doughnut

    pants suit, pantsuit

    plow, plough

    U.S. Weather Bureau, National Weather Service

3-2 Using the stylebook

Correct the following items so that they conform with AP style.

1. The defense department is about to propose a new missele system.

2. F.C.C., hitch-hiker, three dollars, 4 million

3. The three most important people in his life are his wife, son, and mother.

4. part-time, 10 year old child, 5 PM, 5300

5. The cardinals won the last game of the world series, 7 to 5.

6. spring (season), fall (season), south (point on compass), south (region)

7. November 15, the last day of Feb., Mar. 16

8. 13 people travelled to Austin, Tex. for the rally.

9. He had ten cents left in his pocket.

10. home-made, well-known, Italian-American, questionaire

3–3 Using the stylebook

Correct the following items so that they conform with AP style.

1. The U.S. is sometimes not the best market for U.S. products.

2. Circle the correct form:

   upward, upwards

   British (Labour, Labor) Party

   Riverside (Ave., Avenue)

   cupsful, cupfuls

   eying, eyeing

3. The Republican differed from the Democrat many times during the debate.

4. Dr. John Smith and Dr. Mary Wilson preformed the operations.

5. Circle the correct form:

   good will, goodwill (noun)

   USS Eisenhower, U.S.S. Eisenhower

   cigaret, cigarette

   midAmerica, mid-America

6. He said he was neither a Communist or a member of the Communist Party.

7. After her surgery, she had to wear a Pacemaker.

8. "What a hair-brained scheme!" she exclaimed.

9. preempt, speed-up (noun), 55 miles per hour, hookey

10. The underworld, or mafia, was responsible for the murder.

3–4 Using the stylebook

Correct the following items so that they conform with AP style.

1. The first annual rutabaga eating contest was canceled because of averse weather.

2. Its not alright to drink an access of beer before going to the football game.

3. Like Einstein said, all knowledge is relative.

4. The state capital of Alabama is located at 3722 Dagwood Rd.

5. The Mayor refused to go along with the City Council vote. "I descent," he stated.

6. Madonna certainly has a flare for fashion; she always wears expensive outfits.

7. The bomb totally destroyed Senator Kitsmoot's bird cage.

8. My bright green Chevrolet which is in the garage needs a new transmission.

9. Knopke's hilarious joke illicited laughter from the Midville city council.

10. Jones laid on the floor waiting for the job interview to begin.

11. Horowitz, an ethics major, vowed never to compromise his principals.

12. At the end of the book report, Haynes sited the World Book as a source.

3–5 Using the stylebook

Correct the following items so that they conform with AP style.

1. The twenty-five-year-old man wept as he left Hattiesburg, Mississippi.

2. This November 10th will mark our anniversary.

3. Don't park the car on Rodeo Dr. Instead, park it at 12 Davies Street.

4. They spent 130 dollars to buy a new set of nose rings.

5. Smoots moved to the North because the people there are so nice.

6. At 7 p.m. this evening, the rodeo will begin in the Town Square.

7. Yesterday, the Terrorists blew up their home at 123 Melrose St.

8. 22 seamstresses were needed to mend the prom dresses.

9. About 5 percent of the professors have lost their hair.

10. After 2 feet of snow fell at his home in Columbus, Ohio, Jones decided to leave.

11. Miss Smith bet fifty dollars that her brother weighed more than a 1964 Chevy.

12. Guy Reel, the Governor of Calif., set his trailer on fire September 1.

13. A fire began at 3325 McDonald Dr. when an oven full of rutabagas exploded.

14. During the 1970's, everyone wore bell-bottom blue jeans to church.

3-6 Using the stylebook

Correct the following items so that they conform with AP style.

1. In Aug. 1985, Davies rented a rutabaga stand in Augusta, Georgia.

2. Pomerantz tied the beehive to Senator Gramm's cowboy hat.

3. About 1200 easter rabbits were killed in the explosion at Big Dave's Bunny Warehouse, located at 2525 Hackensack Drive.

4. In the 1980's, Davies left the Midwest and moved to the Loire Valley in France.

5. Smoots brought two cups of coffee to the Governor.

6. About eight percent of the cantaloupes have been stuffed with rutabagbas.

7. Jones bet 40 dollars that his roommate had hidden the sandwich.

8. The 3 university professors share a house at 613 25th Avenue.

9. After 2 feet of snow fell at his home in Columbus, Ohio, Davies decided to leave the midwest and move to the South.

10. On December 11th, all classes will been canceled.

11. Yesterday morning, the Mayor skipped her aerobics class.

12. Davies drove 2,000,000 miles in his old Toyota Corolla before it blew up.

13. Doctor Kildare said he had filed a malpractice suit against Marcus Welby.

14. At eight p.m. in the evening, Governor Jim Guy Tucker of Arkansas will give a short speech in front of the Gorgas library.

3–7 Using the stylebook

Correct the following items so that they conform with AP style.

1. Estalene Smoots dropped her french class the 1st day of school.

2. Sadie Hoots won 3,200,000 dollars on Wheel of Fortune.

3. Frustrated that their professor required them to eat fried rutabagas, the students walked out of class at 9 a.m. this morning.

4. The office manager had twenty-one plants, sixty-two cats and two puppies.

5. President Aubrey Lucas is originally from Compton, California.

6. On October 25th, Ruth Ann Bobetski will turn 41.

7. Goober Hicks lives at 10 West Hardy St. He used to live in a run down shack at 2803 Williamsburg Rd.

8. Abby gave birth to a nine pound baby boy.

9. The President invited me to dinner at the white house, but I could not fit it into my schedule.

10. Senator Davies said his earnings had increased 10% in the 1980's.

11. Barney the dinosaur will be executed on Tuesday, November 2.

12. 25 vagabonds attacked me from behind in front of the hub.

13. Miss Snarkle found a 10 inch bug crawling in her spaghetti. "Great! Now I won't need seconds", she exclaimed.

14. All the men in the R.O.T.C. chapter wore red, white, and blue pantyhose to class in Jan. 1991.

15. The Bay City baseball team lost their final game two to one and climbed dejectedly back onto their bus.

3–8 Using the stylebook

Using the AP stylebook, answer the questions or correct the sentences or phrases.

1. What is the acceptable form of abbreviation for miles per hour?

2. What is the difference between civil and criminal cases?

3. **Correct this sentence:** The eye witness found himself in an eye to eye confrontation.

4. If GMT is used on second reference, what must accompany it?

5. When do you capitalize grand jury?

6. Which is correct: Scene two, Scene 2, scene two, or scene 2?

7. Correct the spelling of "cuetips."

8. Which one of these refers to the building where government resides: capital, Capital or capitol?

9. What use of the term "working class" needs a hyphen?

10. Which term is correct: Christian Science Church or Churches or Christ Scientist?

3–9 Using the stylebook

Using the AP stylebook, answer the questions or correct the sentences or phrases.

1. The United States (constitutes, composes, comprises) 50 states.

2. How would you write "In the year of the Lord 33"?

3. What is the correct title for Russian leaders before 1914?

4. What is an acceptable abbreviation for the ocean liner Queen Elizabeth II?

5. Which of the following is incorrect: court-martials or cupfuls?

6. What is the long name for the Machinists union?

7. How should the term "NROTC" be used correctly in journalism?

8. Which of the following is not an acceptable term for the journalist to apply to a religious group: evangelical, Pentecostal, or liberal?

9.Which of these words has to do with flowing water: pour or pore?

10. Where are the headquarters for Northwest Airlines?

3–10 Using the stylebook

Correct the following items so that they conform with AP style.

1. His solution turned out to be the most equal of the two.

2. Ga. Sec. of State George Smith testified at the Congressional hearing.

3. tis, the Gay 1890's, a South America country, 1492 A.D.

4. Write the plurals for the following words:
Eskimo,_____ ; chili, _____ ; memorandum, _____ ; ski, _____

5. The ballif opened the court by saying, "Oyes, oyes, oyes!"

6. He spread out his palate and went to sleep.

7. carry-over (adj.), nitty-gritty, nit-picking, know-how

8. What do the following abbreviations stand for?

   USIA _____ _____

   GOP_____

   EST _____

   TVA _____ _____

   Are any of these abbreviations acceptable for first reference?
   _____

9. The pan had a teflon surface.

10. He was graduated from a teacher's college in the north.

3–11 Using the stylebook

Correct the following items so that they conform with AP style.

1. Write the plurals for the following words: referendum, _____; court martial, _____; 1920, _____; dead end, _____.

2. Daylight savings time begins on the last Sun. in April.

3. He made the Dean's List after Dean Smith talked to him.

4. The game, that was scheduled for to-night, was rained out.

5. He said the car would go further on premium gas.

6. The movie which starred Sam Jones received an r rating.

7. He had run the gauntlet of criticism and abuse for his views.

8. The woman who the article referred to was a German Jewess.

9. judgement, naval orange, resistible, self-defense

10. He played semi-pro baseball for 3 years.

3–12 Using the stylebook

Correct the following story so that it conforms to AP style. The story contains other errors besides style errors that you will need to correct. Use the proper editing marks.

Baseball game

The Bay City Bluebirds rallied from a 3-run defict last night to defeat the Carmel Cardinals 6-3 and win the Western Tri-state division championship.

The bluebirds are now assured a place int eh Tri-state playoffs which begin next week. Their opponent will be determined tonight in a game between the Santa Ana Gnerals and the Redwood Knights.

The cardinals led the bluebirds for most of the game, and they hasa 3-0 lead in the eighth inniny.

In the bluebird hafl of the eighth, Tim Story, the first baseman, walked and stole second. Bill Holden Biff Curbosi was walked intensionally, and both runner moved up a base on a wild pitch by cardinal started ronnie Miller. Miller was then relieved by Chuck Nelson.

Bluebird secondbaseman Carbo Garbey lined Nelson's first pitch into deep centefield, scoring both baserunners. Two pitches later, Garbey stole home to tie the game.

Nelson got the next 2 hitters out, but then Carey Clark, the bluebird catcher, homered to put the bluebirds ahead. The bluebirds added two more runs in the ninth to insure their victory.

3–13 Using the stylebook

Correct the following story so that it conforms to AP style. Use the proper editing marks.

Guilty verdict

    A jury found a Midville man guilty of Second-Degree Manslaughter after an hour's worth of deliberations on Tuesday.

    Johnny Gene Garber was convicted at the end of a 3-day trial which featured his mother testifying against him. He was charged in the death of a thirty-nine year old brickmason, Gardner Jackson, of Number Twelve, Ninth Street in Jonesville.

    Mr. Garber stood sliently as the jury read the verdict. The Presiding Judge, Jonas T. McMillan, set a sentencing hearing for next Monday at eight o'clock in the morning.

    Garber was charged with being druck while driving down highway 69 last March. His car served out of control and ran head on into a car driven by Mr. Jackson, who had been attending services at the Midville Baptist church.

    During the trial, the Prosecution Attory, Able Sasson, called Garber's mother, Mrs. Minnie Lee Garber, to testify that her son had been drinking heavily at there home that evening before the accident occured.

    Garber could recieve a sentence of two to five years in prison for the crime he committed.

3–14 Using the stylebook

Correct the following story so that it conforms to AP style. The story contains other errors besides style errors that you will need to correct. Use the proper editing marks.

City council

The city council passed an ordinance last night requireing people convicted of their second drunk charge to serve a minimum of thirty days in jail and to have their driver's license suspended for six months.

The ordinance was passed by a vote of five to three.   Councilman Clarissa Atwell sponsored the change in the law which wil take effect on December 31st of this year.

"I think this new law will save the lives of a lot of people, Miss Atwell said.

The council chamber was filled to overflowing with people interested in the law. Many of the people there were members of Mothers Against Drunk Driving (M.A.D.D.)

One Councilamn who voted against law, Les Honeycutt, said he felt the laws against drunk driving were strong enough and that they needed to be inforced for rigidly. His comments received hoots and jeers from the crowd, and at one point the council president, Harley Sanders, trhreatened to have some of the audience removed and evicted.

3–15 Using the stylebook

Correct the following story so that it conforms to AP style. Use the proper editing marks.

Power failure

Power was cut off to nearly a 3rd of the residents of Midville, last night, after a violent storm ripped through the city around six o'clock.

Police chief Robert Dye said that power was restored to most homes within about two hours, but "a substantial number of people," had to go without power for most of the night.

Chief Dye said that many of the city's traffic lights were knocked out by the storm, and traffick problems developed on several of the more busy streets.

Chief dye says that everything should be back to normal today.

A power company official said that more than 1500 homes were without electricity for some part of the night. They said that crews worked throughout the entire night to get people's power turned on.

The storm dumped over 2 inches of rain on the city in about 30 minutes. The power failure was due to lighting hitting one of the power companys substations in the Western part of the city.

4

Writing in the media environment

Introduction

On the evening of Nov. 7, 2000, millions of people gathered in front of their televisions sets, tuned in their radios and called up their favorite news web sites. They were seeking the results of the 2000 presidential election and the many local elections that had taken place that day. The next morning, millions of people bought newspapers and read about the continuing saga that resulted from that remarkable day.

Reading and viewing the news about the presidential election were individual acts, but it was also a shared experience. We read and viewed, and then we talked. We may have used the telephone or e-mail or Internet chat rooms to discuss the events with friends, acquaintances or even strangers.

Each of us could form our own opinions and interpretations about why the presidential election ended the way it did. But what we shared was the news.

News is one of the elements that holds a society of diverse people together. The fact that a group of individuals share the same current information allows the group to operate as a community. If we were all hermits, or if we dealt with only the small group of people with whom we have physical contact, news might not matter so much. Our interests extend far beyond our group of acquaintances, however, and one of the ways we establish relationships with those beyond this group is to share the same current information.

This centrality of news makes the news story a fundamental form of writing for the mass media. Those who would write for the mass media in any form must understand the importance of news and should master the news story format.

Writing for the mass media is one of the most important jobs in our society. The people who do this job have a tremendous impact on the shape and direction of the community. They tell us about ourselves. They establish a bond between the individual members of the society and the community and nation as a whole. They must be honest, talented, and dedicated. The job is too important and too difficult for people of lesser qualities.

The writer for the mass media has two jobs. The first is gathering information; the second is putting that information into the form appropriate for the medium in which he or she is working. This chapter explores the environment of writing that is common to most mass media organizations. While not every such organization deals with the political and cultural information we call news, most media organizations have a news and information function that they must perform.

The news culture

Anyone involved with the mass media – even if the person does not work for what we normally think of as a news organization – is part of the news culture and must understand the professional standards and demands that this culture imposes.

The news culture arises from the fact that we deal with information. Media professionals gather and process that information and put it into a form that is distributed to a wide audience for specific purposes. Those purposes can include informing, persuading or entertaining an audience, but information is always at the core of what any media professional does.

Because of this centrality of information, the media professional is governed by a number of considerations.

The first is the need for accurate information. We will discuss the importance of getting good information and presenting it accurately in several parts of this book. Here we should simply say that the quality of information with which the writer must deal is irrevocably tied to the writer's credibility and reputation for fairness. In fact, more than anything else, accurate information determines how good a professional writer is. Getting accurate information and presenting it accurately — no matter what the purpose of the writing — is the writer's first and foremost duty.

Another consideration of the news culture is presenting information efficiently. Many of the forms of writing that we will discuss in this book, whether news, advertising or public relations, are structured to enhance efficient delivery of information.

Tied to this efficiency is yet another consideration of the news culture — the economic health of the organization. In most instances, media professionals work for organizations that are subject to the rules of the marketplace. Their survival depends on their ability to gather the audience, advertisers and income to pay expenses. Writers must understand their role in how an organization functions in the marketplace.

Writers in the news culture must also understand thoroughly the processes of the organization. One of the most important parts of this understanding is the concept of deadlines. Writers must not only produce good work, but they must meet the deadlines that the organization establishes.

Finally, the idea of individual and corporate integrity must be part of the daily life of the media professional. An individual's commitment to honesty, fairness, and ethical standards should be strong, and the writer's confidence in the corporation's standards should be well placed. An individual professional does not have to agree with every decision made at the corporate level, but there should be a degree of confidence in the overall organization that is never violated.

Accuracy, efficiency, processes, deadlines, and ethics are all part of the news culture. Students entering into this discipline must understand their importance, and the demands that are made on individuals who would work in this environment.

News values

What makes an event news? The same thing could happen to two people in two different places, and one would be a news story and the other would not. For instance, if you were involved in a minor automobile accident where there were no injuries, the incident probably would not appear in your local newspaper. If the president were involved in that same type of accident, it would probably be the first story on all the nightly newscasts.

The separation of events into "news" and "not news" categories is a function of what we call news values. These are concepts that help us decide what a mass media audience is or should be interested in. There are millions of events that occur in our society every day. Only those few events editors and news directors select and have at least one of the following criteria can be classified as news.

Impact. Events that change people's lives are classified as news. The event itself might involve only a few people, but the consequences may be wide-ranging. For example, if Congress passes a bill to raise taxes or if a researcher discovers a cure for a form of cancer, both actions will affect larger numbers of people. They have impact, and they would be considered news.

Timeliness. Timeliness is a value common to almost all news stories. It refers to the recency of an event. Without the element of timeliness, most events cannot be considered news. For example, a trial that occurred last year is not news; a trial that is going on right now may be news. How much time has to elapse before an event can no longer be considered news? No one answer applies to every case. Most events that are more than a day to a day-and-a-half old are not thought to be news. (Look in today's newspaper and see if you can find a news story about an event that occurred two days ago.)

Prominence. Prominent people, sometimes even when they are doing trivial things, make news. The president of the United States is a prime example. Whenever he takes a trip — even for purely personal and private reasons — his movements are covered in great detail by the news media. The president is a prominent and important person. Anything he does is likely to have an impact on the country, and people are very interested in his actions. The president is not the only example of a prominent person who often makes news. Movie stars, famous politicians, advo-

Figure 4-1

News values

One of these pictures appeared in newspapers around the world. The other appeared only in a local daily. What news values are at work here?

Photos
from
White House website;
Amy Kilpatrick

cates of social causes — all of these people make news simply because they are very well known.

Proximity. Events occurring close to home are more likely to be news than the same events that occur elsewhere. For example, a car wreck killing two people that happens on a road in your home county is more likely to be reported in the local news media than the same kind of wreck which occurs 1,000 miles away. We are interested in the things that happen around us. If we know a place where something goes on, we are more likely to have a feeling for it and for the people involved.

Conflict. When people disagree, when they fight, when they have arguments — that's news, particularly if one of the other news values, such as prominence, is involved. Conflict is one of the journalist's favorite news values because it generally ensures there is an interesting story to write. One of the reasons trial stories are so popular with newspaper readers and television watchers is that the central drama involves conflict — two competing forces, each vying to defeat the other.

The bizarre or unusual. A rare event is sometimes considered news. There is an adage in journalism that goes, "When a dog bites a man, that's not news; when a man bites a dog, now that's news." These events, though they may have relatively little importance or involve obscure people, are interesting to readers and enliven a publication. For example, it's not news when someone's driver's license is revoked (unless that someone is a prominent person); it is news, however, when a state department of transportation revokes the license of a person called "the worst driver in the state" because he had twenty-two accidents in the last two years.

Currency. Issues that have current interest often have news value, and events surrounding those issues can sometimes be considered news. For example, a panel discussion of doctors may be held in your community. Normally, such a discussion might not provoke much interest from journalists. If the discussion topic were "The Latest Cancer-fighting Drugs," the news value of the event would change, and there would likely be a number of newspaper, radio, and television journalists covering it. Issues that have the value of currency come and go, but there are always many such issues being discussed by the public.

A news writer and editor must make decisions about events based on these news values. News values are also used in deciding the kind of information needed for a story and in helping the writer structure the story so that the most important and interesting information gets to the reader in the most efficient manner.

Gathering the news: Five Ws and One H

Basic to all writing is having the information that you will use in the writing process. Writing for the mass media requires that certain information be gathered at the beginning of the writing process. A journalist gathering information or writing a story tries to answer six basic questions for the reader:

Who. Who are the important people related to the story? Is everyone included so that the story can be accurately and adequately told? Is everyone properly identified?

What. What is the major action or event of the story? What are the actions or events of lesser importance? A journalist ought to be able to state the major action of the story in one sentence, and this should be the theme of the story.

When. When did the event occur? Readers of news stories should have a clear idea of when the story takes place. The when element is rarely the best way to begin a story because it is not often the most important piece of information a journalist has to tell a reader, but it should come early in the story and should be clearly stated.

Where. Where did the event occur? Journalists cannot assume readers will know or be able to figure out where an event takes place. The location or locations of the event or action should be clearly written.

Why and How. The reader deserves explanation about events. If a story is about something bizarre or unusual, the writer should offer some explanation, so the questions the event raises in the reader's mind are answered. The writer also needs to set the events or actions in a story in the proper context. Reference should be made to previous events or actions if they help to explain things to the reader.

Acquiring the information needed to write anything for the mass media is an essential part of the writing process. Information is not always self-evident or readily available. The process of reporting — gathering the information — takes considerable skill, creativity, and tenacity. What the writer needs, of course, depends upon what he or she is writing about, but essentially a writer has three fundamental sources of information: people, records (any information written or stored so others may find it), and personal observation.

Personal sources

Most information in most news stories comes from personal sources — that is, people. A news reporter is likely to spend most of his or her nonwriting time talking to people either face to face or over the telephone. In fact, many would argue that the more people the reporter talks to, the better a story is likely to be, because of the variety of information and views the reporter can obtain.

Here are some examples of paragraphs from news stories in which the information comes from personal sources:

> According to the theater owner, Martin Miller, about 340 attended the first-night showing of the controversial film.
>
> Although he attended the inauguration, the congressman said he disapproved of the amount of money spent on the event.
>
> "I'm against that proposal because it's unfair to the middle class," the senator said.

The first two of the examples are indirect quotations or paraphrases; the third is a direct quotation. The next chapter discusses more fully the handling of direct and indirect quotations.

Interviewing is when a reporter talks to a source. All writers who deal with information — whether they are newspaper reporters, magazine writers or public relations practitioners —

must master the art of interviewing. A reporter tries to determine what information the source has and would be willing to share. Then the reporter attempts to ask the kind of questions that would elicit this information. The techniques of interviewing are discussed more fully in the next section of this chapter.

Journalists develop "sources" among the people whom they contact regularly; that is, the reporters will find people who have information and are willing to talk with the reporter about it. Reporters soon realize that many people can provide them with information and sometimes that information can come from surprising sources. For instance, most reporters who are assigned to a beat — a term in journalism meaning a place or topic a reporter must write regularly about — learn that secretaries, rather than their bosses, are the best sources of information. Secretaries often know what is happening before their bosses do. Consequently, many reporters get to know the secretaries on their beats very well. As reporters and sources deal with each other, they should develop a relationship of mutual understanding. Reporters find out whom they can trust among their sources, and sources realize the information they give to reporters will be used wisely.

One general rule governs the relationships reporters have with their sources — reporters should always identify themselves clearly to their sources. Sources should know before they talk to reporters the information they give may be used in a news story. Sources should have the opportunity not to talk with news reporters if they do not want to.

Attribution in a news story means telling readers where information comes from. Attribution phrases are those such as "he said," "she said," and "according to officials." Most of the major information in a news story needs to have some attribution, particularly information that comes from personal sources.

Interviewing

Interviewing ranks at the top of the most important activities a mass media professional can undertake. Talking with people is the chief way we have of gathering current information about almost any topic. Within the daily press, more information is collected through interviews than by any other method.

News stories use two kinds of quoted material — direct quotations and indirect quotations. Direct quotations are those words that the source has used to express an idea; those words should be surrounded by quotation marks.

```
"I believe the tax reform proposal would
wreck our economic recovery," the presi-
dent said.
```

Indirect quotations, or paraphrases, express what the source said but use different words from those the source used.

```
         The president expressed his oppo-
         sition to the tax reform proposal cur-
         rently before Congress, saying it would
         hurt the nation's economic recovery.
```

A paraphrase may use some of the exact words of the source, and the writer may want to put those inside quotation marks.

```
         The president expressed his oppo-
         sition to the tax reform proposal cur-
         rently before Congress, saying it would
         "wreck our economic recovery."
```

The qualities of the "good" interview (from the standpoint of the journalist) mirror the qualities of any good conversation. The participants quickly reach an understanding about why they are talking with one another. They exchange views and information. They learn something about one another. They share nonverbal gestures, such as smiles or frowns.

Yet, interviewing for the journalist is not just having a good conversation. The journalist's purpose in an interview is to gain information and material for an article that will be disseminated to others. Because of that purpose, a journalist needs to develop interviewing skills that include not only proper conduct during the face-to-face conversation but also proper preparation and follow-up. The following are some of the steps a journalist should take in having successful interviews.

The first step in interviewing is deciding, sometimes simultaneously, what information is needed and who would be the best source for that information. A journalist should have a clear idea of what information it will take to make a good article. Developing that kind of clear idea takes some experience, but it is certainly within the grasp of the beginning reporter. The information that a reporter needs will often dictate who the best source is to provide that information, but the selection of the source may depend on other factors as well. For instance, the best source for certain information might not be available or might be hesitant to talk with a journalist. These are situations in which journalists might have to find other sources of information.

The second step to a successful interview is preparing for the conversation. This preparation may include doing research on the topic of the interview or on the person to be interviewed. In general, the more the journalist knows about both, the more successful the interview is likely to be. In the world of daily journalism, time and deadline pressure may not permit much preparation. In such instances, the journalist must draw upon his or her experience and the cooperation of the source.

Another part of the preparation phase of the interview is figuring out what questions to ask. The questions, of course, will depend on the information needed, but they will also depend on the willingness of the source to give information. Information that is simple and not necessarily controversial can usually be gained from clear, straightforward, and efficient questions, as in the following exchange:

> Reporter: Can you tell me how the wreck occurred?
>
> Police officer: Well, the witnesses said it wasn't raining but the roads were pretty wet from a thunderstorm that had just come through the area. The car traveling in the westbound lane put its brakes on for some reason and the car skidded out of control and into the eastbound lane.
>
> Reporter: Why did the car brake?
>
> Police officer: We're not sure. Maybe an animal ran across the road. Sometimes at night, especially in wet conditions, you think you see things that aren't there and you hit the brakes.
>
> Reporter: What happened when the car skidded?
>
> Police officer: It skidded about fifty feet and slammed into a car in the eastbound lane. A third car, also traveling eastbound, then crashed into those cars. Fortunately for everyone else, those were the only three cars involved in the wreck.
>
> Reporter: Was anyone hurt?
>
> Police officer: Yeah, two people were hurt pretty bad, and two others were injured. Everyone was alive when we got them to the hospital. You'll have to check with the hospital to see how they are doing. . . .

This short exchange has given the reporter a lot of information (though certainly not everything) that can be included in a story. Chances are the reporter did not have much time to prepare for this interview. But the reporter understands news values and story construction well enough to ask relevant and productive questions.

Sometimes the information a reporter seeks is much more controversial and the source is not as adept or as willing to give the information. Journalists should be sensitive and empathetic with their sources, but they should also remember their professional responsibilities.

Interviewers have different methods of asking questions, and they will employ these methods when they are appropriate for the situation. Here are some of the various types of questions they can ask:

Closed-ended questions: These usually require very short answers or the question itself may contain a choice of answers from which the respondent will choose. How often do you travel out of town? Do you feel good or bad about the way things turned out?

Open-ended questions: Sometimes an interviewer will want to give a subject the chance to say anything he or she wants.

Open-ended questions allow this to happen. What do you think is the most important issue facing the city council now? When you think about a person who is homeless, what picture comes into your mind?

Hypothetical questions: These are questions that set up a situation or condition and ask the interviewee to respond to it. They are sometimes known as "what if" questions. If someone came to you and asked your help in finding a job, what would you tell that person?

Agree-disagree questions: As the name implies, these questions ask respondents to express agreement or disagreement with a statement or action. Some people say Congressmen should be prevented from serving more than two terms. Do you agree or disagree with that?

Figure 4-2

Interviewing tips

1. Think of your audience in preparing questions.

2. Prepare at least 20 questions in advance.

3. Avoid asking yes/no questions.

4. Start with the 5 W's and H questions.

5. Don't be afraid to leave your set of questions if your interview goes off on an interesting or newsworthy tangent.

6. Be on time for the interview. Dress appropriately.

7. At first, introduce yourself and state the purpose for your interview.

8. Break the ice with light conversation before beginning questions.

9. Let your subject do the talking.

10. Listen carefully to your subject's answers and take very good notes. Develop an efficient note-taking system.

11. Get at least three good, insightful direct quotes.

12. Write down exact spellings of names. Double check them. Then triple check them.

13. Ask for permission to telephone your source later for more information if necessary.

14. Know the background of the person you are interviewing.

15. Collect more information than you think you'll need.

16. Don't be bashful about asking the person to repeat something important.

17. Be aware of your surroundings during the interview. A few notes about the room and other surroundings may be useful in a feature story to help set the mood of your piece.

18. Leave the most difficult questions for last.

Probes: These are questions that follow up on something the interviewee has said. They can be neutral (Can you tell me more about that?), provocative (Are you saying you will never do that?), or challenging (I think a lot of people will find that difficult to believe.). The purpose of a probe is to get the interviewee to give more information about what he or she has just said.

Personal questions: These questions have to do with the personal life of a subject. They may be very relevant to the article the journalist must do, but these questions need to be approached carefully. Most experienced interviewers agree such questions should be left until the middle or end of the interview, giving the respondent a chance to establish some trust in the interviewer.

One of the most important products of planning an interview is for the journalist to have a list of questions that will be asked when the interview takes place. Because interviews are not always predictable, it may not be feasible or necessary to ask every question — and it may be that unplanned questions arise — but a journalist should always have some kind of a plan for the interview session.

The next step in the interview process is to establish contact with the source and to set up some mutually agreeable time and place to conduct the interview. When a reporter is working near a daily deadline, he or she may insist the interview be conducted immediately on the phone. In other instances, however, a source should be told who wants to conduct the interview, for what publication it will be conducted, and what information, in general, the reporter needs. The reporter should be flexible about the time and the place of the interview so that it is as convenient for the source as possible.

During the interview itself, a reporter should keep in mind why the interview is taking place: to obtain certain information but also to remain open to possibilities that other, more interesting or important information may be obtained. If a source decides to offer some new or surprising information, the reporter should be able to evaluate the worth of the information and handle it appropriately. Most of the time, however, a reporter's planning will pay off with an efficient and productive interview. The following are a number of things that an interviewer should keep in mind about an interviewing situation:

• Control the situation. Keep the conversation on track by remembering what you came for and what information you need to get from the source. Refer to your notes or questions.

• Normally, the first few questions will set the tone for the interview, so the reporter should think carefully about how the interview should be structured. If there are difficult questions the reporter needs to ask — questions that would make the source uncomfortable — they are usually not the questions that should be asked first. Those questions will be easier to ask and answer later in the interview when the reporter and source have established some rapport.

• Take notes. Do so as unobtrusively as possible, but if you are there as a journalist, the source will expect you to do this. Write down the key words and phrases that the source uses if you

Figure 4-3

Tom Clancy, author of *The Hunt for Red October,* on writing and interviewing

Every person you meet—and everything you do in life—is an opportunity to learn something. That's important to all of us, but most of all to a writer because as a writer you can use anything . . . I never even got aboard a nuclear sub until *Red October* was in final editing. On the other hand, I have talked with a lot of people who are or were in this line of work.

cannot get every word. Concentrate on what is being said so you can reconstruct an accurate quote later. Even during the interview session you should begin thinking about what information and direct quotations you will use in your article.

• If you don't understand what a source has said, ask that the quote be repeated. Read back what you have written to make sure that you have it right. If you don't understand a word or phrase the source has used, ask about it. It is better you show your ignorance to the source than to thousands of readers or viewers when you do your story.

• If a source attacks or criticizes you, try to respond as little as possible. Remember you are there to get information, not to defend yourself.

• Use a tape recorder only if you have the permission of the source. Ask the source's permission before you turn it on. If the source is reluctant, you might say, "This will help me make sure I get everything you say correctly." If the source will not permit the use of the tape recorder, do not use it.

• Even if you use a tape recorder, always take notes. A tape recorder may not work, or the tape may be bad. Any number of things can happen.

• Sometime during the interview, take note of something other than what is being said such as gestures or other physical details of the source, pictures or awards on the wall, or other objects in the room. You may see something you want to ask about or something you will want to use in your article.

• Always be courteous and professional.

As soon as possible after the interview, you should go over your notes and listen to your tape recording. Many reporters will listen to a tape and fill in their notes. If there is no tape, it is a good idea to read your notes carefully and fill in parts of the interview you may want to use in your article.

If possible, a reporter should check important information that the source has given with another source to verify it. Many reporters have been taken in by sources who sounded as if they knew exactly what they were talking about. These reporters have looked foolish in print or on the air when they used the information they had obtained.

Finally, a reporter should never hesitate to call a source back for more information or for clarification of information or discrepancies. These callbacks show that a reporter is serious about producing an accurate report, and sources who are honest will not mind helping the reporter in this effort.

Observation

The second major source of information for the news reporter is observation. Whenever possible, news reporters attend the events they are writing about. They like to see for themselves what happens, even though they rarely write from a first person point of view. Here are some examples of news reports that have used observational sources:

> The anti-abortion rally drew people from many areas of the Midwest. Cars in the parking lot bore license tags from Missouri to West Virginia.

> Bailey High's Sam Love kicked a 14-yard field goal in the first period, and Mateo Central's Jack Mayo had a 34-yarder in the second period to account for the second-lowest scoring first half in the history of the championship game.

> The packed courtroom listened, in a hushed silence, as the defendant took the witness stand and began to tell her story.

In each of these cases, it is clear that the reporters attended the events they described. One indication of this is the lack of attribution in each of these paragraphs.

Observing is more than just watching an event or being there. Good reporters are active observers. They often enter a situation knowing what they want to watch for and what information they need for an article. They also remain open to bizarre or unusual events, so that such events can be included in what they write.

Good observation requires the reporter to develop a sense of what is significant. The fact that two members of a city council confer before a vote is taken and then vote the same way may raise a question in the mind of a reporter — a question that he or she will want to find the answer to after the meeting has occurred. If the reporter had not seen the conference, no question would have been raised, and something significant might have been missed.

Good reporters also put themselves in a position to see what they need to see. Physical positioning is a key part of good reporting. A reporter who wants to do a story on what it is like to be on the sidelines at a football game would not stay in the press box during the game. Visiting a scene before an event takes place — if possible — is a good idea and usually allows a reporter to gain insight about an event.

News reporters are obligated to put what they see into their stories whether or not it makes the people they are writing about look "good" or "bad." Some actions or information may be embarrassing to people, even those in authority. A reporter must not make a judgment about what to include in a news report based on that. The reporter's obligation is to the readers who are expecting an accurate account of an event.

Generally, reporters do not participate in events. If the event is a demonstration, they do not carry signs and march with a group. At a city council meeting where citizens are asking questions or making statements to the council, they do not join in by asking their own questions. At the same time, reporters should not leave their humanity behind. If they can prevent injury or help out in an emergency situation, they should certainly do so.

Stored sources of information

"You can look it up!" Casey Stengel used to tell reporters who gathered around him in the manager's office of the New York Yankees baseball team. Stengel, who led the Yankees to a record string of championships in the 1940s and 1950s, was known for his long, involved answers to the simplest questions. He would often end his circumlocutions by saying, "You can look it up!" — a challenge to those who might not believe what he had just said.

What Stengel told reporters is what most of us already know: a vast amount of information is available to be "looked up." This stored information includes any books, reports, articles, press releases, documents, and computer-stored information to which a reporter has access. Here are some examples of reporters using stored sources:

```
Furillo, who died Sunday, played right
field for the Brooklyn and Los Angeles
Dodgers from 1946 through 1960. He won
the NL batting title with a .344 average
in 1953, when he missed the last few
weeks of the season because of a broken
hand he sustained during a fight with
manager Leo Durocher.
```

Figure 4-4

Ten basic references you should know

CURRENT BIOGRAPHY. This monthly publication contains excellent biographical pieces on notable personalities. A typical entry runs 3000-3500 words and contains personal information such as birthplace, birthdate, names of family members as well as thorough coverage of a person's career. Another source, called *Biography Index* is also useful for finding magazine profiles of individuals.

ENCYCLOPEDIA OF ASSOCIATIONS. This publication contains entries for thousands of social, political, medical, religious, labor, legal, cultural, scientific, educational associations, and groups. Also it includes fan clubs and hobbyist groups. Each entry includes a description of the group's mission, names of executives, the number of members, and the size

"You can look it up!"

— **Casey Stengel**

of the group's budget. The companion volumes, *Research Centers Directory, Government Research Directory* and *International Organizations* are also useful.

FACTS ON FILE. An indispensable source of news information, *Facts on File* is a weekly publication containing detailed summaries of the past week's stories. There are weekly, annual and five-year indexes.

OFFICIAL CONGRESSIONAL DIRECTORY. This is the official source for basic information on Congress. It in-cludes biographical sketches of members with descriptions of their congressional districts, committee assignments and committee staff, and maps of congressional districts. The name, address and phone number of foreign ambassadors and consular offices in the United States as well as a list of U.S. Ambassadors abroad are also here.

READER'S GUIDE TO PERIODICAL LITERATURE. This is an index to general interest magazines such as *Time, Life, Newsweek, Business Week, Fortune,* and *Forbes* and it is a good place to start research on any subject. Another index, called *Public Affairs Information Service* (PAIS) is an index to more specialized sources of information primarily concerning public policy issues.

STATISTICAL ABSTRACT OF THE UNITED STATES. The standard summary of U.S. government statistics, the *Statistical Abstract,* has been published annually for 109 years. Use it to find data on population, birth, marriage, divorce and death rates, educational statistics such as enrollment figures and graduation rates, crime rates, unemployment rates, GNP, poverty rates, consumer price indexes, interest rates, housing, business, agriculture, and selected comparative international statistics.

THE UNITED STATES GOVERNMENT MANUAL. This is the official handbook of the federal government and provides comprehensive information on judicial, legislative, and executive branch agencies. Use this book to find out a particular agency's official name, its mission, when it was founded, how it is organized, and who its key officials are.

WHO'S WHO. Just because someone is not in the current edition of *Who's Who in America* does not mean they aren't in another edition. There are multiple Who's Whos (*Who's Who of the South, Who's Who of the East,* etc.)

THE WORLD ALMANAC AND BOOK OF FACTS. Useful features include a chronology of the year's major news stories, population, sports, weather, economic statistics, presidential biographies, maps, basic information on cities, states, and nations, U.S. and world history, weights and measurements conversion tables, a perpetual calendar, lists of prize winners, colleges and universities, and a list of noted personalities with their places of birth and birth dates. It also has the text of the Constitution, the Declaration of Independence, and the Gettysburg Address.

```
A City Social Services Department report
estimated that more than 10,000 people
were "without permanent or temporary
shelter" in the city last year.

A statement issued by the new adminis-
tration said that foreign policy prob-
lems would be high on the president's
agenda.
```

Stored sources are located in many places — government documents, company records, books, magazines, and so on. A news
reporter should be familiar with the holdings of the local public
library because that can be a major source of stored information.

Chances are, however, the modern journalist has a library as
close as the keyboard of his or her computer. That library, of
course, is the World Wide Web, or the Internet. Most libaries and
many businesses are connected to the internet so that employees
can "look it up" more easily than ever before.

Akin to the Internet is the stored information that is found in
on-line or electronic information services. Such services provide
subscribers with fingertip access to a wide range of information,
such as newspapers, magazines, television transcripts, governmental reports, legal opinions, encyclopedias, library card catalogues and many other sources. These services come through
telephone lines from central data banks to personal computers.
People who work with information, particularly those in the mass
media, are relying more and more heavily on these on-line data
bases.

In most cases, information that comes from stored sources —
like that which comes from personal sources — should be attributed. In two of the examples above, the attribution is clear.
Occasionally, as in the first example, the information may either
be common knowledge or be available in many references so that
telling the reader the source is not that important.

Stored information, whether it comes from a library or from
the Internet, presents the reporter with two basic problems. The
first problem is management — how do you find what you need?
Sometimes, just "looking it up" is not nearly as simple as it
sounds, and when you are faced with the enormous amount of
information that is available through the Internet, the problem is
compounded. Most reporters develop strategies for exploring
information sources mainly through experience. The more a
reporter uses a library or an internet search engine, the more he
or she will understand what information is available and where it
is more likely to reside.

The second problem is that of reliability. Is the information
that you get correct? How do you know? Assessing the reliability
of information has always been a problem for reporters, but it,
too, has been compounded by the expansion of information that
is available. Reporters should consider carefully the source of the
information in assessing its reliability. They should also try to
find the same information from another source, if possible and if

there is some doubt about the original source. They should remember that just because something is in a book in the library — or posted on a Web page on the Internet — does not make it accurate.

The importance of accuracy

The overriding goal of the writer for the mass media is accuracy. The attempt to be accurate must govern all of the actions of the writer, from the way he or she gathers information to the language that is used to convey that information. Previous chapters have discussed the necessity of using the language precisely and about the attention that a writer must give to the format, style, and usage in writing. These efforts are important because ultimately they help increase the accuracy of the writing that is produced.

This attention to precise writing should be preceded by an attention to the details of reporting. Developing good habits in gathering information will pay off for the reporter in many ways. The following are some of the areas of reporting that deserve the special effort of a reporter.

Spell names correctly. One of the most important possessions a person has is his or her name. The misspelling of a name is more likely to offend someone than almost any other mistake. Consequently, news reporters should take special care to make sure they have the correct spelling for the names they use in their stories. They should never assume they can spell a name correctly. For instance, "John Smith" may really be

John Smithe
John Smythe
John Smyth
Jon Smith

The person whose name you are spelling is the best source for the correct spelling, and you should never be afraid or embarrassed to ask. In fact, asking specifically often demonstrates that you are trying to be careful and increases the confidence that source has in you.

Checking with the person may not always be possible, however. In that case, telephone directories and city directories are generally reliable sources for correctly spelled names. The people who put these directories together are professionals and understand that they are creating a resource that will be checked by others. Police reports, printed programs and other such material are not reliable sources, and they should not be used for name checking.

Quote your sources correctly. This chapter has already discussed gathering and using quoted material, and more discussion will follow in the next chapter. The point here is to make sure you get it right. Many people who are used as sources in news reports complain about being "misquoted" or "quoted out of context." Often that is a way for the source to back away from what he or she has said after it has been printed or broadcast. On the other hand, news reporters do make mistakes, and it is their responsibility — not that of the source — to make sure they have heard and understood what the source has said. The simplest remedy to not understanding what the source has said is to ask. Make sure you know not only what words the source has used but the meaning that the source has given to them.

Get information from more than one source if possible. As a general rule, news stories are better if reporters get information from more than one source. Different people know various things about a situation, or they may have differing viewpoints about it. The more people a news reporter talks to about a story, and the more records that he or she checks, the more likely he or she will be to understand the story fully.

Getting information from multiple sources sometimes will saddle the reporter with contradictory information. Where the contradictions are apparent and important, the reporter should attempt to resolve them among the sources; otherwise, the reporter will have to choose which source he or she feels is the most reliable. Either way, the process of resolving contradictions will usually deepen a reporter's understanding of the information.

Make sure that the numbers in a story add up correctly. Numbers don't have to throw journalists, but they often do. For instance, consider this paragraph about a student election that appeared in a college newspaper:

```
Officials said a total of 5,865 ballots
were cast, representing a 34.2 percent
turnout. Smith defeated Jones by receiv-
ing 3,077 votes to Jones' 2,385, a mar-
gin of 393 votes.
```

The reporter should have done two things with this story. He or she should have added up to the totals for the two candidates to make sure that total matched the total number of ballots cast. If the numbers did not match, the news reporter should have found out why. Second, the story says that "officials" said there was a 34.2 percent turnout. The reporter should have gotten the figures that these officials used and done his or her own calculations. It may be that the 34.2 figure is correct. The reporter should have made sure.

Deadlines

The chief enemy of media writers — and occasionally their friend — is time. No matter what the medium, there comes a point when the writing must be finished and put into production. That point is called a deadline, and almost all writers must adhere to some kind of deadline.

Figure 4-5

A Newsweek graphics journalist takes a ride
By Kevin Hand

On your deathbed there will be moments that flash through your mind in your lingering last minutes. As a journalist, you will probably collect a few. Here's one of my special moments to savor.

During the first week of my job at Newsweek, my boss sent me up in a helicopter to view a house that was part of a crime story we were doing. They had scant reference on the properties, so I agreed and headed for the heliport. When I got there, I teamed up with a freelance photographer who was also shooting for the magazine .

After we got into the air, the helicopter was jolting violently. The pilot said, it will be better once we get away from the city. Melissa, the photographer, smiled with a pleasant, what-am-I-doing-here smile.

When we got to the area of the properties, there was another problem. My boss had told me the day before that the helicopter pilot would know where the house was. He didn't. "We can get you to the exact area, but it's up to you to find the exact house," he said. I had studied the home in the pictures we had, but you can't see street signs from 1,500 ft. I got new contacts, but crap, dude. It took only 15 minutes to get to the area and the pilot said 'OK, the coordinates say we're over the house.' I look down and... thousands of homes... all the same. I panic.

That was the least of my worries.

While, desperately, trying to locate the correct home, I realize that we are circling in a nauseating manner. Actually, my stomach noticed it before I did. Melissa was looking a little green too. I managed to find the home just seconds before the first dry heave.

Melissa saw this and began gagging. I wrestled a small window (the size of half your face) open. My nose, lips, chin and part of my lower eyelids were instantly subject to 30° temperatures while I expulsed my wretched cargo. The pilot, not happy about what I done to the outside of his copter, then told us there were barf bags in the middle compartment.

By the time I turn around to look for the bags, I see the photographer with a hand full of breakfast too. There were no bags. I found a garbage bag in her stuff and held it for her.

Do you want to go back?" the pilot asked. I thought, well, first week on the job. First assignment. First chance to do an important graphic. No, we had to finish. So while snapping four rolls of film, we traded off puking and getting pictures.

It was a real quiet ride back to the heliport. When we got back to Newsweek, we laughed about it and promised not to tell anyone. Somehow, it was mentioned in the news meeting that the new guy had 'tossed his cookies' in the helicopter.

Now, I'm affectionately known as the Barfman. Nice ring.

There is a lesson here.

Kevin Hand is a graphics journalist for Newsweek magazine. He has also worked for the Honolulu Star-Bulletin and the Chicago Tribune.

Deadlines vary according to the type of medium for which you are writing. Broadcasters have some of the most immediate and intense deadlines. A broadcast writer must finish writing sometime before a newscast is aired; otherwise the copy will not be used, and the writer will have worked in vain. Reporters for daily newspapers face at least one and sometimes several deadlines each day. Their deadlines are not as rigid as those of broadcasters. Sometimes they can be missed by a few minutes, and the production of the newspaper will still proceed. Still, the deadline pressure is undeniable. (Try observing a newspaper's newsroom 15 or 20 minutes before a deadline and the increased activity — reporters making phone calls, typing on computer terminals, huddling with editors — will be evident.) Many writers are attracted to magazines because the deadline pressures of their publications do not occur as often as with newspapers or broadcast stations. That is the case, but the deadlines still exist, and when they approach, they too exert great pressure on writers. The same is true for writers in advertising and public relations, who face deadlines on a daily basis.

The one medium in which the deadline pressure seems less is the web. Web site producers are not under the strict time pressures of broadcasters, nor must they conform to the production schedules of newspapers and magazines. Still, they are not deadline free. The pressure on web writers and editors come from users themselves who visit web sites expecting the latest information. Consequently, web writers must work quickly but without many of the internal pressures that face writers for other media.

Deadlines force writers to produce. Few writers for the mass media experience serious cases of "writer's block," the inability to write. Those who work in the mass media simply cannot survive unless they complete their assignments in some form. In fact, the excitement of an approaching deadline can energize a writer, allowing him or her to produce good work in a very short period of time.

Deadlines also allow media organizations to function. They allow production schedules to be set and news broadcasts to be aired. They allow presses to be run at certain times so newspapers can get their issues to their carriers.

But deadlines have serious drawbacks for the writer. They impose a psychological and sometimes physical pressure on the writer that can be wearing and may ultimately lead a writer to quit the mass media altogether. Deadlines also create or encourage a dependency on formula writing. A writer will find it easier to write things as he or she has done it before, rather than to be creative or to let the content of the writing dictate the form. In the news and information business, deadlines sometimes prevent adequate fact-checking and editing of copy, and that has had embarrassing or even legal consequences for the writer and the news organizations. Finally, deadlines shorten the time that a writer has to assimilate the information and ideas that he or she is writing about and to understand their context.

Despite these drawbacks, deadline writing is an irrevocable fact of life for the media writer. No wide-ranging alternatives to deadlines exist, and it is unlikely that any will be developed.

Ethical considerations

Much has been written about the ethics and ethical dilemmas of people who work in mass communication. Professional associations such as the Public Relations Society of America, the American Advertising Federation, and the Society of Professional Journalists have developed codes of ethics or rules of behavior that are supposed to govern the actions and attitudes of their members. Scholars have devoted long years of study to classifying ethical dilemmas and identifying appropriate responses to them. Many journalists, advertisers and public relations practitioners attend professional conferences where ethical issues are strongly debated and discussed.

At its root, however, the issue of ethics in mass communication can be summed up rather simply. It begins with a statement of what we might call an "ideal condition" about communication. From that ideal condition, we can then deduce two statements of admonition for the person who is working as a mass communication professional.

Ideal condition: Communication is the mutually beneficial transaction of information and ideas among its participants; participants assume that the information and ideas are truthful and honestly presented.

This condition arises on what we know as the Golden Rule. A form of the Golden Rule is found in many religions, such as Christianity, Judaism, Hinduism, Confucism, and Buddhism, and in the Greek and Roman ethical teachings. "So, in everything, do to others what you would have them do to you." Matthew 7:12 NIV. "What you do not want done to yourself, do not do to others." The Confucian Analects, bk. 17:6.

By using the term truthful, we do not mean that the information is the literal truth. Rather, it is truthful if the originator of the communication believes that it meets the reasonable expectations of those who receive the communication. It is honestly presented if the communicator does not manipulate the conditions or context of the communication to make it something other than truthful.

From this ideal condition we can deduce two admonitions for professional communicators:

Admonition 1: Professional communicators should present truthful information and ideas and should do so honestly.

Admonition 2: Professional communicators should act in ways that will encourage and reinforce the assumption of truthful information and ideas honestly presented.

Most "codes of ethics" of professional organizations prescribe behavior according to this second admonition. They are filled with items such as the following:

The Advertising Principles of American Business, American Advertising Federation: "Advertising shall avoid price claims which are false or misleading, or savings claims which do not offer provable savings."

Code of Ethics, Society of Professional Journalists: "Journalists should identify sources whenever feasible. The public is entitled to as much information as possible on sources' reliability."

Code of Professional Standards, Public Relations Society of America: "A member shall not knowingly disseminate false or misleading information and shall act promptly to correct erroneous communications for which he or she is responsible."

These items reflect the issues that are relevant to the profession at the time they are written and adopted, and the issues change often. The basic admonition remains the same, however: communicators, no matter what discipline they choose, should be honest and should act that way.

The ideal condition and admonitions presented above are stated absolutely and abstractly. They open many questions about what is "truthful communication" and "honest presentation." What is behavior that will "encourage and reinforce the assumption of truthful information and ideas"? Many situations make it difficult for professional communicators to decide the answers to these questions. Those situations — and the way that people react to them — do not affect the basic truth of the ideal condition or its admonitions.

Writing by example

The first three chapters of this book have attempted to introduce you to some of the characteristics, techniques, and rules of good writing. This chapter has tried to describe some of the aspects of writing in a media environment. As you continue through this text, you will be introduced to some of the forms of writing for the mass media.

The writing you do from here on will require something more than an application of the rules of writing that we have discussed. Writers for media organizations must assimilate information and ideas as well as understand the demands and expectations of the particular medium for which they are writing. In short, while learning about media forms, they must think and make judgments about the information and ideas they have to present.

One way of doing this is what we might call "writing by example." Writers can learn a form of writing by following examples as closely as possible. Students should recognize that this form of learning is not cheating or bending the rules. What you write — as long as you are not copying it word for word — is still your original work. But if you pattern it after a good example, you can learn what it takes to produce a particular form of writing.

The next chapters contain many good examples of writing in various media forms. Study them closely. Try to emulate them and make them your own.

Points for consideration and discussion

1. The author says that writing for the mass media is "one of the most important jobs in our society." Do you agree or disagree?

2. Look at three news stories in your local newspaper. What news values are present in each of them?

3. One of the criticisms of the news media that many people make is that journalists emphasize "bad news" rather than "good news." What do you think people mean by that? Do you agree? Do the news values listed in this chapter mean that journalists are more likely to look for "bad news" than "good news"?

4. The author says that secretaries are often good sources of information. Can you think of other job categories that would make good sources for journalists?

5. Why is it important for a journalist to get information from more than one source?

6. On pages 131-132, the author outlines an ethical scheme for people who work in the mass media. What do you think of that scheme? Has the author left out or ignored any important concept?

Further reading

Douglas A. Anderson and Bruce D. Itule, Writing the News. New York : Random House, 1988.

Walter Fox. Writing the News: A Guide for Print Journalists, 3rd ed., Ames, Iowa: Iowa State University Press, 2000.

Rob Anderson, Robert Dardenne, and George M. Killenberg, The Conversation of Journalism: Communication, Community, and News. Westport, Conn. : Praeger, 1994.

John Joseph Brady, The Craft of Interviewing. New York: Vintage Books, 1977.

Fred Fedler, Reporting for the Print Media, 6th ed., Ft.Worth: Harcourt Brace College Publishers, 1997.

Kelly Leiter, Julian Harriss, and Stanley Johnson, The Complete Reporter, 7th ed., Boston: Allyn and Bacon, 2000.

Ralph S. Izard, Hugh M. Culbertson, and Donald A. Lambert, Fundamentals of News Reporting, 6th ed., Dubuque, IA: Kendall/Hunt, 1994.

George M. Killenberg and Rob Anderson, Before the Story: Interviewing and Communication Skills for Journalists. New York: St. Martin's Press, 1989.

Bruce D. Itule and Douglas A. Anderson, News Writing and Reporting for Today's Media, Boston: McGraw-Hill College, 2000.

Ken Metzler, Creative Interviewing, Englewood Cliffs, NJ: Prentice Hall, 1977.

On the Web: One of the best sites about the news media is Jim Romenesko's MediaNews, http://www.poynter.org/medianews/index.cfm. The site is updated daily.

Chapter 4 Writing in the media environment

Exercises

• *The following section contains a variety of public relations writing exercises. You should follow your instructor's directions in completing them.*

4-1 News values

Read the story and answer the questions below.

CHILLICOTHE, Mo.—A jury has recommended a 69-year-old woman be sentenced to death for the murders of four transient farm workers whose bodies were found buried in northwestern Missouri last year.

Jurors in Livingston County Circuit Court deliberated more than three hours before making the recommendation Tuesday night in the case of Faye Copeland, whom the jury had convicted Saturday of five counts of first-degree murder.

The jury of eight women and four men recommended Copeland be sentenced to life in prison without parole on the fifth murder conviction.

Circuit Judge E. Richard Webber must decide whether to accept the jury's recommendations or to sentence Copeland to life in prison. He ordered a pre-sentence investigation.

If sentenced to death, Copeland will become the oldest person on Missouri's death row.

Copeland's attorney, public defender David Miller, has said he will file a motion for a new trial. Miller said he would appeal the court's refusal to allow a psychologist to testify about "battered-wife syndrome."

Miller had argued Faye Copeland was dominated by her 74-year-old husband, Ray, who is awaiting trial on the same charges, and had only a minor role in the crimes.

Ray Copeland's trial is scheduled to begin Jan. 24 but the court first must determine whether he is mentally competent to assist in his own defense. His attorneys contend Ray Copeland suffers from senile dementia, including an organic brain disorder.

The bodies of the victims were found last year in shallow graves in barns or dumped in wells on farms in Livingston County where Ray Copeland had worked. Investigators said the victims had been shot to death. No bodies were found on the couple's farm near Mooresville, about 65 miles northeast of Kansas City.

The Copelands originally were arrested on charges of conspiracy in an alleged fraudulent cattle-buying conspiracy.

Authorities contended the couple hired the transients to work as cattle buyers, then killed and buried them. Prosecutors said the Copelands netted $32,000 by reselling the cattle. The fraud charges were dismissed after the murder charges were filed.

1. What are the news values that are present in each of the stories?

2. List the who, what, when, where, why, and how elements of each story.

3. Which of the three major types of sources of information are used in these stories?

4. List the sources specifically mentioned in each story. How do you think that the reporters were able to get this information?

5. Based on your limited knowledge about the events, analyze each of the stories for accuracy. Are there points in the story that might not be accurate? If you were the editor, what would you question? What would you want the reporter to double-check?

4-2 News values

Read the story and answer the questions below.

NEW YORK—Federal agents and state police continued digging up a suspected secret mob grave Monday, where the remains of at least three people were found buried in a garage behind a locksmith shop, officials said.

The owner of the shop, convicted bank robber Richard Joseph Beedle Sr., 58, appeared in U.S. District Court in New Haven and was ordered held without bond, said U.S. Attorney Stanley A. Twardy Jr.

The bones of three and perhaps four people believed to be victims of warfare within the Patriarca organized crime family in the Hartford, Conn.–Springfield, Mass., area were found in a garage behind Beedle's home, Twardy said.

Beedle was charged with being an accessory after the fact of a murder committed in aid of racketeering, which is punishable by up to 10 years in federal prison and a $250,000 fine, Twardy said.

Arrested on the same charge Monday was Salvatore "Butch" D'Aquila Jr. of Middletown, 48, who operates Central News, a newspaper and variety store on Main Street in Middletown, Twardy said.

D'Aquila has past convictions on state gambling and fraud charges, said Twardy.

FBI agents discovered the mass grave in a garage behind Beedle's home in Hamden on Friday after searching for weeks with the cooperation of another suspect convicted on racketeering charges.

Jack Johns, a reputed organized crime figure arrested in March in a roundup of the Providence, R.I.–based Patriarca family, told authorities that bodies had been buried in Hamden, but he could not remember the address, Twardy said.

Johns rode through the New Haven suburb with FBI agents and spotted the house Friday, Twardy said.

Beedle was arrested and federal and state investigators with a search warrant and picks and shovels dug up the remains over the weekend.

Beedle, who operated Dick's Locksmith Shop in Hamden, was convicted in a 1970 bank robbery in Allentown, Pa., and was long associated with organized crime, New Haven police said.

The grave had been disturbed earlier in an apparent attempt to remove the remains and no other fragments were found in the search which continued Monday, Twardy said.

Twardy said he could not comment on the possible identities of the victims, but a published report said one of those buried in Hamden may be William Grant, an East Hartford restaurant owner who vanished in 1988.

1. What are the news values that are present in each of the stories?

2. List the who, what, when, where, why, and how elements of each story.

3. Which of the three major types of sources of information are used in these stories?

4. List the sources specifically mentioned in each story. How do you think that the reporters were able to get this information?

5. Based on your limited knowledge about the events, analyze each of the stories for accuracy. Are there points in the story that might not be accurate? If you were the editor, what would you question? What would you want the reporter to double-check?

4-3 News values

Read the story and answer the questions below.

A teenager described as a "good guy" who "wouldn't hurt anybody" took a teacher and about 15 students hostage at gunpoint Monday in a local high school classroom, gradually releasing his captives until the stand-off ended more than eight hours later.

The suspect, Eli Dean, 18, did not fire a shot during the siege at Central High School, and no injuries were reported.

By mid afternoon, Dean, who recently was suspended from school for pranks, had released all but five students from a classroom, and early in the evening released four more hostages, state police Sgt. Martin Jenkins said.

The siege ended about 7:30 p.m. EST when Dean surrendered and released the last student, he said.

The youth was armed with a pistol, believed to be a .44-caliber revolver taken from his stepfather's room, Jenkins said, but no shots were fired throughout the ordeal.

Dean, twice suspended from the school in the last two weeks for setting off a fire alarm and breaking a window, went to the school to speak to Melody Money, 43, a teacher who had counseled him about previous trouble at the school, the state police sergeant said.

Dean walked into Money's classroom about 11:10 a.m. and brandished the revolver in front of her and about 15 students, Jenkins said.

The suspect was persuaded to release most of his captives soon after the siege began, but state police could not give an exact count of the number of hostages freed.

Dean continued holding six students and Money until about 2 p.m., when a freshman, Stacy Medelli, was allowed to leave, followed soon by the teacher, Jenkins said.

Dean made no demands throughout the stand off.

A fellow student, Amanda Garr, said she believed the young gunman was "upset" at the recent suspensions but expressed astonishment at his reaction.

"Eli, to me, is the best guy anybody could ever ask for," Garr said. "Something got in him and he's gone crazy about it. He's a very good guy. He wouldn't hurt anybody."

Garr said she and other students at first thought there had been a bomb threat when the school was evacuated and a police SWAT team moved into place, but later "we found out it was Eli and everybody started crying."

The youth's parents and stepfather, Rocky Williams, were called to the school to help police negotiators. Williams said he believes Dean took his .44-caliber revolver from their home.

1. What are the news values that are present in each of the stories?

2. List the who, what, when, where, why, and how elements of each story.

3. Which of the three major types of sources of information are used in these stories?

4. List the sources specifically mentioned in each story. How do you think that the reporters were able to get this information?

5. Based on your limited knowledge about the events, analyze each of the stories for accuracy. Are there points in the story that might not be accurate? If you were the editor, what would you question? What would you want the reporter to double-check?

4-4 News values

Read the story and answer the questions below.

LISBON, Portugal — An American charter jet filled with Italian tourists slammed into a fog-covered mountain in the Azores today and exploded, and all 144 people on board are feared dead, officials and news reports said.

Maria della Versesi, a spokeswoman at the Italian Embassy in Lisbon, said all 137 passengers were Italian and the seven crew members were American. She did not release any names. The aircraft belonged to the U.S. airline Independent Air Corp., based in Smyrna, Tenn.

The flight originated in Bergamo, Italy, and was to have proceeded to Puerto Plata in the Dominican Republic, and Montego Bay in Jamaica, after making a refueling stop in the Azores.

The Portuguese news agency LUSA quoted an official from the Azores Civil Protection Service as saying about 50 bodies had been recovered and it appeared all on board died. LUSA also quoted an unidentified member of a local flying club as saying all the passengers and crew had been killed.

Afonso Pimentel, a LUSA reporter based in the Azores, said the Boeing 707 was preparing to land at Santa Maria airport when it crashed into Pico Alto, a fog-covered, 1,794-foot-high mountain, and burst into flames. LUSA quoted the civil protection official, who was not identified, as saying the pilot asked the airport to clear a runway for an emergency landing.

The Civil Protection Service is a state body that provides rescue services and assistance in civilian emergencies. A.L. Pittman, president of Independent Air Corp., said in an interview in Smyrna that the 15-year-old company makes 400 to 500 charter flights a year, mostly in the Caribbean and Europe.

Pittman, who declined to identify the seven American crew members, said the 20-year-old jetliner that crashed had a relatively low number of flight hours and no history of trouble. Pittman said the airplane, one of two Boeing 707s owned by the company, had 12,500 cycles, or takeoffs and landings, and less than 50,000 hours in the air.

1. What are the news values that are present in each of the stories?

2. List the who, what, when, where, why, and how elements of each story.

3. Which of the three major types of sources of information are used in these stories?

4. List the sources specifically mentioned in each story. How do you think that the reporters were able to get this information?

5. Based on your limited knowledge about the events, analyze each of the stories for accuracy. Are there points in the story that might not be accurate? If you were the editor, what would you question? What would you want the reporter to double-check?

4-5 Selecting news

You are the editor of your hometown newspaper, and you need to select the stories that will go on the front page for tomorrow's paper. Below are the first two paragraphs of the news stories from which you must make your selection. Which four of the following would you select? In what order? Be prepared to justify your answer.

DEARBORN, Mich. — Ford Motor Co. said Monday it is recalling more than 127,000 1987-model Ford Thunderbirds and Mercury Cougar cars with 3.8 liter V6 engines to correct unacceptable emissions levels.

Dealers will be asked to install free of charge a vacuum retard delay valve and change the ignition timing. Cars affected were built for sale in 49 states, with California and Canadian vehicles not affected.

A Bay Minette woman was uninjured after a fiery one-car accident on Alabama 225 early Monday morning.

The 1987 Chevrolet driven by Janice Singleton, 28, apparently caught fire in the wreck just north of Baldwin 40, a state trooper spokesman said Monday.

Ms. Singleton was able to escape the car and then abandoned it, the spokesman said. She later notified local police that she was unhurt.

MONTGOMERY, Ala. — An 8-month-old North Carolina boy was reunited with his mother, while the Iowa couple accused of abducting him were expected to be returned next week to North Carolina to face kidnapping charges.

The infant's mother, Susan Tarlton of Greensboro, N.C., offered advice to other parents when Larry Wayne Tarlton arrived at a North Carolina airport. The child was abducted three weeks ago.

CAPE HATTERAS, N.C. — The severed bridge that is the only link between Hatteras Island and the mainland could be repaired within 45 days, state officials say.

Previous estimates indicated repairs could take at least six months. A dredge battered the bridge during a Friday storm, causing a 370-foot section of the structure to collapse.

BELLEVUE, Wash. — Government health experts Wednesday launched a nationwide, federally funded program to detect hepatitis B among pregnant women and immunize their infants against the serious liver infection.

Doctors from the U.S. Centers for Disease Control and the National Foundation for Infectious Diseases told public health officials at the first of a series of regional conferences that efforts to stop hepatitis B have largely failed despite the availability since 1981 of safe and effective vaccines.

TORONTO — Union officials representing about 10,000 striking Canadian steelworkers said Monday's tentative settlement with Stelco Inc. that includes full pension-indexing was a major victory for its members.

Leo Gerard, the Ontario director of the United Steelworkers of America, said the union's negotiators had achieved its five major objectives.

4-6 Selecting news

You are the editor of your hometown newspaper, and you need to select the stories that will go on the front page for tomorrow's paper. Below are the first two paragraphs of the news stories from which you must make your selection. Which four of the following would you select? In what order? Be prepared to justify your answer.

NEW YORK —The Daily News accused strikers Monday of dealer intimidation and theft of bundled papers on the street as it continued to publish for the fourth day with a work force of newly hired non-union employees and management.

News spokesman John Sloan made the accusation and said these "crimes"would be dealt with forcefully and effectively.

Record lows in the Midwest and cool weather elsewhere chilled much of the nation Monday with strong winds and storms in the extreme Northwest and Northeast and heavy fog in Southern California.

In New England, skiers hit the slopes as the season's first major snowfall blanketed northern mountains. At least one resort in northern Maine reported 15 inches of new snow.

WASHINGTON — Protesters came to a Ku Klux Klan rally ready for violence, and city officials criticized a judge's ruling that allowed the robed marchers to cover a longer route through downtown of the predominately black city.

Police in riot gear guarded 30 Klan members Sunday on their 1 - mile march to the Capital along Constitution Avenue, while 1,200 protesters battled police in their wake.

An 8-year-old boy was in good condition Wednesday night after his bicycle collided with an ambulance earlier in the day.

The accident happened around 10:12 a.m. at the intersection of LaRua and L streets, said city police officer John Austin.

LONDON — Alcohol-giant Guinness PLC announced plans Tuesday to cut 700 jobs from its whisky business in Scotland over the next two years as part of a reorganization plan.

"This major reorganization and investment program reaffirms our commitment to modernize and upgrade our production facilities for Scotch whisky, and to take the steps we believe are necessary to continue to lead the industry," company chairman Tony Greener said.

DETROIT — A top Nissan executive Tuesday said consumers' demands have moved from a desire for "cheap" cars to one of "quality at a fair price."

"In the '80s, auto manufacturers around the world lost touch with their customers," Earl Hesterberg, vice president and general manager of Nissan Motor Corp. U.S.A., told delegates at the Automotive News World Congress. "Everyone was chasing everyone else's latest, greatest hits. But along the way, we forgot to listen carefully to what our customers wanted."

4-7 Selecting news

You are the news director of your hometown television station, and you need to select the stories that will go on the local news tonight. Below are the first two paragraphs of the news stories from which you must make your selection. Which four of the following would you select? In what order? Be prepared to justify your answer.

A police officer shot a man during a struggle early Tuesday, then had his weapon turned on him before the suspect fled and was overpowered by two other officers, police said.

Officer David Kelley shot Anthony McQueen, 31, of Duval Street, in the left side as they grappled over Kelley's .357-caliber handgun behind a house in the 1000 block of Cherokee Street shortly after 2 a.m., police said.

A 17-year-old British math prodigy has accepted a one-year post as a visiting lecturer at Local University, becoming one of the youngest people ever to be a faculty member, Local officials said Friday.

Ruth J. Lawrence was taught by her father in their home in Huddersfield, England, and had never been to school before she entered Oxford University at age 11 six years ago.

The liver of a baboon transplanted into a 62-year- old man was functioning satisfactorily Tuesday, surgeons at the University Hospital said.

The man, whose identity was not released, remained in critical condition after the world's second such transplant at Presbyterian University

Hospital in a 13-hour operation that ended early Monday. Surgeons said the man was dying from hepatitis B and did not have the option of a human-to-human liver transplant.

Funland, a local amusement park that draws tourists from around the county, will boost its admission prices by $2 for adults and children, a park spokesman said Tuesday.

The new admission prices, which go into effect Nov. 1, are $27.50 for an adult "passport" and $22.50 for children between the ages of 3 and 11, according to spokesman Bob Roth. Children under 3 years old are admitted free.

A local doctor's research says cigarette smoking may hamper a smoker's ability to feel the chest pains that may be an important early warning sign of heart disease.

Researchers from the University Hospital, compared the pain response of 20 male smokers ages 19 to 44 with that of five male non-smokers in the same age range.

A local art collector, William Chase, has acquired a Van Gogh painting from an auction in New York.

The Van Gogh, "Vase With Cornflowers and Poppies," sold for $8 million. Chase also purchased a rare ink sketch by the Dutch master, "Garden of Flowers," valued at $5 million to $7 million.

4-8 Selecting news

You are the news director of your hometown television station, and you need to select the stories that will go on the local news tonight. Below are the first two paragraphs of the news stories from which you must make your selection. Which four of the following would you select? In what order? Be prepared to justify your answer.

Taco Bell, the nation's leading Mexican fast-food restaurant chain, announced a wide range of price cuts Monday coupled with a marketing strategy that groups menu items by price rather than by types of food.

The moves clearly show Taco Bell Corp. is trying to position itself as a low-price leader in the fast-food business, but a spokesman discounted the possibility of a price war breaking out with competitors.

If the city runs out of cash around Dec. 1 as expected, Mayor Wilson Goode expects city employees to work anyway, even if they are not getting paid, a published report said Tuesday.

Labor leaders, however, said the mayor could not force workers to stay on the job because that would violate their labor contract. He can only request that they continue working and hope they do.

An 82-year-old woman filed a $5 million lawsuit against the owner of Nan Seas Restaurant Thursday, alleging that he used a fraudulent deed to her property in seeking zoning changes for the restaurant. Rosalie McGovern alleges that she did not sign the deed to her property filed in courthouse records by Willis Robinson, the owner of Nan Seas Restaurant located at 4170 Bay Front Road in Mobile. Because of an expansion, Robinson applied for rezoning of the restaurant and the surrounding property, including Mrs. McGovern's house on Terrell Road.

A County circuit court jury took less than half an hour Thursday to find James William McGowan guilty of two counts of capital murder.

McGowan was accused of beating Hiram Johnson, 82, and his 79-year-old wife, Mamie Johnson, to death with a hammer in their home in the Antioch community in eastern Conecuh County on July 18, 1994.

Official election returns show voters defeated by a somewhat wider margin than expected a Lincoln county tax issue that could have given the public library enough local support to stay open for the next 20 years.

Certified results show that by a vote of 1166 to 1087, county voters refused to ratify the tax which they approved in 1994. The Alabama attorney general's office last year advised county officials to have the vote ratified because it was not properly advertised for the first election.

County commissioners will vote Tuesday on a garbage-collection plan aimed at making residents forget their much-criticized and short-lived experience with Waste Management of Alabama.

Commissioners said their main intention in providing the service for nearly 21,000 residents is to iron out collection and billing complaints lodged since the company began weekly pickup in unincorporated areas of the county in July 1994.

Storms dumped more than three inches of rain in spots as they rolled through the area Monday, flooding streets and contributing to several traffic problems.

Heavy rains led to high water standing in low places as the storms moved northeastward. A check with law enforcement agencies turned up no reports of major damage as of early Monday night.

4-9 Planning an interview

Plan an interview with the mayor of your city. First, you will need to decide the central reason why you want the interview. It could be that there is some issue facing the city currently that you will want to build your story around. If no such issue exists, you may want to talk to the mayor about what it is like to be mayor—duties, responsibilities, daily schedule, etc. Or you may want to do a personality profile on the mayor, asking about family, friends, recreation, etc.

Once you have decided what the interview is to be about, what background research will you have to do? How will you go about getting the information you need? Be specific about what information you will need and where you can get it.

Finally, formulate a list of tentative questions that you will want to ask the mayor during the interview. This list of questions should be in the approximate order of how you would like to ask the questions.

4-10 Planning an interview

Plan an interview with the president of your college or university. Decide the central reason why you want the interview. It could be that there is some issue facing the university currently that you will want to ask about. If no such issue exists, you may want to talk to the president about what it is like to be president–duties, responsibilities, daily schedule, etc. Or you may want to do a personality profile on the president, asking about family, friends, recreation, etc.

Once you have decided what the interview is to be about, what background research will you have to do? How will you go about getting the information you need? Be specific about what information you will need and where you can get it.

Finally, formulate a list of tentative questions that you will want to ask the mayor during the interview. This list of questions should be in the approximate order of how you would like to ask the questions.

4-11 Paraphrasing

Rewrite the following by paraphrasing the direct quotations. Make what you write no more than half the length of the original quotation. Try to include most of the information that is in the quotation. The first quotation has been paraphrased to give you an example of what is expected.

Tom Nelson, president of the city-wide Parent Teachers Association: "Our major concern this year will be security in the schools, particularly in the high schools. We will be working with school officials on ways we can help create a safer environment for the education of our children. A number of incidents in the past year have been very disturbing to many parents. We are going to try to provide a way for those parents to make a real difference in their local schools."

Paraphrase

Tom Nelson, president of the city Parent Teachers Association, said the chief concern of the organization this year would be security, particularly in the high schools. Nelson said parents would be working with school officials to make the schools safer.

Martin Goldsmith, general manager of the local public radio station: "Our goal in this year's fundraising effort is to raise $100,000, which will be about 15 percent more than we raised last year. The money we are seeking—this $100,000—will go toward our programming efforts. We spent about $130,000 buying programs each year for the station, and those costs are going up each year.

There is a lot that our audience would like to have on the station, and this is the way for them to help pay for it."

Marilyn Wall, president of the Walls Tire Co., a locally owned tire manufacturer: "The current year has been a good one for our company and its employees. Our orders were up about 20 percent over last year, and we were able to recall many of the employees that we had had to lay off during the past three years. In addition, we have expanded our workforce to add about 20 new jobs in various parts of the factory."

Marsha Moss, director of the local symphony orchestra: "The response of the audience to last night's concert was particularly gratifying. They seemed to enjoy everything that we put on the program. I can tell you that playing before an audience like that is a lot more fun than playing to a bunch of critics. It's good to know that people appreciate the many hours of hard work that this orchestra puts into each concert that we do."

4-12 Paraphrasing

Rewrite the following by paraphrasing the direct quotations. Make what you write no more than half the length of the original quotation. Try to include most of the information that is in the quotation. The first quotation in the previous exercise has been paraphrased to give you an example of what is expected.

Jerry Butts, member of the City Council: "Our options were extremely limited this year. We could either grant the police the raise their union requested—one which they deserve, I think, although some might disagree with that—and then raise the property tax to pay for it, or we could have denied the request for a pay raise and kept the tax rates the same as they have been for more than five years. While I think the police do deserve a raise, I am fairly certain that most people would not want them to get it if they thought their taxes would go up to pay for it."

Anita Keller, president of the local Mothers Against Drunk Driving: "For months now, we have attended meetings of committees of state legislators, and we have tried to make the point over and over again that the laws against drunk driving in this state are too lenient. I do not believe that the legislators have gotten that message yet, or else they are being influenced by money from the alcohol industry, which contributed to many of their campaigns, to keep the laws the way they are. In any event, people are dying every day because of it."

Laura Stewart, president of Stewart Advertising Agency: "The business climate in this city is really quite healthy. That is, we seem to be growing every year. I know that my agency increased its gross revenues by over 20 percent last year over the year before, and that is the third time that has happened. Most of our business comes from local businesses, although some of it—may be as much as 25 percent—is from out-of-town clients. Anyway, I think things look pretty good for the local economy."

Bruce Hill, organizer of an antique automobile show set for this weekend: "These old cars are really fun and really interesting, too. I have a 1929 Packard that I have had for years, and I've got it running about as good as it was on the day that it was first brought home from the dealership. A lot of people in the show will be driving British cars—old Triumphs, Jaguars, and the like—and some of those old sportscars can really give you a ride. I mean, they can pick up and move. Folks ought to come out and see our show this Saturday and Sunday because I think they would really be interested in it."

5

Writing for print

Writers for the mass media always work at two tasks: gathering information and putting that information into an acceptable form. Having the proper information — all the relevant facts of a story, the proper identification for the people involved, the times and dates, accurate direct quotations, etc. — is vital to the writing process, but it is only the beginning. There comes a time when the information gathering must cease and the writing must begin.

The ability to write well requires that the writer have a thorough knowledge and understanding of the subject about which he or she is writing. In addition, the writer must understand the basic structure of the news story and the conventions or customs of news writing in order to complete the process.

This chapter focuses on putting information into a form appropriate for the print media. Many forms of writing — or writing structures — populate the print media, but the most common are the news story and the feature story. These forms are found in newspapers, magazines, newsletters, and many other publications. Mastering these two forms will give the person beginning to write for the mass media a good foundation on which to build while learning to write in other forms and for other media.

Characteristics of news stories

All good pieces of writing have one thing in common — a unifying theme. A central idea should govern every book, magazine article, advertisement, or news story that anyone tries to create. The idea of a central theme is important for writers learning the different forms of writing for the mass media and particularly those learning to write a news story. Faced with a mass of information, facts, ideas, quotations, and the like, the news writer can use the central idea to help sort out what should be included in the article and how the various pieces of information should be presented to the reader.

The central idea will usually be expressed early in the story, normally in the first paragraph. This paragraph, called the lead, will set the tone and direction for the story. Lead paragraphs will be examined in more detail later in this chapter, but their importance is noted here. A strong lead that sets forth the central idea of the story will help to unify the writing for the reader.

No two writers will do this is in exactly the same way, so there is no formula that a writer can always use. The information the writer has, the amount of time there is to write the story, and the amount of space available to print the story will be major factors in determining how the story is developed. Still, writers must be aware of the tools and conventions of writing in order to make the story acceptable for the publication for which they are writing. The following are some of those tools and conventions that writers of news stories must use and observe.

Transitions. The relationship between various pieces of information and the central theme is established with the use of transitions. Transitions are a way of tying the information together and tipping the reader off as to what may come next. Readers should not be surprised by a brand new subject in the middle of a news story.

Various types of transitions exist for the writer to use in tying a story together. The following are a few of those types:

Connectors. These are simply words that, in a structural way, help unify the writing. For the most part, they are conjunctions such as and, but, or, thus, however, therefore, meanwhile, on the other hand, likewise, and so on. They do not have great value in terms of the content of the writing, but they are necessary for its flow.

Hooks. Hooks are words or phrases that are repeated throughout an article to give the reader a sense of unity. Look at the example on the next page and notice how many times the word "robbery" is used.

Pronouns. One of the best transitional devices, particularly for writing about people, is the pronoun. We use it naturally so that we can avoid repeating the names of people or things.

Associations. Ideas may be repeated within an article, but the writer may use different words to refer to them. This is called an association. The following example demonstrates this type of transition:

```
        Arnold came in to pitch in the
eighth inning and immediately threw at
the head of the first batter he faced.
Doing so, he thought, would establish
some fear in the minds of the batter.
        Johnson, the first batter and the
one Arnold threw at, didn't pick up on
Arnold's meaning. He lined the next
pitch off the left field wall.
```

The two phrases underlined in that passage represent an association of ideas. Associations are the most subtle of transitional devices, but they can be highly effective in unifying a piece of writing.

Chronology. One of the best transitional devices is a word or phrase that refers to a time. Such devices help the reader establish a sequence for the events that are being written about. Many news stories, such as the one above, are not written strictly in

Figure 5-1

Transitions

While each sentence in a news story should introduce some new information, the story should follow a logical sequence so that the reader is not surprised or shocked. One of the best transitional devices is the use of reference words that refer to things mentioned previously in the story. Some of the referents in this story are marked and tied together with diagonal lines. Another good transitional device is the use of words that refer to the time sequence of the story. Look for words that refer to time, such as "last week" in the seventh paragraph, and notice how they help tie different parts of the story together.

A Brownsville woman received a 20-year prison sentence yesterday for her part in a robbery of the Trust National Bank last year.

Anne Evenson, who lived with her mother on Mine Road before the robbery, wept softly as Circuit Court Judge John Sloan read the verdict to a packed courtroom. The 20-year sentence means that she could be eligible for parole in seven years.

Evenson's attorney, Harriet Braden, said after the court recessed that she is planning to file an appeal.

"I think that we will be able to demonstrate that Miss Yeager was an innocent victim and did not receive a fair trial," she said.

Braden said the appeal will be filed sometime next week.

District Attorney Ed Sims said, however, that he thought the trial had been a fair one and that Yeager had received the sentence she deserved.

Yeager was convicted last week of first degree robbery for driving the get-away car for her boyfriend, Reggie Holder, after he robbed the bank of almost $29,000. Holder was convicted last month for first-degree robbery and also received a 20-year sentence.

Yeager testified during her trial that she drove the car for Holder but that she thought she was simply taking him to the bank to make a deposit and pay some bills.

chronological order, but references to the time of the events can still be helpful to the reader.

Enumeration. Numbering items within your writing is a good way to tie it together. A good example of enumeration is in the following paragraph:

The mayor said there were three reasons why the Pynex Corporation decided to locate the plant in the city. First, the land was available for the plant and possible expansion. Second, the city has a good educational system, and that is important for its employees. Third, the state offered what he called "attractive tax incentives to come to this area."

A news writer must make use of all of these forms of transi-

Figure 5-2

Verbs of attribution

While few verbs are as versatile as said for use in attribution, there are occasions when a writer will need to use something different. At right are some of the most commonly used verbs of attribution. These verbs should be used only when they serve the specific purpose of the writer.

• **Said** is a word that connotes only the fact that words were spoken or written. It says nothing about the way the words were spoken, the circumstances of the utterance, or the attitude of the speaker. The word is a modest one, never calling attention to itself. It can be used repeatedly without disruption to the writing. Consequently, there are few real substitutes for said. There are words you can use in its place, however, when it is proper for you to do so.

• **Explain** means that more facts are being added to make something more understandable. It can be a neutral synonym for said, but it must be used in the right context. It is incorrect to write: "Bill Clinton is our current president," he explained. It would be correct to use explain as the verb of attribution for the following sentence: "The presidency is the nation's most important office," he explained.

• **Relate** means to pass along facts. It implies an absence of opinion on the part of the speaker.

• **Point out** means to call attention to a matter of fact. A speaker can point out that grass is green, but a journalist should not write: "The majority leader pointed out that the president was tough in standing up to the communists." That statement is opinion, not fact.

• **State** should be used for formal speeches or announcements such as the State of the Union address in January. It is incorrect to write: "Smith stated that the party would begin at 8 p.m."

• **Declare,** like state, implies formality.

• **Add** indicates more facts or comment about the same subject or an afterthought, a comment less important than what has been said before. It is incorrect to write: "She said she was unable to finish her paper. 'My typewriter was broken,' she added."

• **Revealed and disclosed** are suitable only when referring to something that previously was unknown or concealed.

• **Exclaim** means to cry out in surprise or sudden emotion. It can easily be overused, so writers should be careful. It is usually written with an exclamation point. It is incorrect to use it in the following way: "The meeting will be at 3 p.m.," she exclaimed.

• **Assert** also implies formality but also an intensity on the part of the speaker.

---

tions. It is not so important to know the different types of transitions as it is to understand when they can be best used.

Attribution. A major convention of news stories is the use of attribution. Attribution simply means telling readers where the information in a story comes from. Attribution is important because it establishes the news report's credibility. Readers are more likely to believe that the publication is trying to be accurate in its reporting if they know clearly the source of the information. News reports in which the information is properly attributed reflect the professionalism of the publication and its reporters.

Another reason for attributing information in a story is to allow the reader to assess the information by assessing its source. Some sources are more credible than others. By telling the reader where information comes from, the news reporter is letting the reader make up his or her mind whether the information can be believed.

Beginning news writers sometimes have trouble with attribution because it can occasionally be awkward to work into a sentence. In most cases, however, the attribution can be included in a natural or unobtrusive way. Look at these examples:

```
        The mayor said the city is facing
a budget crisis.

        According to the police report,
the car skidded 50 feet before stopping.

        The grand jury's report will be
announced tomorrow, the prosecutor said.
```

Most of the major facts in a news story should be attributed to some source (unless they come from an eyewitness account by the reporter), but information that is common knowledge to most readers usually does not have to be attributed. For instance, in the sentence, "A heavy cloud of smog hung over the city today, National Weather Service officials said," the attribution is unnecessary and even silly. As in many other aspects of writing, common sense should prevail. Too much attribution will get in the way of a story; too little attribution will harm the credibility of the story and confuse the reader. The good writer wants neither of these things to happen.

Many writers, particularly beginning journalists, complain that the word "said" is used too much in news stories. It is a colorless word that does not add much to the life of the copy. With this thought in mind, many writers begin the tortuous search for adequate substitutes for said. Surely, they think, the English language can come up with at least a few good words to use in its place.

While English does have many words that can describe the way words are spoken, there is no word that does the job the way said does it. Said is a neutral word. It simply connotes that words have been spoken; it doesn't say anything about the way in which they were spoken. Consequently, it is the kind of word that journalists ought to be using. Another point in the word's favor is that said is fairly unobtrusive in a news story. Even if used repeatedly, it does not jump out at the reader and get in the way of the information that is being transmitted.

Trying to find substitutes for the word said is a dangerous game for the journalist. While there are many words that might be used in its place, writers should remember that they must use words for their exact meaning, not simply for variety's sake. Too often writers misuse these substitutes and create erroneous impressions about what was said. Another danger in the search for substitutes for said is that most substitutes are not neutral. If used, they make a statement about how the journalist feels about what was said. For instance, a person accused of a crime

may "say" that he is innocent, or he may "claim" that he is innocent. That second verb carries a more negative or doubtful con-
notation, one which the journalist should not be implying.

Short sentences, short paragraphs. News stories use short
sentences and short paragraphs. The newswriter tries to get
information to the reader as quickly as possible. That is accomplished more easily if the writer uses short sentences. They are
easier for the reader to digest.

Unlike other forms of expository writing, the news story does
not require that a writer fully develop paragraphs. Paragraph
length usually should be kept to three sentences or less and to
less than 100 words. Again, the goal is getting information to
readers, not fully developing an idea. Another reason for short
paragraphs is that the width of a column of type in a newspaper
is so narrow that a long paragraph is difficult and daunting for
the reader.

Third person. News stories are usually written in the third
person. A writer does not intrude into a story by using first person pronouns (unless they are part of a direct quotation from one
of the story's sources). Except for unusual cases where the writer
witnesses a dramatic event or is somehow a participant in that
event, he or she should not tell the story from the point of view of
the first person.

WRONG: From where I was sitting, it looked like the umpire made
the wrong call.
RIGHT: The manager protested the call by the umpire.

WRONG: The principal said enrollment at our school has gone
down.
RIGHT: The principal said enrollment at Central High has gone
down.

By the same token, news stories rarely directly address the
reader by using the second-person pronoun "you." Occasionally,
lead paragraphs are questions directed at the reader, but this
device can be overused quickly, and it is best avoided when you
are beginning to learn newswriting.

The writer's personal opinions — or what journalists call "edi-
torializing" — should be kept out of news stories. News reporters
should report only what they see and hear. How they feel about
that information is not relevant to the news story. They should
present the information and let the readers make up their own
minds about it.

An attitude for accuracy. Accuracy forms the core of the
writing process. Journalists expend much energy in making certain that all of the information he or she has is correct. Achieving
accuracy is not just a matter of techniques of reporting and writing but a state of mind that the journalist should foster. A journalist should never be satisfied with information about which he
or she has doubts. The journalist has to make every effort to alle-
viate those doubts and to clear up any discrepancies.

This attitude extends not only to the major information that a journalist has but to the smallest bits of a story. Making sure that dates and identifications are correct, that numbers in a story add up properly, that locations are correct — all of these things are part of a journalist's job. Journalists should take special care with the names of people to make sure they are spelled correctly.

Journalists strive for accuracy because they realize that their readers and viewers trust them and expect their reports to be accurate. If those reports are not accurate, journalists will lose that trust and eventually lose their readers.

The inverted pyramid

Once a writer has gathered the information necessary to begin a story, he or she must decide on the structure of the story. The goal of a proper structure is to get information to the reader quickly and to allow the reader to move through the story easily. The reader must be able to see the relationships between the various pieces of information that the reporter has gathered.

The most common structure for writing news stories is called the inverted pyramid. A daily newspaper or web site contains many stories. Most stories must be written so that readers can get the most information in the least time. The inverted pyramid structure concentrates the most interesting and important information at the top of the story so that readers can get the information they need or want and then go on to another story if they choose. Headlines and lead paragraphs should be written to describe what the story contains as succinctly and as interestingly as possible.

The lead, or first paragraph, is the focal point of the basic news story. It is a simple statement of the point of the entire story. Lead paragraphs are discussed more fully in the next section of this chapter.

The second paragraph is almost as important as the lead. It takes some of the information and adds to it. A good second paragraph will put the readers into a story and will give them incentive to read on.

The body of the inverted pyramid story adds detail to information that has been introduced in the lead and the first two or three paragraphs. The body should provide more information, supporting evidence, context, and illumination in the form of more details, direct and indirect quotes, and other description.

The major concept of the inverted pyramid structure is to put the most important and latest information toward the top of the story. As the story continues, the writer should be using information of less importance. There are two reasons for writing a story this way. One is what we have already talked about: Putting the most important information at the top allows a reader to decide quickly whether or not to stick with the story.

The inverted pyramid also organizes the information in such a way that the reader can be efficient. Not every reader will read all of every story in a newspaper. In fact, one of the strengths of

Figure 5-3

The inverted pyramid

Most news stories are structured in the inverted pyramid form; that is, they begin with the most important information, and the information is presented in descending order of importance. To write in this way, the writer must use some judgment about what information is the most important and the most interesting to the reader and what information the reader should have in order to understand the story.

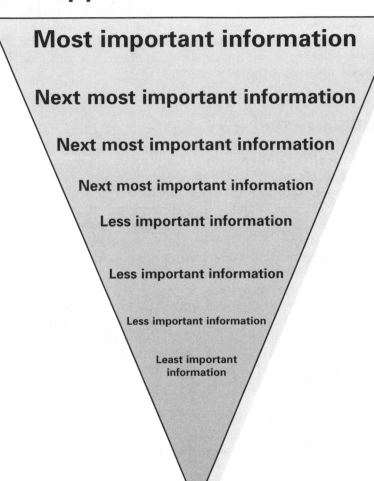

Most important information

Next most important information

Next most important information

Next most important information

Less important information

Less important information

Less important information

Least important information

a newspaper is that it offers a wide variety of information that will appeal to many people. The inverted pyramid structure for news stories allows the readers to get as much of the most important information in that story as quickly as possible; it also allows the readers to stop reading and go on to something else when they have satisfied themselves with that story.

This process would not be possible if all stories were written chronologically. Very often, what happens at or near the end of the story is the most important or interesting thing to the reader. Readers are not accustomed to wading through a lot of less important or less interesting information to get to these parts. Consider a story that begins with the following paragraphs:

The City Council opened its meeting last night with a prayer from the Rev. Jonathan Fowler, pastor of the Canterbury Episcopal Church.

The minutes of the previous meeting were read and accepted without changes.

Mayor H.L. Johnson then called for a report from the city budget director, Hiram Lewis, who said that property tax collections were running behind what had been expected when the budget was adopted last year.

"If property tax collections continue at this rate, the city will be facing a major deficit," he said.

When Councilmember Fred Greenburg asked what that meant, Lewis replied that the city would have to borrow money or cut back on some of its services.

Johnson then proposed that the council raise the property tax rate by 5 percent for most property owners. The new rates would go into effect next year and would last for only one year, he said. This increase would allow the city to continue operating without any cutbacks in service.

Council member Marge Allen objected to the increase, saying the citizens of her district already had too many taxes to pay. She also said that an increase in the property tax would discourage industries from locating in the city. . . .

Think about the reader of that story who is a property owner in the city. Most likely, that person is asking, "Are my taxes going up?" The reader should not have to wait for six or more paragraphs to find out the answer to that question. Instead, the answer should come immediately in the first paragraph:

```
     The City Council voted against
raising property taxes 5 percent last
night, despite warning from officials
that the city faces a cutback in ser-
vices unless it gets more money.
```

Another reason for the inverted pyramid structure is a technical one. When stories are prepared for print publications such as newspapers, they are placed on certain parts of a page. An editor must decide how to fit stories together on a page. Sometimes stories will be longer than the space allotted for them. If this is the case, an editor will try to cut a story from the bottom, knowing that if the story is written properly, none of the essential facts will be lost.

The inverted pyramid structure demands that the writer make judgments about the importance of the information that he or she has gathered—judgments based on the news values discussed in the previous chapter.

The inverted pyramid structure, though it is the most common, is not the only type of story structure that can be used in news writing. There are several others, which are discussed beginning on page 173. These structures are not rigid. If one style alone won't do, a writer should search for combinations of styles which will best fit the information and ideas he or she is trying to organize.

The lead paragraph

The most important part of the news story is the first, or lead (pronounced LEED), paragraph. The lead should tell the reader the most important information in the story. It should be written so that the reader will be interested in going further into the story. Let's go back to the example of the city council story in the previous section. A lead on that story might simply say:

```
The City Council voted against
raising property taxes last night.
```

This lead gives the most important information in this story, but it should also invite the reader to continue reading. Go back to the lead written for this story on page 159. That lead tells the reader the following: There was a debate about this matter, and it has some consequences that you might be interested in.

An otherwise good story will not be read by many people if the lead is dull or confusing. The lead is the first part of the story a reader will come in contact with after the headline, and if the lead does not hold the reader's interest and attention, little else will.

In writing the lead, a reporter must make a judgment on what to put in a lead based on the news values discussed in the previous chapter. The writer must get information to the reader quickly, but also accurately and interestingly. Accuracy, speed, and entertainment are finely balanced in a good lead paragraph.

Leads on news stories generally contain at least four of the five Ws and H that were discussed in the previous chapter. Those four elements are who, what, where, and when. A lead paragraph may emphasize any one of these elements, depending on the facts that are available to the reporter, but usually all four of these questions are answered in the lead. Sometimes the lead will contain or emphasize the why and the how of a story, but such stories are unusual.

Lead paragraphs should say neither too much nor too little. One of the mistakes that beginning news writers often make is that of trying to put too much in a lead. A lead should not be crowded with information; rather, it should tell enough to answer the reader's major questions about a story and to do so in an interesting and efficient way.

Leads can come in a wide variety of forms and styles. While journalistic conventions restrict what writers can do in some ways, there is still plen-

Figure 5-4

Walt Whitman on writing

Write short; to the point; stop when you have done ... Read it over, abridge, and correct it until you get it into the shortest space possible.

ty of room for creativity. The following types of leads and examples demonstrate some of the ways writers can approach a story.

The straight news lead is a just-the-facts approach. It delivers information quickly and concisely to the reader, and does not try to dress up the information. For instance:

```
     Two people were killed and four
were injured today when a truck collided
with a passenger car on Interstate 59
near the Cottondale exit.
```

This straight news approach is the most common type of news lead and lends itself to most of the stories a reporter will have to cover. Because of this, a couple of technical rules have been developed for this kind of story. Such leads should be one sentence long, and they should contain about thirty words (a maximum of thirty-three words). It is particularly important for the beginning writer to master this one-sentence, thirty-word approach because of the discipline of thinking that it requires. A writer must learn that words cannot be wasted, particularly at the beginning of the story.

The summary lead is one in which there may be more than one major fact to be covered. Again, the one-sentence, thirty-word approach should be used even though such an approach may require even more effort on the part of the writer. For example:

```
     A tractor-trailer truck carrying
dangerous chemicals crashed on
Interstate 59 today, killing one person,
injuring four others, and forcing the
evacuation of several hundred people
from their homes.
```

The emphasis in this kind of lead is on outlining the full story for the readers in a brief paragraph. Writers using summary leads need to take care that they do not crowd their leads with too much detail but also that they do not generalize too much. A balance should be achieved between including enough detail to make the story interesting and enough general material to avoid confusing the reader.

Up to this point, we have been dealing with straight leads for the most part. Straight leads give the who, what, when, where, how and why elements of the story to the reader in a straightforward, no-frills fashion. Other types of leads exist, however, and the good news writer should be aware of when they can be used most effectively.

The blind lead is a lead in which the people in the story are not named. The two previous examples are blind leads. This kind of lead is common when the people in the story are not well known. In the last lead about the accident, we assume that none of the people involved in the accident are well known. If one of the people hurt was the mayor of the city, we would not want to write a blind lead. We would want to mention his name in the lead.

Figure 5-5

Rewriting

The lead paragraph is the most important part of a news story. It should present the reader with the most important information in the story. It should be long enough to give the reader a good idea about what is in the story, but short enough to let the reader get through it quickly.

In other words, leads are not easy to write. Quite often, it takes more than one try to write a good lead. On the left are some lead paragraphs as they appeared in print. The writers and editors who produced them did not have the time or make the effort to rewrite them. Below each lead are rewritten versions that are considerable improvements from the first efforts.

• A new law that gives prosecutors additional power to halt the distribution of movies they believe are obscene prompted videotape rental stories in Decatur to pull nearly 2,000 adult films off their shelves.

Rewrite

Owners of videotape rental stores in Decatur have pulled nearly 2,000 tapes off the shelves because of a new law that gives prosecutors more power to halt the sale of obscene materials.

• Several steps are being taken to prevent a repeat of the error that caused an ambulance answering a heart attack call to be sent to the wrong street last week, the Emergency 911 board of directors was told Tuesday.

Rewrite

Emergency 911 is taking several steps to make sure that ambulances are sent to the correct addresses, according to testimony before the E–911 board.

• Civilian unemployment, rising at the fastest clip in more than three years, jumped to 5.3 percent last month, the government said Friday in a report that was taken as the strongest evidence yet of an economic slowdown.

Rewrite

Unemployment is up to 5.3 percent, the steepest rise in three years, according to a government report, and many economists believe that is the strongest sign yet of an economic slowdown.

The direct address lead is one in which the writer speaks directly to the reader. The main characteristic of this lead is the word you, present or implied.

```
If gardening is your hobby, you'll need
to know about Tom Smith.

If you're a property owner in the city,
the City Council is about to take at
least $50 more from you each year.
```

The direct address lead is a good way of getting the reader's attention, but it should be used sparingly. It is also important to follow up a direct address lead quickly in the second and third paragraphs with information about the lead. By implication, the direct address lead promises the reader some immediate information.

The question lead attempts to draw the reader into the story by asking a question.

```
Do you really want to know how hot dogs
are made?

Why doesn't the president tell Congress
how he stands on the pay increase issue?
```

The question lead has some of the same advantages and disadvantages as the direct address lead. It is a good way of getting the attention of the reader. On the other hand, it can easily be overused. It, too, promises to give the reader some immediate information, and the writer should make good on that promise.

The direct address and the question lead also imply that the story has some compelling information for the reader. That's why writers should be careful to use them only when that is the case. Otherwise, the reader will likely be disappointed.

The direct quote lead uses a direct quotation to introduce the story and to gain the reader's attention. The direct quote, of course, should be something that one of the participants in the story said, and it should be compelling and informative enough to serve as the lead.

```
"A city that cares!"
That's what mayoral candidate George
Bramble promised today as he hit the
campaign trail in ..
```

Any of these leads can be used when a writer feels that the facts of a story warrant their use. Writers should be careful, however, not to use one of these leads simply for the sake of using something different and not to use them when a story does not lend itself to their use.

Developing the story

The inverted pyramid requires that writers make judgments not only about what should be at the beginning of the story but also about the relative importance of all the information they present in the story. In other words, writers must decide what the most important information is for the lead, but they must also decide what the second and third most important pieces of information are. Developing the story in a logical and coherent way requires much skill and practice.

If the lead paragraph is the most important part of the news story, the second paragraph is the second most important part of the story. In some ways, it is almost as important as the lead but for different reasons.

A lead paragraph cannot contain all of the information in a news story. If it is written well, it will inform the reader, but it will also raise certain questions in the reader's mind about the story.

How to become your editor's favorite reporter
By Lauren Cabell

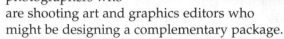

The key to becoming a good writer is finding a good editor. A good editor is a wordsmith who works well not only with stories and ideas, but also with reporters in a patient, cooperative manner. Editors—like everyone—usually play favorites, and reporters who have proven reliable will be assigned the most interesting stories and projects. To endear yourself to editors:

1. Thumb through the newspaper every day. Have a general awareness of the day's topics—in all sections of the paper, not only on your beat.

2. Learn AP style. Editors notice which reporters are diligent in filing clean copy. Study your newspaper's style manual.

3. Reread your stories when they appear in the newspaper. Make a note of changes editors have made—and remember them when writing your next story. If you have questions about why something might have been changed, ask.

4. File your stories on time—or earlier. Unless you are an award-winning columnist, editors will not tolerate reporters who repeatedly miss deadlines.

5. Offer to learn to work on the copy desk for a limited time. It will improve your writing and help you understand the nightly challenges faced by the copy desk. Building relationships with the editors who read your stories will pay off later.

6. Communicate with the people working on your story. This includes photographers who are shooting art and graphics editors who might be designing a complementary package.

7. Support your writing with solid reporting. Do not let Internet research replace traditional reporting skills. Call sources, go to the courthouse, use the library. Confirm information you research on the Internet with a telephone call.

8. Accept every assignment with enthusiasm (feign enthusiasm, if necessary).

9. Use fewer words. Filing a crisp 12-inch story will earn more kudos than turning in a 16-inch story that needs to be trimmed.

10. Don't be afraid to question an editor's decision. Editors sometimes make mistakes too. Constructive dialogue between editors and reporters will improve your story—and prevent errors.

Lauren Cabell started her neighborhood's first handwritten newspaper when she was 9 years old. She earned her master's degree in print journalism from the University of Southern California and has held various editing positions at the Fort Worth Star-Telegram, the Los Angeles Times and the Chicago Tribune, where she is a graphics editor.

Chief among the roles of the second (and succeeding) paragraphs is to answer these questions. The writer does this by providing additional information about the story. The writer must decide what information is most important and what will help the reader to understand the story.

One method that writers use to make these judgments is to

put themselves in the place of the reader and ask, "If I were a reader of this story, what would I want to know next?" For instance, a lead might say

```
Authorities are searching for a state
prison inmate who escaped from a work
crew at the Kidder Correctional Facility
yesterday.
```

That lead gives some information about the story, but it also raises a number of questions, such as:

Who was the inmate?

Why was he in prison?

How long had he been there and how long was his sentence?

How did he escape?

Where is the search for him taking place?

Is the inmate dangerous?

What does he look like?

How have the prison officials explained his escape?

These are just a few of the questions that could be asked about this story. The writer must answer these questions in a logical and coherent manner that will result in a unified and interesting story. The order in which these questions are answered will depend on the specific information that the writer has to work with.

The writer will probably want to give the name of the inmate quickly and the circumstances of the escape. Beyond that, the type of information the writer has will dictate the order in which the questions are answered. For instance, the second paragraph might go something like this:

```
Billy Wayne Hodge, 22, who was convicted
two years ago for armed robbery, walked
away from his work crew yesterday after-
noon at about 3 p.m., according to prison
officials. The crew was picking up trash
along Highway 69 about four miles from
the prison at the time of the escape.
```

This paragraph answers some of the questions but leaves others unanswered. Even though a second paragraph can be longer than the lead, it still cannot answer all of the questions a lead can raise. Now the writer will have to decide what questions he or she will answer in the third paragraph. Again, those decisions will be based on the kind of information the writer has. The writer might want to say something about the search for the prisoner. For instance:

```
Sheriff Will Harper said last night that
he thought the prisoner was still in the
thick woods in the area of the escape.
He said deputies would patrol the area
tonight and a full-scale search would
begin early today.
```

Or the writer may expand on the circumstances of the escape:

```
"It appears that one of our guards wasn't
watching the prisoners as closely as he
should have been," Sam Mayer, the prison
warden, said. "There were 15 men in the
work crew and only two guards."
```

Either choice might be appropriate, depending on the circumstances of the story and the writer's preference. Still, the writer has not answered all of the questions raised by the lead, but the story is becoming more complete.

The following is another example of the way in which a story can be developed:

An automobile accident occurs on a busy street in your city. Three cars are involved. The driver of one of the cars is arrested for drinking and driving. One person is killed and another is seriously injured. The accident occurred during the afternoon rush and tied up traffic for more than an hour.

A reporter covering that accident would get all of the information listed above plus other details. Of all of these facts, however, which one would you say is the most important? Which one would rank as the second most important fact? the third?

Death and personal injury are usually considered the most important facts in a story such as this one. The fact that one person was killed and another seriously injured would be the most important thing that the reporter would have to tell the readers.

The reporter would then have to decide what the second most important fact was. It could be that the arrest of one of the drivers would be second in the mind of the reporter, especially since drinking and driving is in the news a lot these days. Or it might be that the reporter would think that traffic being tied up for so long on a busy street was the second most important fact; a lot of people (and possibly many readers) would have been affected by the traffic jam. A reporter would have to decide about this, and about the other information he or she would gather.

If the fact that one person was killed and another seriously injured is the most important fact, the reporter will want to use that fact to start the lead. But what else will be in the lead? Think about the "what," "when," and "where" or the story. If we put all those things together in one sentence, it might come out like this:

```
    One person was killed and another
seriously injured in a three-car acci-
dent Tuesday afternoon during rush hour
on Chester Street.
```

What do you think? Is this the best lead that could be written for a story like this one, or can you think of a better approach to this story? (One of the most noticeable problems about the way it is written is that it uses the passive voice—something we try to avoid in writing for the mass media.)

Figure 5-7

Organizing a news story

In the colum below is a set of facts that needs to be formed into a news story in the inverted pyramid style. On the right is an example of such a story.

Soccer team from local middle school, Brown Middle School; competed in state middle school tournament this weekend in the state capitol; tournament involved 32 teams in 4 divisions; Brown Middle School played 4 games, 2 on Friday and two on Saturday; won three of the four, the last one they beat Dorchester Middle School three to two for a second place in their division.

Coach Randy Fowler: "This is the best that any middle school of this area has ever done in statewide competition. I'm very proud of our team. They played with a lot of spirit and showed a lot of skill. Our doing this well will help us continue to build a solid soccer program for this area."

Coach Fowler teaches social studies at Brown Middle School

Ray Johnson, one of the team's co-captains: "We had a great time. I think we probably learned a lot, too. Its good to see how other teams from other areas play the game."

On the way back home on Saturday night, after dark: a deer ran across the road in front of the team bus; this happened about quarter after eight, near Risterville on highway 59; bus skidded into a ditch.

Bus driver A.P. Hill: "That thing just come up at us all of a sudden there in the road – wasn't nothing I could do about it. Thank goodness none of the kids was hurt. We just had a few bumps and bruises and scratches, and some of the kids was kinda shook up. Once we knowed they was okay, some of the kids thought it was kinda funny, seeing that old school bus stuck in a ditch. You know how kids are."

State trooper Rose Midgelin: "We got the call about 8:30 and got right out there. I don't think the deer got hit. We didn't find any marks on the bus that would indicate that it did. All the kids were pretty good about it, and of course were glad nobody was hurt."

Wrecker was called to get the bus out of the ditch; team arrived home about midnight.

The Brown Middle School soccer team had a successful trip to the state tournament this weekend in Montgomery and a scare on the bus trip home.

The team bus skidded off Highway 59 near Risterville after a deer ran across the front of the bus. No one was seriously injured in the wreck, but some of the children suffered cuts and bruises.

Bus driver A.P. Hill said the deer dashed in front of the bus before he could stop.

"The thing just came up at us all of a sudden," he said.

The accident occurred about 8:15 p.m., according to state troopers who were called to the scene.

"All the kids were pretty good about it, and of course were glad nobody was hurt," Rose Midgelin, one of the troopers on the scene, said.

The team had been returning from a weekend soccer tournament in Montgomery where it had won three out of four games and finished second in its division.

That finish, according to team coach Randy Fowler, is the best that any middle school has ever done at a state level.

"They played with a lot of spirit and showed a lot of skill," Fowler said. "Our doing this well will help us continue to build a solid soccer program for this area."

In its last game on Saturday, the team beat Dorchester Middle School 3-2 for a second place overall.

"I think we probably learned a lot, too. Its good to see how other teams from other areas play the game," Ray Johnson, one of the co-captains of the team, said.

After the accident, state troopers called a wrecker and pulled the bus out of the ditch. The team arrived in Tuscaloosa about midnight on Saturday.

The paragraph on page 166 is a serviceable lead, but there may be more that can be done with it. Adding a few more details, such as more identification of the person who was killed, might make it more interesting for the reader. Then we might have the following lead:

```
    A Centerville man is dead and
another person seriously injured after a
rush hour collision on Chester Street on
Tuesday afternoon.
```

Or if we wanted to take a different tack and try to work in the fact that one of the drivers was arrested, the lead might read like this:

```
    One person is dead and another
seriously injured after a three-car
accident on Chester Street on Tuesday,
and police later arrested one of the
drivers involved in the collision.
```

As you can tell from this one example, there are many approaches to even the simplest story. Note some things about each of these examples, however. All of them begin with the most important information—the fact that one person was killed and another injured. All of these are one sentence long and contain thirty words or less. And all use simple, straightforward language to give the reader information. The writer does not try to bowl the reader over with fancy words or phrasing but rather tries to keep the language as simple as possible.

Now, for the second and third paragraphs of the story: The reporter would want to give the name and identification of the accident victims and would want to relate a few more details about the events surrounding the accident. A second or third paragraph for this story might read this way:

```
    George Smith, 2629 Silver St., was
killed when the car he was driving crashed
into a telephone pole after being hit by
another car. His wife, Sylvia Smith, was also
injured in the accident and is in serious con-
dition in General Hospital, according to hos-
pital officials.
    Police said they arrested Sam Johnson,
30 Pine Ave., and charged him with driving
under the influence of alcohol in connection
with the accident.
    Sgt. Roland Langley, the officer who
investigated the accident, said the car
Johnson was driving swerved across the road
and hit the Smith vehicle, driving it into a
telephone pole. A third car was also hit, but
no one in that car was injured.
```

Figure 5-8

News story critique

FBI questions two about park death

The FBI has begun questioning two of its most wanted fugitives about the unsolved death of a Memphis woman in the Great Smoky Mountains National Park.

An FBI spokesman, however, was careful not to declare Howard Williams, 44, or his wife, Sarah, 36, suspects in the death of Gladys Roslyn. Roslyn's skeletal remains were found by hikers in the park more than two years ago.

"At this point, they are being regarded as material witnesses, and that's about all that we can say about the case," Larry Tims, assistant special agent in charge of the local FBI office, said Tuesday.

Clark Summerford, a lawyer for the couple, confirmed that the FBI is seeking information from them about the woman's death, but he, too, emphasized that the FBI was not about to charge them with any additional crimes.

"As far as I know, the FBI has no evidence directly linking the Williamses with this woman's death," Summerford said.

The Williamses were captured last week after more than a decade on the run. They were spotted by a local truck driver who said he had seen them on "America's Most Wanted," a television show that features stories about fugitives from justice. The Williamses escaped from a Massachusetts jail more than 10 years ago, after they had been convicted of armed robbery of a bank in Salem, Mass.

On the left is a news story written in a typical inverted pyramid structure. This story demonstrates a number of points that we have made about newswriting in this chapter. Below are some of them. See if you can find others.

• **The lead** summarizes the story and gives the latest and most important information to the reader.

• **Note that FBI is not spelled out,** even on first reference. According the the *AP Stylebook*, FBI is so well known that it does not need to be spelled out on first reference.

• **The second paragraph** builds on the lead paragraph with additional information. By the end of the second paragraph, the reader has most of the major information of this story.

• **Note the use of the direct quotes** in the third and fifth paragraphs. They reinforce information that has been presented previously. The direct quotes also add life to the story; they let the readers know that this story is about real people.

• **The last paragraph** gives the reader some background information on this story. We can assume that the information has already been published, but this paragraph informs the readers who haven't heard about this incident and reminds those who have.

At this point, the writer might want to make the story even more interesting by adding some direct quotations from the news sources.

> "A number of witnesses said they saw Johnson's vehicle swerving all over the road, and it appears that he was going pretty fast, too," Langley said. The police measured 60-foot skid marks made by the Johnson vehicle, Langley added.
>
> A spokesman for the City Jail said Johnson was being held pending other charges that might be lodged against him. A bail hearing for Johnson was set for today.

So far, the story has concentrated on the accident. Now, however, the writer might return to the victims and give more details about them.

> Hospital officials said Smith suffered head injuries, and he died shortly after he arrived at the hospital. Mrs. Smith also suffered injuries to her head and neck and has three broken ribs and a broken arm.
>
> The third car in the accident was driven by Lester Matson, 406 Altus Drive. Matson said Johnson's car smashed into his after it had hit the Smith's car.
>
> "There was simply nothing I could do to get out of the way," he said. "I saw this car up ahead, swerving all around the road, but there were cars all around me, and I couldn't go anywhere." Matson was not hurt, but he said his car was damaged in the accident.

The two examples in this section should give you some idea of how a news story is developed. That development is based on a series of decisions that the writer must make about the information he or she has. Even with simple stories, these decisions are rarely simple ones. They require that the writer understand the news story structure, as well as the facts of a particular story.

How should a news story end? A writer should stop writing when all of the logical questions have been answered and when all of the interesting information has been presented in the story. A writer should not be concerned with concluding or summarizing a story, particularly when he or she is beginning to learn how to write news. Instead, the writer should make sure that the reader can understand and be satisfied with what is written.

Using quotations

One of the most important parts of any news story is the material that writers quote directly or indirectly from their sources. Learning proper newswriting form means understanding how to use quoted material. A good news story usually has a mixture of direct and indirect quotations, and a news writer must have a good sense of when to use a direct or an indirect quotation.

Most news stories will use more indirect quotations than direct quotations. An indirect quotation may contain one or a few of the same words that a speaker has used but will also have words that the speaker did not use.

Indirect quotations should maintain the meaning of what the speaker has said but use fewer words than the speaker has used. Competent writers quickly learn that most people use more words than necessary to say what they have to say. They can paraphrase what people say and be more efficient than the speakers themselves. And as a news writer, you will find that you can get more information into your story if you use indirect quotes.

If that is the case, why worry about using direct quotations at all? Why not just use indirect quotations all of the time?

Direct quotations can be used by the skillful writer to bring a story to life, to show that the people in the story are real, and to enhance the story's readability. Occasionally, people will say something in a memorable or colorful way, and that should be preserved by the writer. Think about some of the famous direct quotations in American history:

> "Give me liberty or give me death." (Patrick Henry)
> "Read my lips. No new taxes." (George Bush)
> "We have nothing to fear but fear itself." (Franklin Roosevelt)
> "Four score and seven years ago. . . ." (Abraham Lincoln)

Another reason for using a direct quotation is that some quotations simply cannot be paraphrased. They are too vivid and colorful and they capture a feeling better than a writer could. For instance, when Heisman Trophy winner Bo Jackson was playing college football, he was once stopped from making a game-winning touchdown near the end of the game. The opposing linebacker who made the hit on Jackson was asked about the play after the game. Still high from his accomplishment, he said, "I waxed the dude!" That quotation would be impossible to paraphrase.

If you are going to use direct quotations in your stories — and you should — you should follow some basic rules.

Use the exact words of the speaker. Anything that is within quotation marks should be the words the speaker said in the order that he or she said them. The words should be the speaker's, not the writer's.

Figure 5-9

The inverted pyramid

The story on the right is written in the inverted pyramid style. Compare this one to the stories in Figures 5-10 (page 174) and 5-11 (page 175), which are about the same event but written in a narrative and eyewitness style.

Violent storm crashes city

A violent thunder and wind storm ripped through the city Tuesday afternoon, downing trees and power lines and causing personal injuries and property damage.

The storm hit about 3 p.m. and took approximately 45 minutes to sweep through the city.

While most of the city felt the storm, the most damaging high winds and sheets of rain were confined to the Hillsdale area west of downtown.

Arthur Major, 227 W. Hill St., was struck by a falling limb and taken to Community Hospital during the storm. He suffered severe head injuries and was in serious but stable condition on Tuesday evening.

Hospital officials said five other people were injured in car accidents caused by the storm. All were treated and released by emergency room doctors.

The storm downed power lines throughout the city. West Point Power Co. officials said at one time during the afternoon, about 30,000 city residents were without electricity. They said power was restored to every part of the city except the Hillsdale area by 9 p.m.

"I don't know when we'll get the lights back on in Hillsdale," Brad Jeffries, a spokesman for the power company, said.

Jeffries said all of the traffic lights in the city are operating. At one point on Tuesday afternoon all of the traffic signals on the west side of town were out.

The storm and high winds damaged a number of cars, houses and businesses. The home of Mary Golightly, 123 Oakdale Rd., suffered major damage when a large oak tree standing near the house was blown over onto the house.

Golightly was in the house at the time but was not injured when parts of the tree came through the roof and windows.

Martin Best, owner of the Best Hardware Store in the Hillsdale Shopping Center, said his building was among those that were damaged.

"The high winds blew off parts of the roofs of several of the businesses in the shopping center," he said.

Dozens of trees lost large limbs, and that caused some roads to be blocked in the Hillsdale area. City Manager Tom Sprightly said all of the roads are now passable. "It's going to cost the city some time and money to get the Hillsdale area cleaned up," he said.

"It will be a long time before we can drive through Hillsdale and not be reminded of this storm," he said.

Use direct quotations sparingly. Good writers will let people speak, but they won't let them ramble on. Most news writers avoid putting one direct quote after another in a story. You should never pile one direct quote onto another in paragraph after paragraph of a story. The writer who does that is not a writer but a stenographer.

Use direct quotations to supplement and clarify the information presented in the indirect quotes. In a news story, a direct quote is rarely used to present new or important information to the reader. It is most commonly used to follow up information that has already been presented.

Knowing how to deal with direct and indirect quotations is one of the most important skills that a newswriter can acquire. It takes some practice to paraphrase accurately and to select the direct quotations that should be used in a story. The key to both is to listen — listen carefully so that you understand what the speaker is saying and so that you remember the exact words that the speaker has used.

The correct sequence for a direct quote and its attribution is DIRECT QUOTE, SPEAKER, VERB. This sequence is generally used in news stories because it follows the inverted pyramid philosophy of putting the most important information first. Usually, what has been said is the most important element a journalist has; who said it, assuming that person has already been identified in the story, is the second most important element; the fact that it was said is the third most important element.

One of the common faults among many writers is the inverted attribution — putting the verb ahead of the subject.

"I do not choose to run," said the president.

There is no good reason for writing this way, and it violates one of the basic structures of English sentence: Subjects precede verbs. Remember, one of the major goals of the journalist is to make the writing of a story unobtrusive and the content of the story dominant. Sticking with basic English forms is one of the ways the journalist can do this.

One additional note: Use the past tense of verbs in news stories unless the action is continuing at the time of publication or unless it will happen in the future. Writing

"I do not choose to run," the president says.

is inaccurate unless the president goes around continually saying it. Chances are that it was said only once. It happened in the past, and that's the way it should be written. Although you would probably be able to find many examples of the use of the present tense in many publications, it is inaccurate when it is referring to things that have happened and to action that has been completed.

Other story structures

The inverted pyramid story structure is not the only form that writers of news and information can use. Sometimes the facts, the publication, or the situation will dictate that a different form be used to present ideas and information. Beginning news writers should first master the inverted pyramid form, but they should also be able to use a different story structure when the

Eyewitness account

The story on the right is written as an eyewitness account. Here the writer centers the story around himself and his experiences. Compare this one to the stories in Figures 5-9 (page 172) and 5-11 (page 175), which are about the same event but written in an inverted pyramid and narrative style.

One man's story
Violent storm crashes city

By Guy Hibbs

I have lived in this city for nearly 20 years, and I've never seen anything like it.

The storm that blew through this city yesterday was the noisiest, most violent roaring of Mother Nature in my memory. Others who have lived here longer than I have have told me the same thing.

Normally, I'm in the office of the Daily News at 3 p.m., usually putting the finishing touches on the day's work and thinking about the evening at home.

But yesterday, when the storm hit, I happened to be driving back to the office from an interview that I conducted for a Sunday feature story.

As I was driving by the Hillsdale shopping center – later to be one of the hardest hit areas – I looked at the sky and noticed a line of thick, dark clouds marching from east to west across the sky. The wind was picking up.

A bad storm, I thought, but nothing too unusual.

Within minutes, I knew I had misjudged the elements. . .

situation calls for it. The following is a brief summary of some of the various story structures that are used in writing for print:

Narrative. As the name suggests, this form uses traditional story-telling techniques, particularly a chronological approach. Instead of a summary lead paragraph, the story begins at the beginning. Events are then related in the order in which they occurred.

The narrative structure demands a strong, interesting lead paragraph to draw the readers into the story, just as the inverted pyramid structure does. It also requires the writer to relate everything to a central theme and to weave the events together so that they have a unity for the reader. Finally, readers must come away from a narrative story with a strong sense of the sequence in which events occur and an understanding of why this sequence is important.

Eyewitness accounts. This approach to news writing can occur in two ways. One is when the reporter is present at the event. This type of eyewitness report requires that the reporter get away from the impersonal approach with which most news is written. It opens up possibilities for the reporter to describe sights, sounds, and smells that might be left out of news stories.

Another type of eyewitness account is for a reporter to collab-

Figure 5-11

Bullet structure

The story on the right is written in the bullet style. The story begins with a summary lead paragraph and then quickly summarizes several pieces of information in the next few paragraphs. Compare this one to the stories in Figures 5-9 (page 172) and 5-10 (page 174), which are about the same event but written in an inverted pyramid and eyewitness style.

30,000 residents without power
Violent storm crashes city

A violent thunder and wind storm ripped through the city Tuesday afternoon, downing trees and power lines and causing personal injuries and property damage.

The storm caused the following injuries, disruptions and damage:

• One man was seriously injured when a tree limb hit him on the head; five others received minor injuries because of car accidents caused by the storm;

• Some 30,000 West Point Power Co. customers were without electricity for part of the evening Tuesday; power has been restored in most areas;

• Several homes and businesses in the Hillsdale area were seriously damaged by the strong winds;

• Traffic signals were out in much of the western part of the city immediately after the storm, but all have been restored.

Arthur Major, 227 W. Hill St., was struck by a falling limb and taken to Community Hospital during the storm. He suffered severe head injuries and was in serious but stable condition on Tuesday evening.

Hospital officials said five other people were injured in car accidents caused by the storm. All were treated and released by emergency room doctors.

The storm downed power lines throughout the city. West Point Power Co. officials said at one time during the afternoon about 30,000 city residents were without electricity. They said power was restored to ever part of the city except the Hillsdale area by 9 p.m.

"I don't know when we'll get the lights back on in Hillsdale," Brad Jeffries, a spokesman for the power company, said. . .

orate with an eyewitness to an event to produce an on-the-scene story about the event. This approach requires more than just interviewing an eyewitness. It means that the reporter should talk with the subject long enough to understand not only what the subject saw and heard but how the subject felt about the event. Before this approach is used, the reporter and the subject should agree on their collaboration. Normally, a reporter will draft an account of the event using the words of the eyewitness as much as possible and writing from that person's point of view. The eyewitness will then review the draft and suggest changes. This process of drafting and reviewing will continue until the article is ready for publication. An eyewitness should always see the final draft before it is published.

Bullet. This structure is useful when several things happen at an event that are not closely related to one another but the event itself needs to be covered in one story. It uses a summary lead to tell the reader what the story is about in general and then a series of short paragraphs — called bullets, and thus the name — summarizing the different events or points that the story will cover. This establishes the structure of the story. Each bullet is then expanded with several paragraphs of explanation. In this structure, the news writer does not have to be closely concerned with transitions or with trying to tie the different parts of the story together for the reader.

Micro-macro. This structure, used most prominently by the Wall Street Journal in its lead articles on page 1 each day, works well when the topic of the story is a large event that affects many people. It begins by focusing on some person or situation that has been affected by the event. This "micro" beginning reflects or demonstrates the larger issue or problem. After describing the person or situation, the story then expands to the larger problem (the "macro") with a transition paragraph that explains what the story is about. This transition paragraph often uses facts and figures that summarize the issue. The subsequent paragraphs continue to discuss the larger issue, although they may refer to the situation presented at the beginning. The story will return to the beginning situation for some type of resolution or ending. These stories take time to develop because the reporter must become familiar enough with the large problem and the small situation to write about both accurately. A lead story in the Wall Street Journal can take as much as three or four months to research and write.

These are just a few of the different approaches that news writers can take to their stories. All of these structures demand that writers adhere to the basic characteristics of good news writing: a goal of accuracy, a knowledge of the language, and an adherence to the rules of style.

Editing and rewriting

Benjamin Franklin would tell the following story:

John Thompson, a hatter, was about to open his first shop. He made a sign to put in front of his business that read, "John Thompson, hatter, makes and sells hats for ready money." He was proud of his sign and showed it to his friends. One friend said it was a fine sign, but the word "hatter" was unnecessary because the sign also said "makes and sells hats." Another friend said "makes" could be dropped. Yet another friend said the phrase "for ready money" could be eliminated because it could be assumed that people would pay money for the hats. The word "sells" could also be dropped, another friend pointed out, because it could also be assumed. With all these suggestions, Thompson remade the sign to read, "John Thompson, hatter." Then a friend suggested that a picture of a hat could replace the word, "hatter." The sign was redone again, hung outside the shop, and Thompson had a long and prosperous business.

The point is this: All writers need an editor (even if they are your neighbors). The nature of writing is that first drafts are rarely satisfactory. They do not often accomplish what the authors intend.

Editing and rewriting are integral parts of the writing process. A writer who finishes an initial draft has the responsibility to try to improve it, and most writers readily recognize this necessity.

In writing for the mass media, editing and rewriting in some form are usually part of the production process. News organizations employ people to edit copy just as they employ reporters to write it. These copy editors, many of whom have experience as news reporters, develop an expertise in the techniques of copy editing. They can edit under deadline pressure, just as writers must learn to write under those same pressures.

The first responsibility for editing lies with the writer. A writer should develop a good understanding of the purpose and techniques of copy editing. The writer should also acquire good editing habits that, when put to use, will improve what has been written.

Two general types of editing can occur: copy editing and rewriting. Copy editing involves various techniques and operations that change and improve copy but do not alter its basic structure and approach. Rewriting, just as its name implies, means rewording large portions of the copy and reexamining it structure. Rewriting produces a different piece of copy, and its purpose is to make it more suitable for the medium in which it is to be used. Both copy editing and rewriting should be done when the copy demands it, but the amount of time available for these activities will often dictate how much can be done.

Given that time is not often available to rewrite completely every piece of copy, the following are some of the things that writers should look for first in articles they have drafted:

Spelling, grammar, and style mistakes. No mistakes are more embarrassing or more harmful to the writer than spelling and grammar mistakes. Such mistakes tag the writer as unprofessional or ignorant of the basic tools of the language. These are the mistakes that a writer should look for first. They should look up any words they are not sure about, and they should use every means possible to verify that the proper names in their stories are spelled correctly.

Style mistakes can also be painfully embarrassing to a writer. Ignorance of style rules for a particular medium will signal to other professionals that the writer does not understand the importance of consistency in writing and does not care to learn.

Verbs. The quickest way to improve writing is to improve the verbs. If possible, verbs should be active and descriptive. A writer should look at every instance where he or she has used the passive voice (see page 22) and consider whether or not the passage should be changed to the active voice.

Writing that is laden with linking verbs is probably not going to sound very interesting. These verbs (is, are, was, were, etc.) are useful and necessary at times, but they lack the power that active, descriptive verbs have. Changing linking verbs to descriptive verbs will inject life into a piece of writing.

Wordiness. Some writers delight in finding passages in their own writing that use too many words. They recognize that wordiness — using too many words to say something — is one of the major and consistent problems in writing. Just as the man in Benjamin Franklin's story, every writer could use friends who are good editors to improve copy.

In examining your writing, look at the parts that were difficult for you to write initially. You may have gotten something down to express the idea or information, but chances are you could improve it on a second reading. This improvement will usually involve cutting down on the number of words it takes to express the thought.

Answering all the questions. Writing for the mass media will raise questions in the minds of the readers. Writers must make sure that they answer all of the logical and relevant questions that their articles create. For example, an article may say that three people were hurt in an automobile accident and may give the name of the person hurt seriously enough to remain in the hospital. A natural question from this information would be, who are the other two people? Or, an article may mention that a coastal storm is the second worst such storm in the history of the state. What was the worst storm? The article should tell the reader at some point.

An article that does not answer all of the logical questions often means a reporter has not done a complete job in gathering information about the subject. It is not unusual for a reporter to discover in the editing process that he or she must find out more if the article is to be complete.

Internal consistency. An article should make sense for the reasonable and sensible reader. Figures should add up properly, and times and dates should be logical. Even though most news stories are not written chronologically, a reader should have a good idea of the time sequence of a story. Confusion in the writing often indicates confusion on the part of the writer–and it almost guarantees confusion for the reader.

Looking for the writing problems listed above constitutes the beginning of good copy editing. Given enough time, writers should not stop with these problems. They should judge their copy on its emphasis, tone, and structure. All of these factors need to be correct for writing to be at its best. The best writers avoid falling in love with their copy. In fact, the best writers are among their own worst critics. Good writers are always trying to improve their writing, using whatever means are necessary. A willingness to copy edit and rewrite are two such means that writers should never shy away from.

Feature styles

Dividing feature stories from news stories is misleading. The two actually have a great deal in common. The difference is in emphasis. The styles commonly used for feature stories assume that the reader has more time to read. They still require a central theme. The writer must be able to summarize the point of the story. But the writing may require that the reader go further in order to fully understand the point of the story. Of course, that means the writer must sustain interest for a longer period of time.

Feature writing is a way for both readers and writers to get away from the relevant facts-only approach of most news stories. Feature stories generally contain more detail and description. They go beyond most news stories by trying to discover the interesting or important side of an event that may not be covered by the six basic news values.

Feature stories are also a way of humanizing the news, of breathing life into a publication. Most features center around people and their activities and interests. A good way for a feature writer to approach the job is to believe that every person is worth at least one good feature story.

Feature stories not only vary in content but also vary in structure. The following is a brief discussion of some of the structures a feature writer may use. Feature stories have no single structure that is used most of the time. Feature writers are freer to adapt whatever structure is suitable to the story they are trying to tell.

Anecdotal features. This style usually begins with a story of some kind and usually will follow with a statement of facts to support the point of the story. Quotations, anecdotes, and facts then weave in and out of one another throughout the story. The trick is to keep the quotes and the anecdotes relevant to the point of focus and to keep the story interesting without making it trite.

Suspended interest features. This style is often used for producing some special effect. Usually it is used for a short story with a punch line. But sometimes it is drawn out into a much longer story. In either case, the style requires the writer to lead readers through a series of paragraphs that may raise questions in the minds of the reader while at the same time keeping readers interested in solving the puzzle. At the end, the story is resolved in an unexpected way.

The question and answer. This is a simple style used for a specific effect. An explanatory paragraph usually starts the story. Then the interviewer's questions are followed by the interviewee's answers word for word. Using this style requires articulate participants in the interview. Sometimes, however, it makes clear how inarticulate an interviewee is about a topic. In any case, it is effective for showing the reader an unfiltered view of the interviewee's use of language.

Characteristics of feature writing

To the reader, the feature story seems to exhibit a more relaxed style of writing than a news story. It may be easier to read

Figure 5-12

Feature styles

At right are the beginnings of two feature articles. Take a close look at each of them. Any feature story can be approached and written in a variety of ways. Note the approach of each. What are the attention-getting devices? What are the sources of information in each article? Do you have any changes that you would suggest for any of these articles?

She spends most of her day in her six-by-ten-foot cell, reading her Bible, writing a letter occasionally, and walking back and forth a little. She rarely speaks to other inmates at the Miranda State Women's Prison even when she has the chance. She prefers to keep to herself.

"All my life I've been around other people. I never had any privacy," she says. "That's the one good thing about being in this place all alone."

"This place" for Wendy Hoffman is Death Row, an isolated corner of the third floor of one of Miranda's cellblocks. She's "all alone" because she is currently the only woman in the state living under a death sentence.

Hoffman has been there for six months now, ever since the end of her celebrated trial in Molene. There she was convicted of shooting 13-year-old Chrissy Staten on the orders of her husband. The trial generated a barrage of international publicity for everyone involved, including Dax Hoffman, who is also living under a death sentence at the Norton Jones State Prison, about 100 miles away ...

Norma Sasser is determined that next Wednesday will be like any other day has been for the last 45 years. She'll walk into her first-grade classroom at Rockwood Elementary, give her students their final report cards and wish them a happy summer.

The problem is that however much "Miss Norma" follows her routine, it won't be the same. It will be her last day of teaching kids to read, write, count and be still.

She knows that, and even though she dreads the last day, she's looking forward to what comes after that: lots of travel, time to read and gardening, she says.

The day might be more normal if all she had to do was meet with this year's students. But soon after they've received their grades, a day-long celebration will begin at the school, all in her honor. More than 1,000 of her former students will be there, some of whom will travel from distant parts of the country.

"That's the part I dread, not leaving the classroom for the last time," she said ...

than a news story, and because of its content it may be more entertaining. Feature writers, however, work just as hard and are just as disciplined as news writers. They may work under a slightly different set of rules than news writers, but the goals of a feature writer are essentially the same ones that a news writer has: to tell a story accurately and to write well.

The main thing that sets feature stories apart from news stories is the greater amount of detail and description features contain. This difference is the backbone of a good feature story. While the news story writer wishes to transmit a basic set of facts to the reader as quickly as possible, the feature writer tries to enhance those facts with details and description so that the reader will be able to see a more complete picture of an event or a person. For instance, while the news writer might refer to "a desk" in a news story, the feature writer will want to go beyond that simple reference by telling the reader something more — "a mahogany desk" or "a dark mahogany desk." Or better yet, the writer might rely on verbs to enhance the descriptions of the subject: "A large, soft executive chair enveloped him as he sat behind a dark mahogany desk."

The three major kinds of descriptions that should be contained in a feature story are description of actions, description of people, and description of places. All of these are important to a good feature story, but the description that makes for the strongest writing is generally the description of action. Telling about events, telling what has happened, telling what people are doing—these things make compelling reading. Descriptions of this type help readers to see a story, not just read about it. In addition, feature writers should make sure that readers see the people in their stories, just as the writers themselves have seen the people. Feature writers also need to describe adequately the places where the stories occur. Readers need an idea of the surroundings of a story to draw a complete picture of the story in their minds.

A couple of tips will help writers attain more vivid descriptions in their stories. One is the reliance on nouns and verbs. Beginning writers sometimes feel that they should use as many adjectives and adverbs as possible to enhance their writing, and in doing so, they rely on dull and overused nouns and verbs. That approach is a wrong turn on the road to producing lively, descriptive writing. A second tip for writers is to remember the five senses. Often writers simply describe the way things look, and they forget about the way things sound, feel, taste, or smell. Incorporating the five senses into a story will help make a description come alive for a reader.

Feature stories often contain more quotations and even dialogue than news stories. News writers use direct quotations to enhance and illuminate the facts they are trying to present. Feature writers go beyond this by using quotations to say something about the people who are in their stories. Quoted material is generally used much more freely in feature stories, although, as in news stories, dumping a load of quotes on a reader without a break often puts too heavy a burden on the reader. Dialogue and dialect are other devices a feature writer may use if the story calls for them.

One of the charms of feature writing for many writers is that they can put more of themselves into a story. Unlike news stories, in which writers stay out of sight as much as they can, feature writers are somewhat freer to inject themselves and their opinions into a story. While feature writers have a little more latitude in this regard, they must use this latitude wisely and make sure that a feature story does not become a story about themselves rather than about the subject they are trying to cover.

Parts of a feature story

Feature stories generally have four parts: a lead, an engine paragraph, a body, and an ending. Each needs special handling by the writer.

As in a news story, the lead of a feature story is its most important part. Feature writers are not bound by the one sentence, thirty-word lead paragraph structure that newswriters must often follow. A lead in a feature story may be several sentences or paragraphs long. From the beginning sentence, however, the feature writer must capture the reader's attention and give the reader some information of substance—or at least promise some information of substance. A news writer can depend on the story's subject to compel the reader's interest. A feature writer must sell the reader on the subject in the first few words or sentences.

A good lead uses the first words or sentences of a story to build interest in the story's subject, but the reader must soon discover some benefit for reading the story. That's why the writer should build a lead toward some initial point that the story is to make, something that will hook the reader for the rest of the story.

The engine paragraph (also called the fat paragraph, the snapper, or the why paragraph) gives the reader this payoff and sets the stage for the rest of the story. It puts the story in some context for the reader and tells the reader why the rest of the story should be read.

The body of the feature story is the middle of the story that expands and details the subjects introduced in the lead. The body should answer every question raised in the lead, and it should fulfill every expectation raised within the reader. Unfortunately, like products bought in a store, features often promise more than they deliver. They tell the reader in the lead that the information they contain will be of interest or help to the reader, and they turn out to be neither interesting nor helpful. The body should contain the substance of the article, and it should be what the reader has been led to expect.

News writers using the inverted pyramid generally do not have to worry about the ending of their stories. Feature writers need to take care as to how a story ends. The ending of a story may be used to put the story in some perspective, to answer any lingering questions that a reader may have, or to make a final point about the story's subject. The major point about an ending is that a writer should not allow a story to go on too long. Like any other writer, the feature writer should stop writing when there is nothing of substance left to say.

Thinking graphically

As we mentioned in the first chapter of this book, the modern writer for the mass media often finds it necessary to think in terms of pictures as well as words. Because of significant changes in technology during the past two decades, most publications can integrate pictures, graphics and other graphic devices into their text. In many cases, writers are no longer wordsmiths. They must have broader skills than just being able to handle the language and the forms of writing for the media in which they work. They must think graphically.

Nowhere is that more apparent than in the news and information business, particularly in publications that deal in news. Writers and reporters must know the standard graphic forms and understand their uses. They must be able to recognize that a pic-

Figure 5-13

Visual and Verbal: The Paradox of the Visual Journalist
By Celeste Bernard

Tell people you work at a newspaper and the first thing they'll likely ask is, "So, are you a reporter?" If you say yes, they'll likely pepper you with questions, berate the media's liberal bent or, if you're lucky, give you a lead on a good story. But respond that you're a visual journalist and you'll get a blank stare followed by a conversation-ending "Oh."

I know, because I've been there.

The problem is everyone understands what a reporter, editor or photographer does, but not a visual journalist. The title sounds vague and seems to imply that words aren't an essential part of the job.

Not true. Not by a long shot.

Careful reporting and writing is behind every respectable graphic, for obvious reasons. Diagrams can't be drawn unless the concepts or processes they illustrate are fully understood. Charts can't be plotted without considering the source of the data —

nor can they be explained without context. Most importantly, graphics won't do their job if the information contained in them is obscured by bad writing or editing, regardless how beautiful the image.

This is why good writing is so critical. Visual journalists must craft words that thread together concepts, pictures or trends. They must do so carefully, so as not to blatantly repeat the lead of the story or dilute the point of the graphic. It is difficult work and usually means a day's worth of reporting is boiled down to a few well-chosen words. But it serves the readers, who are pressed for time but still crave knowledge.

Now when people ask me if I'm a reporter, I always say yes. Then I explain that I'm the person behind all those maps, charts and diagrams they see in the paper each day. Their response is usually, "Cool."

And it is. By a long shot.

Celeste Bernard is the graphics editor of the Seattle Post-Intelligencer. She is the former associate editor for news graphics at the Chicago Tribune.

ture or graphic might be a better way of conveying information than a sentence or paragraph.

The graphic forms that are in use in the mass media today are many and varied – too many to discuss fully here. They are generally categorized into four types: text-based graphics; chart-based graphics; illustration-based graphics; and maps, graphics that represent geographic or physical locations.

Text-based graphics are page design devices such as drop caps, pull quotes, and others shown in Figure 5-14. Unless a writer is involved with the layout and design of the article, he or she is unlikely to be very concerned with these types of graphics specifically. They are often drawn from what the writer has already written by the person who is designing the page.

Writers are more likely to be called upon to create – or to provide information for – chart-based graphics. These graphics use some sort of graphic form to represent information. They are likely to require text also to help the reader understand the information, but the graphic form is the main device that they use. Chart-based graphics can be divided into two major groups: those that represent numbers and those that do not. The chart-based graphics that represent numbers are what we are most likely to think of when we talk about informational graphics.

Information for graphics

What are the graphic possibilities for a story? Many writers are trained to think in terms of words and text structures. They gather information they know will fit into paragraph form, and they often ignore information that might require other forms. The well-rounded writer, particularly in an age when many forms of information presentation are used, must think more broadly.

In putting together a news story, the writer should consider the following possibilities for graphics that would support the story.

Numbers. Are there numbers that need to shown with this story? Will showing the numbers add to the reader's understanding? We're talking basic bar, line, and pie charts here, along with tables.

Location. Does the story need a map? Should it be a simple locator or does it need to be married with some other information? Is a data map called for -- does the geography relate to the numbers?

History and context. A timeline is the first thing that springs to mind. How did the events of the story get to this point? Is there a history that the reader needs to know about? Another form that this takes is the fact or profile box. Can we add to the reader's understanding of an organization or person that would not be included in a story?

Process. Should we show the reader how something works? Sometimes we can do that with text or text married with pictures.

Figure 5-14

Type-based graphics

Type-based graphics come in a wide variety of forms. To the right are examples of a few: (clockwise from top left) drop cap, index, refer, and pull quote.

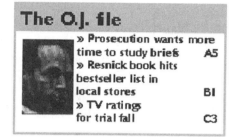

Procedure. Is there a step-by-step procedure that shows how something happened? Somewhat akin to a timeline, a procedural chart can show how an event occurred. (While the words process and procedure may be interchangeable, I distinguish them in this context in the following way: a process refers to something that is not unusual and happens periodically; a procedure refers to a single, often unique, event.)

Profile. This might be thought of as "information-plus." A organization, company, person or almost any element in a story can be outlined or explained with extra information in a variety of ways.

Forms of graphic presentation

Writers for the mass media should understand thoroughly the four most commonly used types of numerical chart-based graphics: the bar chart, the line chart, the pie chart and the map.

The bar chart uses rectangles to represent numbers. These rectangles may be either horizontal or vertical. (Bar charts that

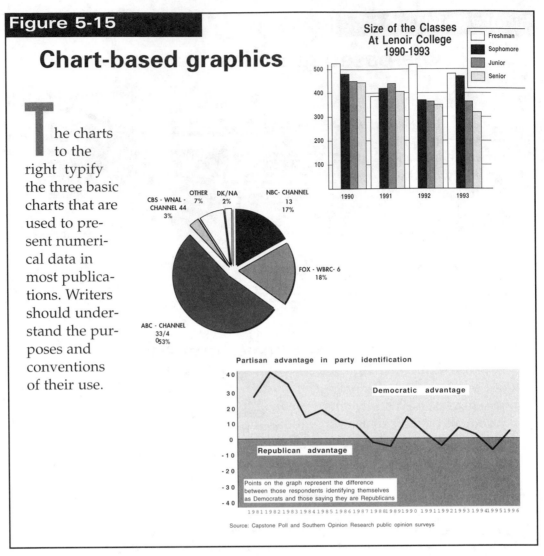

Figure 5-15

Chart-based graphics

The charts to the right typify the three basic charts that are used to present numerical data in most publications. Writers should understand the purposes and conventions of their use.

Size of the Classes At Lenoir College 1990-1993

Legend: Freshman, Sophomore, Junior, Senior

1990, 1991, 1992, 1993

CBS - WNAL - CHANNEL 44 3%
OTHER 7%
DK/NA 2%
NBC- CHANNEL 13 17%
FOX - WBRC- 6 18%
ABC - CHANNEL 33/4 053%

Partisan advantage in party identification

Democratic advantage

Republican advantage

Points on the graph represent the difference between those respondents identifying themselves as Democrats and those saying they are Republicans

1981 1982 1983 1984 1985 1986 1987 1988 1989 1990 1991 1992 1993 1994 1995 1996

Source: Capstone Poll and Southern Opinion Research public opinion surveys

use vertical rectangles are sometimes called column charts.) These rectangles are drawn in relation to one another. That is, the rectangle that represents 10 of something should be twice the length of the one that represents five. Bar charts are an excellent means of representing units of numerical data so that they can be compared with one another. Bar charts are usually simple to construct and easy to understand. They give readers an impression about the information as well as the information itself.

The line chart has a specific purpose: to represent change over time. The line chart uses lines that are drawn from left to right over some sort of grid. The numbers or units that run horizontally across the chart represent units of time. The numbers or units that run vertically represent the units of data that you are attempting to show to the reader. The major purpose of this chart is to allow the reader to compare the data at different points in time. Sometimes a line chart will use more than one line, which means that it is representing more than one set of data. Such multi-line charts increase the levels of comparison: a reader can compare one set of data with another and can compare both sets to the time units represented on the chart.

Figure 5-16

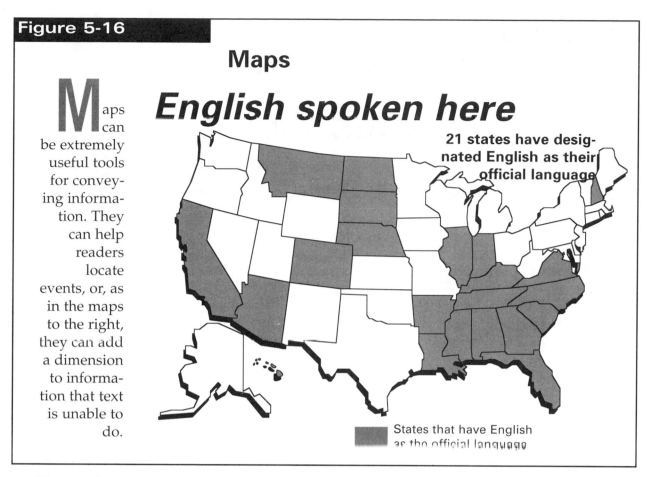

Maps

English spoken here

21 states have designated English as their official language

Maps can be extremely useful tools for conveying information. They can help readers locate events, or, as in the maps to the right, they can add a dimension to information that text is unable to do.

States that have English as the official language

The pie chart shows how something is divided. In order for a pie chart to work properly, whatever is being shown must be completely represented; nothing should be left out. For instance, if a city's population is divided into ethnic groups and then represented by a pie chart, everyone in the city should be represented by one of the sections of the pie (see Figure 5-15). The information in a pie chart is usually expressed in percentages, and those percentages must add up to 100. Pie charts are an excellent means of letting readers compare the parts of a whole unit.

One of the oldest, most common and most enduring forms of graphics is the map. Maps represent geographic or physical locations; they are geographic if they represent parts of the earth, physical if they represent something other than that. A set of house plans is a physical map. Humans have been drawing maps for thousands of years, and in that time, certain conventions concerning maps have evolved. One is that, particularly for geographic maps, the northern most part of what is represented is at the top of the map, west is on the left and east is on the right. Another convention is that maps should represent their subjects proportionally. That is, the east-west axis should be on the same scale as the north-south axis, and the map should be about what we would see if we were high enough above the earth to see it.

Two types of maps are used most often by the print media: locator maps and data maps. Locator maps give readers an idea of the location of an event in relation to some place they may already know. When a news event occurs in a small town, a loca-

Figure 5-17

Illustration-based graphics

A strong illustration, such as the one used with the story on the right, can be both attention-getting and content-laden. The illustrator definitely had something to say about this subject.

THE DAILY NEWS, SEPTEMBER 8, 1993,   PAGE 3

Unbanned

Penn. judges dismisses complaints against book

By United Press International

A Pennsylvania judge has dismissed the case of a Pentecostal minister who wanted the Apollo-Ridge School District to ban an award-winning children's book, "Dragonwings."

Sylvia Hall argued the use of author Lawrence Yepp's book in eighth- grade classes violated the U.S. Constitution because it promoted Taoism, reincarnation and secular humanism. Hall, of Kiski, Pa., said the beliefs were inconsistent with her Fundamentalist Christian faith.

The American Civil Liberties Union argued the case on behalf of the school district.

Armstrong County President Judge Joseph Nickleach ruled Wednesday "neither the book nor the teachers who taught it expounded a particular religion as the only correct belief or even the preferred belief," and therefore did not violate the Constitution.

The ACLU said the judge reaffirmed the longstanding legal precedent that simply discussing in school different religious beliefs in a historical or literary context does not violate the Constitution.

"So long as religious dogma is not promoted in any way nor one's religious beliefs hindered or criticized, the Establishment Clause (of the constitution) is not violated," Nichleach wrote.

The book, published in 1975, tells the story of a Chinese boy who comes to live with his father in Chinatown in San Francisco during the early 1900s.

Hall in May asked the Apollo-Ridge school board to ban the book because it contained the word "demon," a translation of the Chinese word "kuei" meaning ghost or spirit. Chinese characters in the book used the word demon to describe Caucasians because of their light skin.

The ACLU said it applauded the decision.

The civil rights organization said 24 years ago the U.S. Supreme Court struck down an anti-evolution statute and stated a school curriculum could not betailored to satisfy the beliefs of any particular religious group, for that in itself would violate the Constitution.

The ACLU said Nickleach's ruling vindicated that "vitally important principle."

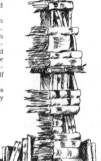

tor map is often used that will include a larger city, so that readers can get an idea of where it is. Even when news occurs locally, locator maps are used to pinpoint the place where it happened.

Data maps combine some other type of information to geography. By using different shades or colors for geographic units, the mapmaker can give the reader some information about the data that he or she is presenting. Data maps are widely used, but they take some skill to construct, and the information in them must be accurate. That's where the writer comes in. Often, it is the job of the writer to gather the information that is presented in a data map.

The final major type of graphic that we mentioned earlier is the illustration-based graphic. These graphics use illustration — often a drawing of some type — as the major part of the graphic. The purpose of these graphics is not so much to give readers specific information about a story but to offer the reader an impression about this story. Writers, unless they have special skills artistically, are not usually called upon to produce these graphics, but they may be asked to give their ideas to an illustrator.

The challenge of writing

Writing for print encapsulates most of the challenges that a media writer will face — gathering information, learning the appropriate structures and writing conventions, and understanding the graphic devices that may enhance the writing. The type of writing that we have discussed in this chapter occurs every day in newspapers, magazines, newsletters, web sites, and many other forms of media. The professional writer is always faced with the same task — to present information accurately, completely, precisely and efficiently. Learning to do this takes reading, analysis, study and practice.

Points for discussion

1. Some critics argue that the inverted pyramid news story structure should be abandoned by newspapers. They say that television and radio deliver news much faster than newspapers; therefore, newspapers should not be concerned so much with getting information to readers quickly as with getting more complete and accurate information. What do you think?

2. Chapter 3 discussed journalistic style and the conventions of journalism. How does what you learned in that chapter fit in with the principles presented in this chapter?

3. The author says you shouldn't go out of your way to find substitutes for the verb said. Do you think that is good advice?

4. The text says that a direct quote "should be the exact words of the speaker." Can you think of any circumstances where this would not be true?

Further reading

Bruce J. Evensen, The Responsible Reporter. Northport, Ala.: Vision Press, 1995

Everette E. Dennis and Arnold H. Ismach, Reporting Processes and Practices: Newswriting for Today's Readers, Belmont, CA: Wadsworth, 1981.

Catherine C. Mitchell and Mark D. West, The News Formula. New York: St. Martin's Press, 1996

M. L. Stein, Getting and Writing the News, New York: Longman, 1985.

Stovall, James Glen. Infographics: A Journalist's Guide. Boston: Allyn and Bacon, 1997.

On the Web: One place to start learning about journalism is the journalism section of the WWW Virtual Library, www.cais. com/makulow/vlj.html. For student journalists, there is the National Scholastic Press Association and the Associated Collegiate Press website located at studentpress.journ.umn.edu/. The Society of Professional Journalist website is at www.spj.org.

Chapter 5 Writing for print

Exercises

• *A NOTE TO THE STUDENTS: The following section contains a variety of exercises for news and feature writing. You should follow your instructor's directions in completing them. Some of the exercises are written in sentence fragments while others are written in complete sentences, often in narrative form. If you are assigned to write news stories from the exercises in this section, you should use the information but not the exact wording contained in the exercises (except for the direct quotes). Many of the exercises are badly written on purpose. It will be your job to rewrite the information you have so that it is better written than the exercise material.*

5–1 Writing leads

Write a lead paragraph from each set of facts.

Crash

• Happened today at noon.
• Killed: Rufus N. Hebernowski, an Air Force major
• happened at the Super Shopping Mall, a huge new mall on the western edge of town.
• the jet aircraft he was piloting crashed.
• fortunately no one on the ground was injured or killed.
• 15 cars were destroyed in the mall's northern parking lot when the aircraft crashed into them.
• Hebernowski had no known connections locally. He was killed.
• He was stationed at Little Rock Air Force Base.

City council

• City council met this morning
• 10 percent increase in city property taxes
• increase will cause average taxes to

go up by about $50 yearly.
• higher rate takes effect at the first of next month.
• tax will be used to pay for doubling the size of the city park.

University raises

• Harold R. Drazsnzak, university vice president for finance
• made an announcement at a press conference on the front steps of the university Administration Building.
• he said that all faculty and staff will get 15 percent pay raises
• will take effect this fall.
• said the raise is possible because of increased revenues from the state.
• "Without a doubt, our faculty is long overdue to get a raise," he said.
• first raise for the faculty in two years.

Journalism students meet

• Journalism Student Association met today at noon. About 200 students attended.
• meeting began with Pledge of

Allegiance, followed by a group song: "America the Beautiful."

- Journalism Student Association treasurer Rufus L. McSnorkel reported that the organization has a balance in its bank account of $725.35.
- Members voted to hold their next regular meeting two weeks from today.
- Members decided to organize a boycott of all journalism classes tomorrow to protest university tuition increase. Tuition is supposed to go up by 10 percent beginning in the fall semester.
- David S. Kuykendall, Journalism Student Association president, said: "We are confident that all journalism students will boycott all classes."

5–2 Writing leads

Write a lead paragraph from each set of facts.

Plant accident

- Duane LaChance, 53, of Petal, a pipe fitter employed by Gross Engineers
- company based in Petal, Miss.
- LaChance suffered third-degree burns and was listed in serious condition tonight in the intensive care unit at Methodist Hospital.
- Happened 3 p.m. today at Petal Municipal Power Plant, 222 Power Drive.
- LaChance installing new pipes on the roof of the plant when he accidentally touched a power line carrying 15,000 volts with a wrench.
- Source for this information is Henry Rosen, project manager for Gross Engineers.

McCartney illness

- Peter McCartney, famous rock singer.
- entered Riverside Hospital for exploratory throat surgery today.
- voice had been reduced to a whisper following Bennett Auditorium performance in front of capacity crowd of 1,000 fans tonight.
- checked in the hospital late tonight; surgery is scheduled tomorrow.

Perot World

- press conference held at University Administration Building.
- Ross Perot, Texas billionaire, held the press conference. Press conference held in third-floor conference room.
- Announced plans to buy local City Park and convert it into a theme park.
- Park will be called Perot World.

BOE meeting

- Hattiesburg Board of Education met this morning. All members were present.
- Assistant Superintendent Max Hoemmeldorfer reported that enrollment this school year dropped by 200 students to 1,050.
- "This is the third year we've lost enrollment. The future looks bleak," Hoemmeldorfer said.
- board accepted report, and then passed a group of new rules proposed by the administration.
- new rules will prohibit female students from wearing miniskirts and will prohibit all students from wearing blue jeans. Male students will not be allowed to wear their hair below their ears.
- board then accepted a low bid from Farmer's Dairy to provide milk to the schools at one-half cent a pint.

- *Hint: Do not try to put all of the available information into the lead. Be selective. Use proper style and copy editing symbols. Double check facts and spelling of proper names before turning your story in. Copyediting symbols can be found on page 395.*

5–3 Writing leads

Write a lead paragraph from each set of facts.

Faculty in plane crash

- Associate Professor of Rural Sociology John Dumont and associate professor of English George Johnson, both from Backwater State University
- were returning Thursday night from separate conferences in New York City.
- were aboard the same TWA jet
- crashed on takeoff at Kennedy International Airport
- 45 passengers and crew members aboard. Five persons were killed.
- two from Backwater escaped injury.

You are a reporter for the Backwater State student newspaper, The Backwash.

Mailer speaks

- Noted author Norman Mailer, winner of the Pulitzer Prize
- spoke at 4:30 pm. in Room 111 of the William Oxley Thomson Memorial Library Sunday
- told his audience of 67, mostly English students:
- "You can't be a great writer by imitating the styles of prize-winning authors. You've got to get out and sample life, learn how other people live, and then let your inner feelings pour out. These parodies they assign in college English courses are a bunch of hogwash."

Professor wins award

- The Freedoms Foundation at Valley Forge announced its annual George Washington Honor Medal winners
- at ceremony in Pennsylvania last week
- among the 32 winners was Clement Crabtree, a professor of horticulture.
- Crabtree was cited for his essay called "Plan for Peace," in which he urged distribution of free packets of red, white and blue flower seeds in foreign nations.

5–4 Leads and follow-up paragraphs

Write a lead and second paragraph for each of the following sets of information.

Curriculum changes

- recent study showed only 15 percent of students took a foreign language course and only 20 percent took a math course while at the University
- University president announces changes in requirements for graduation
- students entering next fall must take one math, computer science, and foreign language course
- President: "We feel that these new course requirements will allow us to turn out better educated persons."
- president's name is French English

Arrest

- Cathy Bensen, 22-year-old senior
- daughter of locally prominent attorney Jim Bensen, 211 Green Grove Drive
- mother, Sharon Bensen, lives in Canada
- arrested for driving under the influence of alcohol for third time in six months last night
- Cathy was this year's Homecoming Queen; has been cheerleader; straight-A student
- going to Vanderbilt University for graduate studies in biology

Record weather

- It is warm
- students keep talking about the unseasonable weather. Your editor tells you to find out what the temperature is and to write a story about the weather.
- You call the Port Columbus weather office and learn that that high yesterday was 82 degrees at 3:30 p.m.
- It was the hottest temperature for this date since 1888.

5–5 Leads and follow-up paragraphs

Write a lead and a second paragraph for each of the following sets of information.

Protest

- group of citizens angry because University biology class is teaching evolution
- group led by Wilbur Straking, pastor of the Ever-Faithful Church of the Living Water
- Straking: "I plan to lead a group of 25 dedicated Christians to the state capital next Monday to speak with legislators about this problem. We believe the teaching of evolution is against the principles of this Christian country, and we want to put a stop to it."
- class they're objecting to is taught by Laura Cliff, associate professor of biology; she wouldn't comment on the group's charges
- neither would University president

Law suit

- suit filed in Circuit Court today; for $100,000
- against Amburn's Produce Market
- by Ellie Maston, 313 Journey Road
- charges market with negligence; suit says green beans left on floor of market; she walked through them and slipped and broke her hip
- suit says she "suffered permanent bodily and mental injuries, incurred medical expenses and lost income."
- accident happened April 1 this year

Agreement announced

- Clyde Parris, president of Ambrose Steel Company, and Charles Pointer, president of United Steelworkers Local 923, make joint announcement
- company and union have reached collective bargaining agreement
- strike set for midnight tonight has been called off
- strike would have stopped production at Ambrose and put 457 steelworkers off the job
- terms of agreement will be read tonight to a meeting of the union, Pointer says
- Parris says contract includes "substantial wage agreement" but won't say how much; that will be announced tonight
- union will vote on contract next week
- Pointer says contract "the best we can get out of the company"

5–6 Leads and follow-up paragraphs

Write a lead and a second paragraph for each of the following sets of information.

Malpractice suit

- two doctors being sued for malpractice; Barney Olive and Stephen Rogers, both of whom practice at Riverside Hospital
- William Hamilton, lawyer for plaintiff, Bertie McNicholls, 623 Leanto Road
- Hamilton, beginning final arguments in case, has heart attack
- quick work of Olive and Rogers save his life
- Hamilton, 73, now recovering at Riverside Hospital
- trial to resume next week

Alumni festival

- University Alumni Association planning spring festival for April
- games, contests will be held on football field
- barbeque lunch and exhibition baseball game
- all proceeds to go to school library, plus alumni hoping to raise more money through pledges
- date depends on whether or not baseball team makes it to playoffs this year
- alumni president Bobby Don Willis: "This kind of activity is one of the positive things we can do to make this university a better educational institution."

Website policy

- lots of people at Backwater University are building websites
- University says 50 to 100 people using University connection to establish website
- University has looked at these websites and found that many contain pornographic pictures and other material
- University announcing policy to inspect and approve website before they are put on the University's web connection
- Sperling Sprinter, University public relations officer: "This type of stuff isn't good for Backwater University. We had to put a stop to it."
- Art Waddell, associate professor in the art department
- Waddell is planning to sue University if it tries to enforce the policy.

5–7 Writing news stories

Write the information given below as a three paragraph inverted pyramid story.

An accident report gives the following information:

- Incident: Two car accident on Hwy 14 and Gilmore Ave.
- Time and date: 2:45 AM, Oct. 8
- Involved: Carol Gleson, 19, Saint Mary's College Student
- Home town: Minneapolis, MN.
- Driving a 1983 Toyota Tercel; Northbound on Hwy 14.
- Minor injuries: Treated and released from Winona Hospital.

- Involved: Candy Floss 17, Daughter of Daryl and Stacy Floss, 1352 Broadway, Winona, MN. Driving a 1990 Chevrolet Camaro; Westbound on Gilmore Avenue. Drugs were recovered from the Floss Car. Did not require hospitalization. Released to parents at police station.

In an interview with a State Police Trooper William Troutner at the scene of the accident the officer says, "Y'know the girl who walked away was the daughter of the president of the local school board? She just pulled right out in front of the kid from Saint Mary's. I'll tell you one thing that's just a shame, she had more drugs in her car than you could sell in a month. You don't use my name. You media ghouls are all alike."

5–8 Writing news stories

Write the information given below as a three paragraph inverted pyramid story.

An arrest report gives the following information:

- Incident: An assault and battery at Watter's Hall.
- Time and date: 2:45 a.m., February 26, 1991.
- Involved: Sharron Peters, 19, Saint Mary's College Student
- Home town: Minneapolis, MN. Daughter of Wm. Peters, SMC Vice-President of Student Life.
- Minor injuries: Treated and released from Winona Hospital.

- Involved: Thomas Harnell 21, Son of Sherman and Tricia Harnell, 1352 Broadway, Winona, MN. Reported driving a 1990 Chevrolet Camaro. Arrested on Gilmore Avenue at 2:50 a.m. and charged with assault and battery.

As police led away Harnell, he shouted, "She owed me money, man! Those Saint Mary's brats think they own us."

In an interview with a State Police Trooper William Troutner at the scene of the arrest the officer says, "Y'know the girl who got attacked was the daughter of the vice-president of Saint Mary's? I'll tell you one thing that's just a shame, she had more drugs in her purse than you could sell in a month. Because we were on private property we couldn't make an arrest. You don't use my name. You media ghouls are all alike."

5–9 Writing news stories

Write a news story from the following set of facts

Murder

Francie Franklin, proprietor of a small bakery in Pleasant Grove, was killed during the night. Police Chief Wilburn Cole tells you over the phone that Miss Franklin did not deliver a wedding cake as expected this morning, and when the bride's mother went to the bake shop in Miss Franklin's home to check, she found the front door open and a display case smashed. "She didn't go no further," Cole says. "When we got there we found Miss Francie in the kitchen. She was shot dead." The little shop is in a shambles when you go by to check and you note the contrast to the neat tidy operation the woman kept. You can't find the chief, but the radio dispatcher reads this memo to you: "Francie's body was taken to Smith's Funeral Parlor where they'll do an autopsy. It must have happened before midnight because her television set was still on and she always turns it off after the late movie. She was shot once in the chest and her pistol is missing from the drawer under the cash register. Money was scattered around but they probably got away with some." Kenton County Homicide Investigator Kelton Kelly says she was shot with a .22 calibre bullet and that they didn't find any fingerprints. However, a strange, unidentified red wool ski cap was found under the body. Kenton County Coroner Ransom Cranwell tells you that death was from a single gunshot wound and that there were no other injuries. "It was crazy the way they messed up the place though," he adds. "She was always so proud of it. She was just an old maid who loved everyone and everyone loved her." Arrangements are pending. No known survivors. Age 68. Address, 504 Ash St. She started the business 20 years ago under the name Francie's Fancies. She recently expanded by building a small service area at the front of the house.

5–10 Writing news stories

Write a news story from the following set of facts.

Prosper

Prosper is a mining town of 909 people in the northeast corner of Crocker County. Since the deep-shaft coal mine was opened in 1901, it has provided a major source of employment for the town's people, and in the last 18 years has brought more than 800 people from other towns to work every day at the mine, United Coal Company's Mine No. 3, known locally as Hellpit. The company announced yesterday that the mine will close in two weeks for an indefinite period. Since 1980, when Prosper was incorporated and became eligible for coal tax revenue, its budget has risen from $40,000 to $300,000 ($125,000 in coal severance tax monies, $125,000 in federal matching money for capital improvements). Mayor Lester Jenkins tells you that "With the mine closed, our revenue is just about gone." Some tax money will continue to dribble in as stockpiles of coal are depleted, but Wilma Foster, the city clerk, foresees a cutback for the fiscal year, which starts in 30 days, to $60,000. "That will cover essential services like police protection and utilities at city hall and at the new ball park," she adds. Councilman Ed Barnes tells you that most of the coal money went into building projects. "And we've got the city hall and the park paid for, so at least we're not in debt." The town council will talk about a new budget at its meeting tomorrow night. The mine employed 1,000 people. The shaft is a quarter mile deep, the deepest in the state. Company officials cannot be reached by phone, but a statement delivered to you gives the reason for the closing as a severe cutback in demand for coal because of a shutdown in manufacturing nationwide. It quotes Wilson Standridge, company president: "We hope to see an increase in demand, but until we do, the mine will remain sealed."

5–11 Writing news stories

Write a news story from the following set of facts.

Shooting

On your regular telephone rounds of the area police and sheriff departments, you talk with Sheriff Carmen Townsend of Sevier County. He says: "Yeah, we had a pretty bad incident here last night. A Mrs. Bertie Clancy was shot and killed by her husband. At least, I think she was killed. The hospital didn't expect her to live long. They lived on Caney Creek Road near Pigeon Forge. She was sixty-eight years old. The way I understand it, they had this kid — Randy — and he's the kind of kid who ain't all there, you know what I mean. Anyway, he and his old man, a fellow named Darris Clancy, got into an argument. Randy was all the time coming around, asking for money. He was drawing some disability money from the government, about $300 a month, but that was never enough. He was always hitting his folks up for some more, and as I understand it, they usually gave it to him. Well, they got into this argument, and the old man pointed a gun at Randy. The old lady tried to break it up and got in between them and the gun went off. She was hit in the head and the shoulder. Well, you can imagine how the son felt and what it was like in the house then, so I guess what happened was that Randy grabbed the gun away from his daddy and shot him. It was a shotgun. Anyway, the old man dropped dead as a doornail. There wasn't even no use in taking him to the hospital. We just called the coroner and took him over to the funeral home."

A sheriff's deputy tells you that Randy Clancy is being held in the county jail without bond. His arraignment will be sometime this afternoon.

You call the hospital and a spokesman there says Mrs. Clancy has died. She died just a few minutes after she arrived at about 11 o'clock last night.

James Clancy, another son and an employee of the local Stokely canning company, tells you the following things about what happened: "No, Randy never was exactly right, but he was a good kid. I wasn't there. I just talked with him a little while after it happened. He says he don't remember much, but he said he couldn't live without mama. He was always her favorite, but he and daddy hadn't gotten along too well lately. I guess it happened about like the sheriff told you. I had talked with Randy earlier in the day, and he told me he was going up to see mama and daddy because he needed some money 'cause he was getting into some trouble with some people he had borrowed from. I think he was going to ask them for about $200. Daddy used to get really mad when he would ask for money. He got there about 9 o'clock. He told me that after the shooting he went upstairs to what used to be his bedroom and tore all the pictures off the wall. Then he went out into the yard and smashed the shotgun on a fence post. I found it later and showed it to the sheriff. As I understand it, after he had done that, he went to a neighbor's house and called the sheriff and told him to come get him.

The neighbor, Will O'Reilly, who lives next door to the Clancy couple on Caney Creek Road, tells you that's what happened: "I heard a lot of arguing coming from their house, I guess it was about 9 o'clock or maybe a little afterwards. Then I heard these shots, and I told my wife, 'There's trouble up there,' but she said I'd better not leave the house. Pretty soon, Randy come knocking on the door and asked to use the phone. I remember he was wearing a tee shirt with the words 'Gospel Baptist Church' on it. He was pretty calm, but I heard him tell the sheriff what happened and for them to come and get him."

Employee records at the Stokely plant show that Darris Clancy was 64 years old and had worked as a driver at the plant off and on for more than 20 years. He quit seven years ago because of arthritis and had been drawing disability payments ever since.

Bertie Clancy had lived all her life in the Pigeon Forge area but had never been employed anywhere for any length of time.

Caney Creek Road is a winding mountain road, and the dead couple had lived there for about 25 years.

5–12 Writing news stories

Write a news story from the following set of facts.

City council

Here's what happened at the city council meeting last night.

The meeting started about five minutes late because city council member Harvey Haddix couldn't find a place to park. He came rushing in and made a comment about how the city police were going to have to crack down on illegal parkers. That brought a laugh from the overflow crowd of over two hundred people there. Mayor Ray Sadecki called the meeting to order, and Wilber Mizell, the minister of the Vinegar Bend Baptist Church, started the meeting with prayer. The minutes of the last meeting of the council were read, and no one had any additions or corrections to them.

The first item of business was a report from the Metropolitan Zoning Commission. Bobby Thompson, who is the chairman of the Zoning Commission, said the commission had met two days ago to consider a request by a local developer to move a cemetery so that he can build a supermarket. The developer's name is Carl Erskine. The cemetery is located in the 2800 block of Forbes Street, much of which is zoned for commercial purposes now. Erskine told the council that he will pay all the costs of having the graves relocated in Peaceful Rest Cemetery, which is located about a mile away from the present site. "I think rezoning will be good for the neighborhood and good for the city," Erskine said. "There's not another supermarket for at least a mile and a half in any direction." Thompson said: "We've studied the traffic patterns along Forbes Street, and we don't believe the supermarket will cause any problems." After several more questions by various council members, the mayor asked for any questions or comments from those in the audience. About twenty people spoke, and all but two of them were against the rezoning. It took about an hour. Here are some of the comments:

Early Wynn, 122 Forbes Street: "This thing is going to destroy our neighborhood. It's pretty quiet there now, but if you get this thing in there, it's going to turn noisy."

Dick Groat, 1811 Polo Grounds Road: "Nobody on my street wants the supermarket. We have plenty of places to go to shop. We don't need this. Besides, some of those graves are pretty old, and I don't think it would be the same if you moved them."

Sarah Yawkey, 555 Bosox Drive: "I just can't believe you'd do this. Anybody who'd do this would steal the dimes off a dead man's eyes."

Walt Dropo, 611 Forbes Street and president of the Forbes Street Residents Association: "We've been fighting this thing for two years now. All the zoning commission did was study the traffic patterns. They didn't consider what it would do to the neighborhood. Besides, that cemetery has some of the oldest graves in the city in it -- some of those people helped found this city. I'm sure that if you tried to move some of those stones, they would crumble in your hands. I can promise you that we will mount a campaign to recall any councilmember who votes for this thing." (That comment drew lots of applause from the people who were there.)

Harry Walker, 610 Forbes Street: "I'm afraid Walt's gone overboard on this one, like he usually does. I think our neighborhood needs a supermarket. We've got lots of people who have trouble getting around. Walt's one of these people who's against anything that is progress. He just wants to get some publicity for himself."

When the speakers were done, the council voted 5-2 against the rezoning petition. At that the crowd cheered, and most of them filed out, leaving a small audience of only about 35 or 40 people.

The next item of business was a one-cent sales tax proposed by councilwoman Wilma Rudolph. "The city desperately needs this money," said Rudolph, "or there is a chance that we'll have to start laying off workers next year." Mr. Joe Black, the city treasurer, agreed, saying the city's financial condition was pretty bad. A one-cent sales tax would raise about $400,000 for the city next year, and not only would that mean there would be no layoffs, but it's possible that the city could expand some services, such as having garbage pickups twice a week instead of just once a week, he said. "Besides, we figure that such a tax will only cost the average family in the city about $75 a year," Black pointed out. Mayor Sadecki is against the tax. He said, "I believe the people are taxed too heavily now. I don't believe they want this. I think they want to look at our budget and see where we can cut back." But the majority of the council didn't agree with the mayor, and they voted for the tax 5-2. Those voting for the tax were Rudolph, Haddix, Sam Jones, Eddie Matthews, and Lew

Burdette; those against were Sadecki and Bill Mazeroski.

The last item of business was a proposal from councilman Mazeroski to license morticians in the city. "The state gives us the power to do this, and I think we should take advantage of it," he said. He said his proposal would assess an annual license fee that morticians would have to pay every year. Mazeroski said, "We've got more than 30 mortuaries in the city now, and assessing a fee from them would bring in a considerable amount of revenue." His bill calls for a $150 fee per mortuary per year. Several morticians were in the audience and spoke against Mazeroski's proposals. Don Blasingame, who owns Blasingame Mortuary and who is president of the city's Mortician Society, said: "We don't believe Mr. Mazeroski is correct when he says the state gives the city the power to do this. The state licenses morticians and gives the city the power to enforce this licensing procedure if it chooses to do so. Otherwise, the state enforces the licensing. I believe that if the city did this, it would just have to turn the money over to the state." Harold Reece, the city attorney, said there is some question about this in the law, and he has asked the state attorney general to give an opinion on it. Mazeroski said, "I don't believe we should wait for the opinion. I think we should go ahead and do it." Burdette made a motion to table the proposal, and that passed by a vote of six to one.

With that, Mayor Sadecki adjourned the meeting.

You find out later that when councilman Haddix got to his car after the meeting, there was a parking ticket on it.

5–13 Writing news stories

Write a news story from the following set of facts.

Development

About six months ago the Roberts Development Company announced that it wanted to build an apartment complex on Park Lane, a residential area of the local community. The complex would be, a spokesman said at the time, about 120 units and would be built on a farm owned by P.T. Rodney, who had agreed to sell it for that purpose. The complex would cover about 15 acres. In order to get permission to build the complex, the company had to apply to the City Council for a rezoning of the area from "R–1," which allows only single-family residences, to "R–2," which would allow the apartment complex to be built.

Immediately after the announcement, the Park Lane Residents Association said it opposed the complex and would ask the City Council not to grant the rezoning request. The association's president is George Houghton. The association was joined in its opposition by the City Neighborhood Preservation Association. Both groups appeared before the council to fight the rezoning. The council voted 7-0 not to rezone the property, but Roberts Development said it would try to work out a compromise with both groups and resubmit the rezoning application.

Today, six months after this happened, you (a reporter for the local newspaper) receive a call from the president of the City Neighborhood Preservation Association, whose name is John Hedrick, saying his group is no longer opposed to the rezoning. Hedrick says, "We've had several meetings with Roberts Development people, and they have given us assurances about what will happen to the property. We're satisfied that the neighborhood will retain its character, so we will be backing them up when they go to the City Commission tomorrow to ask for another rezoning of the property." Hedrick said the reason for the turnaround by his group is that Roberts had redesigned much of their original plans so that the apartment complex would be more architecturally compatible with the neighborhood.

The city commission meeting is tomorrow morning, and you have to do a story on this situation for this afternoon's paper.

Olin Millsaps, president of Roberts Development Company, tells you, "We're very pleased with the preservation association's support. I think we have a shot at turning this thing around at the meeting tomorrow."

Gardner Houghton, who is president of the Park Lane Residents Association, says, however, that his group is still opposed to the petition. "I don't think the development people have changed their plans that much. What they are trying to do would still disrupt the neighborhood. The way the streets are now, they just can't hold the traffic an apartment complex like that would generate. Frankly, and I don't have any evidence to back this up, I think the neighborhood preservation people sold out to the development company. I wouldn't be surprised if Roberts made a big contribution to their treasury."

The president of the city council, Harvey Latton, says he can't predict how the vote will go.

After numerous calls, you reach the other six council members, and none of them will tell you how he or she will vote on the issue. They all say they will wait until tomorrow before making up their minds.

5–14 Writing news stories

Write a news story from the following set of facts.

Athlete lawsuit

Several months ago, last fall, the local newspaper printed a story about your university's basketball team. The story was written by the sports editor, William Sonoma, and it said that five members of the team were being investigated in a cheating and grade-fixing scheme and might not be returning to the team.

Here's what part of the story said:

Sources within the university said the players conspired with the registrars at their high schools and junior colleges to have their transcripts reflect that they took courses they did not take and that in some of the courses they did take, they made passing rather than failing grades.

A spokesperson for the athletic department would have no comment on the investigation.

"The policy of the university is that student records are private matter," John Balk of the athletic department said. "We can neither confirm nor deny any of the details about this story."

The story made quite a splash. Newspapers and television stations all over the state carried it, and even ESPN's SportsCenter ran a couple of stories.

The newspaper continued to run stories about it for several days, but the names of the students under investigation were never revealed.

A month later the athletic department announced that two players would not be returning to the team this year. They were Tad Rankin and André Johnson, two stars that had been recruited from a large high school in the state's largest city. The announcement that they would not return did not say why they would not return. Reporters asked if this had anything to do with the cheating investigation, and the athletic department people would not comment on that. All of the stuff about the investigation was dredged up again by the newspaper.

Right after the first of the year, three members of the basketball team – Pettus Ford, Joseph Garfield, and Marcus Van Buren – sued the newspaper for invasion of privacy. The suit asked for an apology by the paper, and it asked that the university be ordered to state the names of the players that were being investigated. It also asked for $100,000 in damages from the papers.

Here's what Pettus Ford said at the time the suit was filed: "We were treated very unfairly by the newspaper when it talked about five basketball players. There are only fourteen of us on the team, and we had to spend the next few months telling people that we were not one of those who was being investigated. The university did not give us much help either. We think our reputations have been tarnished and our privacy has been invaded by these stories, and we want the newspaper and the court to set things right. We want people to know that we were not the ones being investigated." The players' attorney, O'Banin Dirsky, said at the time that precedents in the law provided for suits such as this one. He cited the part of privacy law that deals with embarrassing private facts. "A member of a small group who has been unfairly tarnished by something that was said about the group has some recourse in the court," he said.

Today, a judge granted a motion for summary judgment, dismissing the case against the newspaper. Summary judgment occurs when a judge finds that no facts are in dispute and there is nothing to litigate. In a short opinion that the judge read in court, he said: "While the facts show that the plaintiffs were embarrassed by the newspaper stories, there is simply no legal basis for a suit against the newspaper, and the law offers them no relief. Life sometimes is not fair, and there is nothing the law can do about it." The judge's name is Sheila Latham.

Dirsky: "My clients are very disappointed with this ruling. I believe that they had a legitimate case that should have been tried on its merits. Unfortunately, the judge did not think so."

Sonoma: "This is exactly what we had been hoping for. This thing has taken up a lot more time than it should have and so far has cost the newspaper about $10,000 in legal fees. I'm glad the judge put an end to it."

Ford: "None of us believe the judge gave this case a fair hearing. We still have this thing hanging over our heads, and we want to clear our names. We're going to talk with our lawyer about an appeal."

Randall Flowers, a friend of Ford who appeared outside the courtroom with him: "This is a travesty. To me, the judge's opinion showed him to be senile and in the pocket of the university. They didn't want any of this to come out so they can protect their precious image. They don't care about the players, just how they look."

5–15 Writing news stories

Write a news story from the following set of facts.

IN THE COUNTY COURT OF FORREST COUNTY, MISSISSIPPI

CAUSE NO. 37,733

VICTORIA FULTON VICUNA,   VERSUS   MILTON JEROME FINE,
PLAINTIFF   DEFENDANT

COMPLAINT

Plaintiff, Victoria Fulton Vicuna, sues the Defendant, Milton Jerome Fine, on the following grounds:

1.   Plaintiff is an adult resident citizen of United States of America, presently domiciled in New York City, New York.

2.   Defendant, Milton Jerome Fine, is an adult resident citizen of Forrest County, Mississippi, residing at 113 South 22nd Avenue, Hattiesburg, Mississippi.

3.   That on or about the first part of May, 1989, the Plaintiff left her dog, one Chinese Shar-Pei male dog (named Ming-Ming-Jai) in the care and custody of the Defendant. The dog was left with the Defendant on a temporary basis and at no time was the dog intended to be given to the Defendant.

4.   But since the above referenced date, the Plaintiff has repeated demands for said dog, has offered to pay reasonable boarding expenses and has agreed to reimburse the Defendant for any veterinarian medicine and expenses which he has incurred.

5.   That Plaintiff claims that she is the rightful owner of aforementioned dog pursuant to the Certificate of Pedigree which is attached hereto and marked as Exhibit A.

6.   Plaintiff is entitled to immediate possession of the above referenced dog, yet the Defendant unlawfully withholds possession of the dog from the Plaintiff within the jurisdiction of this Court.

7.   Plaintiff tenders herein a surety bond in the amount of $4,000.00 which amount is equal to double the value of the dog.

WHEREFORE, Plaintiff prays that this Court will examine the allegations of this Complaint and all documentary evidence exhibited with this Complaint, will satisfy itself that Plaintiff has a prima facie claim to possession of the dog described in the Complaint and will order the immediate issuance of a Writ of Replevin conditioned upon Plaintiff's posting of the Security Bond described above, and will further schedule a hearing to determine the rights of the parties to the possession of the described dog within the time and manner provided by law.

Respectfully submitted,

Victoria Fulton Vicuna

5–16 Writing news stories

Write a news story from the following set of facts

Local student and school administrator killed

The press release and quotations were supplied to you by a reporter who has just returned from an accident in front of Davies High School. The reporter has turned the material over to you to write a finished story for tomorrow's newspaper (Saturday, April 8, 1994.) You are to use the following information to write a two-to three-page news story.

Press Release
Issued by Davies High School
For immediate release

For more information, contact:
Roscoe L. Drazsnzak, principal,
Davies High School

Sometimes unfortunate events occur in the lifetime of any high school, even as great a high school as Davies High School. It happens that such an event has happened today, April 7, at our very own Davies High.

What happened was that there was an accident in front of the school. The accident occurred at approximately 8 a.m. today. There were two people killed, and one of them was the assistant principal, David R. Smoots. Smoots was 36 years of age. The other person killed was a student, Janice Snorgrass, a senior. She was 17 years of age.

This is a very unfortunate accident and the school regrets it very much. Davies High School has established the Smoots-Snorgrass Trust Fund to collect money for the victims' families. Anyone interested in contributing to the fund should send their check or money orders to the Smoots-Snorgrass Trust Fund, P.O. Box 43102, Hattiesburg, Mississippi, 39401.

What happened is this: Smoots and Snorgrass were talking in front of the Davies High School building next to the school driveway just before class began. A school bus arriving at the school came down the drive, jumped the curb and hit the two. Both were killed. The brakes on the bus apparently failed, and the brake failure is apparently what caused the accident.

The following are verbatim interviews conducted by your reporter. You should feel free to use the material below for inclusion in your story:

Roscoe L. Drazsnzak, principal, Davies High School: "I was standing next to the entrance of the high school when the accident occurred. Mr. Smoots and Janice were standing there on the sidewalk talking when the school bus drove up. It didn't stop at the curb like it was supposed to. Instead, it drove up onto the sidewalk and struck Mr. Smoots and Janice. It was the worst thing I have ever seen. Smoots had been assistant principal for five years. He was one of the best-loved administrators that we have ever had on this campus. Janice was a straight-A student who was Student Council president this school year. Both will be sorely missed. After the accident occurred, we canceled classes for the rest of the day. Classes will also be closed Monday for the funeral."

Capt. George Frangoulis, Hattiesburg Police Department: "We have investigated the accident fully and have determined that the driver was not at fault. It appears that the bus driver, James L. Loudermilk, who is 25 years of age, was driving up to the curb at a slow rate of speed, and when he tried to stop the bus the brakes failed. We have checked the brakes and determined that a brake fluid line had ruptured. This is what caused the brakes to fail. None of the 25 high school students on the bus were injured when the accident occurred. No charges will be filed."

Roy Benham, spokesman for Benham Funeral Home: "Funeral for Smoots will be at 2 p.m. Monday at the Church of the Ascension Episcopal Church. Funeral for Snorgrass will be at 10 a.m. Monday at First United Methodist Church."

Luke Spivey, vice president, Student Council: "The campus is in shock. Smoots was a popular administrator and teacher, and Janice was the school's most popular student. The Student Council has organized a memorial service Monday night at 7 p.m. in the auditorium of Davies High. This is undoubtedly one of the saddest events ever to occur at our school. We wish everyone would come to the memorial service to pay their last respects to their dearly departed friends."

5–17 Writing news stories

Write a news story from the following set of facts

Snowstorm

This is what you know by 6 p.m. on March 5.

Major late season snowstorm; 8" fell between midnight and 3 a.m.; unexpected, caught city by surprise; most forecasts evening before predicted some rain and sleet.

Art Carrie, meteorologist at local National Weather Service center: "We had been saying there was a slight possibility of snow, but the upper atmospheric temperature must have dropped more suddenly than we figured." Sounded slightly embarrassed and somewhat defensive.

Felicity Ryan, mayor: "I got a call from the police about 2 this morning telling me about the snow. We tried to get some plows and salting trucks out on the streets as soon as possible, but we weren't very successful. Some of our equipment was in for repairs. We figured it was safe to start doing that since it rarely, if ever, snows this late in the season. In fact, I can't recall a March snowstorm for many years."

Mayor is right; worst March snowstorm in 50 years; last one occurred in 1980 but accumulation only 1"; 1954 saw 12" fall on Mar. 1; this storm is historical record snowfall for city for this date; source of this info in National Weather Service center.

Wayne Tisdale, chief of police: "It's been a mess all day long. This city doesn't do well trafficwise when it snows anyway, and this one really caught us all off guard. Lots of people were on the road for no good reason. All of the roads in the city were officially closed until about 2 p.m. today. When that happens people shouldn't try to get out. For one thing, many auto insurance policies will not pay off when a driver has an accident on a road that has been officially closed. I'm afraid a lot of people are going to find that out the hard way today." Police reports indicate 119 accidents reported between midnight and 3 p.m.; dispatcher says on a clear day there are about twenty to thirty; tells you about Elmer, the guardian angel with the towtruck. "He really helped us and a lot of other people out today."

School superintendent Buddy McMartin says schools shut down today and tomorrow; decision about shutting down the rest of the week will be made tomorrow; if temperatures stay around freezing as predicted, that's probably what will happen. Local university also shut its doors; first time in 20 years that that has happened. You drove through the campus today and can describe what you saw.

National Association of City Planners national convention meeting in downtown Sheraton Inn; more than 800 city planners from around the country; today was last day of three-day national convention; many stuck here for extra day because airport closed. Melodie Goldstein, executive director of the association: "This has been a disappointment. Most of us were ready to go home, but even if we had been able to get to the airport, it would have been hard to make connections." Much of this part of the country is affected by this storm, and most airports experienced flight

delays. You asked Goldstein how she thought the city responded to the storm, and she said, "Not very well. People around here don't seem to know how to handle it."
City Central Hospital emergency room spokesperson: "dramatic increase" in number of broken bones treated; 70 to 80 people treated for this by mid-day. "Usually we only have two or three at the most." Seven people treated for heart attacks or chest pains contracted while shoveling snow. One of these seven died, and two are in critical condition; hospital won't release names. Dr. Sandra Smith, local cardiologist, had this to say about shoveling snow: "Shoveling snow is one of the most strenuous activities you can undertake and under some of the worst conditions imaginable. You shouldn't try it unless you are used to doing that type of thing."

Dolores Bunker estimates that fewer than half of the city's workforce made it to work today. She is executive director of the Chamber of Commerce. A spot check of some of the city's businesses is what she bases her estimate on. She says storm will mean substantial losses for many businesses, but usually such losses are made up by increased business when the storm is over. "We think people ought not to try to get out unless it's safe."

Elmer's Garage towtruck seen around the city streets around the city today, pulling people out who had gotten themselves stuck. One woman who had been helped called you. "I was driving down 15th Street trying to get to work this morning. There was no one on the street. I hit my breaks and skidded into a ditch. The wheels just kept spinning. I sat there for a few minutes wondering how I was going to get out and whether or not I was going to freeze to death. Then I heard this truck coming along. Elmer pulled me out and had me back on the road in just a few minutes. And, you know, he wouldn't let me pay him anything." You talk with Elmer Burton, owner of Elmer's Garage. He estimates that he pulled out "fifty or sixty" cars from being stuck between about 6 a.m. and 1 p.m. You ask him what he charged for doing this and say he must have made a lot of money. "Naw, I didn't charge nuthin'. I just enjoyed helping people out. Besides, maybe next time when people need help they'll remember old Elmer." He adds that one person he helped called him a "guardian angel." Has he done this before when it snows? "No, this is the first time. You don't get too many chances around here. But I'll probably do it again next time."

5–18 Writing news stories

Write a news story from the following set of facts

Chicken truck causes pile-up

25 people got hurt. A pile-up happened on Mcfarland Blvd. at about 6 in the evening. It was yesterday.

It happened at the corner of Mcfarland and 15th. Police say eleven cars were involved. Sergeant John Jones tells you that a semi-truck carrying chickens (laying hens) made an illegal left turn causing the accident.

The chicken truck driver got hurt. His name - Jeff Johnson. He's 45. Ambulance transported him to DCH. He had bruises and a possible broken ankle. He lives in Alberta City with his wife, three children. Jones reports this.

The chickens, police say, may be as many as 300, also suffered. The truck turned on its side making a sharp turn. At least 30 are dead. Many others trapped in the vehicle until firemen arrived. Several, as many as 40, remain at large.

Jones also notes that Sarah Bernell was hurt. She, at age 63, is a retired local kindergarten teacher. Miss Bernell was riding in the car driven by her nephew, Mike Kenyon. She was taken to the hospital.

The animals are the property of the chicken company, Alabama Poultry, Inc., and should be returned if found, Jones stresses.

Clarence DiMotta reports Johnson is in good condition. Clarence is the hospital spokesperson. Also, the teacher has a slight concussion and is also in good condition.

Jones says "It was the biggest pile-up I've ever seen. Lots and lots of smashed bumpers but the worst part was the screams of the chickens. Those things sure do make a lotta noise, you know."

The chickens were on the way to one of the company's new farms near Gadsden.

Only other injuries to the 23 others in the cars were bruises. None admitted.

The chicken company pres. Carlton Fitzsimmons reports the dead and missing chickens are worth over 700 dollars. Each chicken was insured for 10 bucks. His company's chickens - the farm holds about 20,000 - supply eggs to IGA stores across the south.

Other damages to the 12 cars in the accident were minor, police report said.

Several smashed eggs were also found in the wreckage of the truck. "It was so hot out there I thought we might have fried eggs for dinner" Jones adds.

5–19 Writing news stories

Write a story for tomorrow morning's newspaper.

Russel

Last New Year's Eve, John Page was found shot to death in his home. At first, the police and the coroner ruled the death a suicide, but that changed when they later found that Page had withdrawn a large amount of money from his bank account on the day that he died. Page is the owner of Page Auto Parts Store. He is also a real estate developer, a deacon in the First Baptist Church, a city councilman, and generally thought to be one of the wealthiest citizens in town. The amount of money Page withdrew from the bank that day was $10,000. Page's wife told the police that he had been depressed for some weeks before his death, but she didn't believe that he committed suicide.

Page's death and all of the subsequent events, including the police investigation and the trial, received a great amount of publicity from the city's newspapers and television stations.

A month after Page's death, the police arrested William Russel and charged him with first degree murder. William Russel is owner of Russel Realty, and even though they were competitors in business, Page and Russel were known to be good friends. They grew up together, and their families had been friends. Police said that several clues pointed to Russel as the murderer. Russel had been seen leaving the Page home late New Year's Eve by a neighbor who

had been walking his dog. The bank provided the police with serial numbers of the money it had given to Page, and most of that money was found in Russel's house.

During the trial, which began a month ago, it came out that Russel had been having an affair with Page's wife, Geneveve. The district attorney, Hix Bradfield, tried to paint Russel as a desperate man whose business was failing and who was blackmailing Page. The key witness in his case was Page's wife, who said that Russel had threatened Page by saying he would "tell everybody in town about your slutty little wife" if he wouldn't pay. She said Page was worried that his reputation in the community would be damaged and it would mean the end to his political career. She said he had been planning to run for Congress next year.

Russel took the stand in his own defense and denied killing Page, and he denied having an affair with Page's wife. He said Page had asked him to keep the money because of a business deal he was about to make, but he didn't know any of the details. He said Page had been despondent because he had found out that his wife had been having affairs with other men. "I felt sorry for John," he said. "He married a little slut. I suspect that she was blackmailing him." Russel said he went to talk with Page on New Year's Eve but found him too depressed to talk. When he left, Russel said, Page was drinking heavily. Russel said he didn't tell the police about the visit or the money because "I got scared. It was a stupid thing to do."

Yesterday, after three days of deliberating, the jury found Russel guilty. Russel broke down and cried when he heard the verdict.

This morning, Judge Cecil Andrews sentenced Russel to death in the electric chair. In handing out the sentence, Andrews said, "This was a heinous crime — one that merits swift and severe retribution. The victim was a leading citizen in the community, a man who had made many contributions. In a cold-blooded way, the defendant ended his life while posing as his good friend. He has shown no remorse for his deed and has, in fact, lied about it. He showed no mercy to his victim, and I, in turn, can show no mercy to him." Russel, who looked pale and puffy-eyed when he came into the courtroom, had to be helped out.

Outside the court, Regina Wright, Russel's lawyer, said she would file an immediate appeal both of the verdict and the sentence. "Mr. Russel didn't get a fair trial. The massive amount of pretrial publicity surrounding this case prevented that. Early on, we asked for a change of venue, but that motion was denied. There was just no way that a person accused of killing a popular man like John Page was going to get a fair trial in this town." Asked about the sentence, Wright said, "I just can't believe he was given the death penalty. I believe Judge Andrews had it in for my client. He should have disqualified himself because he was a friend of John Page. He should have granted our change-of-venue motion. He did neither, and then he winds up sentencing my client to death."

After the sentencing, Bradfield said, "The sentence was a harsh one — not the one we would have recommended. We would have preferred a life-without-parole sentence, but I'll go along with what the judge said. It was an awful crime, and John Page was one of our leading citizens."

You try to get a comment from Mrs. Page, but her attorney, Frank Story, tells you she left immediately after the sentencing for New York to discuss writing a book about the trial and her experiences.

5–20 Writing news stories

Write a news story from the following set of facts

Tornado

Yesterday afternoon was unseasonably warm for this time of year. Early in the afternoon, the temperature reached 70 degrees, and the people at the Weather Bureau became concerned. There was a lot of moisture in the air, and the conditions seemed just right for a tornado. At two o'clock they issued a tornado warning because of some buildup of moisture west of here.

At three p.m., after receiving several reports of funnel clouds, Lee Harper, chief meteorologist at the weather bureau, issued a tornado warning. Funnel clouds had been sighted just south of Midville, and there was one report that a barn had been damaged and some cows had been killed. The tornado watch was to stay in effect for one hour.

At 3:33 a tornado touched down on Cleveland Street, a street with a lot of businesses and homes on it. The tornado damaged the following businesses: the Cleveland Street branch of the Trust National Bank; Red Cedar's used car lot; the Jiffy-Kwik 24-hour food store; and the Big Bank Sound Record Shop, which is located in the same building as the food store. Also, several homes were damaged, including that of Robert T. Mellon, the mayor. The bank was being housed in a mobile home while a permanent structure was built. There was no damage to the building site, which was located nearby. The mobile home was lifted completely off its foundation, however, and was totally destroyed. Clyde Plenty, vice president of the Trust National Bank said the following: "Thank goodness, the tornado hit when it did. We had closed up about three o'clock, and nobody was in the building." Some of the records housed in the building were destroyed, but Clyde said nothing of importance had been lost permanently, and all the records could be duplicated. There was also no money in the building to speak of.

The people at Jiffy-Kwik and the record shop weren't so lucky. At least four people had to go to the hospital to be treated for injuries due to flying debris and broken glass, according to hospital officials. Mr. and Mrs. George Jones -- his wife's name is Thelma -- were treated for minor cuts and lacerations and then released at Good Hope Hospital, and Irving Smalley was being kept overnight because of more serious cuts. He's listed in good condition. He lives at 123 Urban Street. The Joneses live at 1311 13th Avenue. Anna Patton had major injuries after being buried by an aisle of canned goods; she had just come out of surgery at 8 o'clock last night and was listed in critical condition. She lives at 12 Pinto Avenue. Killed was Evelyn Morrison as she was coming out of the record shop and getting into her car. She was a teller who worked at the Trust Bank, the same one that had been damaged by the tornado. She was on her way home. She lived at 67 Kent Street. She was dead on arrival at the hospital and her body was taken to Green Acres Chapel. None of the funeral arrangements have been set.

Holbert Morrison, manager of the Jiffy-Kwik, said his store was not a total loss, but the damage was several thousand dollar's worth. "The worst thing was the looters," he said. "I just couldn't believe that some people would steal from us after something like this had happened." Police Chief Robert Sykes said they had arrested several youths for looting after the tornado hit, but they weren't going to release their names yet. Bill Belson, the manager of the record store and a noted area record collector, also said the damage to his shop would go into thousands of dollars. "Fortunately, none of my most valuable records were damaged."

Red Cedar said that one of his cars was damaged when some limbs fell on it, but otherwise nothing was hurt. Three homes in the next block of Cleveland Street were damaged, including that of Mayor Mellon. The roof was torn off of his home. "We were lucky because no one was home. I just feel awful about Miss Morrison, though. She was an old friend and a life-long resident of the town. Lots of people knew her, and I think it's tragic. You know, she used to be a teacher -- was a teacher at Elmwood Elementary School about ten years ago. She taught there for about 20 years before retiring and going to work for the bank. She didn't have much family, but everybody in town knew her." The roofs of the other homes on Cleveland Street were damaged by flying limbs, but none of the owners reported serious damage.

The police chief said the total amount of damage done by the tornado would come to about $150,000. "That part of Cleveland Street looks like a bomb has been dropped on it. It's going to take us several days to get it all cleared. It's amazing that all this damage was done in less than two minutes. I feel awfully bad about Miss Morrison, but we were lucky

that more people weren't hurt. There were quite a few people in the area at the time." One of the people who was in the record store at the time said the noise right before the tornado hit was the "scariest thing." He was Josh Gibson. "It was like the loudest drum roll I ever heard. Then there was sounds of glass breaking and things crashing around you."

That night Dan Rather devotes about 30 seconds to the tornado. Your editor tells you that it is the first time the town has ever been mentioned on a network newscast.

Harper said this tornado was the only one that did any damage. At least three others were sighted during the afternoon.

5–21 Features

Write a short feature story on each of the following sets of information.

Bank robbery

- man named Jesse James tried to rob First Fidelity bank this morning
- caught by passing policeman as he backed out the door
- had $20,000
- same bank had been robbed nearly 100 years ago by real Jesse James and his brother Frank; they too had been caught. Suspect says: "Jesse James was my great-great uncle. I was just trying to finish the job he started."
- Police Chief Weldon Freeman: "This man has no sense of history."

Noise abatement

- City Civil Court this morning
- Judge Jan Sommerfelt
- suit involved Lakeshore subdivision residents suing Weatherford Construction Co.
- company was building a road near subdivision
- residents complained that noise the construction company was making violated city ordinances against loud noises
- judge ruled in favor of the residents but refused to stop the construction; said construction company would have to give earplugs to anyone who complained about the noise

Student sit-up

- local high school student Bobby Lott, junior at City Central, now sitting in tree in front of school
- will sit there until Friday's football game with County Central, City's arch-rival; winner of the game goes to state championship
- climbed into tree at 9 a.m.
- Principal Dick Barrett says Lott is a good student, "has his parents permission to do this," and "I won't make him come down. I don't think he'll get behind in his school work." Friends taking class notes for him, handing him food
- Lott says this is his way of showing support for the team; he won't come down except to go to the bathroom; says he won't stay in the tree if there's a lightning storm. "I may be crazy, but I'm not stupid."

5–22 Features II

Write feature stories based on the following sets of information.

Tennis player

Bucky Haskiell is a tennis pro who graduated from your college two years ago. While in college, he led the team to the conference championship during his senior year and was named the conference's best player. When he graduated, he turned pro.

During this year's Wimbledon tennis tournament in London, England, Haskiell held the limelight briefly when he had to play John McElroy, the eventual champion, during the first round. Haskiell lost to McElroy, but only after he and the champion had played five full sets. The match was also highlighted by one of the fiercest temper tantrums McElroy had ever thrown. At one point during the match, McElroy stormed around the court cursing the officials and nearly got himself eliminated.

Haskiell has returned to the college for an exhibition tournament to raise money for the college tennis team's travel expenses. You are sent to interview him and here's how the interview goes.

What was it like playing John McElroy during the first round at Wimbledon?

Very hard (he says, laughing). In some ways McElroy is much like any other tennis player — only he's very, very good. When he concentrates on tennis alone, there aren't many people who can beat him. When he gets distracted, he tends to let down. But even then, he's hard to beat. I guess I found that out.

Was it the first time you had played him?

No, I had played him once before in a tournament in South Carolina. I beat him the first two sets, but he came back and won the last three to take the match.

Did he throw any tantrums that day?

No, he was pretty calm.

Do you think that the fit he threw at Wimbledon hurt your game that day?

I'm not sure. I've thought about that a lot. I don't think I played as well after he had finished his argument with the line judge as I had been playing. But I don't know if I was tired or what. I didn't really think about it at the time. I was trying to concentrate on my game.

Do you know McElroy personally?

Yes, I've been with him on several occasions. He's really a nice guy off the court and doesn't deserve his 'bad boy' image. Once he even gave me some pointers about how I was serving that really helped my game.

What was Wimbledon like? Everybody says it's a great place to be.

Well (laughing), I really wasn't there that long. As a player, it's not a great tournament because of the grass courts, which most of us aren't use to, and the accommodations aren't as good as some we've had at other tournaments. But the atmosphere at Wimbledon is hard to beat. There's so much tradition there — it makes you feel good just having a chance to play. Of course, next year I would like to win a match or two.

Do you expect to be invited back to Wimbledon next year?

I hope so. I'm having a pretty good year. I've won one tournament and have finished in the semi-finals in at least four others. My ranking with the tennis association is better than last year, so maybe I'll get back there. **What's it like having been a tennis pro for two years?**

I really enjoy it, but it's not what people think. Tennis pros aren't pampered people. All of us have to work very hard just to maintain our forms. And we're required to travel a lot — it's not like being a tourist either. It's just one hotel or motel after another. The time you might spend seeing the sights is time you should spend practicing — and you do if you want to be any good. For instance, I saw relatively little of London when I was there for Wimbledon. I'd like to go back sometime when there's not a tournament.

Oldest tree

A plaque marking the oldest tree on campus will be dedicated today. Ceremonies for the dedication will take place under the tree at 10 a.m., and the event will also be used to announce a fund-raising drive by the alumni association for the school. A news story has already been written about this event. Your job is to write a feature story about the tree which will be used as a sidebar (a journalistic term for a secondary story) with the news story. You gather the following information about the tree:

The tree is a water oak and is thought to be about 100 years old. University records show that the tree was probably planted by students who had been hired to do some work on the campus. One record says that during the same spring 50 trees were planted in that area of the campus.

Marcus Maxwell, professor of history and University historian: "The University used to hire students to do odd jobs around the campus, so we think students planted this tree. There is no exact record of what was planted and by whom, so we're not sure about it.

"A number of buildings have been built in the area of the tree, but none has come so close to it that the tree had to be destroyed. The tree has some significance in university history. The first troop of soldiers that gathered at the University to fight in World War I assembled under that tree right before they left by train to report to their army base. A crowd of people gathered, a band played, and some politicians made speeches. It was a pretty festive occasion.

"Likewise, when the first of the University's reserve units was activated right after the beginning of World War II, they also gathered under the tree for a send off. I understand that it wasn't such a festive occasion then."

Elmer Hinton, a retired bicycle repairman in the town, was among the soldiers who started for World War I at the tree. He tells you: "It was hot as blazes that day, even though it was April. Fortunately, we got to stand in the shade, and I remember being thankful of that. I enjoyed the music the band played, but I coulda done without the speeches. Lots of people thought this war was going to be a lark — that all we had to do was show up and the Germans would fade away. It turned out not to be like that at all. The part of World War I I saw was pretty rough."

A number of legends exist about the tree. One is that a man was lynched on the tree around the turn of the century. He had killed the family of the mayor of the town, and one night an angry crowd broke into the jail, took him out and hung him.

Newspaper accounts say that a man named Josiah Lindy was hung by an angry crowd in 1901; he was accused of killing the family of Mayor Tyree Jones — Jones's wife and two daughters – after the wife had let him in the house and given him something to eat. The news account doesn't say exactly where the lynching took place. Nor does it say that Mayor Jones was part of the crowd.

Another legend that was once popular with students is that the girl who walked under the lowest branch of the tree on the night of the full moon before the homecoming queen election would win that election. That legend became so popular in the 1920s and 1930s that students had a ritual of requiring all homecoming queen candidates to walk under the tree on the night before the election. That ritual died out during World War II.

Flora Handle, a professor in the biology department, says: "The tree is a good example of one of the major types of trees of this area. It is in remarkably good shape for a tree of its age. Usually a tree that old will have too many limbs and not enough foliage to support the whole system. That's not the case with this one. If something doesn't happen — if the tree isn't struck by a disease or by lightning — it should live another 50 or 75 years. It must be trimmed properly."

Your story should include a description of the tree and its location. (For that, you may pick any large tree on your campus.)

Hiker

A local high school teacher, Will Henderson, was lost for four days last week while hiking in the Great Smoky Mountains National Park. Henderson had been hiking along the Appalachian Trail and had gotten off the trail near a place known as Gregory Bald. After a couple of hours of walking off the trail, Henderson tried to cross a stream when he slipped and broke his leg.

Henderson is an experienced hiker. He is a member of the National Hiking Association. He had plenty of food with him at the time. He had been hiking for about 10 days before the accident. He had started in Georgia and was in Tennessee at the time of the accident.

After his fall, Henderson used some sticks and string to make a splint for his leg. He then began four days of crawling, pushing his 40-pound hiking pack in front of him. He crawled through a lot of thick underbrush. Finally, he made it back to the main part of the Appalachian Trail and was soon found by two other hikers.

The Appalachian Trail is nearly 3,000 miles long, stretching from Georgia to Maine. It is one of the most popular hiking trails in the country.

Henderson teaches biology at Jefferson High School. He is 39 and has been hiking since he was a boy of 10.

Henderson was hospitalized for several days in Knoxville during which time a number of stories were written about his ordeal. Now he is back home, recuperating in a local hospital, and your newspaper sends you to interview him. Here's some of what he tells you:

"I never doubted that I would be found. I got discouraged sometimes, but I figured that I had plenty of food and thought that if I could get back to a trail – particularly the main Appalachian Trail because it's so busy – somebody would come along before long.

"I'll tell you though, I sure was happy when I heard those first footsteps coming up behind me. Those guys thought I was some kind of animal at first. I guess I looked pretty rough. They kind of hesitated in approaching me, but when I said, 'Help' a couple of times, they came running.

"One of the guys stayed with me while the other went for help. They kept telling me not to go to sleep, and I didn't. I was so happy then that I probably couldn't have, even if I had wanted to. I'll never forget the feeling I had when they found me, not if I live to be a hundred. Those guys are going to get mentioned in my will.

"The hardest thing about being lost was thinking that other people might be worrying about me. I was supposed to meet some friends in Gatlinburg a couple of days after I got lost. As it turned out, they weren't worried but said if I had been gone another day, they would have contacted the park rangers and started a search.

"After a day or so of crawling, I had to discard most of my clothes and most of the other things in my pack. They had gotten too wet and heavy for me to push. Of course, I kept all of the food I had. It was mostly dry stuff – crackers, fruit, peanut butter, things like that.

"The mountain foliage was like a jungle. There had been a lot of rain up there this year, and it was really thick. If I had stayed where I was when I fell, I probably would still be there. At least, that's what one of the park rangers said. I think I knew that instinctively when I fell, so I never thought about staying put. I knew that I had better get somewhere where people could find me.

"Besides food, I did manage to keep a few small things with me. I had several pictures of my wife and two little girls. I looked at them a lot, especially when I got discouraged. I would spend a little time looking at those pictures, and then I would crawl a little bit more.

"I broke the first rule of hiking, of course. I hiked alone. If you're on the Appalachian Trail, it doesn't matter because you're not really alone. There are so many people on that trail. But when you get off the beaten track – that's when you need to be with somebody. I learned my lesson about that. My goal is still to hike the entire trail, but I guess I'll have to wait until I get my leg in shape."

5–23 Magazine writing

Travel article

A travel magazine is running a series of short pieces on several cities in your area. The series is geared toward college students and is trying to tell them things they would want to know if they visited them. Write about 300 words about the city where your college or university is located. Include some basic information about the city and the colleges and universities located there; also tell about places which are popular with students; finally, include something about places in the city that any tourist would want to visit.

Student budget

Write a short article (about 300 words) on how to live on a limited budget during your first year in college. This article is for a magazine which goes to high school students. You should talk about some of the unexpected expenses a new college student encounters as well as give some advice on how to save money on books, food, or other expenses.

A story with a moral

Write a short story, possibly based on some incident in your life, that has a moral to it. The story, which should be about 300 words long, is for a religious publication which is geared to teenagers. The story should not be heavily theological, but it should contain some moral message. The story can be completely fictional or based totally on a real incident.

Professor

The alumni magazine of your college or university wants stories on file about the professors who have been selected as the school's outstanding teachers: you have been asked to write one of them. (You will have to select the professor on whom you do the story.) There are four professors who have been awarded the Outstanding Teacher Award, and the editor wants a 400-word article on each of them. Be sure to include information about the teacher's background, research, personal activities and interests, and what makes this teacher outstanding.

"My Most Unforgettable Character"

Reader's Digest runs a regular feature article called "My Most Unforgettable Character." It is a character sketch about the author's encounter with an unusual and interesting character. Write a 400-word article on your most unforgettable character. What was your relationship with the person? What makes the person unforgettable?

6 Writing for the Web

Introduction

The editors of Newsweek magazine struggled with a problem on the third weekend in January of 1998. It was Saturday, when the final decisions are made for the next week's issue of the newsmagazine. Reporter Michael Isikoff, who had been covering the Kenneth Starr investigation of President Bill Clinton, had unearthed information that the president had been having a sexual affair with a White House intern.

No one at Newsweek thought the story was untrue. The president's rakish reputation had conditioned Washington insiders to believe that Clinton would do something like this during his term. Isikoff's reputation as a thorough reporter meant that the information he had gathered was probably correct.

But there were other considerations. The Starr investigation had challenged the White House, and Clinton's operatives were fighting back. The story Newsweek was about to run would put the magazine on one side of that fight, rather than watching from the sidelines. If even one minor part of the story was incorrect, the whole thing could be discredited.

By the end of the day, the editors had "spiked" the story. ("Spiked" is an old newspaper term for holding or killing a story.) They would give themselves and their reporter one more week just to make sure everything they were about to print was correct.

That, they thought, was the end of the story for the moment. It was about 6 p.m.

But what they had just done — a major newsmagazine killing a story about a president's adulterous affair — was itself a story. At least, that's how Matt Drudge saw it.

Drudge produced a one-person, gossip-filled Web site from a small office in Hollywood, California. His brief moment of notoriety until that time was a story that he had run saying Sidney Blumenthal, a White House aide, had beat his wife. Blumenthal had filed a $30 million libel suit against him.

Drudge had developed many sources in Washington, and through one of them he heard what Newsweek had done. He decided the world should know that a big news organization had killed an important story. But in telling that story, he would also have to tell the story of the president's affair.

Unlike the Newsweek editors, Drudge did not struggle. He

checked with "multiple sources," according to his account, and then put his own story on the Web site.

During the rest of that night and early Sunday morning, Drudge's story was picked up by a variety of newsgroups and reposted. On ABC's This Week with Sam Donaldson and Cokie Roberts, a Sunday talk show about public affairs, one anti-Clinton guest mentioned the Drudge story during the discussion. Other talk shows then picked it up, with opinion mixing freely with facts.

The attention of the nation's babelratti (a term for incessant guests on political talk shows) quickly shifted from Newsweek to the president's alleged affair. By Wednesday, it was being reported by major news organizations. The reports of an affair eventually led to a harsh denial by the president, increased fervor by the special prosecutor, and a political firestorm that resulted in impeachment by the U.S. House of Representatives and a trial in the U.S. Senate. President Clinton survived to finish his term in office, but the political landscape had changed irrevocably.

The actions by Newsweek editors and Matt Drudge on January 17, 1998, have been the subject of many debates on journalism ethics and practices. Those debates continue. But more than any single event to that point, they demonstrated the power of the World Wide Web. The ability of an individual to communicate with so many people so quickly outside of the mainstream media had never had such a startling and profound effect.

The World Wide Web continues to grow and change — and to have a profound influence on our lives. It attracts an increasing number of Web sites and users. The United States government, along with many states, has set as its goal the wiring of every school building to the Web, so that its vast educational advantages can be available to all children. The Web has altered the way we trade stocks, the way we do our banking, the way people shop, the way many people get their music and even the way some people listen to baseball games.

So what is it about the Web that it is having this impact? Isn't it like broadcasting because you see all this stuff on your computer screen? Or, isn't it like newspapers and magazines because you can read all the copy and look at the pictures?

The answer to both of those questions is yes and no. The Web is like broadcasting and newspapers, but it is also something quite different. While it shares many of the characteristics of other media, it has qualities that make it unique. Those qualities are immediacy, permanency, capacity and interactivity.

Immediacy. It is much easier and less time-consuming to "broadcast" or "publish" on the Web than in the traditional broadcasting or print media. Certainly, broadcasters can go on the air quickly when news occurs. But what they broadcast may have little substance, or they are often reduced to showing live camera shots when nothing is happening. In less frenetic times, broadcasters spent a great deal of time and effort in preparing material for their shows.

The publishing process for the print media involves several

unavoidable steps. Whatever is being published must be in printable form, it must be duplicated by some machine (a photocopier, printer or printing press) and then distributed to an audience.

With the Web, once information is available in some form, it can be loaded onto a Web site within a few seconds. The president could go on television to declare war, and before the statement is finished, it would be on the Web and reaction to it could be coming in. The Web does not require the personnel or equipment that broadcasting needs, and it does not have the distribution problems of print.

Permanency. Unless we turn our videotape machines on every time we turn on the television, there is little about broadcasting that is permanent for the user. We certainly cannot (again, unless we happen to be taping) go back to re-view a story by Dan Rather or part of a Friends episode. Once these are broadcast, they are gone.

While we can re-read stories in newspapers and magazines, we generally do not save everything we get. Lack of storage space would quickly overwhelm us (not to mention the tag of "eccentric" that our neighbors would hang on us). Printed materials are certainly more lasting than broadcasting, but their life and usefulness is limited.

With the Web, however, material can remain in place and accessible as long as the Web server and electronic storage space exist. While many Web sites — particularly news Web sites — change their content every day, the previous day's stories, pictures, graphics, video, etc. can remain available as long as the Webmaster wishes. Even when the server ceases to exist, material can be stored in a variety of ways so that it can be accessible to users.

Capacity. Most news organizations produce more than they can show or print. Broadcasting is limited by time. Print media are limited by space. The Web races past these problems with its ability to keep and show huge amounts of text and image material.

Not only can a news Web site load a story about an event, but it can also offer pictures, video, audio, graphics, and ancillary text. It can even set up a forum so that visitors can react to the event and see the reactions of others. Professional communicators are now faced with the problem of figuring out the best way to present the material they have — a problem we will discuss later in this chapter — rather than what material to leave out.

And then there is storage. We have already alluded to what your neighbors might do if you keep too many newspapers and magazines around your place. This is a problem of capacity. You are probably running out of room in your house, apartment or dorm room. So is the Library of Congress. No one has enough physical space to store copies of all of the books, magazines, newspapers, videotapes, audio tapes, pictures, and other material that are being produced.

The Web and other technological advances have alleviated the space problem by enhancing our ability to store more in smaller spaces and by centralizing information so that it is available from one location to people anywhere in the world. You no longer have to keep a copy of Shakespeare's plays and poems on your bookshelf. You can access them from any number of sites in just a few seconds.

Interactivity. Broadcasting in its traditional forms has a low level of interactivity with its listeners and viewers. People can change television or radio stations and the sound volume with the ease of a clicker, but they have no control over what they receive from those stations.

Newspapers, magazines and other printed media are highly interactive in at least one sense. Readers can select what they will read and look at and what they won't. Choosing, however, can be slow and cumbersome. And in doing so, readers do not communicate directly with the media they are using or with the people who have produced the material.

The technology of the Web offers a level of interactivity between producers and consumers that goes far beyond print media. The wide variety of material on a site can offer visitors many more choices than they would get if they were reading a magazine or a newspaper. Linking to other material on other sites is another way visitors can interact with what they are seeing.

Visitors can choose the parts of the Web site they want to see, and producers can track those choices. Software can record "hits" for various pages within a site, and they can show site managers the sequence of those hits and the amount of time visitors spend on a page.

Visitors can communicate directly through e-mail or other means set up by the producers. They can send producers their money, as many commercial sites hope they will do. And they can communicate with other visitors to share thoughts and reactions about what is on the site.

With all of these characteristics and differences, the Web remains a medium of words, images and sounds — especially words. The Web requires people who understand the language and are skilled in using it.

The Audience

Who uses the Web? What do users expect? What do they do when they use it?

Demographically, most research shows that Web users tend to be younger and male. But those findings are not much help to those writing for individual Web sites, and the demographics themselves are likely to change. The Web is quickly becoming a pervasive medium that is available at home, work, shopping, and leisure venues.

Most Web sites are developed to satisfy a particular audience, usually an audience that shares a common interest and a limited set of demographics. Sites present specialized information, sometimes in a specialized way, to a limited audience. (News Web sites, those devoted to showing the latest in news, information, and sports, seek a broader audience, just as general interest newspapers and magazines try to satisfy many demographic categories.)

The single thing that people of all demographic categories expect from the sites that they visit is information. (A secondary and overlapping expectation is "entertainment," but the focus of this chapter will be on information.) People visit Web sites because they want to know certain things. They often want this information for a particular purpose — to further investigate some news item they heard about, to help them solve a problem, to buy something, etc.

And that leads to another characteristic about Web users. They often know the type of information they are seeking. A user might visit a Web site to see if it sells a certain product or contains a set of instructions or has the latest information about a celebrity. It is important that Web site developers and writers understand that many visitors come to a site committed to finding something. The task of developers and writers is to figure out what visitors are seeking and how to give it to them in the best way.

Web surfers, in a relatively short time, have come to agree on a common set of expectations for almost all Web sites. Those expectations include the following:

Speed. Web sites are thought to be bad or amateurish if they do not load quickly and if their links do not respond instantly. The desire for speed is often a technical and a design problem. But the whole concept of speed has great implications for the work of the writer.

Visual logic. That simply means that a visitor should be able to figure out a Web site quickly and easily. It should be clear what the Web site is about, what it contains and who produced it. While this expectation, too, is a designer's problem, it is also the responsibility of the writer, as we shall see later in this chapter.

Simple organization and navigation. A well-organized Web site is one where the visitor has a good idea about what it contains from the very beginning of the visit. It also means that information is presented in logical layers and that getting to those layers is a straightforward process.

Depth. Web sites that are speedy, visually logical and easy to navigate will be incomplete and often die from lack of visitors because they simply do not contain enough information. The hard part about Web site development is not the design or navigation. It is gathering the information necessary to sustain the site and organizing and presenting information in a way that allows visitors to access and use it.

News. Not every Web site is a news site, but almost all sites need to present new and updated information. A static Web site

Figure 6-1

Splash pages

A good splash page has to give a Web visitor just the right information about what is on the Web site and how to get to the different parts of it.

Most splash pages fails. They do not inform the reader efficiently, and they are not visually intuitive. That is, it is not apparent what the reader is supposed to do when he or she gets to the page.

This second failure is a design problem, but the first is a writing problem. Copy for a splash page must be accurate and efficient. In just a few words, it must say exactly the right thing.

Copy for a splash page is often divided into two parts. The first is a **general introduction** that describes the Web

FROM JESUS to CHRIST

THE FIRST CHRISTIANS

Jesus' Many Faces
How well do the archaeological clues historians are uncovering match up with the story Christians have long told each other?

A Portrait of Jesus' World
His was a deeply religious generation, spiraling toward war amid expectations of a coming cosmic battle of the Sons of Light against the Sons of Darkness

The Story of the Storytellers
The first gospel was written almost 40 years after Jesus' death. Were they historically accurate, objective accounts? Or intended as proclamations of faith?

The First Christians
The clash of customs and cultures among early Christians yielded a Jesus of many different interpretations and multiple messages

Why Did Christianity Succeed?
How did this small Jewish sect become the Christian church, embraced by the Empire that had sent Jesus to his death?

Maps, Archaeology & Sources   Discussion   Biblical Quiz   A Follow-Up Symposium

This FRONTLINE series is an intellectual and visual guide to the new and controversial historical evidence which challenges familiar assumptions about the life of Jesus and the epic rise of Christianity.

For an overview of the series read the Synopsis. It includes links to some of the stories and material on this web site which expand the narrative.

This site is anchored by the testimony of New Testament theologians, archaeologists and historians who serve as both critics and storytellers. They address dozens of key issues, disagreements and critical problems relating to Jesus' life and the evolution of Christianity. Throughout the site, maps, charts (for example, the fortress of Masada), ancient texts (including Perpetua's diary), pictures of the archaeological discoveries, ancient imagery, and audio excerpts from the television program complement and illuminate the scholars' commentary.

A new addition to this site is the edited transcript of a two-day symposium at Harvard University. This symposium was a follow-up to the FRONTLINE broadcast and featured scholars' presentations, workshops and audience discussion.

FRONTLINE:http://www.pbs.org/wgbh/pages/frontline/shows/religion/

Used by permission

page and what it contains. Without being too specific, the introduction must give enough detailed information to make the page interesting for the reader. The example on this page is taken from a Web sites developed for the Public Broadcasting System's Frontline series.

Read the introduction for the series PBS did on early Christianity. The introduction begins with a sentence about what the Web site is. Almost immediately thereafter, it direct the attention of the reader to different parts of the Web site and gives information about those sections. Notice, too, that the writer embeds links to different parts of the Web site where it is appropriate.

Another part of a splash page is the **introduction to the individual sections** of the Web site. Look again at the examples from the Early Christianity Web site. The writer of these introductions sums up the pages in one sentence. The longest of these is 23 words. That's not much when you are trying to accurately describe a large amount of material.

— one that changes so little that visitors see the same things when they return — will not hold or increase its audience. The people who produce the news, the new information for Web sites — not the people who design the site — are the ones who do the heavy lifting for the site.

Given these expectations, what do users do when they get to a site? They do two things: scan and read.

While studies of user behavior have been limited, they have begun to give us some insight into how users operate when they get to a Web site. As with any other activity where people are given a set of options and expected to make a choice, users tend to look around a site before landing (or fixating) on a particular part of the screen. They scan the terrain, so to speak, to see what their choices are and what interests them.

Images are thought to have a powerful draw for most users. Many designers believe that strong images are likely to catch and hold the eye of the visitor. An ongoing set of studies by the Poynter Institute in St. Petersburg, Fla., and Stanford University have tracked eye movement and fixations of those looking at a Web site and found that text, not an image, is what is likely to hold the attention of the visitors. They do jump around, but when they land, they are likely to land on text, on words.

Creating content

If the chief purpose of Web sites is to offer information and the chief form of that information is text, then it is writing for the Web — not design and not flashy programming — that becomes the all-important activity in producing a Web site. In some quarters this is known as "creating content," not a very satisfying term but one that is useful in that it helps us distinguish writing from design. (Some, such as Web writing guru Jakob Nielsen, have gone so far as to separate "macrocontent" from "microcontent," the former being large blocks of text, such as full news article and the latter shorter pieces of text such as labels, headlines and summaries.)

Whatever it is called, writers must understand that they are writing for an audience, just as newspaper and magazine writers write for an audience. They must have credibility, and they must be masters of the language. Their writing must display the same characteristics of all media writing: accuracy, completeness, precision and efficiency (see Chapter 1).

The forms of writing, however, are somewhat different from what we have learned so far in writing for print. (They are quite different in writing for broadcast, writing for advertising and writing for public relations, as we will see in subsequent chapters of this book.) Because of the physical nature of a Web site and the varied expectations of Web site visitors, writers must present their information in different ways.

One structure of writing that the Web shares with print is the inverted pyramid. Presenting the most important information first, without introduction and without much verbal baggage, satisfies the Web's demand for speed and efficiency. In previous chapters, we have discussed the inverted pyramid structure as a good way to present news, but its essential element — ordering information from most important to least important — is applicable to many other writing tasks.

Take, for instance, the problem of writing an introductory statement about a company or organization for its Web site. The writer must decide what is the most important thing that the visitor needs to know about the company:

```
The Mercedes Widget Company is the old-
est and largest widget company in
America.
```

Or:

```
The Mercedes Widget Company manufactures
a complete line of widgets that will
meet every widget need.
```

Or:

```
The quality of the widgets produced by
the Mercedes Widget Company has been
unsurpassed for more than 150 years.
```

Each of these sentences presents information of value to the Web site visitor. What the writer will have to balance is the desire of the company to present information about itself and the needs and expectations of the visitor for a particular type of information.

As with news stories, the writer still has the job of ordering the information and putting it together in a simple prose form that is interesting and readable. This kind of writing also requires another characteristic that most other media writing also demands: impersonality. The writer should use simple, clear language that is unadorned with personal opinions or personal writing style. As with news stories, the reader is interested in getting the information, not the writer's point of view.

Concision

Students who are new to writing for the mass media probably struggle with one of its major characteristics — efficiency — more than any other. To write efficiently, to use the fewest words to present the most information, is not the type of writing that most students have been taught in English grammar and literature classes. To write less and say more is a difficult skill to develop. Writing efficiently is time consuming because it involves editing and rewriting. Most of us use too many words when we put together our first drafts (as we discussed in Chapter 1), and those drafts need to be edited and rewritten.

The Web demands efficient writing, but it goes further because of the forms and structures of writing that are used. We can call what the Web demands concision because these forms ask writers to determine the essence of the information and to present that succinctly.

Just what are these forms and structures? A description some of them is below.

In examining them, it is helpful to remember that many are designed to help the Web visitor do what he or she is inclined to do: scan. These forms give readers places for their eyes to land, and when they do land, they present information that the reader will want, or they give readers a clue to the information that is available at that point.

Keywords. These are words within text that are most likely to tell the reader what the text is about. They are usually nouns or verbs specific enough to indicate the information being present-ed. Designers will highlight keywords by using boldface or colored type.

```
The Mercedes Widget Company manufactures
a complete line of widgets that will
meet every widget need.
```

A reader could glance at this sentence and without reading it understand that it was about widgets.

On many Web sites, keywords represent links that visitors can use to jump to additional information about that subject. Used in a limited way, keyword links can indicate to the visitor that the site has depth; overused, they can give the reader too many options and become distracting or confusing. Too many boldfaced keywords will leave the reader wondering what is real-ly important about the text. With only one or two, there is much less confusion. For instance, look at the first paragraph of Lincoln's Gettysburg Address:

```
Four score and seven years ago, our
fathers brought forth on this continent
a new nation, conceived in liberty and
dedicated to the proposition that all
men are created equal.
```

What's important here? By boldfacing many of the important words in this sentence, the writer has not aided the reader much. Now look at the same sentence:

```
Four score and seven years ago, our
fathers brought forth on this continent
a new nation, conceived in liberty and
dedicated to the proposition that all
men are created equal.
```

Here the writer has zeroed in on the two ideas about the sentence

Figure 6-2

Keywords, indentions, bullets

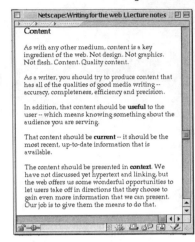

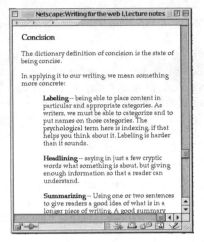

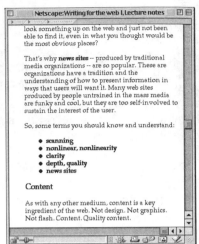

The examples above show the visual nature of keywords (left), indentions (center), and bulleted lists (right). Each of these are techniques that emphasize certain parts of the copy on a Web site and thus help readers when they are scanning.

that he or she believes to be the most important ones — the ones the writer wants the reader to pay attention to.

Short paragraphs. This is something you didn't learn in literature class: write in short paragraphs (when it is appropriate), using three to four sentences at the most. Short paragraphs are visible enticements for the reader to read. If they have a line of white space above and below them, they can be especially easy for the reader to digest.

Short paragraphs make for easier reading, but they demand disciplined thinking on the part of the writer. Information must be broken into bits that the writer can put together in small portions but also in a manner that is logical and effective.

With this type of writing, transitions are particularly important (see Chapter 4). The writing must tie together the information tightly so the readers can easily follow it. A new paragraph should be introduced in a way that follows from the previous paragraph; new paragraphs should not surprise or confuse the reader.

Indentions. Material that can be set off from the main text, such as a block quotation, can be indented to provide another visual cue for the readers. The indention must be logical, however. That is, it should be readily apparent to the reader why the material is set off and that it actually fits together.

Bulleted and numbered lists. The bulleted list is one step beyond the indention. Bulleted lists are indented and use black dots in front of individual items on the list. If the material that the writer is using lends itself to such a list, a list is relatively easy to set up in HTML (Hypertext Mark-up Language, the tagged format that most Web sites use). A bulleted list implies that there is no particular order for the items on the list.

A numbered list is the same as a bulleted list but uses numbers instead of dots. The numbered list implies an order for the items on the list and that the number of items itself may have some importance.

All of the structures mentioned above will help writers conform to some of the demands of writing for the Web. These forms also help writers deal with large blocks of prose that can be daunting, particularly if it appears in small type on a screen. They aid the reader in scanning information and in deciding what information is relevant to their needs. They should be used only when appropriate, however, because the form should support content, not control it.

Writers must also master other forms that demand succinct use of the language. These forms are difficult for the unskilled, particularly those who have not developed a practiced use of the language. These forms include labels, headlines, secondary headlines, introductions, summaries, and subheads.

Labels. These are the one- and two-word monikers that indicate the overall organization of the Web site. Because of their brevity, they do not contain much specific information for the reader. Rather, they are general guidelines that tell the reader where he or she is or is going in the site.

Still, they must be accurate and as specific as possible. Writers must understand the widely accepted meanings and implications of words, not just their strict dictionary definitions. They should understand that within some contexts, words that may seem the same carry different connotations. One example of such a pair of words is "story" and "article." Within the confines of some parts of journalism, a "story" is likely to refer to something in a newspaper while an "article" is a magazine piece. In the U.S. Navy, a "ship" refers to a surface vehicle while a "boat" refers to a submarine.

Applying the correct labels to Web site content and categories is an important task and sometimes more difficult than it first appears.

Headlines. Most of us are familiar with headlines as they appear in newspapers, magazines and newsletters. They are cryptic summaries of information that indicate the content of a longer piece of prose. The form that a headline usually takes is that of a complete sentence with a subject and a verb:

    President threatens veto of new tax bill

Sometimes a verb or part of a verb form is understood but not explicitly stated:

```
Midville man charged with larceny

Smith on team's final roster
```

(In each of the headlines, the verb "is" is missing.)

Notice a couple of things about these examples and the ones you see in the illustrations. First, the headlines are written with present tense verbs. Second, articles (a, an, the) are missing. The third characteristic is specificity; even though just a few words are used, the headline contains specific meaningful information.

Though brief, headlines are not easy to write. They first require that the writer understand thoroughly the article that the headline is for, which requires reading the article carefully, of course. Headlines should not mimic the beginning or lead paragraph of the article, so if the writer wants to use the idea in the lead for the headline, he or she needs to find different words to express it. Many journalists consider the headline to be a sales pitch for a story. The headline should be interesting enough to engage a reader and help him or her decide to read a story. For that, the headline needs specific information and concrete wording. Vague or abstract words do not help build interest.

Most Web sites will develop a style and set of requirements for headlines. The New York Times news site (nytimes.com) requires its headline writers to meet the same standards that print headlines meet; other newspaper sites are not as restrictive and demanding.

Secondary headlines. Less cryptic than headlines, secondary headlines are often complete sentences, using full verb forms and articles.

Secondary headlines assume the presence of a main headline. They do not stand by themselves. They give information that is additional to the main headline; writers should be careful not to repeat information that is in the headline.

A secondary headline is yet another layer of textual information that can lead the reader further into an article.

Intros and summaries. An intro, short for introduction, is a one- or two-sentence paragraph that tries to sell the visitor on reading an article. While giving the reader some information, it attempts to raise a question about the article that the reader will want to get answered. Consider this intro for a review of the movie The Perfect Storm from Salon (salon.com):

```
"The Perfect Storm" Special effects!
Massive waves! George Clooney! Weathered
fishermen! A pall of despair!!!
```

Or this one from Arts and Letters Daily (cybereditions.com/aldaily):

```
Today's magazine editors can polish
blurbs and make cute pop culture refer-
```

Figure 6-3

Labels, headlines and summaries

This example shows how lables, headlines and summaries can give readers layers of infomration and help them choose what parts of a Web site they want to explore and read. The labels "News" and "Special" give readers a general idea of what the item is about; the headlines give more specific information; and the summaries offer precise information about the item.

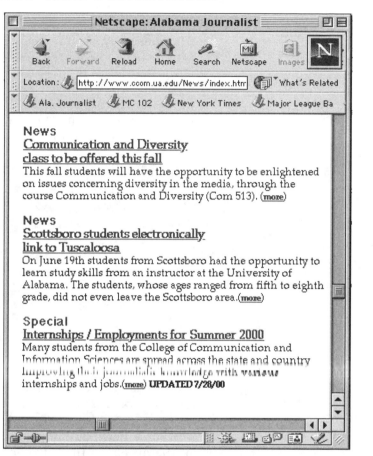

ences. But they can't edit a long story. Some may have never even read one... [more]

Or this set of intros from Slate magazine (slate.com):

the week/the spin Michael Brus
De-institutionalizing the Institutional Revolutionary Party, and more spins on the week's news.

in other magazines Jeremy Derfner and David Plotz
Time reveals how the Pentagon is rigging a crucial missile-defense test, plus what's in Newsweek, U.S. News, etc.

news quiz Randy Cohen
America rejoices as new Harry Potter book bursts in midair.

```
readme Michael Kinsley
The triumph of political discipline in
the Republicans' support for George W.
Bush
```

Intros are open sales pitches for an article. They are successful when they arouse enough curiosity within the reader to get him or her to begin reading the entire article.

A summary is more straightforward and simply tries to tell what an article or Web page is about. Its purpose, rather than inducing visitors to read the article, is to help readers decide if they want to read it. The New York Times Web site (nytimes.com) uses summaries to inform visitors about stories:

```
Mexico, New Leader Voted In,
Begins a Political Sea Change
By SAM DILLON
FROM TUESDAY'S TIMES
President-elect Vicente Fox Quesada began
the transition from a republic headed
for decades by autocratic presidents to
one in which political power suddenly
seemed up for grabs. Go to Article
```

Or this example from the Washington Post (washingtonpost.com):

```
Mexicans Celebrate Win
Euphoria sweeps the nation as Vincente
Fox starts transition.
```

Some news organizations attempt to use the lead paragraph of the article as the intro or summary. This practice is easier on editors than writing something new, but it is ultimately unsatisfying for the reader. Lead paragraphs are written to go with the full article, not to stand by themselves on the front page of a Web site. The best practice is to write a separate intro or summary.

Subheads. A subhead is a line of type within the body copy of an article that informs the reader what is coming up next within the copy. They also break up the copy, introducing more white space and making articles easier to read.

Subheads are best used at natural breaks within the article rather than being arbitrarily inserted every few paragraphs. They should help the reader through the article rather than interrupting the flow of the prose.

Like all forms of concision, they can be difficult to write. They require that the editor read the copy closely enough to capture the essence or the most important idea of the paragraphs to which the subheads refer. Then the editor must state that idea in just a few words — usually no more than three or four.

All of these forms of concision require a great deal from a writer:

Figure 6-3

Writing tightly in Cyberspace
By Joe Frisaro

Internet users are in a hurry. Keep that in mind when you write in cyberspace. Users want information, and they want it presented in a fast, clear, and concise manner. Ramble on aimlessly with drawn out sentences, and you will find yourself stuck in the slow lane on the Information Superhighway.

For best readership results, have something to say and say it. Make key points in the first two paragraphs, back them up with essential facts or salient opinions, then call it a wrap. Users want a fresh, original voice. Use strong verbs and powerful nouns.

Simple sentence structure is essential. Best readership results, studies show, are stories with short sentences. Story lengths should be in the 350-500 word range. Less is more when you are logged on.

Time is of the essence. If a user spends two minutes on a story, it's a lot. One minute or less is the average. Many sites are elated if a visitor surfs around the entire site for 8-10 minutes.

With millions of web sites available, users have choices. Lots of choices. Writers face a daunting challenge — keeping a user from clicking away.

Therefore, you need to figure out new, creative ways to engage a user. Remember, by its nature, the Internet is interactive. If possible, write in the second person. Make users feel attached to the story.

Think of writing for the Internet as talking directly, face-to-face, with someone. You want their undivided attention. If you stumble over your words, you'll lose them in seconds. Once you've turned off users in cyberspace, it's hard to get them back.

That's life in the fast lane.

Joe Frisaro is 1982 graduate of the University of Miami. Frisaro has spent nearly 10 years writing for daily newspapers, including 10 at the Tampa Tribune. For the last three years, he has been managing editor of United Sports Fans of America (www.usfans.com) web site. He has written for a number of web sites, including MSNBC.com, Fox Sports and The Sporting News.

- full understanding of what the writer is writing about;
- skill at using the language efficiently
- the ability to edit and rewrite
- a willingness to spend the time it takes to write succinctly.

Thinking laterally

As a medium, the Web allows us to go beyond the few forms of information presentation that confine other media. We are not limited to prose, whether it is in the inverted pyramid or some other structure. The Web lets us think laterally about what information a reader might need or want and what form that information should take. Editors and writers for the Web — if they are to take full advantage of their medium and if they want to attract and hold a large audience — must consider these forms and must tailor their reporting, writing, and editing efforts to produce them when necessary.

Just what forms are we talking about? The following is a partial list, some of which are very much part of other media (pictures in printed media and video in broadcast, for instance) and some are particularly applicable to the Web.

Background, details and lists. Most reporters have far more information than they can appropriately put in their inverted pyramid stories. This kind of information includes names, addresses, telephone numbers and e-mail and Web site addresses of people and organizations involved in the news. A reporter who had covered previous events that have led up to a story may not be able to put all of that in a straight inverted pyramid structure but could build a timeline. The possibilities for this kind of information are many and vary from situation to situation. What a reporter or writer should do is consider what would be useful to Web site visitors.

Pictures. Photographs allow readers to visualize the subjects of a story. They are popular in the print media and are just as effective on a Web site. In addition, a Web site is not confined by the same space considerations that newspapers, magazines and newsletters have, so pictures may be used much more extensively. More and more, the profession of journalism is demanding that the reporter report not just with words but also with a camera.

Graphics. Some of the forms of graphic presentation of information are discussed in Chapter 5. Graphics are particularly suitable for presenting numerical information. They can also illustrate events, processes, and procedures that cannot be photographed.

Maps. Location is an important concept for many people in understanding information. We like to know where things are and where events occur. Providing maps, either geographic or illustrative, can give a reader a greater sense of understanding about a story.

Documents. A reporter who covers a speech for a newspaper is generally confined to writing an inverted pyramid-style story about that speech. An editor, if there is space in the paper, may run a photograph along with the story. But what if the reader reads the story and then wants to read the full text of the speech? A newspaper generally does not have the space to do that, but it can be put on a Web site.

Court opinions, laws, policy statements, organizational reports — all of these can be included with a news report. Some book review sections are including the full text of the first chapter of books they review. (This must be done with the permission of the publisher, of course, but many publishers consent because they feel this will help sell copies of the book.) A set of instructions on how to use, assemble or build a product referred to in a story is another type of document that might be included on a site.

Previous stories. One of the easiest things to produce is a list of previous stories that a Web site has published about an event. This list, appropriately linked, gives the reader some background and context without a great deal of effort on the part of the writer or editor.

Audio and video clips. The Web allows a true merger of broadcast and print journalism by letting reporters and editors include audio and video with their stories. Thus, a reporter covering a city council meeting can write a full story on the meeting and include a clip of some of the debate on the most important issues. Currently, the practice is to keep these clips relatively brief — less than two minutes — because of their size (they can take up a lot of room of a server) and because readers may not have computers that allow them to download and view large audio or video packages.

Links to other Web sites. A good Web site on a particular topic can provide a great deal of information for the reader, but editors and writers should be careful about linking to other sites for the following reasons:

First, links can take the reader out of the news Web site, and they might not return. This tendency can be limited somewhat with pop-up windows and frames, but sometimes these devices are irritating to readers.

Second, another Web site may not be as substantial as it appears. You do not want to promise the reader something and then not deliver it.

Figuring out where to put links is another issue in placing links on a page. Some people prefer that they be within the text, so that a reader can have instant access to them. Others maintain that a list of links at the side of an article is less distracting and just as useful. Still other editors and writers, prefer a list of related links at the end of the story so that once a reader finishing reading the entire piece, he or she can go somewhere else.

E-polls. An e-poll or on-line survey offers readers a question and a set of responses. The reader can click on a response and submit that to the site. Readers can also see how others have responded to the same question. E-polls are not scientific samplings of general public opinion or even the opinions of those who have visited the site, but they are highly popular items for many news sites because they are a quick and easy way of allowing readers to respond to what they read.

Discussion forums. These, too, are popular interactive devices for readers, and many news sites are finding ways to take advantage of them. A discussion forum allows readers to respond to an event, issue or topic of current debate. Those responses are posted on a part of the Web site where everyone can see them and give their own responses. The responses may monitored by an editor (although not always), and inappropriate or irrelevant responses are not allowed.

A chat room allows users to enter into an e-mail-type discussion with others interested in the topic at hand. The chat room is usually conducted on a real-time basis. That is, statements and responses can be seen immediately, and the discussion can be ongoing.

A variation on the discussion forum is the question-and-answer forum that a site may conduct. This involves a reporter or someone familiar with an event or topic who can answer questions about that subject. Discussions can be viewed live (that is, text can be read as it is being created), giving viewers an added sense of participation. The text can then be preserved so it can be read later.

Setting up the forms of information and presentation that we are discussing in this section is not particularly difficult technically. The hard work is thinking about what information might be helpful to a visitor, gathering that information, and putting it into a form that would be useful. News sites find themselves limited not by the technology it takes to present information, but the manpower and brainpower required to gather, organize and prepare it.

E-mail

The Web has fostered one of the most important sub-media of mass communication: e-mail. Its importance is increasing as people discover its speed and efficiency and as technical advances continue to open up more possibilities for its use. E-mail, once viewed as a personal convenience, has become a tool of mass communication.

As such, professional writers are finding that the informal, grammar-less style with which they began using e-mail needs to be set aside for a more formal, disciplined approach to the writing. As with any writing, e-mails should be clear in their context and their structure. Writers of e-mail messages should consider the reader — what does the reader need to know about the message to response appropriately to it? Cryptic, non-grammatical, messages without context may be fine for communicating between friends or even in chat room settings, but they simply won't do in a professional environment.

E-mail newsletters are an increasingly popular form of keeping those with a common interest informed. Many news Web sites have established e-mail headline services that tell readers about new and interesting features on the site. Usually, these take the form of headlines and intros or summaries, along with links that allow receivers to go directly to articles and pages being referred to. Other e-mail newsletters, such as A Word A Day (www.word smith.org/), present a single new item each day and are short enough to be read easily and quickly.

Wanted for the Web: Writers and Editors

In one major sense, the World Wide Web is no different from any other mass medium: it uses words and images to convey information. Words are its chief tool. Words — not images and not increasingly sophisticated technology — are the way in which Web sites convey information, ideas and meaning.

The Web is voracious in its appetite for words and information. Every Web site becomes a beast, and it is imperative for the producers of the site to "feed the beast." Many people who begin Web sites do not understand this dynamic, believing that once a site is up, it can be left alone, and it will gain an audience. What they discover is that information can quickly become stale, and it is often perishable. New information must constantly be prepared.

That is why the Web is being inherited by people who can gather information, make sense of it and present it to an audience in a satisfying way. The Web will always need writers and good writing.

Points for consideration and discussion

1. What Web site do you regularly visit? Why?

2. Do you use the Web to find specific material or just to surf and see what's there?

3. Do you have an idea for a Web site that no one else has done? What kind of information would that site contain? How would it be written and reported?

4. Some people say that loading time — the time it takes for a site to appear fully on a computer screen — is critical to a site's retaining visitors. Others argue that loading time is not nearly as critical as some believe. What do you think? How patient are you in letting sites load onto your computer?

Chapter 6   Writing for the Web

Exercises

• *A NOTE TO THE STUDENTS: The following section contains a variety of exercises for news and feature writing. You should follow your instructor's directions in completing them. Some of the exercises are written in sentence fragments while others are written in complete sentences, often in narrative form. If you are assigned to write news stories from the exercises in this section, you should use the information but not the exact wording contained in the exercises (except for the direct quotes). Many of the exercises are badly written on purpose. It will be your job to rewrite the information you have so that it is better written than the exercise material.*

6–1 Writing headlines and summaries

Write an inverted pyramid news story as assigned by your instructor.

When you have finished, do the following things.

• **Write a headline** of a maximum seven to eight words. The headline must be a complete sentence; that is, it must have a subject and a verb (or an implied verb) and express a complete thought. However, as headlines are, it must be cryptic (don't use articles, for instance). The headline must be accurate and give the reader an overall summary of the story. It must also be written in the present tense.

Look at the examples in this chapter.

• **Write a concise summary of the story.** This is a summary, not the lead paragraph. It should be no more than 25 words and two sentences long. A summary has two purposes: to give enough information so that the reader will know what the story is about and to help persuade readers to read the story. The summary should display the following characteristics:

- It should be accurate (as well as complete, efficient and precise).
- It should summarize; that is, it should give a good overview of the story in just a few words.
- It should be grammatical and not cryptic.
- The best summaries are persuasive; they try to draw readers into the story.

Don't do this page!

6-2 Who are we statement

Write a "Who we are" or "About us" statement for a Web site. The writer must first decide if the statement is for the Web site itself or for the organization that sponsors the Web site. Such a statement will likely include:

Introduction -- a short statement describing the site or the organization.

Purpose -- a statement on why the site/organization exists. There may be more than one reason. The purpose should be stated succinctly. Sometimes, it is appropriate to state what is not the purpose of a site or an organization. A good statement of purpose will often emphasize the benefits to the user.

Process -- how does the Web site work; what are visitors supposed to do; what should be the outcome of visiting or using the Web site. Emphasizing ease of use for a Web site is certainly appropriate.

Conclusion -- ending statement that tells the visitor what to do or what may be the future of the Web site.

A good "who we are" statement is direct, efficient and factual, not self-indulgent. It gives the reader relevant, useful information about an organization or Web site. It exudes a confidence from the writer about the site and its purpose. It also enhances the site's credibility overtly with a persuasive statement of the site's purpose and covertly with sharp, succinct writing and useful information.

A must for this assignment is **concise,** efficient writing.

Write a "who we are" state using the information using the information on the next page.

Alabama Journalist
News site of the Department of Journalism, University of Alabama

Last updated ????? ?????? 16?00160000

News
Students
Faculty
College
Alumni
Specials
Who we are
Contact us
Journalism

The Alabama Journalist

Who we are

The Alabama Journalist is the news web site of the Department of Journalism at the University of Alabama. It was launched as a prototype web site during the week of February 14, 2000.

The Journalist provides a publication outlet for the best work of students studying journalism in our department; it also allows the department to present the best work of the faculty, alumni and others. Our goal is produce the best journalism possible for the University of Alabama campus and beyond.

As a daily news web site, we are committed to bringing readers the latest information about the department, college, campus and community. We seek to present this information in a variety of forms: news stories, feature articles, news graphics, photos, audio and video. Good journalism, in whatever form, demands accuracy, completeness, precision and efficiency, and those are the characteristics of reporting, writing and presentation that we seek to achieve.

As a visitor, we hope that you will explore this site fully. You find the latest news of the department, college and campus here, but you will find much more -- from profile stories by JN311 Reporting students to op-ed pieces by faculty members, from local breaking news to commentaries on national issues.

If you represent a news organization (such as a weekly or daily newspaper) and would like to use our information or reprint our articles and reports, you are welcome to do so except where specific restrictions are stated. We ask that you credit the Alabama Journalist and maintain the byline of the writer -- and that you let us know.

We hope that you will find this web site useful and enjoyable.

Visit us daily. Bookmark this site. And let us know what you think.

Sandi Lent Jewelers

We are a third-generation jewelry store located at 1299 U.S. Highway 1 in Boynton Beach, Florida. We have been in business for 60 years in the same location. Sixty years ago Sandi Lent, a world-renown jewelry designer, opened for business at the end of the Great Depression. It was a risk, but it paid off. Six decades later, our store has expanded from a 1,200-feet store to a 25,000-foot showroom. Our customers happen to be a mixture of loyal locals, devoted snow birds, and savvy international visitors. For that reason, we decided to go on-line this year. At that time we want to open our showroom to the world. We specialize in estate and antique jewelry. Most items are one-of-a-kind finds. We sell loose diamonds, rubies, amethysts, garnets, sapphires, opals, and emeralds. We sell antique platinum rings for men and women, brooches, men's watches, and women's watches. We offer a wide selection of cameos, with and without people on them. We even have cameos made from beautiful pink coral. We have Victorian cameos, cameo bracelets, cameo necklaces, cameo pendants, cameo earrings, cameo rings, cameo cufflinks, and cameo lavaliers. We offer antique pocket watches, including an 18-karat gold Cartier super-thin pocket watch and a Longines pocket watch. We have open-face and key-wind pocket watches. For men, we offer platinum bands; rings with diamonds, quartz, opals, onyx, bloodstones, and sapphires. We also have antique platinum money clips, cigar cutters, and bracelets. For ladies, we sell platinum bracelets with diamonds and/or sapphires, bands, brooches, and pendants. We sell vintage and antique ladies watches, including a 14-karat gold Rolex, and platinum Elgin, Bulova, Hamilton, and Girard Perregaux watches. Other Victorian and vintage jewelry includes filigree amethyst and diamond rings, an engraved ruby ring, filigree onyx ring, brooches, lockets, a 14-karat Victorian bracelet, and a turquoise and pearl bar pin. Our stock list changes and is updated online daily. We also offer unique hand-crafted jewelry, including design award-winning pieces created by Sandi herself more than 40 years ago. We offer weekly specials in our store and online. We will help any nervous groom pick out the perfect antique wedding ring or band. We also offer expert diamond advice for loose diamond purchases. We offer a secure on-line server to order items from. We accept Visa, MasterCard, Discover, and American Express credit cards. We send confirmation on all orders soon after the order is placed. We also accept payment by check or money order through the postal service. If mailed, we will confirm shipment 24 hours after items are shipped. Payment for the items must be received seven days after order or the item will be held. We ship items by USPS regular mail, certified return mail, insured mail, UPS 2nd Day Air, or FedEX Overnight. Returns are handled through our toll free number: 1-800-555-GEMS. Our e-mail address is antiquejeweler@sandilent.com. Mail returns to Sandi Lent Returns, 1299 U.S. Highway 1, Boynton Beach, Florida. We must be notified within 48 hours concerning any return or refund situation. Gift wrapping is available upon request for a nominal charge of $3 per package. We also repair the jewelry we sell and don't sell.

This assignment was written by Beverly Piotrowski.

6–3 Writing a splash page

For a Web site on roller coasters at Six Flags Over Georgia, write a general introduction and an introduction to the individual sections that the Web site will contain.

The general introduction should be 75 to 100 words. The section introductions should be no more than 25 words. They should have a label and a headline.

Roller Coasters at Six Flags Over Georgia

For thrill seekers everywhere, the amusement park of Six Flags Over Georgia, a member of Six Flags Theme Parks, Inc., now boasts eight roller coasters. The newest is the one called The Georgia Scorcher. The oldest is the Dahlonega Mine Train, which was built the year the park was opened in 1967. So, that makes it the park's oldest roller coaster. A "mine train" isn't just a cute name associated with the gold rush history of its north Georgia town namesake, it's also a type of roller coaster. A mine train roller coaster is one in which riders experience the sensation of what it must be like to ride in a runaway mine train. These types of coasters typically hug the ground and make quick, jerky, small turns and drops on a narrow track. The Dahlonega Mine Train is made out of steel. Its highest point is 37 feet, its top speed is almost 30 mph, and it lasts just shy of 3 minutes (2 minutes, 51 seconds). The Mine Train is a favorite for kids tall enough to make its 42-inch height requirement. Parents can also ride with their kids on this roller coaster, making it great fun for the whole entire family. The coaster carries 2,200 passengers each hour, on its busiest days. Another oldie, but goodie roller coaster at Six Flags Over Georgia is the Great American Scream Machine. It's so famous, its name is a registered trademark. The Scream Machine was opened in April 1973. It is made of wood. Its top speed is 57 mph, breaking the speed limit of most highways during the time it was built. When it opened in the early 70s, it was listed in the Guinness World Book of Records as being the world's largest and tallest roller coaster. The Scream Machine's length is 3,800 feet and its top height, which is on the first hill passenger's climb, towers in at 105 feet. That's over 10 stories high. Not the tallest in the park these days, but impressive for the mid-70s. A ride one the Scream Machine lasts only two minutes. It's still one of the world's longest and tallest wooden roller coasters. One of the newest roller coasters at Six Flags Over Georgia, Batman the Ride, is a first for the southeastern part of the United States. It is the only suspended, outside-looping ride of its kind in the southeast. Suspended roller coasters feature ìtrainsî that carry passengers underneath the tracks, rather than the usual above-the-track mode of transport. This means passengers' feet dangle freely beneath them as they soar more than 109 feet above the ground and then barely skim the ground on their way around the ride's post and infrastructure close to the ground. Suspended tracks are designed to heighten a passenger's experience of the track's banks and turns. Batman the Ride's top speed is 50 mph. It gets up to a maximum of four Gs at some point during the ride. People must be at least 54 inches tall to ride this ride. Batman the Ride is made of steel. It was opened in May of 1997. It is named after a Warner Brothers comic book character. Its length is 2,700 feet long. But the newest roller coaster at Six Flags Over Georgia is The

Georgia Scorcher. It opened in May of 1999. It is unique in that the passengers don't sit through this ride, they stand. In fact, it is the tallest and fastest stand-up roller coaster in the entire southeastern portion of the United States. The Georgia Scorcher's tallest point is at 107 feet, which is more than 10 stories tall, and it can zoom up to speeds of 54 mph. It, too, can top four on the G-force scale. It is made of steel. The Georgia Scorcher features high-speed spirals and a figure eight design, both of which help give it its four Gs effect. The Georgia Scorcher makes the No. 8 roller coaster at Six Flags Over Georgia. Its speed, however, does not exceed that of the Great American Scream Machine or The Viper, another speedy roller coaster at the park. Both roller coasters hit top speeds of 57 mph. But both of these don't top the fastest roller coaster in the United States. Currently the fastest roller coaster is the Superman The Escape ride at Six Flags Magic Mountain in California. This $20 million ride pushes 100 mph. But it isn't a full-fledged roller coaster. Superman The Escape is more of a fast drop on tracks for passengers, which could explain its top speeds. The Viper at Six Flags Over Georgia takes passengers from a stand-still stop to almost 60 mph in less than 6 seconds. The Viper is a shuttle, loop roller coaster. A shuttle roller coaster isn't like most other coasters. It doesn't run on a continuous track. Instead, it travels to the end of the track and then returns riders back where they started from. On The Viper, for instance, passengers soar inside a 76-foot vertical loop at up to four Gs, then zoom up a 142-foot incline that drops them backward toward the ground right back through the 76-foot loop, ending where they began. The Viper can handle up to 1,300 riders per hour during the peak times at the park. Passengers must be 42 inches tall or taller to ride this ride. The Viper is made of steel. It opened in 1995. In March of 1990 Six Flags Over Georgia debuted The Georgia Cyclone. The Georgia Cyclone is a wooden roller coaster just like the Great American Scream Machine. The Cyclone is named for

and modeled in the likeness of the old Coney Island Cyclone. In fact, the name cyclone is considered a category for a certain type of roller coaster. All cyclone coasters feature a track layout designed like the Coney Island Cyclone. The Georgia Cyclone reaches heights of 95 feet and travels at a speed up to 50 mph. This ride lasts 1 hour and 48 seconds. Riders must be 48 inches or taller to ride this roller coaster. The Georgia Cyclone can handle up to 1,200 passengers in one hour. Another first at Six Flags Over Georgia came in 1978 when it opened The Mind Bender. The Mind Bender had the honor being the first triple-loop roller coaster in North America. The highest point on the roller coaster is 80 feet, the loops tower above the ground at 56 feet. Each train can carry up to 28 riders. The Mind Bender's length is 3200 feet, and it can entertain up to 1,200 passengers per hour during the peak periods at the park. A ride on this coaster lasts all of 2 minutes, 33 seconds. Anton Schwartzkopf of Germany designed The Mind Bender. This roller coaster uses shoulder restraints to help hold passengers down and in during the upside-down, high point of each of its three loops. The Mind Bender consists of a structure that is made with 400,000 pounds steel. Another speedy roller coaster at Six Flags Over Georgia that turns its riders upside-down is the Ninja. The Ninja towers at its highest point at more than 12 stories high. That height makes it the tallest roller coaster to be built at Six Flags Over Georgia. The Ninja's top speed is at 52 mph. Passengers on the Ninja experience being turned upside-down no less than five times. Six Flags Over Georgia calls the Ninja, "the black belt of roller coasters." It was debuted in April 1992. The Ninja is one of the quickest roller coasters at the park. It only takes passengers 1 minute and 20 seconds to experience. Riders must be at least 48 inches tall to ride this ride.

This assignment was written by Beverly Piotrowski.

6–4 Writing a splash page

For a Web site on roller coasters at ~~Six Flags Over Georgia~~ *Cherokee Nation*, write a general introduction and an introduction to the individual sections that the Web site will contain.

The general introduction should be 75 to 100 words. The section introductions should be no more than 25 words. They should have a label and a headline.

The Cherokee Nation

Cherokees are considered to be a southern group of Iroquois descent in heritage and in the language they use. At one time, Cherokee villages could be found in the states of Tennessee, North Carolina, South Carolina, Georgia, Virginia, and Alabama. Before they were influenced by European explorers and pioneers, Cherokee villages constructed their homes in a square or rectangular shape formed by a frame consisting of vertical poles. They covered the outside of their homes with bark, wood, or a woven material. They also coated the outside sides with clay or mud from the ground. After they were exposed to the ways of the white man, Cherokee Indians began building log cabins much like the settlers built. The Cherokee log cabins had one door, a hole in the roof for smoke to escape when they cooked, and no windows. The roof was covered with bark. Not much of the early history of the Cherokee Indians, along with other Native American Indians in the southeast, is known. It is known that they were a temple and mound-building culture. Ceremonial and pyramid-shape temples were built much like the ones constructed by the early Mayas in Mexico. This Cherokee and southeastern Native American Indian culture is thought to have reached its peak in the 14th century. Only remnants of what is called the Mound Builders' culture remained in the south by the time white men arrived more than 300 years later. They subsisted by farming corn, beans, and squash. When necessary they also hunted for deer, elk, and bear, and fished. Indians in the Southeast, such as the Cherokee, also raised tobacco, nuts, and sunflowers. They also picked berries to eat when available. Along with the Choctows, Chicksaws, Creeks, and Seminoles, Cherokee Indians were considered part of "The Five Civilized Tribes," mostly because they adopted the ways of the white man so easily. Apart from building homes like the white man, southeastern Indians also were known to own slaves, raise livestock, and work large farms. The only domesticated animal they raised before European influence was the dog. Dogs were used as beasts of burden by Indian tribes. Other ways they followed the white man's lead was in how they dressed, their pursuit of commerce, and their acceptance of Christianity. The Cherokees took it one step further by adopting their own formal constitution modeled on the one adopted by the United States, complete with a legislature. Southeastern Indians often had a lot of tattoos on their bodies. Indians in the Southeast played a ball game similar to the game of lacrosse played today. But the Indians of the Southeast used two sticks, instead of the one used today. The Indian version is also said to have been much more violent that the version of lacrosse played today. Prior to the American Revolution, Cherokees were governed by two groups: the Red and the White. When a town was in a state of conflict, or during war, the Red group was in control of its political affairs. During times of peace, the White group was in charge. The tribes would perform certain rituals or ceremonies to mark the transition between the Red and White towns' rule. A supreme war chief was in charge of the Red towns, while the supreme peace chief oversaw the White towns. Two of the most important ceremonies for the Cherokee were the "green corn ceremony," or harvest feast, which was held after the corn was harvested and ready to eat. This was a time for towns to clean themselves up, break old pottery, extinguish ceremonial fires, and start anew. The New Year Fire, or New Year, was also observed. Both of these ceremonies lasted about three weeks and involved an elimination of old bad feelings within the towns. In February 1828, the first Native American Indian newspaper was started. It was called the Cherokee Phoenix. In 1821, several years before the paper was started, a man by the name of Sequoyah, who was half-Cherokee, created a Cherokee alphabet. This, in turn, helped lead to the first newspaper and the a heightened level of literacy among the entire Cherokee tribe. When gold was discovered on land owned by Cherokee Indians in Georgia, the Cherokee challenged the state's right to take away their land, taking the case all the way to the Supreme Court of the United States. In Cherokee Nation v. Georgia in 1831 the court ruled the Indians had a right to occupy their land. But they only had a right to occupancy. The state of Georgia refused to honor the court's decision, evicting the Cherokees under the Indian Removal Act of 1830. Seven thousand troops gathered about 15,000 Cherokees together to make the trek to Oklahoma in what came to be known as the "trail of tears." In the winter of 1838-39, about 4,000 Cherokee died making the trek from Georgia to Oklahoma. The freezing cold conditions proved too much for most of those who died. The intense pressure to follow the troops' orders not to rest when hurt or tired also killed some. In Oklahoma, the Cherokee joined other tribes that had been driven out of their homelands: Creek,

Chickasaw, Choctaw, and Seminoles. Each of the tribes was forced to leave their homelands in the Southeast. Each tribe was given a land allotment and was able to live under tribal governments until they were dissolved, for the most part, in 1906. The "reservations" Indian tribes live on today are just another name for tribal landholdings. When Cherokees were threatened with losing their land just after the American Revolution began, they let it be known that they supported the British. But, in the end, the Cherokees were wiped out by the loss by the British. The Cherokees were then forced to giving up a large amount of territory in North Carolina and South Carolina, under the Treaty of DeWitt's Corner in May of 1777 and the Treaty of Long Island of Holston in July of 1777. Prior to the influence of the European white man, Cherokees used various stone tools, such as knives, axes, and chisels. They also wove baskets and made pottery. During the time of the "trail of tears," hundreds of Cherokee ran away to the Great Smoky Mountains in western North Carolina, where they established a community that still exists there today. By the early 1800s, Cherokees owned a number of prosperous, privately owned plantations. According to one report, by 1825 Cherokees owned more than 1,200 slaves. Of the Cherokee who owned plantations, many were half-Cherokee, while others had come from positions of influence through the ranks of Cherokee politics. The organization of Red towns and White towns was created in an effort to fight the white man's westward advance. With more and more threats by European settlers being made on their frontier homes and villages, the Cherokee had to centralize their tribal politics. The Cherokee used the method of slash and burn to keep weeds and forest fire numbers down, which, in turn, would help with their agricultural efforts. In order to help clear the land, they stripped the trees' bark off and then burned the trees. This method of slash and burn was not favored by the white settlers. In the 1700s, runaway Creeks from Georgia and Alabama moved to Florida. Once in Florida, they joined runaway black slaves and members of the original Florida tribes to create a new population that came to be called the Seminoles. About 47,000 descendants of the Cherokees who were forced to relocate to eastern Oklahoma were living in the late 20th century, 15,000 of those full-blooded Cherokee. By the late 20th century, about 3,000 Cherokee are still living in the Great Smoky Mountain area of North Carolina. They are the descendants of the runaways during the "trail of tears."

This assignment was written by Beverly Piotrowski.

7

Writing for broadcast

Introduction

Broadcasting is the world's most pervasive medium of mass communication. It is not unusual for the American home to receive 50 or more television channels from its cable system or satellite dish. A wide variety of radio stations has been available to anyone with a receiver since the early days of the medium. Underdeveloped areas that cannot get access to even a newspaper will usually have a transistor radio to link it with the rest of the world. Satellite broadcasting has drawn the world closer together (although not always with positive results) by ensuring that we have instant, live coverage of major news events from almost anywhere in the world and even beyond. Consider the following:

• When Americans first landed on the moon in 1969, a television camera was positioned outside the lunar lander to record the event.

• When Prince Charles of England married Princess Diana in 1981, television cameras were at every part of the event.

• In late 1992, when U.S. marines invaded Somalia, their landing was met not by hostile forces but by American, European and Asian television crews who broadcast live pictures of the event all around the world. (The Marines, in fact, complained that the television lights made them more vulnerable to hostile fire.)

• The automobile accident in Paris that took the life of Princess Diana in 1997 was not recorded, of course, but her funeral a week later was watched by people in almost every part of the world.

In America, broadcasting delivers information with immediacy and impact. Most Americans get their news from a variety of sources, and it would be a mistake to believe that broadcasting is always the dominant medium in this regard. Newspapers, newsmagazines and web sites deliver a large amount of information to the American public and will continue to do so, but broadcasting is often perceived as dominant. More than 6,000 local radio and television stations in America (and thousands more shortwave radio operators) are broadcasting, as opposed to 1,700 daily newspapers.

A person who wants to succeed in the field of broadcasting needs to have intelligence, diligence, dependability — and the ability to write. Even though broadcasting is an audio-visual medium, almost everything you hear or see in the way of news or entertainment has been written down. The occasions for ad libbing before the cameras are relatively rare, and even the "spontaneous" lines delivered by some broadcasters are written and rehearsed. Broadcasters consider air time too valuable to leave to chance. Even reporters doing live news spots often work from notes and have a good understanding of the forms of writing for the medium.

Broadcasters look for the same qualities in writers that have been discussed in other parts of this book. They want people who know the language and its rules of usage; who are willing to research their subjects thoroughly and understand them well enough to report on them with clarity; who do not mind working hard; and who are willing to rewrite their work and have it rewritten by others. In addition, they are particularly interested in people who can write under pressure and can meet deadlines.

Writing for broadcasting is similar in many ways to writing for the print media, but there are some important differences. Those differences concern the way news is selected for broadcast, the characteristics of writing and story structure and the style with which the information is presented.

Selection of news

Most of the same news values discussed in Chapter 4 apply to news selection for broadcasting. Broadcast journalists are interested in events that have a wide impact, people in the news, current issues, events that happen close to home and conflicts or unusual happenings. Because of the opportunities and limitations of their medium, however, broadcasters are likely to view such events in different ways than their counterparts in print or web journalism. The following are some of the factors that broadcasters use to select news.

Timeliness. Because of the nature of their medium, broadcasters often consider timeliness the most important news value. Broadcasters work on hourly, or less than hourly, cycles. A news broadcaster may go on the air several times a day. The news must be up-to-the-minute. News that is more than an hour or two old may be too stale for the broadcaster. When you listen to a news report on a breaking news story, you expect to hear the very latest news —what happened just a few minutes before.

Information, not explanation. Broadcasters look for stories that do not need a lot of explanation in order for listeners or viewers to understand them. They prefer stories that are simple and can be told in a straightforward manner. The maximum length for almost any story on a television newscast is two minutes; the more normal length is twenty to thirty seconds. In some larger markets, radio reporters are being told to reduce their story lengths to ten seconds and actualities (using the actual voice of

Figure 7-1

Local news

Most television stations depend on a local news operation to establish a presence in the community, provide service and draw in local viewers. The news operation is the centerpiece of many local stations.

Photo by Jeff Stovall

the source) to five seconds. That amount of time is not enough to explain a complex story. It is only enough time to give the listener or viewer a few pertinent facts. Of course, some stories are both complex and important, and explanation cannot be avoided. Still, even with complex and important stories, the broadcast writer must wrestle with condensing these stories to their essence.

Audio or visual impact. Broadcasters want stories that their audience can hear or see. Playing a part of the president's state of the union address is more dramatic than a news reporter talking about it; pictures of a flood are more likely to be watched than an anchorman's description of it. Broadcasters often choose stories for their newscasts because they have sound or pictures, even though the stories themselves might not merit such attention otherwise. This is one of the major criticisms of broadcast news, but it remains one of the chief factors in news story selection.

Characteristics of writing

A 1960s edition of the UPI Broadcast Stylebook says that while print journalism has the five Ws, broadcast journalism has the Four Cs — correctness, clarity, conciseness and color. These four Cs still serve as the basis for broadcast writing and form a good framework for talking about broadcast writing styles.

The first commitment of the broadcast journalist is to correctness, or accuracy. Everything a broadcast journalist does must contribute to the telling of an accurate story. Even though the broadcast journalist must observe some strict rules about how stories are written, these rules should contribute to, not prevent, an accurate account of an event.

One of the most admirable characteristics of good broadcast writing is its clarity. Good broadcast writers employ clear, precise language that contains no ambiguity. Clarity is an absolute requirement for broadcast writing. Listeners and viewers cannot go back and re-hear a news broadcast as they might be able to read a newspaper account more than once. They must understand what is said the first time. Broadcast writers achieve this kind of clarity by using simple sentences and familiar words, by

Figure 7-2

Broadcast copy

This is the script sheet for the beginning of a local news broadcast that leads off with a national story. The directions on the left indicate that videotape or film is being shown while the announcer is speaking.

Thanks to Janet Hall, WBRC-News, Birmingham

Slug ___SHUTTLE LANDS___   Page ___1___

Directions	Script	
TWO SHOT	(2 shot) (s) GOOD EVENING, I'M RICHARD SCOTT. (J) AND I'M HALLIE JONES *****	1
ON JONES/ FF SHUTTLE LANDING	MERCURY WELCOME BACK. THOSE WERE THE SWEET WORDS FROM MISSION CONTROL TODAY AS THE SPACE SHUTTLE MERCURY MADE A PICTURE PERFECT LAND-ING IN THE CALIFORNIA DESERT.	
ROLLCSS--VO---- FT. EDWARDS AIR FORCE BASE	THIS WAS THE MOMENT NASA HAD WORKED SO HARD FOR IN THE FACE OF MOUNTING OPPOSI-TION TO THE SHUTTLE PROGRAM. THE SHUTTLE CREW STEPPED OUT OF THE SPACE SHIP WAVING A LARGE AMERICAN FLAG AS SOME 340 THOUSAND SPECTATORS CHEERED. VICE PRESIDENT AL GORE AND SEVERAL NASA OFFICIALS WERE THE FIRST TO GREET THE ASTRONAUTS.	
ON JONES/CU	NASA ADMINISTRATOR JAMES JONATHAN SAID QUOTE, "THIS IS A BANNER DAY FOR ALL OF US AT NASA AND WE'RE VERY HAPPY THIS ONE WORKED SO WELL." (2 SHOT) (S)	

avoiding the use of pronouns and repeating proper nouns if necessary and by keeping the subject close to the verb in their sentences. Most of all, however, they achieve clarity by thoroughly knowing and understanding their subject.

Another important characteristic of writing for broadcast is its conversational style. Even the clearest, simplest newspaper style tends to sound stilted when it is read aloud. Broadcast writing must sound more conversational because people will be reading it aloud. Broadcast news should be written for the ear, not the eye. The writer should keep in mind that someone is going to say the words and others will listen to them.

This casual or conversational style, however, does not give the writer freedom to break the rules of grammar, to use slang or off-color phrasing or to use language that might be offensive to listeners. As with all writing, the broadcast writer should try to focus attention on the content of the writing and not the writing itself. Nor is casual–sounding prose particularly easy to produce. It takes a finely-honed ear for the language and a conciseness that we do not normally apply to writing.

Another characteristic of writing for broadcast is the emphasis on the immediate. While past tense verbs are preferred in the print media, broadcasters use the present tense as much as possible. A newspaper or Web site story might begin something like this:

```
The president said Tuesday that he will
support some limited tax increase pro-
posals when Congress reconvenes this
week. . . .
```

A broadcast news story might begin with this:

```
The president says he's for higher
taxes. . .
```

Another way of emphasizing the immediate is to omit the time element in the news story and assume that everything has happened close to the time of the broadcast. In the example above, the broadcast version has no time element since it would probably be heard on the day the president made that statement. The elimination of the time element cannot occur in every story. Sometimes the time element is important and must be mentioned.

The tight phrasing that characterizes broadcast writing is one of its chief assets and one of the most difficult qualities for a beginning writer to achieve. Because time is so short, the broadcaster cannot waste words. The broadcaster must work constantly to simplify and condense. There are a number of techniques for achieving this conciseness. One technique is the elimination of all but the most necessary adjectives and adverbs. Broadcasters know that their stories are built on nouns and verbs, the strongest words in the language. They avoid using the passive voice. Instead they rely on strong, active verbs that will allow the listener to form a picture of the story.

Another technique of broadcast writing is the use of short, simple sentences. Broadcasters do not need the variety of length and type of sentences that print journalists need to make their copy interesting. Broadcasters can more readily fire information at their readers like bullets in short, simple sentences.

The fourth C of the UPI Stylebook — color — refers to writing that allows the listener to paint a picture of the story or event being reported. This picture can be achieved in a variety of ways, such as the inclusion of pertinent and insightful details in the story or allowing the personality of the writer or news reader to come through in a story. The nature of the broadcast medium allows for humor and human interest to inject itself into many stories.

A final characteristic of broadcast writing is its almost complete subjugation to deadlines. Broadcast copy is often written in an atmosphere in which a deadline is imminent. Broadcast writers have to learn to produce in a highly pressurized atmosphere. Unless broadcast writers are able to meet deadline, their compact, understandable prose will never be heard.

Story structure

The most common structure for broadcast news is called dramatic unity. This structure has three parts: climax, cause and effect. The climax of the story gives the listener the point of the story in about the same way the lead of a print news story does; it tells the listener what happened. The cause portion of the story tells why it happened — the circumstances surrounding the event. The effect portion of the story gives the listener the context of the story and possibly some insight about what the story means. The following examples will show how dramatic unity works (note, too, some difference in style rules from print):

Climax   Taxpayers in the state will be paying an average of 15 dollars more in income taxes next year.

Cause   The state senate defeated several delaying amendments this afternoon and passed the governor's controversial revenue-raising bill by a 15 to 14 vote. The bill had been the subject of intense debate for more than a week.

Effect   The bill now goes to the governor for his signature. Estimates are that the measure will raise about 40 million dollars in new revenue for the state next year. Elementary and secondary education will get most of that money. Passage of the bill is a major victory for the governor and his education program.

Climax
    Many children in the city school system will begin their classes at least a half hour later next year.

Cause
    The City School Board last night voted to rearrange the school bus schedule for next year as a cost-cutting measure.

Effect
    The new schedule will require most elementary school children to begin school one half hour later than they do now. Most high school students will begin one half hour earlier.

Broadcast journalists think of their stories as completed circles rather than inverted pyramids. While the pyramid may be cut without losing the essential facts, the broadcast story, if written in this unified fashion, cannot be cut from the bottom or anywhere else. It stands as a unit. Broadcast journalists and their editors are not concerned with cutting stories after they have been written to make them fit into a news broadcast. Rather, stories should be written to fit into an amount of time designated by the editor or news director. For instance, an editor may allot twenty-five seconds for a story. The writer will know this and will write a story that can be read in twenty-five seconds. If the story is longer than it should be, the editor will ask that it be rewritten.

Because they are so brief, broadcast news stories must gain the attention of the listener from the beginning. The first words in the story are extremely important. Getting the attention of the listener is sometimes more important than summarizing the story or giving the most important facts of the story. The broadcast news lead may be short on facts, but if it captures the attention of the reader, it has served its purpose. Here is an example:

    The lame duck keeps limping along.
    Congress met for the third day of its lame-duck session today, and again failed to act on the president's gas tax proposals.

The first sentence has very little in the way of facts, but it gets the listener into the story. This sort of story structure is only appropriate for certain stories, however. If the facts of the story are strong enough to gain the listener's attention, they should be used to open the story. For example:

    The five-cents-a-gallon gas tax is law.
    The president signed the bill authorizing the tax today while vacationing in Florida.

In both of these examples, the writer has not attempted to tell the whole story in the first sentence. Rather, the stories have attention-getting leads and are then supported by facts and details in subsequent sentences. This structure for broadcast news writing is a common one that should be mastered by the beginning student. Here are some more examples of newspaper stories and the attention-getting leads that could be written for broadcast:

Newspaper lead   Americans overwhelmingly oppose the taxation of employee benefits, and congressmen who tamper with such tax-free worker benefits may face trouble at the polls, two Roper Organization surveys say.

Broadcast lead   Keep your hands off employee benefits.
That's what Americans are willing to tell congressmen who want to tax things like retirement payments and educational allowances.

Newspaper lead   The United States is turning out inferior products that are too costly for foreign customers and the problems go beyond a strong dollar, high wages and high taxes, a presidential commission reports.

Broadcast lead   Many American products aren't worth what we are asking for them.

Newspaper lead   A lone juror, a city sanitation department supervisor, forced a hung jury and a mistrial of Midville Mayor Reggie Holder's trial on perjury and conspiracy charges involving alleged illegal campaign contributions.

Broadcast lead   One man has made the difference in the perjury and conspiracy trial of Midville Mayor Reggie Holder.

Stories are measured in time — minutes and seconds. While a newspaper can devote 300 words to a story, a broadcaster may have only twenty to thirty seconds for it. The broadcast writer must keep this time factor in mind during every stage of the writing and editing process. Broadcast news stories cannot go into the detail and explanation that print or web stories can. The broadcast writer has to omit certain facts and explanations if the story is to fit into the time allowed.

Broadcast writing style

The style and customs of broadcast writing differ somewhat from the style you have learned for print and web journalism. While the AP Stylebook is still consulted for many usage questions, broadcast writing has some and conventions of its own. The following is a list of some of those conventions.

Titles usually come before names. Just as in print stories, most people mentioned in broadcast stories need to be identified. In broadcast news writing, however, titles almost always precede a name. Consequently, while a print story might have "James Baker, former secretary of state," the broadcast journalist would say, "former Secretary of State James Baker."

Avoid abbreviations, even on second reference. Only the most commonly known abbreviations should be used in broadcast writing. The FBI and UN are two examples. FTC, however, should be spelled out as the Federal Trade Commission.

Avoid direct quotations if possible. Broadcast writers prefer paraphrasing rather than using direct quotations. Direct quotations are hard to handle in broadcast copy because signaling the listener that the statement is a direct quotation is difficult.

Sometimes a direct quotation is essential and should be used. When that is the case, the writer needs to tip the listener off to the fact that a direct quotation is being used. The use of the phrase "quote . . . unquote" is awkward and should be avoided. Instead, phrases like "in the words of the speaker," "in his own words," "used these words," and "as she put it."

Attribution should come before a quotation, not after it. The sequence of direct quote-speaker-verb that is the standard in print journalism is not useful for the broadcast writer. Tagging an attribution onto the end of a direct or paraphrased quote is confusing to the listener. The listener should know where the quotation is coming from before hearing the quote.

Use as little punctuation as possible but enough to help the newscaster through the copy. Remember that broadcast news copy will be read by only one person, the news reader. That person should be able to read through the copy as easily as possible. The excessive use of commas, dashes and semicolons will not help the newscaster.

Numbers and statistics should be rounded off. While a print journalist will want to use an exact figure, a broadcast journalist will be satisfied with a more general figure. Consequently, $4,101,696 in print becomes "more than four million dollars" in broadcast copy.

Numbers themselves are handled somewhat differently than the AP Stylebook dictates for print journalists. Here are a few rules about handling numbers in broadcast copy: numbers one through nine should be spelled out; numbers 10 through 999 should be written as numerals; write out hundred, thousand, million, billion, and use a combination of numerals with these numbers where appropriate (for example, 15-hundred, 10-billion); don't write "a million" or "a billion," but rather use the word "one" ("a" sounds like "eight").

Personalize the news when possible and appropriate. In the example on page 259 the lead sentence could read, "Gas is going to cost you five cents more a gallon . . . ." Where possible and appropriate, broadcast stories should draw the listeners into the story by telling how the story might affect them.

Avoid extended description. "President and chief executive officer of International Widgets John Smith said today . . ." would become "International Widgets President John Smith says . . ."

Figure 7-3

Live reports

This script sheet shows a lead-in for a live report. The reporter will appear live on camera via satellite and give his report.

Slug GADSDEN POLICE CHIEF		Page _____1_____
Directions	**Script**	

ON HALL/ FF SKYLINK 6	(J)
	   THE CITY OF GADSDEN HAS A NEW POLICE CHIEF TONIGHT DESPITE THE CONTROVERSY THAT SURROUNDED HIS HIRING.
	   FORMER BIRMINGHAM POLICE INSPECTOR JOHNNY MORRIS WAS SWORN IN AS POLICE CHIEF THIS AFTERNOON.
		1

ON HALL/LIVE RON	WE SENT OUR NEW SKYLINK 6 SATELLITE TRUCK TO GADSDEN TODAY ... RON FUDGE JOINS US NOW VIA SATELLITE. RON, WHAT'S THE REACTION THERE TO THE NEW CHIEF TONIGHT?	
TAKE LIVE FULL SPR: SKYLINK 6 / GADSDEN SPR: SKYLINK 6 / RON FUDGE	(LIVE FULL)	

Avoid using symbols when you write. The dollar sign should never be used. Nor should the percent sign be used. Spell these words out so there will be no mistake on the part of the news reader.

Use phonetic spelling for unfamiliar and hard to pronounce names and words. Again, you are trying to be helpful to the newscaster. Writing "California governor George Duekmejian (Dook-MAY-gen) said today he will propose . . ." helps the newscaster get over a difficult name. Notice that the syllable which is emphasized in pronunciation is written in capital letters. Difficult place names also need phonetic spellings. "A car bomb exploded in downtown Caracas (ka-RAH-kus) today . . ." Writers should also be knowledgeable about local pronunciations of place names. For instance, most people know that Louisville, Kentucky is pronounced (LU-ee-vil); but most people do not know that residents of Louisville, Tennessee pronounce the name of their community as (LU-iss-vil). Pronunciation to the broadcast writer is like spelling to the print journalist. It should always be checked if there is any doubt.

Avoid pronouns, and when you have to use them, make sure the referents are clear to the listener. Putting too many pronouns in a story can be an obstacle to the kind of clarity a broadcaster must achieve. For instance, in the following sentences, it is unclear to whom the pronoun is referring: The president and the chief foreign affairs advisor met yesterday. They discussed his recent trip to the Mideast.

Avoid apposition. An apposition is a word or set of words that renames a noun. In "Tom Smith, mayor of Midville, said today . . ." the phrase "mayor of Midville" is an appositional phrase. These phrases are deadly in broadcast writing. They slow the newscaster down and confuse to the listener. Appositions, when they are found in the middle of sentences, are surrounded by commas. Listeners to broadcast stories do not have the advantage of those commas, however. Consequently, they may hear the example above as ". . . Midville said today . . ." Broadcast writers should keep subjects and verbs as close together as possible.

Use the present tense when it is appropriate. Using the present tense ("the president says" rather than "the president said") is one way broadcast writers have of bringing immediacy to their writing. Care should be taken, however, that using the present tense does not make the broadcaster sound foolish. For instance, if the president made a statement yesterday, a broadcast news story probably should not have the attribution in the present tense. The past tense would be more appropriate. The present tense should be used for action that is very recent or that is continuing.

Avoid dependent clauses at the beginning of sentences. Dependent clauses are troublesome to the broadcast writer because they are confusing and tend to hide the subject of the sentence. For instance, "Stopping on the first leg of his European tour today, the president said he . . ." gives the listener too much to digest before getting to the main point of the story. The broadcast writer should always remember that the simple sentence—subject, verb, object—is the best format to use.

Broadcast copy preparation

Copy is prepared for one person, the announcer. The copy should be presented in a way to make the announcer's job as easy as possible. Different stations and news organizations will have rules about how to prepare copy. The list below should give you an idea of the kind of rules the station will employ:

• Type only one story on a page. A story should have some ending mark, such as "—30—", at the end.

• Use caps and lower case. An old style of broadcast writing (and the one you see in some of the examples in this chapter) was to capitalize everything. That is changing. The all caps style is hard to read.

• Don't carry over a paragraph to another page. If a story is more than a page long, end the page at the end of a paragraph; begin the next page with a new paragraph.

• Don't hyphenate at the end of a line.

• Broadcasters often want to work tapes (either audio or video) of interviews into their stories. The following example shows you how to indicate this on your copy.

```
People who want to buy a Chevrolet next
year are going to have to pay more.
That's what company spokesman John Smith
said today in Detroit. The new cars will
cost about seven percent more than last
year's cars. Smith blamed the increase
on the new contract recently negotiated
with the United Auto Workers.

ROLL TAPE: The workers are getting more.
. . .
END TAPE: . . . really no way of avoid-
ing this.
[ :15]

Labor leaders disputed this reasoning,
however. Local auto workers president
Stanley Porter said Chevrolet was rais-
ing its prices just to make the union
look bad. At a separate news conference
```

```
in Detroit, he called on Chevrolet to
roll back its prices.

ROLL TAPE: The union gave up a lot. . .
      .
END TAPE:  . . .without good reason.[
:18]
```

The number in each of the sets of parentheses indicates the number of seconds of each tape.

Putting together a newscast

Broadcast journalists work with and against time. They use time to measure their stories, but they are also always working against time in the form of tight deadlines. Their stories must be completed for the next newscast. People working in radio feel this pressure keenly because of the hourly news shows that many radio stations produce. Many local television stations are also producing such hourly newscasts. For the broadcast journalist, the clock is always ticking toward a deadline, and the deadline cannot be delayed.

Many broadcast journalists — even those who are fairly new in the business — must worry not only about writing their stories but also about putting together a newscast. Producing such a newscast, whether it is a forty-five second news brief or a half-hour telecast, involves many of the skills learned as a news writer.

The first such skill is that of exercising news judgment about what to include in the newscast. Writers must use traditional news values in deciding what events constitute news. Editors and producers use those same values in deciding what goes into a newscast. The key element in putting together newscasts is the timeliness of the stories. A newscast producer looks at the stories available and often decides which ones to run based on how recent the stories are. Because broadcasting is a medium that can emphasize the immediate, news producers often take advantage of this quality by telling listeners and viewers what happened only minutes before a newscast.

Timeliness is not the only news value used in these decisions. A story that is the most recent one available will not necessarily be the first one used in a newscast. Stories that have more impact or involve more prominent people may take precedence. All of the other news values come into play in putting together a newscast.

Another element that news producers use in deciding what to put into a newscast is the availability of audio tapes, slides, film and videotapes. One of the criticisms of broadcast journalism is that decisions about what to run and what not to run are based on the availability of such aids. It is true that often such decisions are made, but broadcast journalists — especially television journalists — feel that they must take advantage of their medium to show a story rather than just tell it. Pictures compel viewers to watch, and the feeling of many in television is that the "talking head," the news announcer with no visual aid, is not as compelling to the viewer as the "talking head" with a picture or slide.

Time is the pervasive fact in putting together a newscast. Not only must stories be timely in themselves, but they must be written to fill a certain amount of air time. The producer or news director is generally the one who assigns the amount of time for a story to fill. The writer must then write a story which can be read in that time. The producer, of course, must have enough copy to fill up the time allotted for the newscast. Sometimes, however, even with the most careful planning, a newscast producer will come up a few seconds short. The producer should always give the announcer one or two more stories than he or she will need in order to fill this time.

A news director for radio or television has a variety of formats from which to choose in putting together a newscast. The following is a brief description of some of those formats for radio. Generally, each of these formats, except the mini-documentary, runs for less than a minute.

Written copy/voicers. This format is a story without actualities or sound-bites.

Sound bite or actuality. When possible and appropriate, a radio news writer will want to include some sort of sound effects from the event that is covered. This actuality may be someone speaking or it may be some other identifiable sound, such as gunshots or crowd noise, that will give the listeners an added dimension to the story. News anchors introduce the soundbite with the copy they read.

Wrap-around. A news anchor briefly introduces a story and the reporter. The reporter then gives the story and includes a sound-bite. The sound-bite is followed by the reporter giving a conclusion or "tag line."

Mini-documentary. This format allows a story to run for more than a minute, and some run for as much as fifteen minutes. They may include several sound-bites with a variety of sources or sounds, such as interviews, noise from events or even music. A reporter will weave in and out of the mini-documentary, guiding it along for the listener. A news anchor usually introduces a mini-documentary with a short lead-in that sets up what the listener is about to hear. This format is most commonly used on public radio news broadcasts.

Television newscasts can use any of the following formats:

Reader copy. This format is a story read by an anchor or reporter without visual or audio aid. It may have a slide or graphic in the background.

Voice-overs. A videotape of an event is shown with the sound of the event turned down. An anchor or reporter speaks over the

Figure 7-4

Writing for the ear
By Debbie Elliott

Working in radio is unique. You have only one shot at reaching your listener. Print journalism offers the option to refer back, or re-read information that might have been overlooked the first time around. Television can use pictures to get the point across. But in radio, every word has to count the first time. Your writing must be clear and engaging.

The best way to connect with radio listeners is to have a conversation with them. Think about how you might tell a story. For example, explain to your Mom what it was like attending your first college class. Or tell your best friend from home about your first campus party. What kind of language would you use? Would you be formal, or casual? How would you describe the people you met? What would you say about the places you've been? That's the style you should strive for when writing for radio.

Always keep it conversational — using common, easy-to-understand language. Don't speak down from the authoritative "radio tower." And never fall into the trap of using the "lingo" of what you're writing

about. Consider the following two sentences:

The sick smoker sued for a million dollars.

The plaintiff filed a smoking and health claim for a million dollars in compensatory damages.

The first is simple, clear, and to the point. The second is dull, wordy, and could be a major tune-out.

Choose your words carefully. And never use something that you wouldn't say in every-day conversation, even if it does look good on paper. Remember, you're writing for the ear, not the eye.

Debbie Elliott is a reporter with National Public Radio. She covers the Gulf South region and tobacco litigation for NPR News. She's a graduate of the University of Alabama.

tape to talk about what the viewer is seeing.

Voice-over to sound-bite. An anchor or reporter speaks over a videotape that includes someone talking. The news copy is timed so that when the reporter stops, the sound on the tape is turned up and the person on the tape is heard speaking.

Package stories. An anchor, using what is called a "lead-in," introduces a story and the reporter. The pre-recorded piece then includes a mix of video, sound-bites, voice-overs, and a "stand-up" from the reporter who explains some element of the story or summarizes the entire story. These packages may run for as long as two and a half minutes.

Live shots. An anchor will introduce a reporter who is shown live at the scene of some news event. The reporter can then do one of several things: present a simple stand-up, interview someone, introduce and voice-over a videotape, or answer questions from the anchor. Satellite technology now allows even local news departments to use such live shots frequently.

Conclusion

The nature of broadcast news is changing dramatically, and the technology that is developing for broadcasters is placing new demands on broadcast journalists. Computer editing stations — allowing the reporter to do all of the editing of both videotape and copy on a single workstation — will give reporters more direct control in producing their stories. These systems will also allow reporters to call up file footage—videotapes that may have run in previous stories—for use or reference. Those entering the field of broadcast news must be increasingly computer-oriented.

Another development is the increased use of satellite technology to produce live shots from the scene of news events. This means that reporters will be called upon to do more stand-ups and that they must develop the ability to think on their feet, outline stories quickly, and read unobtrusively from their notes. Reporters must understand the forms and formats of broadcast news to be able to put these shots together. Even though it may occur in a different form, the ability to write clearly and concisely will continue to be a must of the broadcast news reporter.

Still another development is the merging of broadcast and print news under a single roof. The Chicago Tribune has a broadcast news studio built into its newsroom; it owns CLTV, a 24-hour news channel that is carried by many Chicago area cable companies, and well as WGN radio and television stations. News reporters for the Tribune often wear two hats. They write their copy for print, and then they do a standup spot for broadcast outlets. The Tribune is one of many newspaper/broadcast combinations that are developing throughout the nation. Increasingly, writers will have to know how to construct news in both print and broadcast form.

All of these characteristics of broadcast writing place a heavy burden on the writer of broadcast copy. Producing such copy is no easy task. The person who can do it consistently and well, however, is likely to have a large audience for his or her work.

Points for consideration and discussion

1. The author begins the chapter by saying that many people believe that the broadcast medium is the most important medium of mass communication. Do you agree or disagree?

2. List the major differences between writing news for broadcast and writing news for print. Which of these differences makes writing for broadcast more difficult than writing for print? Which makes it easier?

3. Take a story from the front page of your local newspaper. Read it through completely. Now list, as briefly as possible, the three major facts of that story. That's the kind of thing a broadcast journalist must do. Try to write a thirty-second story using the three facts that you have listed.

4. Look at the lead paragraph of each of the stories in the figures in this chapter (pages 256 and 262). What devices did the reporters use in writing these leads? Do you consider these leads good ones?

5. Make a list of names of local personalities that might be hard to pronounce for broadcasts. Then write their phonetic spellings.

Further reading

Edward Bliss, Edward, Now the News : The Story of Broadcast Journalism. New York : Columbia University Press, 1991.

Carl Hausman, Crafting News for Electronic Media, Belmont, CA: Wadsworth Publishing Co., 1992

Robert L. Hilliard, Writing for Television, Radio and New Media, 7th ed., Belmont, CA: Wadsworth-Thomson Learning, 2000.

Peter E. Mayeux, Writing for the Broadcast Media, Madison: Brown and Benchmark, 1994.

Marcus D. Rosenbaum and John Dinges (eds.), Sound Reporting: The National Public Radio Guide to Radio Journalism and Production. Dubuque, IA: Kendall-Hunt Publishing Co. 1992.

Frederick Shook, Dan Lattimore and James Redmond, The Broadcast News Process, 6th ed., Englewood, CO: Morton Publishing Co., 2001.

Mitchell Stephens, Broadcast News, 3rd ed., Harcourt Brace Jovanovich, 1993.

On the Web: If you're interested in finding out more about broadcasting, visit the National Association of Broadcasters Website at www.nab.org.

Chapter 7 Writing for broadcast

Exercises

• *The following section contains a variety of broadcast writing exercises. You should follow your instructor's directions in completing them.*

7–1 Writing broadcast stories

Write a 30-second broadcast news story based on the following sets of information.

Wreck

Two trucks collided on I-59 last night

Caused a traffic jam because the road was blocked both ways for about 45 minutes

Fuel from both trucks spilled onto the highway and caused a big oil slick

One truck was refrigerated and most of the contents thawed, causing a loss of an estimated $10,000 worth of goods.

Accident happened on a part of I-59 undergoing repairs, so it was two lanes at that point; the trucks met head on.

Honor society

Alpha Alpha, university honor society, to hold inductions next Friday

5 sophomores, 20 juniors, 10 seniors will be named

names will be kept secret until ceremony

ceremony will be at 10 AM at Student Center

New course

Political science department announces new course, "Communism and Socialism," to begin next semester

Open to juniors and seniors who have had the freshman level beginning political science course

taught by Jerald Wiseman, associate professor

Wiseman: "These two political theories have been major forces in helping develop our 20th century political world."

Poll

Local polling firm, City Research Associates

poll of more than 500 city residents

completed last week

showed 65 percent of citizens "satisfied" or "very satisfied" with the quality of life in the city; showed 75 percent of those with school-age children "satisfied" or "very satisfied" with city school system

poll sponsored by Chamber of Commerce

7–2 Writing broadcast stories

Write a 30-second broadcast news story based on the following sets of information.

Faculty death

Education prof. Elizabeth Billson, dead at age 58

had taught here for 36 years

estimated to have taught 10,000 future teachers during her years

awarded University's "Outstanding Professor" award last year

had suffered from cancer for 10 years

Baseball star

Junior baseball star drafted by St. Louis Cardinals

Willie Ames says he won't turn pro this year but will stay in school

Ames says Mom advised him to stay in school: "She was never able to finish high school. It's important to her for me to get my education. I can play baseball later."

Ames was reportedly offered a signing bonus of $15,000 by the Cardinals

Computer donation

Mike McCracken, president of Computer Corporation of America, headquartered in the city, made this announcement this morning

his company donating 10 computers to local high school; donation worth more than $30,000

Schools Supt. Harvey Butterworth says computers will be used to teach word processing and business programs

computers should be in use by the fall term

Drinking bill

State legislature just finished marathon debate; 30 straight hours in the senate and then 30 hours in the house

bill would raise drinking age in state from 19 to 21

bill passed by house, 55-40, early today; passed by senate, 18-12, yesterday

bill sponsored by local legislator, Representative Tom Hartley

7–3 Writing broadcast stories

Write a 30-second broadcast news story based on the following sets of information.

Water alert

Brownsville, twenty miles south of your city

last week placed on a "water alert" by state health commission because of "parasitic contamination"

alert lifted by commission

Jones Lamson, head of commission, says testing by commission shows the danger has passed. Residents had been boiling their water since the alert began

Theft investigation

Police chief Clayton Wheat, at press conference this morning

talks about department's continuing investigation into auto theft ring

says ring responsible for 200 to 300 auto thefts in city last year

says investigation has been expanded into surrounding counties

says most cars were disassembled and sold for parts

Industry returning

Local group of investors, lead by First Trust Bank president Joe E. Jamison

announcement made this morning

buying abandoned Lochs Papermill plant

investor to team up with Textron Corp. to start a machine tool plant

refurbishing the plant will take about a year

when machine tool plant is opened it will employ about 200 people

Football game

School's football team defeats arch-rival, 2-0

final game of the season

only score, safety, comes with 5 seconds left on the clock

breaks 3-game losing streak

arch-rival unbeaten this season until this game

7–4 Writing broadcast stories

Write a 30-second broadcast story for each of the following sets of information.

FCC official

James Graybeard, congressional liaison for Federal Communication Commission

Speaking to meeting of State Broadcasters, meeting in town today

"We are on a brink of new era in communication...new technology are not all that new–what's different is that costs are lower. Many more people can now use technology because the prices are going down and because equipment is easier to operate. Every day, engineers are making technology more accessible. Direct broadcast satellites (DBS) will soon be available to everyone in the U.S. for the price of a television set."

Car telephones

Survey by local telephone company

Number car telephones in area doubled last year

948 last year; 2110 this year

Survey shows mostly used by businesses for business purposes; personal use of car telephone limited but growing

Homecoming

Pep rally on Friday right before Saturday's homecoming football game

Begins at 7:30 p.m.

Featuring bonfire and music by pep band

For the first time this year a fireworks show, produced by fireworks artist Larry Lain, who designs fireworks for world's fairs

Fireworks to begin about 9 p.m.

Country music songwriter

Bill Gillespie, country music song writer; resident of Nashville; spoke to university music appreciation class today

Told students to "write if you feel like it; don't write if you don't"

Gillespie has written hit songs for Dolly Parton, Buck Owens, Charlie Pride

Most recent hit: "Sell Your Soul to the Devil"

House fire

House valued at $150,783 burned completely this morning

Address: 716 Ruppert Street, in Woodland Lake subdivision

Owner: George Mason, vice president of the First Trust Bank

No one at home at the time of the fire

Three engines fought the fire for more than an hour

Don Kerlinger, photographer for local paper, hurt by falling timbers as he tried to take pictures of the blaze; in satisfactory condition at local hospital with minor burns and bruises

Historic document

Letter signed by Robert E. Lee found by local woman this morning

Mattie Harrington, 718 Donald Avenue

She was going through some papers in a trunk in her attic

Says letter was written to her great-grandfather after the battle of Gettysburg

Says Lee talked about the battle, saying he had made some mistakes during the battle but still expressed optimism about the outcome of the war

Letter dated August 17, 1863

Letter now in the custody of the university history department;

Dr. Robert Weir checking its authenticity

Absence policy

New absence policy being considered by university

More than four absences from class during the semester will result in automatic failing grade

Neil Hendron, president of the Student Government Association, said today the policy is "unreasonable" and "outrageous." "I don't think it can or will be enforced."

Faculty senate last week passed a resolution endorsing the policy.

7–5 Writing a newscast

(handwritten: new page for each story 2 min ve)

(handwritten: What goes first?)

Construct a two-minute newscast based on the following items.

Capsize

A fifteen-foot boat capsized in rough waters off Point Lookout yesterday evening. Two men—Terry Reston, twenty-three, and Will Bendix, twenty-five—were in the boat. The men said offshore winds increased wave heights and capsized their boat. The men were picked up by a Coast Guard boat after an hour in the water. Both were hospitalized for observation, but the hospital lists their condition today as good. The men say they were hunting sharks about 200 yards offshore.

Basketball death

A fifteen-year-old freshman basketball player died this morning during practice at Central High School. The freshman, Todd White, collapsed while running during a practice game. White had not had any known illness, according to trainer Mike Way. White was pronounced dead at Central Valley Memorial Hospital after all efforts to revive him failed. An autopsy will be performed by the county coroner today.

Energy plan

The secretary of the interior announced a new $800 million energy plan while traveling through the western United States on a busy three-day tour. The secretary of the interior announced his plan at a Western Governor's Conference meeting in Salt Lake City. The plan calls for a five-year program to ease strains brought on by strip mining and other energy ventures.

Abuse acquittal

A fourth-grade school teacher in Midville has been acquitted of child abuse for spanking a ten-year-old girl with a wooden paddle after the girl lied about having gum in her mouth. The District Court jury returned a verdict of not guilty after deliberating three hours. Lynda Kristle had been charged with child abuse after parents noted bruises on the child's buttocks.

Hotel opening

The world's largest casino-hotel opened yesterday in Reno, Nev. The MGM Grand is on a 145-acre site and will accommodate more than 1,500 persons. It has nineteen bars. Prices for rooms range from fifty dollars to $250 per day.

7–6 Writing a newscast

Construct a two-minute newscast based on the following items.

Retirement

The speaker of the state House of Representatives, Milton Bradford, has announced that he will not seek re-election. He has served in the state house for twenty-seven years and has been speaker for the past ten years. He is a Democrat from Logansville. He has always been closely aligned with the state's education lobby and has recently worked for substantial pay raises for the state's elementary and secondary school teachers.

New runway

The Airport Authority has announced that a new runway will be built some time next year. The airport now has three runways, and this fourth one will increase the airport's capacity. The new runway is being built to meet increased demands from airlines that want to schedule more flights into the city. The costs of construction for the new runway will be about $3 million, but Sam Peck, chairman of the Airport Authority, says the airport should recover the costs within about three and a half years.

Strike

Machinists Union Local 333 has called for an indefinite walkout of all local members against the city's General Motors plant. The walkout was called because the contract that GM has with the machinists expired last Friday. Since then, workers have been working without a contract, and Barney Olive, president of the union, said this situation cannot continue. "We have bargained in good faith, but we can see no evidence that General Motors is doing the same thing." General Motors spokesmen refused to comment about the walkout but said the plant will maintain its operation. The plant manufactures hubcaps for GM tires.

Concert

The City Community Orchestra and the City Chorus will combine forces this Sunday and present a joint concert which will feature the last movement of Beethoven's Ninth Symphony. Lister Banks and Quenton Hill are leaders of the orchestra and chorus, respectively. Banks said this is the first time the two organizations have performed jointly. In addition to the Beethoven symphony, the chorus will perform works by Bach and the symphony will play works by Brahms. The concert will be at the City Auditorium at 3 p.m. Sunday. Admission is two dollars for adults and a dollar for students.

Custody battle

Bobby Ray Hacks, a native of the city and now a famous songwriter in Nashville, has said he will try to disprove a child-molesting charge and regain custody of his twelve-year-old son. In a Nashville courtroom, Hacks vowed to fight the charges brought against him by his former wife. They were divorced last year. He was convicted of child molesting last week, and his sentence hearing was today.

He received a six-month suspended sentence but was also told that he had to give up custody of his son.

7–7 Writing a newscast

Construct a two-minute newscast using the following information.

Bank robbery

The city hasn't had a bank robbery for six months. That changed this morning when two men, both wearing ski masks, entered the Fidelity Federal Bank, the downtown branch, just after it opened this morning. Police Chief Arthur Shultz said the men must have been waiting for the bank to open. They took $22,000 in cash and an undetermined amount in checks and securities, according to the bank's manager Jack Sherry. The men came into the bank brandishing shotguns, and one of them fired a couple of shots into the air. They made all the people in the bank lie down on the floor except for Sherry. "Fortunately, we hadn't taken all of the money we would have out of the vault, and they seemed interested only in the money they could see." Both men were tall and wearing leather jackets. They ran out of the bank and jumped into a red, four-door Chevrolet with a New York license plate. The county sheriff, Pat Gibson, said that roadblocks have been set up on all main roads leading out of the west of the county. That's all you have right now. A reporter from your station is working on the story.

Donations

The county's United Way drive has been going on for three months. Today it was brought to a close offi-cially by this year's chairman, Sara Morris, a local attorney. She said that a record had been set. The county United Way raised $455,789.03. More than a hundred thousand people contributed. That's a record, too, according to Morris. "We couldn't be happier with the progress that we have made in this year's fund drive. The people of this city and county have responded far beyond our expectations." Last year's drive netted just over $400,000, and the goal this year was $400,000 again. United Way helps various community charitable and service organizations. Morris said the United Way board will meet soon to decide on how the money will be allocated.

Reactions

Don Seigel, the press secretary to the mayor, says that the mayor's office has received "literally hundreds" of phone calls this morning. Most of the people calling are mad because of the increase in property tax the city council voted last night. The council voted to increase property tax 10 percent across the board. That means everyone who owns property in the city will have to pay 10 percent more in taxes. "Actually, a 10 percent increase isn't that much because our property tax base is so low now," Seigel said. Mayor Lyle Fester proposed the tax, and after a heated debate, it passed 5-2. A number of people have called the radio station this morning complaining about the tax. It will go into effect next July 1. One citizen's group, the Taxpayer's Union, has announced that it is planning a recall movement against the mayor because of the part he played in proposing the tax. Seigel says, "We knew people would be upset. It was a tough decision, but it was the right thing to do. Most of this new money will go the the city school system, and they need it bad."

Books gift

Stanley Minion taught journalism at the local university for more than 30 years. He retired last year. Yesterday, the university announced that he had donated his entire collection of books and newspapers to the library. Minion was a noted collector of newspaper front pages, and his collection includes many pre-Revolutionary War newspapers. Quincy Mundt, the university librarian, said he is "thrilled" about the gift. "Dr. Minion has some newspapers that aren't available anywhere else that I know of. His collection is one of the best. We are looking into plans to remodel one floor of the library to house the collection. We would like to make the newspapers available to the public for viewing as well as to researchers." Minion's donation includes more than 7,000 books and 10,301 newspapers. Mundt said the collection is worth at least $133,000.

Traffic lights

A violent rainstorm passed over the city early this morning. It didn't last long, only a few minutes. But lightning struck one of the power company's substations and knocked out the traffic lights on one of the city's busy streets, McTerril Boulevard. Traffic was backed up for several blocks during rush hour, and several accidents were reported. At least three of them were caused by the lights being out, according to the police chief. Your reporter on the scene says traffic delays of up to

forty-five minutes were reported in some areas. "The wet streets from the rainstorm didn't help us any," the police chief said. The power was restored by 8:30.

History of the county

The county historical society has been working on a comprehensive history of the county for several years. This morning, Lila Bancroft, president of the society, announced that the project has been completed and that a history of the county will be published some time early next year. She said many of the members of the society contributed to the work, but the main author was John Widner, a retired history professor at the university and a native of the county. The book will cover county history from the earliest settlers in the 1700s to the present day. "It's going to be a beautiful book–very well written and with lots of illustrations," according to Bancroft. The pre-publication price will be $17.50; after publication, the price will be $25. It will be available in all the local bookstores.

7–8 Writing a newscast

Don't do this

Construct a two-minute newscast using the following information.

Canine pacemaker

Last week, Marie Bruton's dog was sick. This week it's better. In fact, it's up and running around—"chasing the cat," she says. The reason is because the dog has had a pacemaker inserted to keep its heart going. Dr. Charles Eulau, a local vet, did the surgery, and he says it's the first time anything like this has been done in this area. Mrs. Bruton: "Wrangler had been pretty listless. Then last week he just collapsed. I didn't know he had a heart problem until I took him to the vet. Now he's doing fine. I think he knows that something has happened to him—that he's been given a new lease on life." Eulau says he used an old pacemaker provided to him by the local hospital. It cost about $100, and he charged $50 for the operation. Mrs. Bruton is a legal secretary for a local law firm.

Sentencing

A local man has been on trial for several months, accused of poisoning some Halloween candy. His name is Sam Gather. Two days ago a jury convicted him after a week-long trial. His attorney argued that he was insane, but the jury did not accept that defense. Less than an hour ago, Judge Harvey Eagle sentenced him to five years in prison. This was the maximum sentence the judge could give him since he wasn't trying to kill the

children, just make them sick. At least ten children got sick from eating the candy given to them by Gather. He had put some cleaning fluid onto some hard candy, which he then gave to the kids.

Beerless St. Patrick's Day

M.A.D.D. stands for Mothers Against Drunk Driving. This organization is working to get drunken drivers off the road and to strengthen laws against them. It also helps victims and families of victims of drunken-driving accidents. Denise Clearly, president of the local chapter, has announced a "beerless St. Patrick's Day party." The party will be on March 17 at Palisades Park. It will feature a cookout and entertainment by a local bluegrass group, Ham'n Eggs. It will start at 5 p.m., and according to Clearly, "Everybody is invited. We want to show people that they can have fun without having to drink." She said that information about M.A.D.D. will be available at the party, and interested people may join. The annual dues are ten dollars a year.

Stabbing deaths

Frederic Church, a local contractor, and his wife, Sarah, were found in their $300,000 home Sunday, beaten and stabbed to death. Their home is on Lake Smith. Police say they think the couple surprised a burglar because some jewelry and other valuable items were stolen. This morning the police announced that they had arrested and charged a 15-year-old boy with the crimes. They said he is a local youth, but his name is being withheld at this time. His name should be available from the district attorney's office later in the day. The police said he was seen by neighbors leaving the house on Sunday, and they said footprints in the mud outside the house matched a shoe belonging to the boy.

Depositors

Two months ago the Trust National Bank was declared bankrupt by the U.S. government. The bank was a state bank and not federally insured, so a lot of people lost their money. A number of people had their life savings invested in the bank, and they have been wondering about it ever since. Today the state claims board, which handles these kinds of things, announced that the state would provide about $60 million to pay back the investors. This amount of money would mean that investors would get about forty cents back for every dollar they had in the bank. The money would be paid out over a period of three years. The state legislature must still approve the plan.

Resignation

The state treasurer is a man named Manness Manford. He has been state treasurer for twenty years, which means that he has been elected to the post four straight times. Today, at the state capital, Mr. Manford announced that he is leaving office at the end of this month. He had just been re-elected to the position last November. He is leaving to become president of Fidelity National Bank in the capital city. Mr. Manford is from your town and a lot of people there

know him. He is credited with revising the accounting procedures for the state, making it easier for the state legislature to predict the amounts of funding that will be available for the upcoming fiscal years. There have been rumors that he has been ill and not able to do his job. The governor made the following statement: "We believe that Manness Manford has served the state well. He has approached his job with imagination and foresight, and he has made the job of everyone in state government easier. He's my good friend, and I hate to have the state lose his services, but I can understand his desire to go into private business. We all wish him well."

7–9 More broadcast writing

Handwritten note in margin: 2 for each TV & radio

Rewrite into radio and television style these stories from a newspaper. Make a special effort to boil them down into capsule form. Watch for errors in style.

Hurricane

MIAMI, Fla.—Hurricane Nancy lurched toward the United States today after a brief pause last night during which she whipped up 160-mile-an-hour winds and developed into the most intense storm since 1935.

As the huge storm swung into motion, hurricane watchers warned persons in the target area of the possibility of monster tides being pushed ahead of Nancy.

Officials at the National Hurricane Center here said the storm was about 325 miles south of Pensacola, headed for the Florida Panhandle at a speed of twelve mph. At that speed she would strike the mainland tonight.

She was expected to hit the Panhandle with wind speeds of up to 156 mph.

Residents and travelers were told to move from low and exposed places which the up-to-15-foot tides could cut off from escape routes.

"Nancy is now very similar to the 1935 storm," said Dr. Robert H. Simpson, head of the National Hurricane Center. "She has a very large fury concentrated in an exceedingly small area."

Seismography report

WASHINGTON, D.C.—One hundred seismograph stations could keep Russia from violating an atomic test ban and at the same time provide new knowledge of how the earth is put together. This view was expressed by seismologist Frank Press of the California Institute of Technology at the annual meeting of the National Academy of Sciences.

Earth waves generated by quakes or large explosions provide science with a tool for studying the planet's structure from crust to core. Such waves are recorded by seismographs. Dr. Press said a network of 100 special seismograph stations could be established in a country the size of the USSR for less than $10 million and "operated at an annual cost of several million dollars." Such a system would spot any sneak atomic tests and at the same time, by recording earthquakes, provide a scientific bonus which "would justify much of the cost."

Authorities agree that no nation could start undetected tests of large nuclear weapons. But in the absence of a monitoring system small underground shots "present the possibility of evasion," Press said.

Collision prevention

SACRAMENTO—A device that has the capability of preventing in-flight airplane collisions through use of infrared rays has been described to a radio engineers conference here. The gadget, designed and developed by the Aerojet-General Corp. of

Sacramento, uses invisible heat rays received from the oncoming aircraft to trigger an alarm.

Robert G. Richards, operations analyst for Aerojet's Avionics Division, told the Seventh Regional Conference and Trade Show of the Institute of Radio Engineers yesterday that the invisible heat rays are sent out by all engines, motors, electrical apparatus, or anything having a source of heat as part of its makeup.

It took about fourteen years of research to develop the device which, Richards explained, would have provided a warning in the case of the Grand Canyon disaster more than three minutes before the collision.

7–10 Interviewing for broadcast

Highway deaths

The State Department of Transportation today said that the total number of traffic deaths on the state's highways was 120. This is the lowest total in ten years. Your station sends you to do an interview with the State Transportation Commissioner Dick Blocker about why this occurred.

Having the lowest highway death total in ten years is quite an accomplishment.

That's right, it is. I think the people of the state are to be commended for it. I think we must be doing something right.

What do you think we are doing right?

Several things. For one thing, I think people are just being more careful, observing the speed limit, having their cars checked, watching out for hazardous conditions – things like that.

The fifty-five-mile-an-hour speed limit – do you think that's had an effect?

Well, the fifty-five-mile-an-hour speed limit has been in place for more than a decade, so last year's low figure wouldn't necessarily be due to that. You know, it's interesting about the fifty-five limit. It was originally established to conserve fuel, but it's real effect has been to save lives. It's not that everyone is observing the fifty-five limit per se. But I think the fifty-five limit has made people drive more slowly than they would other-

wise. So now, instead of the average speed being seventy-five, it might only be sixty-five—and that's an improvement.

Do you know of any specific reason that the death total should have been so low last year?

We're looking into that. One reason has to be the good weather we had generally last year. Hazardous weather conditions create a lot of accidents, and we didn't have much of that last year. Another reason has to be the tough new car safety inspection law the governor proposed and the legislature passed three years ago. I think that's gotten a lot of cars off the road that might have caused accidents.

Is drinking and driving a problem in the state?

Yes, definitely. Eighty out of the 120 people who were killed in automobile accidents in the state last year were killed in accidents where alcohol was involved. Alcohol is still the major safety problem in this state.

What's being done about that?

As you probably know, the governor has sponsored legislation to increase the penalties for those convicted of drunk driving. We were joined in this by M.A.D.D., Mothers Against Drunk Driving. We have also sponsored legislation that would raise the legal drinking age from nineteen to twenty-one. Unfortunately, neither measure was passed by the legislature this session, but we'll be trying against next session.

7–11 Interviewing for broadcast

Hall of Fame

A local resident, George M. "Bucky" Barnett, has just been elected to Baseball's Hall of Fame. Barnett spent most of his career as a shortstop for the St. Louis Cardinals, from 1933 to 1946. He also played with the Boston Red Sox before he retired in 1949. He then spent twenty years as a coach and minor-league manager and has been living in your city since leaving baseball. Barnett was best known as a fielder. Grantland Rice, the famed sportswriter, once described Barnett as "personified lightning" on the field. In fact, he had the highest fielding percentage of any shortstop, .993 (fielding percentage is the number of chances handled without making an error). He had a lifetime batting average of .310. Your station sends you to interview him.

How did you get interested in baseball?

When I was growing up, you didn't get interested in baseball. Baseball was just there-kind of like milk. I don't guess it ever occurred to most of us not to be interested in baseball.

What's different about kids growing up today? Why aren't they as interested in baseball as your generation seems to have been?

There are a lot of distractions, I think. When I was growing up, baseball was about all you had, and you simply tried to survive the winter waiting for spring training to begin.

Now kids have basketball and football and television to look at if they want to.

I take it you don't think much of football?

I don't have anything against football. It's just that I love baseball so much. Nothing comes as close to being a perfect game as baseball. A good baseball game has lots of little dramas going on on the field at the same time, and it takes a keen, intelligent eye to see just a few of them. I'm sorry that many kids today seem to have adopted another sport. I think they're settling for second best.

What was the greatest thrill of your baseball career?

I think it was when the Cardinals won the World Series from the Boston Red Sox in 1946. The Red Sox had a great team with Ted Williams as their leading hitter. I don't think anything in my playing career gave me so much joy as beating the Red Sox that year.

People have said that you were the greatest fielding shortstop in the history of baseball.

That's flattering, but I'm not sure it's true. The game has produced several great men at short. It's funny because I always thought fielding was the easiest part of the game. It was just a matter of staying alert, knowing the hitters, and moving with the pitch. Usually, I just wound up where the ball was. Hitting was always the hardest part of the game for me – something I really had to work at. I think I was lucky to have such a high hitting percentage.

not this page

8 Writing advertising copy

Introduction

Advertising pervades every part of society. The products we use in our homes, the clothes we wear, the programs we watch on television, the books we read, the places we shop and go for recreation — all of these things are affected by advertising.

Advertising is one of the country's major industries. One estimate put the money spent on advertising in 1999 at $134.3 billion in the United States alone. General Motors, the nation's largest advertiser in 1997, spent $2.9 billion in 1997, while Procter and Gamble, the second largest advertiser, spent $2.6 billion. Major companies routinely spend thousands of dollars on the production of advertisements, and the costs of buying time in the mass media can be astronomical. In late 2000, Toyota launched a $20 million ad campaign to persuade young people to buy its entry-level economy car, the Echo.

Charges for network television advertising time can also boggle the mind. In 1983, thirty seconds of air time during the Super Bowl cost $330,000. For the 1993 Super Bowl, those charges had risen to nearly $900,000. One of the most watched programs in television history, the final episode of "MASH" in the spring of 1983, cost advertisers about $450,000 for thirty seconds of air time.

But those costs pale in the light of more modern figures. During the 2000 season, thirty seconds on NBC's top-rate ER series was $620,000, and thirty seconds on Friends cost $540,000. An average thirty-second prime-time television announcement costs more than $200,000 to produce. The cost of thirty seconds of advertising on the Super Bowl in 200 had soared past $1.5 million.

People who spend that much money obviously expect a return, and they often get it. Most companies recognize the need to advertise and the benefits of doing so, and they are willing to pay a price for it. Because advertising is so costly, however, there is little room for error or waste. This chapter discusses the writing of advertising copy, but the writing of the ad is only a part of the marketing strategy of a company. Writers of advertising copy must have more on their minds than how the ad will look and what the ad will say.

A love-hate relationship

Americans have a love-hate relationship with advertising. Many people claim that they never pay attention to advertising. They say they leave the room when a commercial comes on television, and they never read the ads in newspapers or magazines. They never click on banner ads on web sites. Many will tell you they never make consumer decisions based on the ads — as if admitting to that would mean something is wrong with them.

More sophisticated critics of advertisements put them down as insulting and degrading. They criticize ads for creating desires and needs that are wasteful and unhealthy. Advertisers, they believe, use false, misleading, or deceptive measures to foist products on an unsuspecting public. Advertisers, critics say, pollute the public's mind and its environment with their messages.

Figure 8-1

Information advertising

Many advertisements merely try to get information about products and services to potential customers.

If all you got at Lanier's this week was a bag full of apples, it would be a bargain.

But don't stop there.

Pears	$.35/lb	Grapes	$.59/lb
Eggs	$1.50/doz	Pecan	$1.10/lb
Bananas	$.15/lb	Oranges (navel)	$.25/each
Lettuce	$.75/head	Apples (gold. delicious)	$.45/lb

Lanier's Produce, 108 South Main, 689-1112

Despite these criticisms, advertising is one of the vital links in the modern economic chain. It is a major way of getting information to a consumer — information that a consumer often wants and needs. For example, a billboard near an interstate highway telling the location of a gas station may be an eyesore to some, but to the driver who is low on gas, it provides a vital piece of information.

Those who say that they never pay attention to advertising are not being honest. To live in today's society means receiving the messages of advertisers. There are few places people can go where advertising will not reach them. Even the "non-commercial" public broadcasting system contains advertisements in the form of credits to those who contribute to its programming and promotional spots for upcoming shows. One estimate has the individual consumer confronted with 1,600 advertising messages every day.

Not only do people pay attention to advertising messages, but they often act according to those messages. Advertising works. Check around any room in your house, and you will find plenty of items purchased, in part at least, because of the advertising you have encountered.

The field of advertising

The person who wants to enter the field of advertising has chosen an exciting and challenging profession. Advertising copywriters must be willing to work long and difficult hours researching their products and audiences and straining their creative forces to be successful. Like other writers for the mass media, they must understand the language and be willing caretakers of it. They must be willing to change their creativity into forms that others are willing to pay for and support. The rewards to the few who are able to do well in this profession are great.

Two concepts should form the base of a student's thinking about writing advertising copy.

Advertising copy is a different form of writing than the ones that we have studied in other parts of this book. Its purpose is to persuade and motivate. The basic precepts of good writing — simplicity, brevity, accuracy, word precision — remain in force with writing advertising copy as they do with all other forms of writing.

Advertising is based on the assumption that words have the power to produce a change — a change in thinking, attitudes, beliefs, and ultimately, behavior. Advertising that does not accomplish this, or aid in accomplishing it, is worthless. Copywriters must select the words and ideas that will help produce this change.

The process of advertising copywriting is in many ways the same as the process of news writing. The copywriter must process information and put it into an acceptable form for its medium. Like the newswriter, the advertising copywriter must conduct research before the writing begins. He or she must decide what is important enough to use and what should be left out. The copywriter must choose the words and the structure for the copy that will best fit the product, media, and purpose for the advertising. The copywriter, like the newswriter, is subject to many editors — not the least of whom is the client who is paying for the advertising and whose ideas about advertising copy may differ radically from those of the copywriter.

But what about the creative process? Doesn't advertising copy require more creativity on the part of the writer than newswriting? In some respects, it does. Ad copywriters have a greater variety of forms for their work than do newswriters, and they have more tools with which to work.

Those entering the field of advertising make a serious mistake, however, if they believe that because advertising requires creativity, they have complete license to write what they want when they want. A prime example of what many would consider a lack of creativity is found in the advertising for many Proctor and Gamble products — household items such as Tide and toothpaste such as Crest. Advertisements for these products rarely win awards given to the more "creative" or attention-getting ads for the competition. Yet many of these products, backed by a large advertising budget, take a lion's share of their market, and Proctor and Gamble remains one of the biggest spenders in the advertising industry. The evidence at the cash register is that the ads for these products work, despite their lack of creativity. That is the kind of evidence that a client wants.

On the other hand, highly innovative approaches for ads are often effective, especially when products have established and well-rooted competition and when the purpose of the ad is to gain the consumer's attention. Possibly the leading proponent of the off-the-wall approach is Joe Sedelmaier of Sedelmaier Productions in Chicago. In 1984, Sedelmaier created an ad for Wendy's fast food chain that had an elderly lady in front of a fast food counter (at the competition's store, not Wendy's) shouting, "Where's the beef?!" That cry was taken up by a presidential candidate that year and became part of the national lexicon. More importantly for Wendy's and Sedelmaier, revenues for the fast food chain jumped 31 percent, net income went up 24 percent, and average sales per restaurant rose 13 percent from the previous year. Much of the credit for these increases was given to Sedelmaier's off-beat approach — one that he has repeated for clients such as Federal Express and General Motors Acceptance Corp.

Sedelmaier demands total creative control as a condition for taking on a client. His agency is one of the few that can do that. Most clients, whether they are spending a large or small amount of money on the advertising, want a say in the final production of the ad. A copywriter must take copy through a variety of approval stages, a process that demands a great deal of research and discipline. The creative process is a part of the process of producing copy, but it is only a part, and sometimes only a small part, of it.

Beginning the process: needs and appeals

The process of writing advertising copy begins with a recognition on the part of the copywriter that all humans have certain needs and desires. Effective advertising appeals to these needs and desires in a way that will make people act positively toward a product or an idea. We live in a consumer-oriented society where the list of needs and desires is a fairly long one. The first step in producing advertising copy is to examine some of the needs and desires of humans in a very general way.

Food and drink. The need for food and drink is among the most basic and universal needs that we have. We must have food and water daily to sustain ourselves. Beyond that, we want food and drink that is nourishing and palatable.

Shelter, security and comfort. Next to food and drink, one of our most basic needs is for shelter. We need a way of protecting ourselves from the elements.

Following closely on to the need for shelter is the need for security, the need to feel that we are protected from various dangers. Rational people understand that they cannot insulate themselves from every danger, but they can take some steps to ensure that they are not victims of certain calamities.

Once shelter and security are established, people want to feel comfortable. Physically, they want to be without pain, they want to be warm when it is cold and cool when it is hot. They want to live, work, and play in a comfortable and pleasing environment.

Sex, intimacy and social contact. Most people need to have contact with other people. That contact can take various forms in various stages of our lives. Our social relationships are important to us, no matter what form they take. They can be based on sexual intimacy, friendship, or casual contact. Whatever they are, we remain social beings, and lack of such contact can have physical as well as emotional consequences.

Independence, privacy, self-fulfillment and power. While we need social contact, we also have a countervailing need for independence and privacy. We need privacy even from those to whom we feel the closest. We have the urge to "get away from it all," and occasionally we do that, even if that means we simply draw inward rather than removing ourselves physically.

Related to this need is that for independence. Although we are social beings, we are also individuals, and we need to feel that we can develop our own personalities. This need for individual development continues through adulthood and governs many of our actions. We are all different from one another, and we need to confirm that to ourselves.

Independence is part of a greater need for self-fulfillment, much of which is met often by occupation. We need to be engaged in constructive activity that will give us satisfaction and confirm our worth as individuals. For many, the highest fulfillment of this need lies in the work we choose as adults.

At its best, the need for power means that we are able to make our own decisions and in some way control our own environments. Some child psychologists argue this need is one of the most important that children have. At a very early age, children need to be able to make choices — even if they are very small ones — so that they can develop their individuality. Adults also need to feel that they are in control of their lives and their surroundings. This need, of course, can develop into a need to control the lives of others. Many of us have this tendency to some degree, and our places in society may dictate that we exercise this power. Parents, particularly, feel the need to control the environment and actions of their children.

Stimulation. The need to be stimulated — to find life interesting — is one of the most important that we have. Despite the habits and routines that people have for themselves, they need to feel that life holds a variety of experiences. They read books, watch television, go to parties, shop, and engage in a many other activities in part to entertain themselves. Occasionally, they need to be excited, to have the feeling that something is going to offer them special enjoyment or a unique feeling.

Acquisition. The number and variety of goods and services that are available to those in Western industrial societies in particular would boggle the minds of people in other cultures and from other centuries. The availability of those goods and services has stimulated within many a need to acquire things. Part of our development as individuals is the acquisition of goods that go beyond basic needs of food, clothing, and shelter.

On occasion the need overcomes common sense and the bounds of rationality. For instance, news reports coming from the Philippines in 1985 said that Imelda Marcos, wife of the deposed dictator of that country, had a closet full of shoes — more than 3,000 pairs. Her shoe collection became one of the standing jokes of the year, and she became a symbol of a consumer who was beyond conspicuous. What possible use, many wondered, could she have had for so many shoes?

Yet there is some of Imelda Marcos in many of us. Many people acquire things for the sake of acquiring them, not because they are useful or because we need them for basic purposes. Children "collect" things like dolls, baseball cards, rocks, etc., and that collecting syndrome carries over into adulthood.

The foregoing list contains just a few of the needs that we all have. There are many others. The consideration of needs is one of the most important parts of the process of developing effective advertising copy. To understand that people need, or feel they need, certain things is vital to formulating the appeals that advertising can use.

Appeals are the words, phrases, and ideas used by advertising copywriters to tap into the needs of the audience. It is in formulating these appeals that copywriters must choose their language carefully. They must understand that certain words, even those that may have similar meanings, can evoke strikingly different images. The copywriter must have a highly developed ear for the language to couple with an understanding of the needs of the audience.

Just what needs are most salient to an audience? The next section discusses how marketers find this out.

The audience

Most manufacturers and advertisers want to sell as many units of their product as possible. They recognize, however, that most products are not universal; that is, not everyone will want what they sell. In addition, distributing a product to a massive audience can be costly. Consequently, it is not efficient to try to sell most products to everyone. Marketing a product or service begins with deciding what part of the population is most likely to buy it.

Figure 8-2

Needs and appeals

What need is this ad addressing? What kind of appeal is it making? How effective do you think it is?

Ready for a little peace and quiet?

You're ready for Ticonderoga County.

In Ticonderoga County, you can walk in the woods. Think. Breath. Discover places you thought were lost forever.

TICONDEROGA COUNTY VISITORS BUREAU
IT'S NOT FAR — ONLY ABOUT A MILLION MILES

In considering the audience for a product, advertisers need to think about two groups. One is the people who are already using the product. They cannot be taken for granted. Many advertisements are directed at reinforcing the behavior of people who have already bought a product. (For instance, readers of car advertisements in magazines are often those who have already bought the car; they are simply trying to reinforce their belief that they made the correct decision.) Advertisers need to have some idea of how strong a user's loyalty is to a product.

The second group is people who do not use the product but are most likely to. These potential users provide the greatest opportunity for product sales to grow. Finding out who they are and what kind of advertising message is most likely to motivate them is the job of market research, and the answers have a direct effect on the advertising copywriter.

How does an advertiser get this information? Researchers can employ a variety of methods for this purpose. They may include personal interview surveys, telephone surveys, mail surveys, focus-group interviews, consumer product testing, intercept interviewing (the kind of interviewing conducted by people in shopping malls), and many other methods. The data produced by this research are vital to the advertising copywriter.

The major concept that the beginning advertising copywriter must understand is that of demographics. Demographics is a way of dividing the population into groups. People who share many of the same demographic characteristics are likely to share many consumer behaviors. In the 1980s, the term "yuppie" was coined to describe an important segment of the population. A yuppie is a young, upwardly mobile professional. Later there was Generation X, members of whom were thought to share attitudes and behavior. After that came Generation Y. In politics we have had "angry white males" and "soccer moms." All of these categories have particular demographic characteristics, and they provide researchers with a way of looking at different segments of the population.

There are many demographic categories. The following section discusses some of the most basic demographic characteristics.

Age. How old people are is one of the most common determinants of how likely they are to use many products and services. Our needs and desires change as we get older, and often they change in the same way for most of us. Most children want toys, but as they get older, the desire for toys decreases and the desire for other products increases. The changes that accompany age are not only physical but also psychological and emotional.

Gender. Boys and girls are different; men and women are different. These differences are of primary importance to the advertiser. These groups have different needs and desires, due not only to different physical characteristics but also to differing roles they are likely to play in society. For instance, within a household, a man is more likely to earn more money, but a woman is more likely to make most of the household buying decisions.

Income. How much money people have to spend is important in determining how likely they are to buy a product. Some products and services are marketed to people who do not have as much income as others, and the appeal the advertisers use is often based on price. This kind of appeal is likely to motivate potential customers. On the other hand, many producers want to direct their advertising toward an "upscale" audience, those who have high incomes or whose incomes are likely to increase.

Education. Education is an important demographic variable for two reasons. One is based on the assumption that education changes people; it changes their attitudes and values. For instance, the more education people have, the more likely they are to place a value on getting an education. The second is that education is often related to the demographic characteristic of income. The more education a person has, the more likely that person is to have a higher income.

Marital status. If a person is married, that means he or she is in a household. That inevitably leads to different consumer behavior than if that person were single. Knowing whether or not a person is married is important for the advertiser because of the different appeals that may be used to sell a product.

There are many other demographic characteristics that advertisers may need to consider in finding the consumers for their products. For instance, race, home ownership, number of adults and children in a household, occupation, place of residence, and type of housing are just a few of the many variables that can be examined by researchers.

As a step in developing an advertisement, an advertiser might want to draw a demographic profile of those who use the product already or those who are potential users. For instance, a manufacturer might find that those who have used the product are women between the ages of eighteen and thirty, single, with at least a high school education. Chances are that not all consumers who fit this profile are buying the product, so advertising directed at this group might not only persuade others to buy it but also reinforce those who already do. On the other hand, an advertiser may decide that the product could be marketed to older women as well as to those already likely to buy it. In that case, the advertiser might use a different appeal — one that would work for women thirty — one to forty years old.

In addition to these demographic factors, advertisers must also take into account psychographic variables. In general, psychographic variables refer to the values and attitudes of people and how they feel toward various things in their environment. Market researchers want to know what people feel is important and valuable. If people use a product, they want to know how they feel about that product and if they are likely to use it again.

As you can tell, making decisions based on just this small amount of information is not a simple task. An advertiser may take a variety of routes in marketing a product. Good research is essential to making the correct decisions about marketing and advertising. But the audience is only one factor to be considered in trying to sell a product; of equal importance is the product itself.

The product

Along with knowing who the audience is for a product, the advertising copywriter must know the product itself. To say this is to state the obvious, but knowledge of the product — particularly from the standpoint of developing advertising for it — is not as simple as it might first seem. (Note here that when we talk about a product, we are speaking of anything the advertising is designed to promote. It could be a product, such as a vacuum cleaner, a business, such as an auto body repair shop, or an idea, such as quitting smoking.)

The advertising copywriter must ask, "What is it about this

Figure 8-3

Demographics

This advertisement is appealing to an audience with a specific set of demographics. What do you think they are?

The man who has everything.

He may want something else this Father's Day.

He's busy and successful and maddening. He never gives you a clue about what he wants. Surprise him this Father's Day with a Martin fountain pen. Simple. Elegant. A beauty he'll use every day. And think about you while he's doing it.

Martin Fountain Pens

Starting at $60.
At fine stores everywhere

---

product that I am trying to sell?" The answer may come from a close examination of the product, and it may be surprising.

First, the copywriter should know what the product does. A vacuum cleaner may clean a floor, but how it cleans the floor may be important to the advertising of the product. Does it introduce some new cleaning method, something that no other vacuum cleaner on the market does? A line of sofas may come in fifteen different patterns; it may also be comfortable to sit on. Which one does the copywriter emphasize? A copywriter may find that there are a number of advertisable facts about any product, and some-one — the copywriter, the advertiser or a combination of them — will have to decide what it is about the product that will be adver-tised.

The physical characteristics of the product also provide the copywriter with some useful considerations in developing the advertising. Sometimes a product will be designed to do a job more efficiently than competing products. Sometimes it will be designed to do a part of a job. Small, hand-held vacuum cleaners are vacuum cleaners, but they're not meant to vacuum an entire house, or even an entire room. They're for small jobs that need to be done quickly. The physical characteristics of the product help promote the feeling that the product can do the job.

Sometimes the physical characteristics of a product can have little to do with how the product works, but they can still be use-ful in helping to sell the product. When the Macintosh computer was introduced by the Apple Computer Company in 1984 (with an engrossing surreal commercial aired only once, during the Super Bowl that year), one of the characteristics that helped set the Macintosh apart from other computers was its unique, small, box-like design. That design helped establish the Macintosh as "the computer for the rest of us," as its advertising slogan said. One of the most legendary campaigns in the history of advertis-ing, the 1960s promotion of the Volkswagen Beetle, also used the car's unique shape to distinguish it from other cars. Some of the ads even poked some good-natured fun at the car in order to establish this difference in the minds of the consumers.

The history and reputation of a product are characteristics that also need consideration when formulating advertising. A product may have a long history, and that may be something that a copywriter will want to emphasize. Many businesses use the phrase, "Established in —— (year)" to let people know that they have been around for a long time and thus can be considered reli-able and stable. If a product has existed only a short time but has gained a good reputation, the advertisement may reflect that rep-utation.

Sometimes an advertising campaign will be designed to over-come the history or reputation of a product. It could be that the product has not worked particularly well, and a manufacturer has taken steps to correct that. Or, it may be that manufacturers want to sell the product to a different audience. One classic case of this redefinition of a product was done by Miller Brewing Company. For many years, its main product had been known as the "Champagne of Bottled Beers." The slogan had little appeal for the Sunday afternoon, football-watching crowd, who were mostly men. When Miller began making a low calorie beer, Miller Light, the company sponsored a series of commercials that had ex-athletes arguing as to whether the product "tastes great" or was "less filling." The commercials were good entertainment in themselves, but they also established Miller Light as a beer that could be enjoyed while watching a football game.

Another classic advertising campaign that reestablished a product was the one the Chicago-based advertising agency Leo Burnett developed for Marlboro cigarettes. Marlboro had been a red-filtered cigarette when filtered cigarettes were thought to be products for women. Marlboro also had the slogan "mild as the month of May." Burnett developed a series of ads that put the cigarette in the hands of men and put those men outdoors. Eventually, the Marlboro Man, a rugged outdoorsman (usually a cowboy with a horse), became a staple of the advertising industry. The campaign was so successful that the Marlboro Man is still with us today, more than thirty years after he was created.

The manufacturer of a product is another characteristic about a product that an advertising copywriter may want to give attention to. Many products are indistinguishable from their competition, but if the manufacturer is well-known and has a reputation for reliability and stability, that can help set the product apart. International Business Machines (IBM) has a reputation for servicing its products, and that has established for IBM a broader reputation for reliability. IBM often uses this reputation in advertising its individual products. More recently IBM advertising has tried to build on this reputation by emphasizing its ability to find innovative solutions to computing problems.

Many advertising and marketing campaigns emphasize the brand name of a product. This emphasis occurs for a number of reasons. Consumers often exercise what is called "brand loyalty". Having made a decision to buy a product at some point, many people are reluctant to change. A brand may also be positively associated with other products that carry the name. Nabisco, for example, appears on a number of crackers and cookies because of the strong brand identification that name has. Such identification makes a product, especially a new one, easier to sell.

One of the most important product characteristics is price. People want to know how much something costs. They also want to believe that they are getting the best product for the money they spend. Sometimes, price is the most notable factor about a product, and it will be the characteristic the copywriter will want to feature.

Another factor copywriters will want to consider is the competition that a product has. Much of what we have already said has made reference to a product's competition and the means by which advertising can distinguish it from others like it. Rarely is a product the only one of its kind. It may have some distinguishing characteristics, but there are usually other items that will accomplish the same task. One of the copywriter's main jobs is to set a product apart from its competition.

The list of product characteristics just discussed is only an indication of the many variables that may be considered in developing advertising for a product. The key here is that the copywriter should know as much about the product as possible so that the best characteristics may be selected for the advertising.

In advertising terms, this process is called finding the Unique Selling Proposition (USP). A product's USP will give potential consumers their first clue as to why they should want to buy that product. Once a USP has been identified, the selling process has begun.

Finally, advertisers must recognize the social aspects of their advertising, that is how their products and advertising fit into society and whether or not the approaches they use are appropriate. For example, many women feel that much of the advertising for and about them is degrading. One watchdog group, Women Against Pornography, annually gives awards to advertisers who use non-sexist approaches in their advertising, and at the same time the group criticizes advertisers who, according to the group, degrade women. In 1983, the group criticized the Hanes company for the way it implied in its hosiery ads that men preferred women with "shapely, sexy, silky legs."

More recently, the British auto maker Austin Rover received many complaints about an ad that focused on the walnut interior of one of its models and quoted an old English saying, "A woman, a dog, a walnut tree, the more you beat them, the better they'll be." The makers of Opium and Obsession perfumes have also been criticized by those who believe that the names of these products and their advertising glamorizes degrading conditions within society.

The Center for Science in the Public Interest has criticized the alcoholic beverage industry for ads which it said were aimed at starting young people to drink and at inducing alcoholics to return to the bottle. Ethnic minorities are often sensitive to the way in which they are portrayed, and advertisers are wise to be aware of their concerns.

This is not to say that advertising should always avoid controversy and that advertisers should construct ads so bland that absolutely no one will be offended. Controversy might well be an advisable marketing strategy, as when Burger King directly criticized McDonald's in one of its advertising campaigns. The point here is that advertisers should never be surprised at the effects of their ads. They should know what society, or groups in society, expect of them, and they should have thought through their advertising campaigns well enough so that the ads produce the intended results.

The advertising situation

The marketing environment is an important consideration in the development of an ad. This environment is created by the audience and product — factors which have already been discussed — but also by the more immediate situation surrounding the advertisement. We are at the point where the copywriter is beginning to make decisions that will determine the content of the ad.

First, ad writers must know and be able to state the key fact about an advertising situation. This key fact sets the stage for the thinking about an ad, and writers who do not have a key fact clearly in mind will be confused and prone to wander in several directions. The key fact may involve the competition: A new product may have entered the market two years ago and now accounts for more than fifty percent of the sales in the market. The key fact may involve the audience: Few people know about the product. The key fact could involve the product itself: Some improvements have been made in the product. Discovering this key fact is sometimes difficult and time consuming. It often takes extensive research and discussion with the manufacturers. But being able to write down the key fact of the situation orders the thinking of the advertiser and helps to produce effective ads more efficiently.

Distilling the key fact of the advertising situation leads directly to the next step in the process of ad development: stating the problem that the ad should solve. The problem statement should be a specific one and should evolve from the key fact. For example, the key fact may be: A product's percentage of the market is down. The problem then would be: The product's share of the market needs to be raised. Problems may also involve the product itself: The product has a bad reputation; or the product costs more than its competitors.

If the key fact and the problem of the advertising situation are clear in an advertising copywriter's mind, the third step in the process should follow: the objective of the advertisement. The objective needs to be stated clearly and precisely. Just what is the advertisement supposed to do? The following are some statements of advertising objectives: the ad should make people aware of the product; the ad should change people's attitudes toward the product; the ad should tell consumers of the product's improvements; the ad should encourage people to shift from buying another product to buying this product.

Once an advertiser has thought through to this point — and assuming that the proper amount of research has been done — the next step is to develop a copy platform.

Copy platforms

A copy platform is a way of getting the ideas and information of an advertising situation down on paper and of organizing those ideas in such a way that effective advertising copy can be produced from them. A copy platform is not an ad itself, but it will contain many of the ideas that will later appear in the ad, and it will provide valuable information for the ad copywriter. One version of a copy platform is on page 306 in this book, but it is not the only type of copy platform. Copy platforms vary according to the advertising agency and the advertiser, but most contain the same basic information.

The copy platform is where many of the factors in developing an ad begin to come together. The copywriter must finally commit what he or she has learned about a product and about an audience to paper and develop ideas from the information that is there. The example of the copy platform in this chapter shows some of the elements that make up the platform. Note that the advertising problem is the first piece of information that is called for in the copy platform. Stating this problem directly and simply sets the stage for many of the other ideas that will appear on the copy platform. A problem may be encountering a number of different advertising situations, but generally the copywriter will zero in on just one — the one that the advertiser considers the most important. The product characteristics are those that might be helpful in formulating the ad. This list cannot be all-inclusive; the copywriter will have to limit the list to those items that relate directly to the advertising problem and items that might otherwise make the product distinctive and beneficial to the consumer.

The advertising objective is then drawn directly from the advertising problem. The objective should be a way of solving the problem.

Figure 8-4

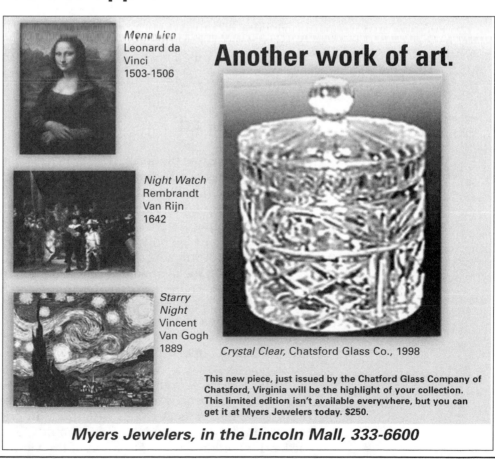

Needs and appeals

Look at this ad and see if you can figure out what the advertising situation is and what problem needs to be solved.

Mona Lisa Leonard da Vinci 1503-1506

Night Watch Rembrandt Van Rijn 1642

Starry Night Vincent Van Gogh 1889

Another work of art.

Crystal Clear, Chatsford Glass Co., 1998

This new piece, just issued by the Chatford Glass Company of Chatsford, Virginia will be the highlight of your collection. This limited edition isn't available everywhere, but you can get it at Myers Jewelers today. $250.

Myers Jewelers, in the Lincoln Mall, 333-6600

The target market is the audience to whom the advertising will be directed. A description of this audience should be stated as simply and specifically as possible. Knowing exactly who the audience is will help the copywriter in coming up with the next, and most important, part of the copy platform — the statement of benefit and appeal.

Advertising should tell its audience the benefit of a product, the "what's in it for me." The advertising should state, implicitly or explicitly, why the product or service is good for the consumer, why the consumer should buy it, or what the consumer can expect from it. This statement of benefit and appeal is the most persuasive part of an advertisement, and its importance cannot be overestimated. Here are a few examples:

You'll save money if you buy our product.
You'll be safer if you use our product.
You'll live in more comfort if you have our product.

These benefits relate directly to the discussion of needs and wants at the beginning of this chapter. Such appeals are highly potent ones for advertising, and they have been highly effective in many advertising campaigns.

The creative theme in a copy platform allows the copywriter to use some imagination in formulating the appeals of the advertising. The creative theme might be a slogan, or it might be a description of the way in which the advertising will be presented.

Supportive selling points is a list of product characteristics or factors about the advertising situation that will help sell a product. They may vary somewhat from the main statement of benefit, but they can be used to reinforce a tendency to use the product.

Writing the ad

With the copy platform in place, the copywriter is almost ready to write an ad. Among the decisions that still need to be made are which medium the advertisements will appear in, how many ads there will be for a product, when they will be placed, how large or long the ads will be, etc. All of these are marketing decisions that go beyond the scope of this book. Our focus here is the writing of the advertisement.

This section looks at some of the common ad writing practices and guidelines. There are few rules in the writing of an advertisement, and there are no dominant structures for ads as there are for news stories and for broadcast news. Instead, each ad is a combination of the factors already discussed in this chapter, plus the limits and opportunities provided by the medium in which the ad is placed.

Still, there are some things that we can say generally about the writing of advertisements. One of the oldest advertising copywriting formulas is A-I-D-A: attention, interest, desire, action. According to this formula, an ad should do four things, in this order. It should gain the attention of the viewer or listener. An ad that doesn't do at least this is not going to be able to do anything else.

After getting the consumer's attention, the ad must hold his or her interest. The ad should use words and pictures that will draw the reader or listener into the ideas that the ad is trying to present. An ad may be about an interesting or important subject, but it can be so dull that the consumer is lost before the message gets across.

The ad should create a desire for the product, service, or idea presented in the ad. It is important for the copywriter to choose the appeal, the benefits, and the proper words that will develop this desire.

Finally, the ad should stimulate the consumer to some action. In most cases, what you want the consumer to do is go out and buy the product.

With this formula in mind, we will look at some of the commonly accepted guidelines for writing effective advertisements.

Use clear, simple English. This rule reappears throughout this book. It is basic to communication in the mass media. Obscure words and complex sentences will not encourage people to read an advertisement. You cannot impress someone with your wide vocabulary in an advertisement.

Another reason for using simple language, particularly in advertising, is that it is more believable. People will tend to believe advertising messages that are presented to them in language they use or are used to hearing.

Pay attention to the verbs. Verbs are the most important part of the language. If your ad has mostly "to be" verb forms (is, are, was, were, etc.), the ad will probably sound flat and lifeless. If it contains mostly action verbs, it will be alive and interesting.

Good copywriters use verbs, rather than adjectives, to describe their product. They associate verbs with how the product looks, what it does, and how it makes the user feel. A list of those verbs helps them develop good advertising copy.

Another rule about the verbs in advertising copy is to stick with the present tense (whenever appropriate) and the active voice (almost always). The present tense implies immediacy and puts the reader into an advertisement more quickly. The active voice allows the writer to make a stronger statement than the passive voice.

Be as specific as possible, but don't let too many details get in the way of the advertising message. An advertisement should be balanced. Facts — specifics — are more likely to sell a product than general ideas or concepts. Yet too many facts are likely to confuse the reader or listener. Consumers like to have reasons to buy a product, and an ad should give them enough of those reasons that they will be motivated to do so.

Be precise in the use of the language. Here's where intelligence, art, and creativity mix together for the copywriter. The copywriter needs to know the language intimately. He or she should be sensitive to the subtle meanings of words—not just their dictionary meanings but the images they provoke.

For example, the words "laugh," "giggle," and "guffaw" have essentially the same meaning, but they provoke different images. Most of us laugh; little boys and girls giggle; old men don't usually giggle but guffaw; and so on. Writers need to understand the subtle differences between words and to take unusual care with them. They need to select the words for their copy that evoke exactly the images that they want to convey; that will describe the product in exactly the way they mean for it to be described. You should select the words that relate directly to the benefit you are presenting with the product.

Use personal pronouns when appropriate. Let the reader, listener, or viewer of an advertisement know that you are talking directly to him or her. Using personal pronouns, especially "you," is an effective way to do that, but like any good idea, it can be overdone. Occasionally, you should ask a question (although only occasionally; we'll discuss this more in the next section).

Don't be afraid of contractions. Contractions are a good way of making sure that your tone is informal, and the informal tone is preferable in most advertisements. Like personal pronouns, they can be used too much, particularly if they sound forced. A copywriter should develop an "ear" for the language and recognize when a piece of copy "sounds" right or wrong. If a contraction sounds right, use it.

Inspire confidence in the product and the advertiser. Ads should contain messages that will help people believe and trust a product. They should not sacrifice a long-range trust for a short-term goal. They should, however, tell an audience that the product being advertised is one that will benefit them and will live up to expectations. Not only should the messages in an ad inspire such confidence, but the ad itself should contribute toward this goal. Ads that are in good taste, use English properly, are not cutesy or smart-alecky, and do not insult the audience are the kinds of ads that build confidence. A manufacturer should be as proud of the ads commissioned for a product as of the product itself. Advertisement writers should feel that same pride in what they produce.

Give the audience all the information it needs. An ad does not have to tell everything about a product or a manufacturer, but it should not leave hanging any major questions about the product or service being advertised. For example, a power company recently advertised that energy audits were available to its customers. These audits involved representatives of the power company coming to the home, inspecting it, and recommending actions to increase the efficient use of energy. The service was free. What the ad did not say was how a customer could get this service: Whom should the customer call or write; what was the procedure? The ad left the clear impression that the power company was not very interested in having customers take advantage of this service.

Elements of a print ad

Unlike the newspaper reporter, who generally does not have anything to do with the physical appearance of a story in the newspaper, an advertising copywriter must always be aware of the design of an ad. Design is an integral part of the ad writing process, and it often is a determining factor in what the ad says. In this section we will discuss the different parts of a print ad, keeping in mind that, depending on the work situation, it may or may not be the copywriter's job to design the ad as well as write the copy.

Illustration. The illustration an ad uses is often the most important attention-getting item in that ad. It is the part of an ad most likely to achieve the attention-getting part of the A-I-D-A formula. While we are not concerned here with the design of the ad or the selection of the illustration, the copywriter will often write the copy based on the kind of illustration that is used. The illustration, the headline and the body copy — the three most important parts of the ad — must be closely tied to one another. If the relationship between these three elements is not readily apparent, the ad runs the risk of losing the reader who will not want to figure it out.

Headline. After the image, the headline is often the most important part of an ad because it gives the reader the first solid information about the product. The headline will most often achieve the "interest" part of the A-I-D-A formula and will determine whether or not the reader's interest is aroused enough to read the rest of the ad.

The most effective headlines appeal to the self-interest of the reader — the "what's in it for me?" The copywriter must decide what appeal is being made and what benefit is being offered.

The headline should consist of just a few carefully chosen words (many ad writers say the limit is eight words) that will set the tone for the ad and implicitly promise some reward to the reader for reading through the ad. Many advertising copywriters believe that headlines in ads should be treated much like headlines for news stories in newspapers. That is, they should give the reader some information that the reader does not already have. Although this is not the only approach to writing headlines in ads, it is a useful one for many ads.

A headline may deliver a promise about a product. It might challenge an assumption on the part of the reader. It might make a claim about a product. It may play on the reputation of the advertiser. It may simply try to provoke a mood for the reader.

Above all, headlines should involve the reader in the ad quickly. They may do this by asking a question ("When will you get an opportunity like this again?"), offering some information ("How to

Figure 8-5

Copy platforms

The copy platform to the right shows how such a platform should be put together and how it can help the advertising copywriter begin to think about creating the advertisement.

Copy Platform

Ad subject: Blackoak Classic Sports Cars
Ad problem: This specialty car dealership needs to become better known by its target market

Product characteristics:
• dealership is the only one of its kind in the area
• it carries a wide variety of models, such as early Datsuns, Triumphs, Jaguars, Porches, MGs, VWs
• dealership has cars that are fully restored and ready to drive off the lot and cars that are restoration projects
• many of these cars are very reasonably priced; quite a number are less than $10,000 and some are less than $5,000

Advertising objective: Let the target market know that there is an alternative to newer, more expensive sports cars.

Target market: Men, ages 35-55; these are people who have established themselves in their professions; they want something that is fun to drive and that is an inexpensive alternative to the new sports cars on the market

Competition: Mazda and other dealerships that handle new sports cars

Statement of benefit or appeal:
• classic sports cars are fun to drive
• they help drivers re-capture the feeling of when they were young and when driving was fun

Creative theme:
Get the feeling back

Supportive selling points:
• dealership has a good reputation among classic car owners
• it carries many types of cars
• it has a good repairs, parts and replacement service

save money"), or making a provocative statement ("Not all men are created equal").

Finally, caution should be exercised when writing headlines. Some headlines are clearly misleading and inappropriate, and an advertiser uses these at his or her peril. Misleading or deceptive headlines can get an advertiser into legal trouble, and inappropriate headlines can destroy the advertiser's credibility with the reader.

Subheads. Subheads allow the copywriter an opportunity to expand on what has been said in the main headline. They also allow the writer to introduce new material that may draw the reader into an ad. Subheads are set in a smaller size of type than the main headline, and they are generally longer. Most often, the thoughts presented in a subhead are tied to those presented in the main headline. For instance, if the main headline poses a question, the subhead may answer it, as in the following example:

```
IS NOW THE TIME TO BUY A NEW CAR?
  Most experts agree that it is.
```

Not every advertisement needs a subhead. They are not attention-getting devices; rather, they are informational devices, and they should be used only when necessary and appropriate.

Body copy. The body copy is the heart of the advertisement. If the art and headline get the attention of the reader, the body copy is where the reader should be rewarded for taking the time to read the ad. That reward should come in the form of information about the product being advertised and answers to questions raised explicitly and implicitly in the headline.

Writing body copy can take a number of approaches. The factual approach is a direct one. Essentially, it says: Here is some information about the product; here is why you should buy it. The narrative approach is a less direct one. It generally tells a story about the product, emphasizing the selling points of the product. The narrative approach is used when the ad needs to hold the attention of the reader. The stories or situations used in a narrative approach should be projective. That is, they should be situations that the readers can relate to or imagine themselves in.

The rules for writing body copy are the same as those for writing in any part of the mass media — simplicity, brevity, word precision, etc. Ad copywriters take special care with the verbs they use and think of them as the chief descriptors of a product.

Avoid mistakes in grammar. Mistakes call attention to the writing and not to the message. Sentence fragments — one or two words or short phrases that do not make complete sentences — can be acceptable, but they must be deliberate, and the writer should exercise complete control of the language.

Avoid exaggeration. Saying that something is the "greatest in the world" or even "the cheapest in town" is not likely to help sell a product. Readers are more likely to want facts and specifics.

The writer should have a simple message in mind, and everything in the body copy should relate to that message.

Tell the reader what you want him or her to do — "Call today," "Go out and buy it," or "Clip this coupon." Whatever the action is, do not assume that the reader will know it without being told.

Above all, the copy should be interesting or even compelling.

Closings. Closings may be thought of as subheads that come after body copy rather than before it. A closing will make a strong point for the reader. Often it will summarize what the body copy has been implying. Sometimes, it will give a direct command to the reader; at other times, it will only suggest that the reader do something. Like the subhead, a closing may not be necessary for every advertisement.

Mandatories, including legals. Mandatories are items that must be included in the advertisement. For instance, an advertiser may want an ad to mention the name of the company president or that a product is manufactured in a certain area. The words, "an equal opportunity employer," are a mandatory for the employment ads of many organizations.

Legals are items that are required by law to be in an ad. For instance, all cigarette ads must give the Surgeon General's warning; all automobile ads must include the mileage ratings. The Federal Trade Commission and other federal agencies, such as the Food and Drug Administration, have issued many regulations about the content of advertisements. These regulations often require that certain things be in an advertisement. A professional copywriter must be familiar with these regulations if the ads he or she writes are to remain legal.

Slogans, logos, signatures. These items may be included in an ad, although they are necessary in every advertisement. Slogans are short phrases that become identified with products. A slogan should be short, easily understood, and appropriate to the product. Sometimes, whole advertising campaigns are built around slogans, such as Coca-Cola's slogan, "The Real Thing," or that of McDonald's, "You deserve a break today."

A logo is a design that represents a company. The Volkswagen logo, for instance, is a "v" sitting in the middle of a "w," all of which is in a circle. Volkswagen has been using this logo for years. It has become a symbol of the company. Advertisers will want to use well-designed logos in their ads because of the distinctiveness they add to the advertisement. Signatures generally refer to the name and address of the company, which are often necessary or useful in an ad.

Writing advertising for broadcast

Much of the advertising that we pay the most attention to comes from the broadcast media — television and radio. Broadcasting has advantages over print in being able to deliver a message with immediacy and impact. It can bring a product to life and show it in action. But broadcast advertising is expensive to produce and air, especially on television. And broadcast advertising gets only one chance at a time with the listener or viewer. If the message is not delivered immediately, the consumer cannot turn back the page and listen to it again.

Whereas print ads are space oriented, broadcast ads are time oriented. Broadcast ads should be simple. They should be designed to achieve maximum impact in a short amount of time. In addition, copywriters should write for the ear. The visual and oral messages should complement one another. They should key in on the sounds, words, and pictures that will help sell the product.

The copywriter for broadcast advertising has certain tools available, and it would be useful to take a brief look at what they are and how they can be used.

Voices. The most commonly used tool of the broadcast advertiser is the voice. Talking is the most direct and effective form of communication for broadcasting and the easiest to produce. Most of what the advertising copywriter will write for broadcast advertising is a script for what people will say. To write conversational language, however, is neither easy nor simple. It takes practice and much writing and rewriting. The script must be suitable for the voice that is using it as well as the other elements of the ad.

Figure 8-6

Ads without dominant illustration

How effective is this layout for an advertisement for newspaper subscribers? Do you think this is a good use of an illustration?

There's good news, and there's bad news.

Then there's the news.

HARRISON DAILY BANNER

Every day.

Subscribe by call 403-8228

Figure 8-7

The ad in print

T he ad below shows how the copy on the copy sheet on page 306 is translated into a print ad.

Copy Sheet

Product: Blackoak Classic Sports Cars
Medium: Newspaper
Client: Blackoak Classic Sports Cars
Writer: Smith

Headline: No car phones allowed

Subhead:

Body copy:

Remember when a car was something you drove, not an office you rode around in.
Remember the thrill of acceleration, going from second to third, feeling the thrust of a powerful engine.

If you still remember, we've got the cars to make those feelings come alive again.

Subhead or slogan:
Get that feeling back

Signature:
Blackoak Classic Sports Cars, 1818 Blackoak Drive, 555-6666

Sound effects. Like voices, sounds can be a very effective means of communication. Sound effects are often vital to radio ads. Car engines, crowds cheering, quiet walks in the woods, children laughing—all of these sounds can take listeners to the scene of an advertisement. They evoke pictures and images inside the heads of the listeners. They can "demonstrate" the way a product looks or works.

Music. As with sound effects, music can provide the proper background for a commercial, or it can be the main part of the commercial's message. Selecting the proper music for a commercial's background is an important consideration for the producers of an advertisement. The haunting music of Vangelis (part of which was used in the score for the movie Chariots of Fire) was one of the most memorable parts of the famous Ernest and Julio Gallo "Wedding" commercial. The commercial needed only the music, the superb photography, and the tagline, "All the best a wine can be" to get its message across.

In the days when radio was the dominant broadcast medium, the jingle — the one-or two-line musical message about a product—was one of the most popular advertising technique. The jingle is still popular for radio but has also become a staple of the television commercial. In fact, the simple one- or two-line jingle has developed in a number of ways. Some advertisers have produced orchestra-score songs to promote their products, and Coca-Cola's "I'd Like to Teach the World to Sing" became a popular hit when it was recorded and sold to the public.

Pictures. Pictures are not available for radio, of course, but they constitute one of the major advantages of television. Not only can television show pictures, but a well-produced advertisement can direct the eye to exactly the images that it wants the audience to see.

Pictures bring a commercial to life. They can show real people talking to one another and doing real things. While most people realize that commercials are most often dramatic presentations (not pictures of real life), they still have a believability about them that makes people accept them and consider the messages they have to send.

Visual effects. Graphics and special effects have always been a part of television and have proven themselves to be a useful tool in the production of television advertising. Today their value has been enhanced because the computer hardware and software to create complex and eye-popping graphics are readily available and easy to use.

While broadcast commercials can vary widely in approach, there are two basic formats that can be used: dramatic formats and announcer formats. Dramatic formats emphasize the action on the screen or within the script. One of the best and oldest ways to make a point is to tell a story. Radio and television commercials are often small dramas packed into just a few seconds. They may also be just a set of scenes and sounds that lead to a point about a product. While they may use announcers, the announcer plays only a partial role in the ad. There are four types of dramatic formats:

Problem-resolution. Presenting a problem and then resolving it is one of the most common ways of selling a product. The outline for a problem-resolution commercial is a simple one. For instance, a person has a headache; he takes a brand of aspirin; he no longer has a headache. The problem-resolution technique is popular with advertisers because it can make a strong point in a short amount of time.

Whatever the problem is, the commercial is structured so that its solution is directly attributed to the product. You can think of the problem-resolution commercial as a "before" and "after" structure: *Before* using the product, we had this problem; *after* using it, we no longer have the problem.

One of the secrets of the problem-resolution commercial's success is the speed at which a problem can be established. A copywriter can waste no time in letting the audience know what the problem is. Usually, that is done with the very first words and pictures. The idea of the problem has to be clear and simple: The people in the commercial are hungry; or they're uncomfortable; or they're looking for something; and so on. The product then comes to their rescue just as quickly. All this is done usually within the space of thirty seconds, sometimes even fifteen seconds.

Slice of life. Normally, the slice-of-life-commercial shows people doing things in which the advertised product is involved. These may be mini-dramas with a problem and resolution that have little to do with the the product itself, but they show the product in a very good light. Or they may be sketches that revolve around the product. For example, a popular commercial for Coca-Cola shows a baseball team on a bus after a game that the team won; the team is hot and thirsty, and the bus stops at a small diner; the team descends on the diner, and everyone who works at the diner must work harder; finally, the team quenches its thirst with Coca-Cola, and one of the team members gives his baseball cap to one of the waitresses right before the team leaves.

In a similar type of commercial, a father drives his pre-teen daughter and her friends to McDonald's, where they may run into some boys they have been discussing. When they get to McDonald's, the father gets out, and his daughter, horrified, says, "You're not going in, are you?" The father waits in the car, realizing that his daughter is growing up. He takes comfort in eating some McDonald's french fries.

Slice-of-life commercials must be entertaining, but more importantly, they need to identify the product with a situation or feeling that is familiar and comfortable. They try to demonstrate that the product is part of the life that the people on the screen are living, and it should also be part of the viewer's life.

Documentary/demonstration. These kinds of commercials use fewer dramatic techniques than others. They may simply show how a product works (for example, how a fabric cleaner

Provoking action

This ad seeks to deliver a great deal of information and have the consumer act on it. Notice that the phone number appears twice in the ad.

Peperino's Pizza

THE BEST THERE IS

A WEEK OF BARGAINS

Free delivery
428 15th Street
70-PIZZA

Monday Madness	**Two for Tuesday**	**Wild Wednesday**	**Thirsty Thursday**
Beat the clock The time you call is what you pay 5 to 8 p.m.	2 large 1 topping **$11.00**	Large for the price of a small All Day and All Night	1 Large 1 Topping & 2 cans of Coke **$8.00**
Fantastic Friday	**Super Saturday**	**Sunday Savings**	**Peperino's Pizza**
Build your own pizza 1 large up to 5 toppings **$10.99**	Perfect Party Pak 3 Large 1 topping **$19.99**	Take advantage of any Week of Bargains except Monday Madness	*THE BEST THERE IS* Free delivery 428 15th Street 70-PIZZA

"lifts out" the stain from a sweater). They may demonstrate how a product works in comparison to its competition. They put a product in an unusual situation to demonstrate something about the product (such as Timex watch's slogan, "It takes a licking and keeps on ticking," or Master Lock's demonstration of the durability of its lock by firing a rifle bullet into one of them). Occasionally, a commercial will present the way a product is made in order to demonstrate something about the product.

Figure 8-9

Television script sheets

An idea for a television may get its first incarnation as a simple television script sheet such as the one shown here. Later it may become a storyboard. (See page 316.)

Television script sheet

Product: Blackoak Classic Sports Cars
Client: Blackoak Classic Sports Cars
Title: No car phones allowed
Writer: Smith
Length: 30 seconds

[handwritten: past this homework]

Video	Audio
Frame time 5 seconds	SDX: car engine, traveling down the highway
Frame time 5 seconds	Remember when driving was fun. Remember when you could step on the accelerator and feel the engine respond. Remember the power of shifting from second to --
Frame time 3 seconds	SDX: car phone rings.
Frame time 7 seconds	Hello. . . Yes, I remember the meeting. I'll be there in a few minutes (voice fades)
Frame time 5 seconds	At Blackoak Classic Sports Cars, we don't install car phones. We want you to remember when driving was fun.
Frame time 5 seconds	Blackoak Classic Sports Cars, 1818 Blackoak Drive. SDX: car engine up.

Fantasy. Putting people and products in unreal or abnormal situations is another way of making a point about a product. Fantasy also includes the use of animation, such as in commercials for Keebler cookies or Jolly Green Giant products, and special camera techniques, such as dancing cats and talking dogs.

Fantasy characters are not always without controversy. During a mid-1980s campaign, Energizer used a fuzzy, pink bunny beating a small drum to say that its batteries lasted longer than those of the competition. One member of the competition, the Eveready Battery Company, took exception to this message and brought out an ad featuring a garish, hot-pink bunny with sunglasses pounding a bass drum. "For years, one of our com-

Figure 8-10

Radio script sheets

This radio script sheet shows the details that should be specified so that a radio ad can be reduced.

Radio script sheet

Product: Blackoak Classic Sports Cars
Client: Blackoak Classic Sports Cars
Title: No car phones allowed
Writer: Smith
Length: 30 seconds

Source	Audio
	SDX: car engine, traveling down the highway (3 seconds)
ANNC #1	Remember when driving was fun. Remember when you could step on the accelerator and feel the engine respond. Remember the power of shifting from second to --
	SDX: car phone rings.
ANNC #2	Hello. . . Yes, I remember the meeting. I'll be there in a few minutes (voice fades)
ANNC #1	At Blackoak Classic Sports Cars, we don't install car phones. We want you to remember when driving was fun.
	Blackoak Classic Sports Cars, 1818 Blackoak Drive.
	SDX: car engine up.

petitors has been telling you they have the longest lasting battery. But they haven't invited us to the party," the voice-over announcer says. The Energizer bunny has proved to be remarkably long lasting as an advertising character. Several years after it originated, its new tactic was to interrupt fake commercials with the tag line, "Just keeps on going."

Dramatic presentations have either no announcer at all or an announcer who plays only a minor part in the commercial. Announcer formats are those in which the announcer is the main character, or one of the main characters, in the commercial.

Figure 8-11

Television storyboard

Not all radio ads can or should be translated into television advertisements, but occasionally that can happen. This is the television storyboard version of the radio ad on the previous page and the script sheet on page 314.

Television storyboard

Product: Blackoak Classic Sports Cars
Client: Blackoak Classic Sports Cars
Title: No car phones allowed
Writer: Smith
Length: 30 seconds

Video		Audio
Frame time 5 seconds		SDX: car engine, traveling down the highway
Frame time 5 seconds		Remember when driving was fun. Remember when you could step on the accelerator and feel the engine respond. Remember the power of shifting from second to --
Frame time 3 seconds		SDX: car phone rings.
Frame time 7 seconds		Hello. . . Yes, I remember the meeting. I'll be there in a few minutes (voice fades)
Frame time 5 seconds		At Blackoak Classic Sports Cars, we don't install car phones. We want you to remember when driving was fun.
Frame time 5 seconds		Blackoak Classic Sports Cars, 1818 Blackoak Drive.

SDX: car engine up. |

There are two types of announcer formats: the spokesperson and the anonymous announcer.

The spokesperson. The spokesperson is another popular format for broadcast commercials. Spokespersons may range from celebrities to unknown but real people to actors. They may or may not be experts on the product they are advertising. The Federal Trade Commission has a wide variety of rules governing the use of spokespersons in advertisements. In general, celebrities who endorse products have some responsibility for the claims that are made about the products; people who are identified as "real people" or "typical users" in advertisements must be who the ads says they are; actors may play the part of "real people" or "typical users" as long as they are not identified otherwise. In other words, if a commercial identifies a speaker as "Joe Smith of Hoboken, New Jersey," that speaker must be Joe Smith of Hoboken, New Jersey.

Famous people (usually actors but not always) can become spokespersons and even symbols for the manufacturers that hire them for their products. Actors Cliff Robertson and James Garner have become identified with ATT and the beef industry, respectively, because of their appearance in commercials. Jesse White was for two decades the Maytag repairman, "the loneliest guy in the world." The advertising industry took special note when Maytag announced in 1989 that Gordon Jump, a star of the "WKRP" comedy series, would replace White in this role.

Sports figures are especially popular with major advertisers as spokespersons. Michael Jordon's remarkable basketball career made him one of the highest paid ad spokesperson in history. Tiger Woods is another sports figure who stands to make far more from his endorsements than from his sports career.

Testimonial. Closely associated with the use of the spokesperson is the testimonial commercial. The testimonial differs from the spokesperson commercial because of the credibility of the person doing the testimonial. In the testimonial, the person in the commercial is saying, in effect, "I have some expertise about this product, and I think it's the best there is." Sports figures are often asked to endorse sporting goods products because it is believed that they have high credibility in this area. In some cases, their endorsements have gone as far as allowing their names to be placed on the product itself, such as with Michael Jordon's line of sports shoes.

Anonymous announcers. In the anonymous announcer format, the announcer does not appear and is not identified but is only heard. This format is popular with advertisers who want to direct all the attention of the audience to the product itself. The attributes of the product, not the spokesperson, are emphasized.

Sometimes "anonymous" announcers may not be so anonymous. A number of people have such distinctive and widely recognizable voices that viewers of a commercial will know who is speaking even when they are not identified. Burgess Meredith's voice has become closely identified with Honda cars, and Jimmy Stewart has done the voice-over parts for Campbell Soup commercials. This technique of having a recognizable voice in a commercial can heighten the interest in a product without distracting from the message of the commercial.

Students should recognize that many commercials do not fall strictly within the categories just outlined. They are often combinations of two or more of the types of commercials. They use techniques from a number of sources to help sell their products. On the other hand, you should remember that the most common characteristic of a television ad is its simplicity of structure. The time constraints of a television commercial demand that you get the message across to the viewer simply and quickly.

One of the most useful tools that writers of television commercials have is the television storyboard. The storyboard allows a writer to begin visualizing the commercial as it is being written. It uses a series of scenes from the commercial along with the words to give the writer an idea of how the commercial will look when it is produced. An example of a television storyboard can be found on page 316.

Storyboards are useful in other ways. Besides helping the writer visualize the commercial, a storyboard can give a client an idea of what a commercial will be like before any expensive production work has begun. It can also give the producer and director of the commercial insights into what the writer has in mind for the commercial.

No one has to be a good or clever artist to use a storyboard. The most basic drawings of commercial scenes, even using stick figures if necessary, will be sufficient for transmitting the visual ideas in a commercial.

Other media

Three other types of media should be mentioned briefly as part of our overall discussion of advertising. They are point-of-purchase advertising, outdoor advertising, and direct mail. These are important forms of advertising, particularly in supporting advertising campaigns that are carried on in other media. Because they involve many decisions beyond those of the copywriter, however, they are discussed only briefly here.

Point-of-purchase advertising refers to the packaging and display of a product. One study by the Point-of-Purchase Advertising Institute indicated that as many as two-thirds of buying decisions are made after the customer has entered the store. All other advertising is useless unless a product can be found. That means that it must be well packaged and well displayed. It must stand out from other products–particularly the competition, which is likely to be displayed beside it on the store shelves.

Point-of-purchase's effectiveness can be found in the history of one product — Hershey's candy bars. For decades, Hershey's declined to advertise in any media except its own packaging. Its market strategy was known as mass availability. That is, the company tried to place its product at as many locations as it could. That strategy worked, and Hershey's products became some of the most popular in its area. It has only been in recent years that the company has produced mass media advertising.

Outdoor advertising is a multi-million-dollar business. In 1991 advertisers spent about $684 million on this medium. In May 1992 McDonald's bought 20,000 outdoor boards all across the country. Because the messages on almost all types of outdoor advertising must be brief, this medium is also used to supplement advertising campaigns in other media. One of the chief assets of outdoor advertising is its repetitive nature. A person may pass by a poster or billboard many times, and yet the advertiser has made only one advertising purchase.

Finally, **direct mail advertising** offers an advertiser many possibilities and advantages. Direct mail includes a variety of marketing techniques, including sales letters, post cards, pamphlets, and brochures and catalogues. Direct mail allows advertisers to target a very specific audience and to get a message to that audience very quickly. It can carry a great deal of information. One of the problems with direct mail is that it can be very expensive. It can, however, give an advertiser some fairly precise information about how well an advertising campaign has worked.

Conclusion

Writing advertising copy calls for a high degree of intelligence, hard work, creativity, and competitiveness on the part of the writer. It is not a job that everyone can do, but it is one that has great rewards for those who are successful.

Points for consideration and discussion

1. The text lists some major demographic characteristics that advertisers want to know. Can you think of other demographic variables that would be important to advertisers? What would make these important in selling a product?

2. Think of a member of your family. What needs are most important to that person? What advertising appeals would work best to sell a person that product?

3. Take an ad from a magazine. To what audience, in terms of demographic variables, is that ad targeted? What appeals does the ad use?

4. The text says that ads should tell people what they should do (for example, "Go out and buy one today.") Find an ad that does not do this and then find one that does. Which do you think is more effective?

5. Select an ad that you think is a good one from a magazine. List the verbs that are used in the ad. Does this tell you anything about how the ad was written?

6. What characteristics does advertising copy writing have in common with news writing? How are they different?

Further reading

Peter B. Turk, Arnold M. Barban, and Donald W. Jugenheimer, Advertising Media Sourcebook, 4th ed., Lincolnwood, Ill., USA : NTC Business Books, 1997.

Arnold M. Barban, Steven M. Cristol, and Frank J. Kopec. Essentials of Media Planning : A Marketing Viewpoint, 3rd ed. Lincolnwood, Ill., USA : NTC Business Books, 1993.

Philip Ward Burton, Advertising copywriting, 7th ed. Lincolnwood, Ill. : NTC Business Books, 1999.

On the Web: Those interested in finding more out about advertising should visit the following sites: Advertising Age, www.adage.com; and Advertising Media Internet Center, www.amic.com.

Chapter 8   Writing advertising copy
Exercises

• *The following section contains a variety of advertising situations for students to use to practice advertising copy writing. The advertising copy sheets contained in Appendix E may be used for these exercises.*

8–1 Print advertising critique sheet

Answer the questions below about a print advertisement.

Name:_____

Advertisement: _____

1) What is the promise of benefit offered by this headline?

2) How does the illustration demonstrate the product? How does this illustration attract attention?

3) What proofs of the promise of benefit in the headline are offered by the body copy?

4) What action does this ad tell readers to take?

8–2 Radio advertising critique sheet

Answer the questions below about a radio advertisement.

Name: _____

Advertisement: _____

1) What sound effects are used to define location?

2) What sound effects are used to define action?

3) Was the announcer over used?

4) Give two examples of how dialog is used to let the listener know what actions are hapening.

5) What is the target market of the ad?

6) What benefits are offered by the ad?

7) Is there a call to action in the ad?

8–3 Television advertising critique sheet

Answer the questions below about a television advertisement.

Name: _____

Advertisement: _____

1) What visual effects are used to define location?

2) What sound effects are used to define action?

3) What type of format is used?

4) Write a brief (three or four sentences at most) synopsis of the ad.

5) What is the target market of the ad?

6) What benefits are offered by the ad?

7) Is there a call to action in the ad?

[Handwritten annotations in left margin: "split screen", "All caps", "think about appeals/product format", "30 sec = 65 words"]

[Handwritten circled "1" above each column heading]

8–4 Writing advertising copy
[handwritten: "for TV"]

Car repair shop

Wright's Auto Repair, located at 126 Wesley, is the oldest car repair shop in town. It has operated continuously from the same location since 1923. In fact, that makes it one of the oldest businesses in town.

At least, that's what it wants to be known for. Hank Wright, the current proprietor, has just taken over as manager of Wright's from his dad. It was Hank Wright's grandfather who began the business in 1923.

Hank wants a set of advertisements that emphasize the reliability of the work he does. He wants to appeal particularly to those people who have used other repair shops—especially those who use the shops at dealerships where they bought their cars and those who have been dissatisfied with them. Hank says his shop offers not only a guarantee on the work, but also a guarantee on when the work will be finished. If the shop cannot meet that deadline, it will provide a loaner car to the customer, if needed. The shop takes care of all types of car work, from car maintenance (changing oil and filters) to engine and brake repair. They also have a specialist trained to repair car radios and sound systems.

Suggested assignment: Write the copy for three ads. The body copy in each should be from fifty to seventy-five words long. You may want to use the layout sheet for this assignment in Appendix D.

8–5 Writing advertising copy
[handwritten: "for TV"]

College promotion

Pick a slogan or theme for an image advertising campaign for your college or university (example: It's a great place to learn.) and write 200 words of copy for three ads centered around that theme. You will also need to write a four- to ten-word headline for each of the ads.

[Handwritten: "SF State 30 sec = 65 words. Must have slogan"]

8–6 Develop an advertising strategy

CREATIVE WORK PLAN

• Cowabunga Cream Bars

Key fact: Cowabunga Cream Bars are made with all-natural ingredients and packaged using 100% recyclable materials.

Advertising problem: Many people feel that pure ice cream is not healthy, and are switching to yogurts and low calorie products instead.

CREATIVE STRATEGY

Principal competition: Cowabunga Cream Bars are new to the market, but will be priced and marketed similarly with Haagen Daas products. Haagen Daas is the current leading brand among gourmet ice creams.

Customer profile: Men and women age 28-35, with total household income of $50,000 or more. Usually with families.

Customer Benefit: Cowabunga Cream Bars come in seven flavors and are easy to eat, with no messy scooping involved — plus, their packaging is environmentally safe.

Reason why: The makers of Cowabunga Cream Bars care about the environment as well as making the best-tasting ice cream available.

Tone and manner: Advertising messages should be lively and upbeat with humor involved.

Mandatories: Do not mention competitor by name. Do no attack competitor's product. All advertising should use the tag line: "Mooove closer to udder perfection."

Cowabunga Cream Bars come in the following flavors: chocolate, vanilla, banana, coconut, strawberry, boysenberry, and peach.

8–7 Develop a product marketing scheme

- Sponsor: Kraft Foods
- Product: SodaBurst

THE PRODUCT

SodaBurst is an instant ice cream soda consisting of a single unit made of ice cream, syrup, and frozen carbonated water fused together and packaged in a "miniature" cylindrical ice cream container of aluminum foil. The ice cream soda is prepared by slipping the single unit (ice cream, syrup, and frozen carbonated water) from its cylindrical container into a large glass and adding tap water. On contact with the tap water, the frozen carbonated water is released and mixes with the syrup. After one minute of stirring, the soda is ready to serve.

At this time, the product is available in two flavors - chocolate (vanilla ice cream with chocolate syrup) and strawberry (vanilla ice cream with strawberry syrup.) The product will be sold from ice cream cabinets in retail outlets, and must be kept in the freezer section of the home refrigerator until ready for use. SodaBurst will be sold in a 4-soda size carton at a suggested retail price of $2.00. (A package design firm is now completing work on the carton.)

MARKETING RESEARCH

Research conducted in the course of SodaBurst's early product testing indicated that about 70% of adults and 80% of teens and children drink sodas. Research also revealed that on a year-round basis housewives reported their own consumption of ice cream sodas at two per month; other family adults at two per month; children at age 5-11 at three per month; and teens age 12-17 at four per month. No research indicated that a specific socio-geographic area purchased more than any other.

Early exploratory research indicated that housewives did not see the product as a substitute for fountain ice cream sodas, particularly for themselves, because it could not furnish the highly valued "going-out" experience associated with consuming fountain sodas. Rather they saw the product as a family snack, competing with the whole spectrum of at-home snacks from traditional snack foods such as peanuts or corn chips to newly introduced, non-traditional snack foods such as beef jerky. (SodaBurst would be entering a very large and highly competitive category)

In response to questions about what specific things they liked about SodaBurst, housewives, after the home-use test, cited four major areas, flavor/taste, convenience, ease of preparation, and packaging/storage. Exploratory research had also revealed that ice cream sodas, in contrast to many other snack foods, are regarded as wholesome, and SodaBurst was seen by the majority of respondents as "wholesome" and/or "nutritious."

TEST MARKETING PLANS

Because it appears that all family members would be prospects, it has been decided that spending levels will be substantial (at least on a $5 million national level) and varied media will be employed in a mix emphasizing television.

The creative message must be distinctive to "break through" the saturation of the snack product market. After extensive discussions, the following message strategy statement was agreed upon between client and agency:

Advertising copy will be directed to an all-family audience, with particular emphasis on housewives in homes with children aged 5-17.

Copy will be designed to appeal to consumers in all geographic areas and among all socioeconomic groups.

The principal objective of the advertising will be to announce that all the familiar taste enjoyment of an ice cream soda is now quickly and conveniently available at home with SodaBurst.

A secondary objective will be the connivance housewives of the product's quality/wholesomeness that makes it suitable for all-family consumption.

The copy will dramatize the interest and excitement inherent in the totally new product concept represented by SodaBurst.

8–8 Developing print advertisements

Local flower shop

Pearsall Florist Shop, the manager says, "wants to put a flower in every business in town at least once a week." She wants to promote the idea that fresh flowers enliven a business and make both customers and employees feel better about that business. The advertising will be pitched to downtown area businesses where the flower shop is located. (It's at 222 Main Street, and the telephone number is 643-ROSE.) For businesses that order one bouquet of flowers each week for a month, there will be a 20 percent discount. Because the shop is located in the downtown area, it can offer quick delivery to businesses in the area. In fact, they guarantee delivery within two hours of getting a telephone order. The manager says the florists at the shop are experts in designing "specialty bouquets" for special occasions or locations and that they can design something that is appropriate for any business.

Suggested assignment: Design a series of four ads to run in the local newspaper in four succeeding weeks. Each ad should carry the same slogan but have a different headline and body copy. Each block of body copy should be about 50 words long. You may want to keep the same design and illustration for the ads, or you can change things around.

You may use the layout sheet for this assignment in Appendix D.

8–9 Writing advertising copy

Wedding dresses

A local wedding shop wants to run a series of ads in April and May with the idea that it has "the best prices in town" on wedding dresses and accessories. Wedding dress prices begin at $250, and bridesmaids dresses begin at $150. The shop has lots of sizes and colors, and it also carries many accessories for weddings such as veils, ring pillows, etc. The store, the Bride's Boutique, is going to remain open extra hours during these two months for its sale. It will be open until 9 every night and Sunday from 1–5 p.m. One of the owners says she especially wants the ads to mention that brides who have looked everywhere else in town and haven't found what they wanted should come to the Bride's Boutique. They'll probably find something they like.

Suggested assignment: Write four ads which include a headline, sub-head, and 75 words of copy.

8–10 Preparing print advertisements

- Sponsor: Marriot Foods
- Product: The Cardinal Club

THE PRODUCT

The Cardinal Club, located on the first floor of the College Center, is a fast service food cafe. Customers can eat in the dining area or take the food with them.

The cafe is open from 11:30 a.m. to 1 a.m. Monday through Thursday with weekend service. Friday 11:30 a.m. to 2 a.m., Saturday Noon to 2 am, and Sunday Noon to 1 am

Lunches available: Fast foods from the grill. Deep fried specialties: Mozzarella Sticks, Mushrooms, and Onion Rings in addition to French Fries. Soup (changes daily)

Sandwiches: Turkey croissants, ham salad, tuna salad or egg salad croissants.

Garden salads and cottage cheese

Drinks: Coca-Cola products, coffee, tea, milk, Fruit juices.

Specials: Wild Pizza. Hand made crust and sauce. Fresh grilled sausage and meats. Call in number for delivery from 6pm to 1am daily: 1588.

Dole Whip. A frozen fruit drink. Available in a variety of flavors.

The staff made up of students from the college are well known and liked on campus. This personal touch makes for a fun to meet place with the type of foods that are in demand by the students.

Entertainment features of the Cardinal Club include: a big-screen TV, Pool tables, video games.

MARKETING RESEARCH

Research conducted indicated that about 80% of students (but fewer than 40% of faculty and staff have eaten at the Cardinal Club) due to the popularity of the main dining area. Research also revealed that on a year-round basis students tend to use the Cardinal Club more in the winter time than in the fall and spring. Students were likely to use the Club if they did not have a class near lunch time. No research indicated that a specific dormitory purchased more than any other.

Early exploratory research indicated that students see the Cardinal Club as a substitute for the dining hall, particularly for themselves, because it could furnish the highly valued "going-out" experience associated restaurants.

In response to questions about what specific things they liked about The Cardinal Club, students cited four major areas: flavor/taste, convenience, to meet with friends, and pizza.

The creative message must be distinctive to "break through" the saturation of the food vending market. After extensive discussions, the following message strategy statement was agreed upon between client and agency:

Advertising copy will be directed to student and faculty with emphasis on student use.

Copy will be designed to appeal to on-campus consumers who want a place to socialize.

The principal objective of the advertising will be to announce that nutritional foods are available fast.

A secondary objective will be to convince students that the product provides advantages primarily associated with ambiance.

The copy will dramatize interest and excitement.

ASSIGNMENT

You are to prepare a series of print advertisements for this product. Follow the instructions given by your teacher.

8–11 Writing advertising copy

Classical record sale

A local shop, Sound Advice, normally advertises and sells a lot of rock and country recordings. The owner wants to expand his business by offering "the best collection of classical records in the area." He wants you to write some ads promoting this part of his business. But you must be careful, he says, because he doesn't want to drive away his current customers. He is starting the new part of his business by offering all his single classical records and tapes for $1.99 for this weekend only. Come up with a slogan that the owner can use for this expansion in his business and write the ads, which will run in the local paper on Thursday, Friday, and Saturday. The owner says he has a full line of classical music, from Bach to Stravinsky.

8–12 Developing an advertising strategy

Frozen dinners

Good Foods, Inc., is a manufacturer and processor of many foods commonly found in grocery stores. The company produces many canned goods, distributes fresh produce in many areas of the country, and has a large line of individually frozen fruits and vegetables. The company is now seeking to enter the frozen dinner market. The company has done extensive research in this area and has found two major negative characteristics of frozen dinners among consumers. One is that frozen dinners lack taste—the food found in most frozen dinners is simply not very good. The other negative characteristic is that, generally, frozen foods do not have a very good reputation. That is, "good" cooks don't serve frozen dinners to their friends; "good" wives and mothers don't serve frozen dinners to their families. People who serve or eat frozen dinners are thought to be lazy and not very good in the kitchen. Frozen dinners have these reputed characteristics despite the fact that research shows frozen dinners are eaten in the average American home at least once a week.

Good Foods doesn't know which negative characteristic to attack in its advertising and comes to your ad agency asking for prototype ads to help company officials decide which approach to take. Choose one of the negative characteristics above and write some advertising copy designed to counter it. It is up to you to come up with a name for Good Foods' frozen dinners, and the name should help in countering the negative characteristic you choose. Here are some more facts about the advertising situation which are included in a copy platform written by your agency.

Target market: Middle- and upper-middle class women who work but still have the responsibility of fixing meals for their families; age range twenty-five to forty-five.

Competition: Two major brands of frozen foods now dominate the market: Swan Foods has a wide variety of frozen dinners, which are generally advertised as the cheapest on the market; their average price is ninety-one cents per dinner. Wholesome Foods doesn't have as many varieties of dinners but research shows that people generally think they're a little tastier and more nutritious. They cost about $1.59 per dinner. These two companies sell 75 percent of the frozen dinners in America. The rest are sold by a variety of small companies, many of whom specialize in foreign dishes, such as Chinese foods.

Supportive selling points: Good Foods dinners will average about $1.25, making them almost the most expensive on the market. Good Foods will have fewer varieties than Swan but more than Wholesome, with more vitamins and minerals than any dinner on the market. One line of the Good Foods dinners will feature rib-eye steaks which have been pre-cooked "well done," "medium," and "rare." The dinners will also have more vegetables than the dinners now on the market, and Good Foods has come up with a process that will preserve more of the natural flavor of these vegetables.

8–13 Preparing advertising copy

Daycare center

Daycare is one of the fastest growing parts of the service sector. As more and more women work outside the home, the demand for quality, affordable daycare has skyrocketed.

The Sunshine Daycare Center is open from 6:30 a.m. to 6:30 p.m. It is located at 1212 Wiltshire Blvd., one of the city's major thoroughfares, so it is convenient to many people, especially to those who work downtown. The center takes children up through kindergarten ages and has a fully accredited kindergarten class.

The center knows that one of the major concerns that parents have for their child's daycare is to make sure that the child is properly cared for and that the child gets a lot of individual attention. Responding to this concern, the center makes sure that there is at least one adult for every ten children at all times in the center. Most of these adults have some academic or professional training. The center has an open, bright environment inside, with a large, well-equipped playground in the back.

Current advertising should be pitched toward people who work downtown and who are concerned about the quality of care their children receive during the day. These people are not as concerned about price (the Sunshine Daycare Center is one of the most expensive in town) as they are convenience and quality.

Suggested assignment: Write three advertisements using the same theme or slogan. The ads should be at least 75 words each.

8–14 Writing advertising copy

Perfume

The Soft Lights Perfume Company has been marketing Wild Abandon perfume for a number of years, and recently it has found that its share of the perfume market has been decreasing. Essentially, the company wants to advertise a "new and improved" Wild Abandon perfume, but company officials are uncertain exactly how to do this. They tell you that this new perfume, which they want to market under the same name, has a slightly stronger scent and that it comes in a variety of colors, including purple, crimson, and gold. (It used to be transparent.) In a radical move, the company has decided to increase the price of the perfume by 50 percent, so that now it costs sixty-five dollars for a half ounce.

Suggested assignment: Write five advertisements for this product which will run in successive issues of Vogue. Each ad should have a headline and about 50 words of copy. The ads will have a common illustration – a gorgeous woman, dressed in a leopard-skin dress and accompanied by a leopard.

8–15 Developing an advertising strategy

Smart Tops, Inc.

Most men don't wear hats. That's what the research shows. Smart Tops, Inc., is going to try to change that. Smart Tops is a small firm but owned by the clothes conglomerate Giant Size, a respected name in clothes. Giant Size isn't a charity, however, and Smart Tops has been losing money for years. The managers of Smart Tops fear that Giant Size will close the company down unless they can show a profit in the next two years. They have decided to embark on a major advertising campaign and have come to your agency for help.

The research that your agency has done into why men do not wear hats has come up with two major reasons: men don't wear hats because they don't consider them necessary, and they don't wear hats because they think hats are for "older" men. Smart Tops wants to market its hats to younger men, those in the twenty-five-to-forty range. The managers aren't sure which would be the most effective advertising campaign. Should they take on the "old" characteristic directly and try to convince men that wearing a hat is a "young" thing to do? Or, should they try to counter the negative characteristic that hats are unnecessary with some convincing arguments that hats really are necessary?

Your agency wants you to pick one of these advertising strategies and design some advertising for Smart Tops. The following is some information that the agency research office has provided you which may eventually go into a copy platform.

Competition. Smart Tops now has about a 7 percent share of the market,

down from 10 percent two years ago. Almost every other manufacturer of men's hats has seen a drop in sales during the past two years also, so there is no evidence that hat wearers have anything against Smart Tops. The biggest advertiser in the market is Smith, Inc., which manufacturers a line of hats known as Good As Gold. These are some of the most expensive and well-made hats on the market. Other hat manufacturers do relatively little advertising.

Supportive selling points. Smart Tops says that its hats are as well made as the Good As Golds, but they sell for an average of twenty-five percent less. The hats range in price from $15 to $50. All the hats contain at least 50 percent natural fibers, especially cotton and wool. They are extremely well crafted and backed by years of tradition and experience. Smart Tops has been making hats since the 1880s. The hats are guaranteed against any defect in workmanship and against any damage for a year. If a customer is dissatisfied with anything about a Smart Tops hat, all he has to do is send the hat to the company office and he'll receive a full refund. Smart Tops can also be counted on to provide the latest in new styling in men's hats, as well as a wide variety of traditional styles.

Audience. The marketing research has turned up the fact that women make about forty percent of all hat purchases for men.

Your assignment is the following:

Write a slogan for Smart Tops hats that can be used in all their advertising.

Write two print ads, each with a headline and at least 50 words of copy. Be sure to use the slogan you have written.

Write a thirty-second radio spot or a thirty-second TV storyboard, also using the slogan you have written.

8–16 Solving advertising problems

Hershal's Department Store

Hershal's Department Store is one of the largest department stores in town. It's located in the same shopping mall as a Sears and a J.C. Penney store, but Hershal's has a larger variety of clothes than either of these two chain stores. The store's line of women's clothes is especially large, and the store has a reputation for having the most up-to-date styles of women's clothing. It is locally owned and has been in operation for more than fifty years. The president of the board is John Hershal, Jr., the son of the founder. The store's general manager is John Hershal III, the president's son. Hershal's is considered to be the major store in the mall where it is located.

Hershal's recently conducted a marketing survey, as it has for several years, but this survey turned up some surprising results. The survey found that there is a reservoir of good will about the store, something Hershal's has cultivated for many years. For instance, people in the survey said they liked Hershal's refund policy, which has always been a very liberal one. However, the survey found that people did not like a number of things about Hershal's: The store hours were not long enough (Hershal's closes at 8 p.m., while the other stores in the mall stay open until 9 p.m.); it takes too long to check out; many of the departments don't have enough people to wait on the customers adequately; there is some feeling that Hershal's has raised prices more than other stores have; and many younger women try smaller shops, especially those close to the local college campus, before shopping at Hershal's.

In light of these findings, Hershal's has done several things: Store hours will be extended to 9 p.m. beginning next month; new people will be added to departments that have been understaffed; the store, which conducts three major sales each year, will conduct five during the coming year.

Hershal's also wants to increase its advertising and comes to your agency for help.

At this point, you should identify some of the possible advertising problems and follow the directions of your instructor on handling this advertising situation.

8–17 Preparing print advertisements

Baseball team

A National League Baseball franchise has been granted to Washington, D.C. The last time the city had a team was 1971, when the Washington Senators moved to Texas to become the Texas Rangers. The owners of the new team have not selected a name for the team yet, and they want your ad agency to propose a name and design a set of advertisements to promote ticket sales during January and February. Ticket prices are $12.50 for box seats, $10.50 for reserved seats, $6.50 for general admission, and $4 for bleacher seats. Those wanting more information or wanting to buy tickets should write to the Washington National League Baseball Team, Box 3995, Washington, D.C. 20006 or call (202) 555-1212. The owners tell your agency that the ads for tickets should emphasize the advantages of buying early, the excitement of baseball, and the fact that the game is finally back in the nation's capital. Write a headline, subhead, and copy for three ads. The copy should be seventy-five to 100 words long.

8–18 Solving advertising problems

Wayfarer Restaurant

The Wayfarer Restaurant was established in 1865 and is the oldest restaurant in town. It has been in several locations but has been at its present location, 505 Sixth Street, for more than fifty years. The Wayfarer is famous for its breakfasts. It has a tradition of serving the finest country ham in the area, but each item on the menu is of exceptional quality. A food critic for the state's largest newspaper once reviewed the breakfast at the Wayfarer and called it the "best place to wake up in the state."

The Wayfarer Restaurant is small and usually crowded, especially in the morning. It seats only about thirty people, and that's one of the problems. The owners feel that they are losing customers who are put off by the thought that they will have to wait for a while. There is no thought being given to expanding the restaurant, however. There is no room to expand, and if there was, the owners probably wouldn't because they like the cozy, intimate atmosphere the small space affords.

The owners have also noticed that many of the people who eat at the Wayfarer are "regulars," people who come there often. They feel that they should be attracting some new customers, especially younger people, like students from the nearby college.

Finally, one of the "hidden secrets" of the restaurant, according to the owners, is its dinner menu. The owners say they offer the best steaks in town–they reject a lot of the meat the packers offer them because it isn't good enough. Their steaks cost seventy-five cents to one dollar less than comparable steaks in the best restaurants in town.

At this point, you should identify some of the possible advertising problems and follow the directions of your instructor on handling this advertising situation.

9

Writing for public relations

Introduction

Public relations ranges across the organizational map. Public relations means communicating, and in today's business and social community, an organization must communicate at every level. Public relations practitioners are communication specialists, hired by organizations to perform and advise on a variety of communication tasks.

Only a few years ago, many organizations, particularly private businesses, saw no need to have such specialists. They sold their products or performed their services for a specialized public, and they were content to believe that they were doing all of the communicating that they needed to do.

One example is a large corporation that specializes in operating sites around the country that handle toxic chemical waste material for other industries. The company performed this necessary but unpleasant task and did so within the legal regulations that governed such operations. The company felt that it had little need to communicate with the public. After all, it was not trying to sell a service to the general public. It dealt exclusively with other industries. In the last two decades, however, with more public attention focused on the environment —and on dangerous toxic waste sites, such as Love Canal in New York —the company found that it could no longer afford to take such a cavalier attitude about its communication needs. As the issue of hazardous waste disposal has become not only an industrial one but also a political one, this company and many others like it has found itself in the communication business.

This situation has occurred for many organizations. Corporate chiefs are discovering that they need professional communicators as well as budget managers, salespeople, scientists, engineers, and secretaries on their staffs. The field of public relations has expanded a great deal in the last few years, and more and more students are finding excellent employment opportunities in this field. In fact, the public relations major has become one of the most popular fields of study in mass communication.

Traditionally, the career path into public relations has been through journalism programs and working in the mass media. People who had either or both of these credentials were thought to make good public relations practitioners. While this is still the case, many colleges and universities have instituted public relations majors. These programs teach many of the specifics of working in the field of public relations. More and more students are obtaining internships in public relations agencies and PR departments within companies and organizations.

Despite these burgeoning opportunities, public relations remains a very competitive field. The person who would enter this line of work must be intelligent, disciplined, and willing to work difficult and long hours. Public relations jobs carry with them a great deal of responsibility, and the people who accept them must be willing to live up to that responsibility.

The work of the PR practitioner

People who work in public relations jobs do a great many things. In fact, that is one of the attractions of a career in PR. The variety of activities that a practitioner can engage in is enormous. On the other hand, that variety requires that practitioners be skilled in many areas and that they be able to deal with many differing and sometimes conflicting assignments. They should also be comfortable with many different people.

The following are some of the jobs of a public relations practitioner:

Handle communication with the external publics of an organization. The term publics is one that is used often in public relations. External publics are those groups outside of the organization that an organization wants to communicate with. They may include the public at large, buyers of a product, users of a service offered by the organization, potential contributors to the organization, members of the news media on whom the organization depends to distribute its information, or any number of other groups. A public relations practitioner must assist not only in getting information out but also in making sure that information is properly interpreted. Some of the means by which information from an organization is distributed are news releases, letters, brochures, and quarterly and annual reports.

Handle communication with the internal publics of an organization. Just as there are groups outside the organization that need to be reached, there are also groups within the organization that must receive information. These are the internal publics. They can include employees, independent contractors, stockholders, members, and the families of any of these groups. In companies that have a larger number of employees, this communication function is often critical to the organization. Keeping employees properly informed is often vital to the company's health. Associations —those that have memberships who are not part of the day-to-day operation of the organization —also depend on good communication with their members to keep their organizations healthy. Communication with these internal publics can take the form of newsletters, company magazines, letters, notices, memoranda, and periodic reports.

Work with the news media to get information about the organization. In most organizations, one of the chief responsibilities is that of media liaison. The PR person is called on to help find out information about the organization that would be useful to the news reporter in putting together a story. This kind of information goes beyond that produced in a press release. The PR person must find the person within the organization that has the information the reporter wants and must often make arrangements for those people to meet. The other side of this responsibility for the PR practitioner is that of advising the organization's officials on media relations. When and how to release information is often the responsibility of PR practitioners. They may also have to give advice on speeches, press conferences, and interviews that the organization's officials may give. In short, any time the news media deal with an organization, a PR person will be involved.

Help produce public functions and events. Public relations practitioners are often involved in the organization's public activities. A company may announce an advertising campaign; officials of a local charity may hold a news conference to kick off its annual fund drive; a local business may make a donation to a school with a ceremony marking that donation; a university may break ground for a new building. Any number of events may occur, and PR practitioners are usually a part of the planning. They are most likely the ones who see that the public is properly informed about such events. Almost all organizations have the need to produce public events at some point, and the public relations practitioner will have a major responsibility for their success.

These are some of the day-to-day activities that PR practitioners might be involved in. On a more general level, they contribute to their organizations by helping formulate a continuing, long-range public relations plan. That plan may have many parts and may certainly be revised as new needs arise and old needs subside. At this level, most experts agree that public relations consists of four parts:

Planning. An organization should develop a plan for how it intends to deal with its publics. Some means of communication are not appropriate for certain publics, while others are. A well-conceived plan will allow the organization's officials to figure out what publics they need to communicate with and how it should take place. An integral part of planning is setting goals for the various communications with the organization's publics. Planning is a constant process with most organizations.

Research. Hand-in-hand with planning is research. A public relations practitioner may have to find out exactly with whom the organization wishes to communicate. And that person may also have to discover the best means of communicating. These are complex questions for which there are no ready answers. A public relations person will need to have these answers if a plan is to be properly executed.

Another part of the research process is finding out what information the organization wants to communicate or should be communicating. Again, this is no easy or simple task. The process of research may involve talking with people in the organization in order to write a news release. It could mean poring over financial and technical papers and holding long discussions with many of the organization's top officials in order to put together an annual report.

Communication. This is the part of the process that we are concerned with most in this book. Putting information into the proper form —and often doing it very quickly —is one of the most important jobs that the PR person can perform. A PR practitioner's ability to do this, more than anything else, will determine that person's worth to the organization.

Evaluation. The evaluation phase of the practitioner's work is when he or she asks, "Did our plan work? Did we get the right information out to the right publics? Did our efforts have the effect we wanted?" Plans need evaluation to see if they are working, and it is often up to the public relations person to devise a means of evaluation for the plan.

Evaluation, of course, is related to the goals of the plan. If the goal of an organization was to gain new members, evaluation is fairly easy. Looking at the number of new members that joined while the plan was being executed is a straightforward means of evaluating the plan. Sometimes, however, goals are much more complex, and evaluation is more subjective.

Characteristics of the PR practitioner

Whether you work for a major public relations firm, a particular company, a government agency, a hospital, a university, or another institution, if you work in public relations the chances are quite good that you will have to write. The overwhelming majority of jobs in the field of public relations are writing jobs. Public relations departments produce brochures, press releases, letters, speeches, scripts, and public service announcements for television and radio, posters, reports, books, formal documents, magazines, newsletters, newspapers, and information directories on a wide variety of topics. While photographers, artists, designers, production managers and editors may also be required in producing such items, each begins with a writer. Even a flier announcing a company picnic has to be written by someone.

Gathering information and structuring it for specific formats is the basic process for all writing in the mass media. The best people in the public relations profession can take a scribbled set of ideas and produce a fifteen-minute speech for a vice-president to give at a company dinner in much the same way that a good reporter takes a tip from the telephone and eventually produces a polished story. The differences between public relations writing and news writing are primarily differences created by the intent inherent in public relations writing. A public relations writer must bear in mind a complex set of purposes and interests while producing any piece of copy for any particular publication.

If you wish to write in a public relations environment, you should be prepared to work very hard on a relatively small set of assignments directed at a limited audience. It is not unusual for a piece of writing to be scrutinized by several "editors" (that is to say, your bosses), who will criticize and often change your work.

Public relations writing is usually done for an explicit purpose, and the expenditures involved in producing any item must be justified by the degree to which the writing fulfills that purpose. For example, if you are asked to write an article for a company publication outlining a new policy about how raises are awarded, you will be expected not only to write a factually correct story but also to express the attitudes and intentions of management in a manner acceptable to employees.

This idea of intent in public relations writing puts an extra burden on the writer. All of the rules of good grammar, spelling, usage, style and structure apply to public relations writing. The requirements of brevity and clarity that help make for crisp news stories also hold for writing brochures. Above and beyond these considerations, public relations writers must constantly bear in mind the interests of the institutions for which they write and the purposes of their writing.

Public relations writers are not merely propagandists for the people who pay them. Rather, the good public relations writer is a professional, able to write honestly and clearly about complex and varied issues in a manner acceptable to people who may know little or nothing about writing but who know a great deal about what they want to see in print.

Public relations writers have a dual role, however. Their responsibilities extend not only upward to their employers but also outward to those who will read what they write. In a sense, public relations writers act as translators. They must completely understand the company or institution they write about. If it is a company that makes computer parts, they must know a great deal about computers. If it is a hospital, they must have a working knowledge of medical terms and procedures. Yet they must write about these things in ways their readers can understand. Their role becomes much like that of newspaper reporters covering particular beats they know intimately.

This intimate knowledge of the institution a writer "covers" engenders a particular problem with the use of language. Public relations writers should take care not to become so immersed in their topics that they take on the jargon of the company to an inordinate degree. Readers of newspapers that use press releases from a hospital may not know what a "cardiovascular microsurgery specialist" really does unless you explain cardiovascular microsurgery in simple terms. The same is true for any highly specialized topic. Central to this concept is the idea of audience.

As a public relations writer, you will write for a variety of people —company employees, the general public, management, government officials—and the use of language will change depending on who the audience is. A piece intended for the board of trustees of a university will differ substantially in tone and content from something intended for release to state newspapers, even if the topic (the hiring of a new dean, for example) is the same.

A public relations writer must be something of a verbal acrobat, leaping from form to form. One person may be required to write speeches, letters, brochures, news releases, promotional copy and formal reports —all on the same topic and all in the same week! This is particularly true of small firms or departments. Doing this kind of work requires an absolute command of the basic tools of writing, good reporting abilities, and a mental flexibility which allows the writer to think about the same or related topics in a multitude of ways.

A final point should be made about PR writing. Essential to all writing for public relations is understanding the purpose of the communication and knowing who the audience is for the communication. In other words, a writer needs to know why he or she is writing and what the audience is likely to do with that information. That knowledge comes not only from the research the writer does on what he or she is writing but also from a sensitivity and respect the writer has for the audience.

The ability to write —and to use the language effectively —is at the heart of almost all public relations activities, but it is not the only skill necessary for the successful public relations person. That person must also have the ability to deal effectively with many people in various situations. He or she must know how to use tact or persuasion in obtaining information from others within the organization. The PR professional must be able to satisfy the various publics with whom the organization communicates. The professional must also be persuasive with the leaders of an organization in advising them on their public relations efforts. The PR practitioner is often one of the most visible persons within the organization and must keep the purposes and goals of the organization in mind during all of his or her contacts.

The successful PR practitioner must have the ability to organize effectively and work efficiently. That means meeting deadlines that are imposed quickly and arbitrarily. That person must be a quick study—one who is able to quickly grasp an idea or situation and give it form and substance. And that person must be able to make sound judgments about the effectiveness of public relations efforts.

The PR professional should combine a belief in the goals of an organization with a high standard of personal ethics and integrity. In the tenth century, so the story goes, Eric the Red sailed west from his native Iceland and discovered a large, desolate land. He wanted to colonize it, but the land was so forbidding that he felt that even his hearty Icelanders would be reluctant to do so. To make the land more appealing, he named it Greenland. With this name, Eric the Red was able to persuade a number of people to follow him to a place that is covered mostly with snow and ice. Eric the Red, many have said, was one of the world's first flacks.

Public relations has had a widespread reputation of being practiced by "flacks." These are people who stretch or ignore the truth to gain something for their organization. They spout the "company line," knowing but not caring that it is self-serving and inaccurate. They seek only publicity, even if it is bad publicity. These kinds of people, unfortunately, make it into almost every profession, and the public relations field has certainly not been immune to them. Yet, most public relations practitioners consider themselves professionals with high standards of ethics and a deep regard for accuracy. The people who believe in what their organization is doing and make genuine efforts to provide accurate and useful information to the organization's publics make the best PR professionals.

Writing news releases

One of the most common forms of public relations writing is the news release. The news release is information, usually written in the form of a news story, which an organization wishes to make public through the news media. A news release, like a news story, should follow a consistent style; it should be written as concisely and precisely as possible; it should answer all of the pertinent questions about the story; and it should emphasize what an editor will think is the most important part of a story. In short, a good news release differs very little from a good news story.

The last point about news releases—that they should emphasize what an editor will think is the most important part of a story—is one that sometimes gives public relations writers some problems. The first problem can be overcome by knowledge and application of the news values discussed in Chapter 4. The second problem is that corporate managers, who have very little knowledge of news values, will often want to emphasize what they think is important rather than what rates as important to an editor.

This attitude puts the writer in a difficult position. News releases are discarded by editors most of the time. One reason for this is that editors get many news releases every day, and they do not take the time to go through each of them carefully. If a news release does not give the editor some news immediately, the editor is not going to spend much time with it. Another reason that editors discard news releases is a prejudice on the part of many editors against running news releases. News releases are often seen by editors as propaganda or promotion—or even free advertising. The way a writer can overcome these problems is by writing a news release as close to the news story form as possible. Editors are much more likely to use news releases that have the most important information in a simply written lead paragraph and that follow a consistent style than those releases that do not.

Many corporate managers do not understand this, and they

often want a non-newsworthy item emphasized in a release. For instance, a manager may want to announce a new plant opening in the following way:

```
     John Jones, president of the
American South Corporation, announced
today that American South Corporation
will open a new copper-wire manufactur-
ing plant in Midville next year.
     Mr. Jones said the plant will
employ about 75 people initially and
about 250 when it is fully opera-
tional....
```

The public relations writer will have to convince the manager that this style will not help the news release get used. A better way of writing this release would be the following:

```
     A copper-wire manufacturing plant,
which will employ about 250 when it is
fully operational, will open in Midville
next year, according to officials of the
American South Corp.
     The opening was announced by John
Jones, president of the corporation....
```

While the content of a good news release is the same as that of a good news story, the form differs slightly. Generally, a news release should contain three things at the top of the first page. One is a headline or slug-line telling what the story is about. The styles of various public relations departments are different, and the writer must learn what style his or her department uses. In the example above, a headline might look like this:

```
NEW PLANT TO OPEN
IN MIDVILLE NEXT YEAR
```

A second item that should be at the top of a news release is the name and telephone number of a person in the organization who can be contacted for more information. Again, this will differ according to various public relations departments, but it should always be there. Editors who are interested in using a story may want to know more about it. They are more likely to pursue a story if a name and telephone number are easily available to them. The form this information takes could be as simple as the following:

```
For more information contact
James E. Smith
American South Corporation
555-1616
```

A third piece of information that should be at the top of a news release is a release time. This tells the editor when the information may be used. Often, the information may be used as soon as the editor gets it, and in this situation the words "FOR IMMEDIATE RELEASE" should be used. Sometimes, however, editors may be sent releases before they should be used. For instance, some sort of a ceremony in the mayor's office may be set up to announce the new plant mentioned in the example above. It may be that corporate officials do not want word of the plant getting out until the official announcement is made, but they still want to cooperate with editors who have deadlines to meet. In these cases, they will put an embargo on the release. An embargo is simply a time when a piece of information may be used, and it may look like this:

```
For release after 10 a.m.
Friday, October 13
```

Editors will generally abide by embargo times and not release information before they should. There is nothing an organization can do, however, if an editor chooses to run information before an embargo. Consequently, public relations practitioners should be careful in releasing information with an embargo and should do so only to those editors who can be trusted.

News stories are generally written in an inverted pyramid form. The most important information is presented first, and the information comes in a descending order of importance. For the writer of the news release, this means that the background information that often must be included about the organization should come at the end of the story rather than toward the beginning.

The writer of a news release—like the writer of a news story—should keep the commonly accepted news values that contribute to defining news in mind when writing the release. The writer should ask, "Is the story timely? What impact will it have? Is there conflict in this story? Are prominent people involved in the story? Is there something bizarre or unusual about this story?" Reviewing the news values of a news release will help the writer in producing a release that is more likely to be used.

The most important part of a news story—and also a news release—is the lead paragraph. Remember, the first reader of a news release is likely to be a busy editor who must decide whether or not to use it in his or her publication. You should let that editor know quickly what your story is about. Just as a news writer needs to "sell" a story with a lead that is interesting or informative (or even both), the writer of a news release needs to sell an editor on the story in the same way. If the editor thinks the news release is interesting or important, he or she is more likely to use the information.

Another point about news releases should be made here. A news release might have only one reader—the editor or reporter to whom it is sent. Yet, if that person uses the information it contains in a story or uses it as the basis for getting more information, the release has been a success. In most cases—particularly in larger cities—newspapers and trade publications rarely run press releases, so the writer of a news release rarely expects to see his or her own words in print. The purpose of a news release is to get information to the people who work in the mass media. If the information in a news release results in the information being used by the media, the news release has done its job.

The rules about sentence and paragraph structure apply to news releases just as they do to news stories. Sentences should be short, and the paragraphs reasonably brief. Editors, just like newspaper readers, do not like to get involved with long paragraphs.

A news release writer has to pay particular attention to jargon and wordiness that might creep into a news release. Every organization or association develops its own language—abbreviations and acronyms that speed up communication among those with a knowledge or interest in the field. PR practitioners must also know this language in order to communicate within the organization, but they should be careful to use only language that is widely familiar in their news stories.

Wordiness is another danger to the well-written news release. Wordiness is particularly a problem if a news release must be approved by those who are not professional writers. People who do not understand how to use the language often believe that the more words you can use—not the fewer words—the more you will impress the reader and the more likely you are to get your point across. Professional writers know that just the opposite is the case. A news release should use only the number of words it takes to convey the information you want to convey. Anything more is wasted.

News release writers should pay particular attention to proper identification of all the people mentioned in a release. A news release is an official document coming from the organization. Journalists count on a news release to be correct when it mentions information about the organization. Journalists may also want to contact directly the people mentioned in the news release. They assume that those mentioned in a news release are correctly identified and that their names are spelled correctly. A PR practitioner who fails at either of these tasks can cause much embarrassment for everyone involved.

Finally, another form of the news release with which PR practitioners must deal is the video news release. The VNR can range from a short news story produced by the organization on videotape and distributed locally to longer feature items (or even half-hour shows) that large companies distribute nationally. VNRs for news items are written in much the same way as broadcast scripts for news stories are written. They are "reported" by someone within the organization or someone hired by the organization, put on videotapes, and distributed to TV news departments in the area. Larger companies produce longer and more expensive VNRs that are likely to emphasize the generic products they sell rather than the brand names. For instance, a soup manufacturer may produce a tape on the nutritional value of soup, or a brokerage firm might produce a piece on the advantages of buying stock.

From the PR practitioner's point of view, the two major problems with producing VNRs are the expense and the uncertainty of their use. VNRs can take a lot of time and money from an orga-

Figure 9-1

Press releases

This news release has a number of problems. As we noted in the text, the lead emphasizes the wrong details. In paragraph 1, instead of having John Jones' name at the beginning of the lead, the fact that a new plant employing as many as 200 people should begin the story.

In paragraph 3, the facts about the company are too high in the story; they should be moved to the end of the story.

In paragraph 5, some company jargon is beginning to sneak into this story. The writer should make sure that the readers can understand everything that is in the story.

The location of the plant is very important, especially to readers in Midville, where this story is likely to get the most attention (see paragraph 7). This fact should be placed higher in the story. Also, the projected beginning and ending dates of construction should be placed higher in the story.

News from

For more information contact
James E. Smith
American Southern Corporation
(404) 555-1313

For release after 10 a.m.
Friday, October 13

NEW PLANT TO OPEN
IN MIDVILLE NEXT YEAR

John Jones, president of the American Southern Corporation, announced today that American Southern Corporation will open a new copper wire manufacturing plant in Midville next year.

Mr. Jones said the plant will employ about 75 people initially and about 200 people when it is fully operation.

American Southern Corporation has plants in more than 30 states and manufactures a variety of materials that are used for industrial and technological purposes. The company employes more than 15,000 people and is headquartered in Atlanta, Ga.

The copper wire plant planned for Midville will be part of the industrial parts division of the corporation.

"The computerized locating process that will be installed at the Midville plant will be state-of-the-art for this industry," Mr. Jones said in making the announcement in Midville today.

"We plan to hire many people from the Midville area to work in this plant, but a number of them will have to be trained in this process. We will be giving those people that training as soon as possible.

The plant will be located on a 50-acre site on Sherrill Road, five miles south of downtown Midville. Construction of the plant will begin immediately, and company officials estimated that the plant should be fully operational within three months.

"We looked at a number of sites for this plant but chose Midville for a number of reasons," Mr. Jones said. "Among those were Midville's location near some major rail transport sites and the overall quality of life that Midville offers."

---

nization. The people and equipment involved in producing a high-quality VNR can involve thousands of dollars. For a company with many assets, the costs may not seem out of line, but for smaller organizations, spending several thousand dollars—or even several hundred—on a single item like a VNR is not worth it. The second problem is getting VNRs used by television stations. Many stations are unwilling to use material that is not produced by their own news departments. And even where stations are willing to use this material, they may not have the air time to do so.

Despite these problems, VNRs remain a valid tool for information distribution by an organization. With improvements in video technology, the costs of producing and distributing a VNR are coming down, and more and more companies are finding video a useful means of providing information to their publics.

Letters

Despite increased use of the telephone and advances in other forms of communication, letters are still one of the most important and effective means of communicating in the business world today. In fact, they have increased in importance with the installation and use of fax machines. The well-written letter is impressive and appreciated by the receiver. The poorly written letter can establish negative feelings on the part of the receiver that are extremely difficult to overcome. PR practitioners are often called on to write letters for their organizations. These letters may serve a variety of purposes, such as selling a product or idea, explaining company policy, answering complaints, and raising funds. Each of these letters must be carefully crafted to accomplish its purpose.

Letters are a good way to direct a message straight to the persons you want to receive that message. Most people read their mail; at least, they begin to read their mail. If a letter does not quickly give its information and make its point, it is likely to irritate or lose its reader—or both. Letters are expensive for organizations to produce and send. They take time and care to write. Like all other communication, they must accomplish their mission for the organization.

Just as in any other kind of writing, letter writing requires a precise and concise use of the language. Letters require that writers come directly to the point, that they do not waste the time of the receiver. Letter writing requires more, however. The letter is a very personal form of communication. Even if a letter is obviously written for a large number of people, it is still taken very personally by a receiver. Letters, then, should have some personal touch. The reader should get the feeling that the letter was written to and for him or her.

One technical requirement is that letters should never contain any spelling, grammar, or punctuation errors. They should also never show any editing.

The first rule of letter writing is to understand the purpose of the letter. The letter writer should ask, "Why am I writing this letter?" and if necessary should make a list of those reasons. There may be a number of reasons for a letter to be written, but there should be one overriding purpose. If that is not evident from the list the writer makes, then he or she should give some more thought to the letter itself.

Following closely on the purpose for writing the letter is the action expected of the recipient. Again, the letter writer should ask a question: "What do I want the reader to do after reading the letter?" Sometimes the answer is a simple one and comes directly from the purpose of the letter. At other times, the intended action of the reader may not be apparent. Again, the writer should have this clearly in mind before starting to write the letter. In any case, the action of the reader should be as specific as possible.

The table on the next page shows some examples of purposes and intended actions for a letter.

Once the purpose of the letter and the intended action on the part of the reader is established, the writing can begin. One of the first and most important considerations a writer should give to a letter is its tone. The proper tone is essential to the effectiveness of a letter. In most cases of business correspondence, a letter must be both personal and professional; they must show the right mix of these qualities. A letter that is too personal—especially if the writer and recipient are not personal friends—may offend the recipient as an invasion of privacy. A letter that is too formal may make the recipient feel that he or she is not very important to the writer.

What do we mean by being "too personal" in a letter? Here are some things to do to avoid that:

Don't be obsequious. The dictionary defines obsequious as "exhibiting a servile attentiveness or compliance." In letter writing, this means not thanking someone too much (twice is the maximum for a letter; once is better); don't keep apologizing; not saying "please" more than once in a letter; not using or repeating phrases such as "I hope you'll understand." All of these things irritate the reader; most people want to be spoken to, or written to, in a straightforward manner.

Don't be too complimentary. Depending on the purpose of the letter, compliments can ring hollow very quickly. In a letter telling a job applicant that he or she didn't get the job, this might be appropriate:

        The experience listed on your
    resume shows that you are very well
    qualified for a number of positions.

But this would be too much:

        The experience listed on your
    resume shows that you are very well
    qualified for a number of positions. You
    made an excellent impression on all of
    us when you interviewed for the posi-
    tion, and we were glad that you know so
    much about our company. People like you
    would be a credit to our company, and
    we're just sorry that we had only one
    position to fill.

Figure 9-2

Parts of a letter

This graphic shows the different parts of a business letter. Read the letter itself and take note of the straightforward, business-like language that is used. Every sentence in the letter contains some information or asks for action from the reader.

date

inside address

COLLEGE OF COMMUNICATION
BACKWATER UNIVERSITY
Box 870172, Backwater, TN 37207 (615) 348-1111

April 24, 1995

Mr. Harmon S. Boskey
President, Metroline Corp.
Box 5555
Metroline, Alabama 356789

Dear Mr. Boskey:

salutation

Higher education, as I am sure that you are aware, is facing an increasingly difficult task in funding the programs necessary to educate our students. State and federal aid has been reduced in recent years, and the prospects of that situation reversing are slim. Consequently, we are having to seek alternate sources for a variety of needs.

In the first paragraph, the writer attempts to establish some mutuality or common ground with the reader. The writer then goes on to state his reasons for writing. The writer includes some specific information about the subject. The request that the writer makes in the fourth paragraph is simple and to the point. The writer then tells the reader what to do to follow through with that request.

One of those needs has to do directly with what we consider the most important part of our curriculum - writing. With the increasing need for computers in our classrooms and the high ratio of instructors to students that is necessary for our writing classes, we are finding our writing courses more and more expensive. Our freshman level writing course alone costs more than $50,000 a year to operate. To meet those growing expenses, we are establishing an endowment that will support our writing program and insure that we are always able to offer the best instruction in this vital area of our curriculum.

body

This endowment will be named in honor of Prof. David Davies, a man who saw many students - including you - through many of the writing courses in our curriculum.

The College is seeking pledges for this endowment, and we want you to be one of the first to make such a pledge. None of the money that comes in for this endowment will ever be spent; we will only spend the interest that grows from it. In that way, it will be an ever-increasing resource for our College and will also be a way of keeping Prof. Davies' memory alive.

If you are interested in making a pledge to this endowment, give me a call or write to me at the above address. We can discuss the details of the pledge and the plans we have for the use of this endowment.

I look forward to hearing from you.

Sincerely,

complimentary close

Manford Meacham, dean

signature

A letter like that is likely to leave the reader asking, "If they thought so much of me, why didn't I get the job?" In that case, the letter would not have accomplished its purpose. Long compliments are usually reserved for friends. They have only limited effectiveness in a business letter.

Generally, don't try to be funny. Humor is not expected in business correspondence and is likely to get in the way of your purpose for writing the letter. In addition, few people can write humor well enough to be understood, so the best rule is: Don't try.

Avoid referring to the personal characteristics, habits, or feelings of the reader. If you are dealing with someone on a professional basis, you probably do not know much about their personal habits or feelings. And even if you think you do, you shouldn't make too many assumptions about them. In the letter above telling a person that he or she did not get a job, what if the writer had said:

I know this news will disappoint you.

It is possible that the recipient would actually be glad not to have gotten the job offer. The recipient may have gotten a better offer from another company. In that case, the writer looks pretty silly.

To avoid sounding too formal in your letters, here are some things you should consider:

Use personal pronouns. Used appropriately—that is, not too much—personal pronouns can humanize a letter without letting it become too personal. A reader wants to be recognized as a human being with attitudes and feelings. The use of personal pronouns, especially you to address the reader, is a good device for business correspondence.

Avoid impersonal constructions. Impersonal constructions are those such as "It is . . ." and "There is . . ." These constructions also include those that place the blame on "it," as in "It has been decided . . ." "It" does not decide anything; some person or group does. Writers use these constructions in the hope that readers will not attribute an action to a particular person (especially themselves). Readers are usually sharper than that, however, and can see right through this ploy.

Avoid the passive voice. In business letters as in all other forms of writing, the passive voice deadens writing. It robs any piece of writing of its vitality. Active verbs make a letter much more likely to be read and understood.

Be careful about referring to policies, rules, and regulations. If a policy or rule is the reason that something occurred and that needs to be explained in the letter, the policy or rule should be stated in the simplest terms possible. In many large, bureaucratic organizations, such rules are written in an obscure form of bureaucratese. The writer needs to translate this for the reader into the plainest terms possible. In most cases, the writer should not make technical references, such as "Regulation 33.b states. . . ." unless that is something the reader will readily understand.

Avoid using technical language that may mean nothing to the reader. A person who has a complaint will not be pacified by a letter that he or she does not understand. In fact, it is likely to confirm the feeling that the complaint is valid. Such a letter is also likely to offend the reader by its condescending tone.

Avoid wordiness. Lots of words, long sentences, and long paragraphs will obscure the message of the letter. They may sound impressive to the person who writes them, but they will not impress the reader. One of the best ways to strike that mix of the formal and personal necessary to a good letter is to write in simple, down-to-earth language.

Sending letters across the Internet or though some other

Figure 9-3

Purposes and intents of letters

The table to the right shows the variety of purposes and intended actions that letters might have. Letter writers should have a good sense of both of these concepts.

Purposes The purpose of the letter is	Intended actions The intended action on the part of the reader is
to answer a complaint from a customer	to understand why the situation occurred
to explain a policy to a member of the organization	to know what the policy is
to announce a new procedure for applying for promotion	to follow the new procedure when applying for promotion
to persuade someone to subscribe to our magazine	to fill out the subscription card
to ask someone to join our organization	to fill out the membership card
to get someone to pay a bill	to send the payment
to tell someone that he or she did not get a job	to know that he or she didn't get the job but still to feel that he or she received fair treatment

wired or cable communication system is a growing part of business and personal communication. E-mail is a form of communication that professional communicators need to master along with all the others they use.

By and large, e-mail messages are shorter and more succinct than letters. E-mail systems are equipped with a function for "attaching" documents to the e-mail communication so that the main message can remain short and to the point.

One of the factors that contributes to this succinctness is that many e-mail messages are sent as direct replies to a previous e-mail message. The original message can be carried along with the reply. Consequently, there is no need to repeat information that may have been in the original e-mail. In this way, e-mail sometimes resembles ordinary conversation rather than letter writing.

E-mail messages are often less formal than those of ordinary letters. One reason for this is that people who use e-mail assume they have at least one experience in common with their fellow correspondents — both sender and receive use the computer. This common experience puts them on a more intimate or friendly basis with their fellow e-mailers. The fact that e-mail messages can be sent and received very quickly —in many cases almost instantly—also contributes to the lessened formality.

Despite greater directness and less formality, the rules of good writing apply to e-mail messages just as they do any other writing. The writer of an e-mail message must be clear and precise in the use of the language. The words must convey the information and meaning that the writer intends and the receiver will understand. Good e-mail messages are just as important to an organization's and individual's image and goals as good letter writing.

Company publications

News releases and letters are very important and common forms of public relations writing, but they are by no means the only ones. Organizational publications abound, and the public relations people in an organization are usually responsible for them.

In dealing with these publications, the public relations practitioners may be responsible for more than writing. They should know about editing, typography, layout, photo selection and cropping, and other parts of the publication process. Those topics are not covered specifically by this book. Rather, the focus here is on the basic writing skills that are a part of any of these jobs.

Three major kinds of publications that organizations produce are newsletters, pamphlets and brochures, and company reports.

Newsletters. The newsletter is a basic term for a wide variety of publications a company may produce. The newsletter may range from a single photocopied sheet to a slick, full-color magazine. The form that a newsletter takes will depend on the company, the amount of money that is spent on it, and, most importantly, the audience.

Newsletters are directed at a particular audience, and a writer for a newsletter must keep this in mind to be successful. Most company newsletters are internal; that is, they are targeted for audiences within the company. One of the most popular types of newsletters is the employee newsletter. This one is directed toward the employees of an organization, giving them information about the company and focusing on their interests and concerns. Newsletters may be specialized to the point of aiming at a certain set of employees in a company.

The style of writing a newsletter uses will depend on the audience and its purpose. Many newsletters are purely informational. They try to get as many facts to the audience as quickly as possible. Other newsletters are for information and entertainment. Either way, the writing in a newsletter must be concise and precise. No newsletter should waste the reader's time. Few companies will require that their employees read a newsletter. Rather, they are encouraged to do so, and one of the means of encouragement is an efficient writing style.

Because of the advent of desktop publishing (DTP) technology, organizations are more likely to produce newsletters for their publics. Desktop publishing technology is computerized editing equipment that allows the users to write, edit, and design a publication on the same computer screen. With DTP, newsletters are an even more efficient means of getting current information to an audience quickly. DTP allows newsletters to be produced efficiently and at a lower cost than was possible just a few years ago. The leading computer for this activity is the Apple Macintosh, but many other computer hardware and software companies are designing products for the DTP market. An understanding of this technology is necessary for the person wishing to become a PR practitioner. That person needs to know how to write but in addition needs to know how to design and lay out a publication.

Newsletters are most effective when they are consistent in their writing, design, and publication schedule. Those who read them should know what to expect in them and when to expect it. The PR practitioner who publishes a newsletter must understand the value of this consistency to the effectiveness of the newsletter.

Pamphlets and brochures. Unlike newsletters, pamphlets and brochures are usually directed at external audiences—people outside an organization. They are not published periodically as a newsletter is. Rather, they are published once and for a specific purpose. These kinds of publications are important because they are often the first and sometimes the only contact a person may have with an organization. These publications must catch the eye of a potential reader and then deliver content that is substantial and well written. Like an advertisement, the appearance of a pamphlet or brochure will promise something; that promise should be fulfilled by the content. Public relations people are often put in charge of producing as well as writing these publications.

There are two kinds of pamphlets and brochures: informational and persuasive. The informational brochure tells about an organization or procedure. The writing in this kind of brochure must be down to earth, practical, and efficient. A brochure on how to hang wallpaper, for instance, should take the reader through a step-by-step process, giving the reader enough information to do the job but not wasting the reader's time. The persuasive brochure is one that tries to make a point, to sell an idea, or to persuade readers to adopt a certain point of view. Many examples of this kind of brochure exist: an American Cancer Society brochure on the evils of smoking is one; a local chamber of commerce brochure on why businesses should locate in that area; a professional association brochure on why people should join the organization. The writing style may vary in this kind of brochure, but one thing the writer should remember is that opinions should be based on information. A writer may express opinions very strongly, but these expressions are not nearly as persuasive as facts. For instance, a writer may say, "You ought to give up smoking because it is bad for your health." The writer would be more effective by saying, "Doctors say more than half the cases of lung cancer that they treat are caused by smoking." The second statement is much stronger because it gives the reader facts, not just opinions.

(For the rest of this section, the term brochure will refer to both pamphlets and brochures. A pamphlet is usually smaller than a brochure, has a narrower purpose, and often has a shorter life. Beyond that—for the purposes here, at least—the differences between a pamphlet and brochure are not significant.)

The brochure is a common means of introducing an organization to the public. Its strength is that it can be designed for and delivered directly to an audience of the organization's choosing. That means that it is efficient in holding the attention of a particular audience. It can be designed for maximum effect on the audience.

The design is a very important part of a brochure and has a great deal to do with the writing in it. There is a wide variety of formats and an infinite number of designs that can be applied to a brochure. When thinking about putting together a brochure, it is useful to follow the diagram on this page. Those in charge of the production of the brochure need to decide first on the purpose it is to serve. They should ask, "Why is this brochure necessary? What problem will it solve? What audience is it directed to?"

Following closely on these questions is the message that the brochure is to convey. Is the brochure supposed to describe the organization in general, or does it have a more specific message? Is it to persuade its audience to do something, or is it simply to inform? (The thinking that goes into a brochure is much like the thinking that goes into an advertisement. In fact, a brochure can be considered a kind of advertisement for an organization. For a more in-depth review of this process, see Chapter 8.)

Once the purpose and message of a brochure are decided, the design and writing decisions are made. These decisions may be simultaneous; that is, the writing and design may take place at more or less the same time. A PR practitioner who is proficient at both writing and design will often do this. Or one decision could follow the other. For instance, a designer may come up with a design for a brochure and then give it to a copywriter; or a writer may write the copy first and hand it over to the designer. In any case, the design and writing are closely linked.

Many people make the mistake of thinking that simply presenting information is a good persuasive method. While information is necessary for a persuasive argument, it usually needs to be crafted in a way that will emphasize its persuasive factors. Sometimes that can be done by the order in which the information is presented. Very often it is done by the graphic techniques in the brochure. If a PR practitioner is not good with design and layout, he or she needs to find someone who is and work closely with that person.

Annual reports and other types of reports. Companies that sell stock to the public are required by law to produce an annual report. Many other organizations that do not come under this requirement also produce annual reports. These reports give people inside and outside the company an idea of what the company is all about and how the company is doing financially. Many companies, particularly larger companies, consider the annual report one of the most important forms of communication they have. One legal requirement for annual reports is that they must be truthful. While a company may try to put on its "best face" in an annual report, the information the report contains must be factual.

Annual reports must contain financial information about the organization and some descriptive information about the company's structure and activities for the year. Beyond that, companies have wide latitude in what they may include in an annual report. Large organizations sometimes put thousands of dollars into the production of an annual report, and they target these reports for specific audiences and purposes, such as attracting investors, holding onto stockholders, and creating a stable image within a field of competition; for non-profit organizations, the purpose of an annual report might be to attract members, increase visibility in the community, and report on otherwise hidden activities.

The writer of an annual report—usually someone in the company's public relations department—is often required to translate a lot of complicated financial data and industry jargon into a simple, clear account of the company's activities and position. The writer must use understandable English and write for an audience that does not know the ins and outs of the company.

Other kinds of reports a company may require are quarterly or semiannual reports or reports about an organization's activities that are directed to a special audience. Nonprofit organizations may compile these kinds of reports when they embark on fund-raising campaigns. Writing these kinds of reports takes a lot of intelligence and skill in using the language.

Web sites. Another type of publication that may fall under the responsibility of the public relations department is the development, design and maintenance of the organization's Web site on the Internet. Access to the Internet has grown phenomenally, and most organizations believe that they must have a presence on the World Wide Web. A "www" site is an integral part of an organization's public posture.

The people in charge of developing the Web site must have the practical knowledge of how to hook up to the web. Usually, this is done through a local or national Internet access provider. The company providing access to the web will also offer technical assistance about how to establish an Internet site. If the organization decides to maintain its own site (rather than subscontract it another company), someone within the organization will need to learn how to write the Hypertext Mark-up Language (HTML) code that is used to program Internet sites. The technical aspects of creating and putting up a web site are not difficult to execute.

The harder job is to understand the purpose of the web site for the organization and to design it according to that purpose. A web site may exist simply to inform Internet browsers about the organization. It may be intended to sell a product. An organization may want those who visit the site to interact with it. Web sites may serve these and many other purposes. Understanding the purpose of the web site is the first step, because—just as with the brochure—a web site may be a person's first contact with the organization. That first contact is always important.

Whatever the purpose, certain principles hold for all web sites:

Clarity. From the beginning and on each part of the site, it should be clear whose web site it is. Possibly this point is so obvious that many web developers tend to forget it; many web sites on the internet do not show a clear owner. The standard logo of the organization should appear throughout the site.

Speed. A web site should load as quickly as possible and should allow users to advance from page to page quickly. Images should be "lite;" that is, they should not take up a lot of space on a server or hard drive. Large images take more time to load.

While this is a technical problem that must be dealt with by those creating the site, it also has some implications for content. It means that pictures and images should be used judiciously. It also means web developers must rely on text, since text is extremely "lite" compared to pictures.

Navigation. Web sites should be divided into a logical set of parts that a user can understand. They can then select the parts of the organization they want to know something about. Often these divisions will mirror the organizational structure. Sometimes, however, they may not. A college, for instance, may see its web site as a recruiting device, so its web site could allow visitors to find out something about student life, to learn about costs, and to view the catalogue.

Whatever the organization structure and purpose, a site should be easy for a user to navigate and to find information. Labels and headlines should be accurate denotations of the content they represent. They should be words or symbols that are commonly understood. Web sites should also have an internal consistency. If a visitor learns how to do something or go from place to place in one part of a site, those procedures should apply to all parts of the site.

Contact information. One of the most useful parts of a web site is contact information. But this information is often left off a site, leaving users puzzled and frustrated. A web site should contain the physical address and telephone number of the organization, not just its e-mail address. Ideally, it should contain contact information for people within the organization whom the public might want to reach. Talented web site managers understand that information about the organization, its procedures and its people will invite a visitor to return.

Figure 9-4

Web sites as public relations vehicles

Many businesses and organizations — even if they are temporary, such as a political campaign — establish websites as a quick and inexpensive way of communicating with their publics.

New information. One of the qualities of the web is its ability to present information quickly. Consequently, we have come to expect web sites to contain the latest information available about their organization or the subjects with which they deal.

Frequent updating with new information has become a central feature of maintaining a web site. Visitors expect something new when they return to a web site. If they do not get new information, they are not likely to return. That, of course, is where writers are necessary. Any dynamic web site must employ people who can put information into an appropriate form. As with any other type of writing, however, text on the web site should be clear, coherent and efficient. Writers usually have just a few words in which to capture and hold the attention of the browser and to direct the browser to other parts of the site. (See Chapter 6 on Writing for the Web.)

Graphics. A web site should also be graphically attractive. Many web sites are highly graphic, and the expectations of clear, sophisticated graphics have developed among those who use the web. Chances are, the person who is developing and maintaining a web site is not just writing text but is also conceiving many of the graphic images that will be used. The interlinking of text and graphics on web sites is one of the aspects of the Internet.

Oral presentations

Speeches, statements, and other oral presentations are among the most common forms of public relations writing. The major difference between this kind of writing and the writing that we have discussed previously is that, like writing for broadcasting, oral presentations are written for the ear, not the eye. They are written to be spoken, not read silently.

Consequently, many of the principles of broadcast writing apply to this kind of writing. Oral presentations should be written in simple, clear, concise language. Sentences should be short. Modifiers and modifying phrases should be kept to a minimum. The content of the speech should be simple; the points made should be easy to follow.

In writing any oral presentation, the PR practitioner must take three major factors into consideration: the audience, the speaker, and the subject of the presentation.

The writer should know, as precisely as possible, who will be listening to the speech. For instance, a company president may be asked to speak at a high school graduation. The writer should understand that while the speech may be directed to the graduates, the audience will also contain their parents and other relatives. This may make a difference in how the speech is structured. The writer will also need to have some idea of what the audience is "expecting" to hear and how important it is to meet those expectations. For instance, if the local college football coach is asked to make a speech before the Lion's Club in early August, the audience will expect him to comment on the upcoming season. They are likely to be disappointed if most of his speech is devoted to the previous season.

The speaker is an important part of how the writer approaches a speech. His or her personality will have much to do with the content of the speech. For instance, the writer may need to know if the speaker is comfortable telling funny stories or if the speaker likes to quote certain people. The speaker may have some ideas he wishes to use in the speech, or he or she may even want to write a draft of the speech for the writer to polish.

The subject of the oral presentation, of course, is an all-important factor for the writer. The subject matter is usually connected with the position of the speaker, although that is not always the case. In the case of the high school graduation speech just mentioned, the company president is not expected to talk much (if at all) about his company. Too many comments about the organization might be inappropriate in this setting. In other cases, however, the audience will expect to hear about the organization that the speaker represents.

Three of the most common types of oral presentations that PR practitioners are asked to write are slide presentations, statements, and speeches.

The slide presentation is a popular method of presentation with many organizations. Slide shows can be used easily with small groups. They are especially helpful in sales presentations. Slides can supplement the words of the speaker and can help focus the attention of the audience on the points that the speaker wants to make.

Software programs that help produce slide shows have become increasingly sophisticated and easy to use. Microsoft's Power Point and other programs place a variety of visual tools at the fingertips of a presenter, and a PR practitioner needs some advanced knowledge of how these programs work and what they do.

In addition to the visual aspects of slide presentations, the presentation must be conceived and a script must be written. The writer of a script for a slide presentation needs to understand the relationship between the script—that is, what the presenter will say—and the slides themselves. In almost all presentations, the slides are used to supplement and enhance what the speaker is saying, but the main information comes from the speaker. The slides themselves should be simple and uncluttered and should have a consistent format. The script contains the major part of the information in the presentation.

Another concept the writer of a slide script needs to understand is that of pacing. Pacing simply means how fast the slides appear to the audience. Some presentations need to be fast-paced; that is, the slides are shown rapidly throughout the presentation, possibly as many as ten per minute. A fast-paced script means that the slides contain no detailed information that the audience must absorb. If the slides do contain such information—such as graphs that indicate something about an organization's progress—the presentation should be at a slower pace.

Some presentations call for slides to be shown at a rate of only one or two per minute. For most presentations, a minute per slide is probably too slow; the audience will expect a faster pace than that.

A statement is a short oral presentation; its length depends on the forum in which it is presented. A statement that precedes a question-and-answer session at a press conference should be relatively short—one to two pages at most. A statement that is read to a legislative committee might be longer, depending on the subject and the time allotted to the speaker. A statement has few of the formalities of a full-blown speech. It is an attempt to summarize facts and make points as efficiently as possible. It often sets the stage for what is to come later, particularly if it precedes a news conference. A statement should be cleanly and efficiently written. It should present its facts and make its points and then stop.

Speeches come in a wide variety of forms. They may be informative, persuasive, entertaining, or a combination of all three. They may last only a few minutes or all day (although modern Western audiences are likely to think a speech is too long if it exceeds thirty minutes). Many of our most memorable sayings were delivered in speeches. For instance:

And so, my fellow Americans, ask not what your country can do for you; ask what you can do for your country.
> John F. Kennedy
> Inaugural address, 1961

The only thing we have to fear is fear itself.
> Franklin D. Roosevelt
> Inaugural address, 1933

I never met a man I didn't like.
> Will Rogers
> Speech in Boston, 1930

Four score and seven years ago, our fathers brought forth on this continent, a new nation, conceived in Liberty, and dedicated to the proposition that all men are created equal.
> Abraham Lincoln
> Gettysburg Address, 1863

I have a dream.
> The Reverend Martin Luther King, Jr.
> Civil Rights March in Washington, 1963

Writing a speech is not an easy task, but it is a common one for many PR practitioners. Writers may begin their work by thinking of a speech as consisting of three parts: an opening, a middle, and an ending.

The opening should do a number of things. It should allow the speaker to introduce himself or herself to the audience with some sort of personal reference. In most cases, an audience will already know something about a speaker; the speaker may have been formally introduced by someone else. The opening allows the speaker to say something about himself or herself and establish a relationship with the audience.

Many speakers also use the opening to "warm up" the audience with a humorous story. Such a device works best when the point of the story can be directly related to the points that the speaker is trying to make in the speech. A funny story for its own sake may help the speaker get going, but it is not as effective as the one that is part of the speaker's message.

Most important, the opening of a speech should establish the speaker's subject and should give the audience clues to the direction in which the speaker is headed. An audience should detect in a speech a logical progression of thought, and that progression should be evident from the very beginning of the speech.

The middle of the speech should take whatever points are made—or alluded to in the opening—and expand on them. A speaker may use a variety of techniques to do this. One of the most effective is telling a story. People of all ages like to hear stories; they enjoy following narratives. The stories, of course, should support the points that the speaker is trying to make in the speech, and they should do so in a fairly obvious way. A speaker who tells a story and then tries to explain what that has to do with the points in a speech has failed in using this device.

Another useful technique for a speech writer is the striking quotation. A speaker who can use quotations from other sources can add interest, strength, and credibility to his or her own remarks. Consider these remarks from a Vietnam combat veteran who was asked to speak to a local civic club about his war experiences:

> Occasionally, I am asked to describe what it was like to be in Vietnam. From the perspective of those who lived in America during that time, Vietnam was somehow a different kind of war. It has often been pointed out that it was the first war we saw on television. To the combat soldier, however, that made little difference. We knew that all wars are essentially the same. William Tecumseh Sherman, speaking more than a hundred years ago, summed up our feelings about war when he said, "I am tired and sick of war. Its glory is all moonshine. It is only those who neither fired a shot nor heard the shrieks and groans of the wounded who cry aloud for blood, more vengeance, more desolation. War is hell."

Adapting an ancient quote to a modern purpose is another useful way to add interest to speeches. A person speaking on the environment used a biblical quote in this way.

> The Book of Ecclesiastes says there is "a time to cast away stones, and a time to gather stones together." Generations before us in this century have been casting away the stones of our environmental systems. I firmly believe that it is the charge of our generation to gather those stones together. Now is the time.

Making a striking statement is another technique that speakers can use to make a point and gain the attention of their audience. Sometimes that statement can come in the form of challenging conventional wisdom, like the following:

> Most people believe that the Golden Rule—"do unto others as you would have them do unto you"—is the simplest and best formula for good human relations. I'm here to tell you that it isn't. In fact, that formula, despite the best intentions of some people, is a disaster.

Sometimes an obscure but striking fact can gain the attention of the audience in the same way. The following is from a speech about how people can rebound from failures early in life and go on to success later:

> Back in 1919, the New York Yankees were looking for an outfielder who was also a good hitter. They thought they had a promising young man, but he managed only two hits in twenty-two at bats. The Yankees then went out and purchased Babe Ruth from the Boston Red Sox. Everybody knows what Babe Ruth accomplished, of course. But what about that young man who only got the two hits? Whatever happened to him? He decided that baseball wasn't his game after all, so he gave football a try. That game was obviously better suited to his abilities, and he became a star. In fact, many consider him to be the father of professional football. His name was George Halas, the long-time owner of the Chicago Bears.

These are just a few of the techniques that a writer can use to expand the body of a speech. Whatever techniques are used, the speech should follow a logical line—one that the audience can follow, too. If the speech goes off on tangents and never returns, the points will be lost and the audience will be dissatisfied.

The closing of a speech can be used to make the final, major point of the speech or it can offer the audience a summary of what the speaker has already said. The same rhetorical devices that you can use in any other parts of the speech—telling stories, using quotes, making striking statements—can be used to close a speech. Speech writers should remember, however, that a good speech does not need a dramatic flourish at the end. It can simply end with a story that summarizes the subject of the speech, a listing of the points already made by the speaker, or a conclusion that can be logically drawn from what the speaker has said.

Conclusion

Public relations work is mostly writing. Employers will look for people who can write to fill their public relations jobs. Public relations writing requires a versatility on the part of the writer that is demanded in few other jobs. While it is exciting and rewarding, the field of public relations is one that demands intelligence, skill, and hard work.

Points for consideration and discussion

1. At the beginning of this chapter, the author describes the field of public relations and some of the things that public relations practitioners do. From this description and what you know about the field, what is the most attractive thing about public relations work to you? What is the part of the work that you would like the least?

2. Many people who work in journalism and elsewhere have a very negative opinion of the field of public relations. Why do you think they have such an opinion?

3. A public relations practitioner has to have a wide range of knowledge and understanding to do his or her job well. What other courses in the curriculum of your college or university would you think a person should take if he or she is interested in becoming a public relations practitioner?

4. What are the advantages and disadvantages of writing a letter as opposed to making a telephone call when you want to make personal contact with someone?

5. The author says that the design and the content of a brochure or pamphlet are closely related. Try to find some examples of brochures or pamphlets and see if you think the people

who put these together did a good job of relating the design and content.

6. The author lists several techniques for writing speeches, such as adapting ancient quotes and telling personal anecdotes. Can you think of others?

Further reading

Scott M. Cutlip, Allen H. Center and Glen Broom, Effective Public Relations, 8th ed., Upper Saddle River, NJ: Prentice-Hall, 2000.

Scott M. Cutlip, The Unseen Power : Public Relations, A History, Hillsdale, N.J. : L. Erlbaum Associates, 1994.

George A. Douglas, Writing for Public Relations, Columbus, OH: Charles E. Merrill, 1980.

Richard Weiner, Professional's Guide to Public Relations Services, 6th ed. New York: American Management Association, 1988.

James J. Welsh, The Speech Writing Guide, Huntington, NY: R.E. Krieger Pub. Co., 1979.

On the Web: Many web sites are devoted to the field of public relations. Here are a couple: Public Relations Society of American, www.prsa.org; and PR Resources, www.webcom.com/impulse/prlist.html.

Chapter 9   Writing for public relations

Exercises

• *The following section contains a variety of public relations writing exercises. You should follow your instructor's directions in completing them.*

9–1 News releases

Write news releases based on the following information. Follow the directions given to you by your instructor.

YMCA

You work for the YMCA in your city, and as part of your job you have to write news releases about the organization's many recreational and educational programs. One such program is an on-going series of swimming lessons for children, young people, and adults. You have to write a release including the following information about the fall series:

Children's classes begin August 25 and are held on Mondays, Wednesdays, and Fridays. One class is held for each of five different age groups: tiny tots (ages one to three); kindergarten (ages four to six); elementary (six to nine); youth (ages ten to thirteen); and teens (ages fourteen to seventeen). All of these classes meet twice each week until November 30 on the following schedule:

Tiny tots meet on Mondays and Wednesdays from 1 p.m. until 2 p.m.

The kindergarten class meets on Mondays and Wednesdays from 2 p.m. until 3 p.m.

Elementary students meet from 3:30 p.m. until 4:30 p.m. on Mondays and Wednesdays.

The youth class runs from 4:30 p.m. until 5:30 p.m. on Mondays and Fridays

The teen class meets from 5:30 p.m. until 6:30 p.m. on Mondays and Wednesdays.

Two classes are held for adults (ages eighteen and older). One meets on Monday and Tuesday nights from 7 p.m. until 8 p.m. The other meets on Saturday from 1 p.m. until 3 p.m.

Registration will be held at the YMCA office from August 15 until August 22. Classes are limited to fifteen students each, and the registration cost is twenty dollars per child or twenty-five dollars per adult for YMCA members, thirty dollars per child or thirty-five dollars per adult for non-members.

Information: Mrs. Bertha Bucher, 774-4567.

Registration: See Mr. Bob Driver at the YMCA office.

No cash refunds for registration fees will be given. Those who register for classes but find it necessary to cancel should be sure to notify Mrs. Bucher immediately so that a credit memo may be issued for the amount of the registration fee. This memo can be applied to registration for other YMCA classes at some future date.

Department head leaves

You are public relations director for a local private hospital, Mountain

East Medical Center. During the past few months, there has been considerable friction between the hospital's board of directors and the head of the purchasing department, Bob Wilkinson. Wilkinson's tight-fisted purchasing practices have been criticized by some of the medical staff in spite of the fact that the board of directors had ordered him to cut costs by 15 percent.

Write a press release using whatever of the following information you feel is important.

Wilkinson's resignation is effective immediately. He will be replaced by the assistant head of the department, Johnny Toler, who has been with the hospital for thirteen years.

Wilkinson was a 1972 graduate of the state university's school of hospital administration. He came to Mountain East Medical Center in 1975 after working for a small rural community hospital as purchasing chief. He will take a job as a purchasing agent with the City Memorial Hospital.

Toler's background is in pharmacy. He began as an assistant druggist in the hospital pharmacy 13 years ago and was moved to the purchasing department in 1978 as an assistant after the hospital pharmacy closed. Toler's wife, Carolyn, is head of the gynecology department at MEMC. They have two children.

Hospital administrator Harry Illscott had this comment: "Bob's abilities will be greatly missed at this hospital, but I know that Johnny Toler is a person we can all depend on to do whatever is necessary to keep his department going. I have great faith in him and in this hospital."

Toler gave the following statement: "This hospital means a great deal to me and my family, and I will give my best efforts to making our purchasing department the best. I learned from a fine man–Bob Wilkinson-and I hope I can continue to build on the foundation he established."

Honorary degrees

Each year, your university awards honorary degrees to people who have made outstanding contributions to the state or to society in some way. This year two honorary degrees will be awarded at the commencement exercises, which will be held at 11 a.m. on May 14 in Memorial Coliseum.

You work part-time at the university's public relations department, and your boss asks you to write a press release announcing that the following people will be receiving honorary doctorates at the Saturday morning ceremony:

George T. Hale, sixty-three, a 1945 graduate of the university who established the state's first cable television system back in the early 1960s, will be cited for his "ability to envision the future and make it a reality for the state's telecommunications industry." When he retired from the presidency of Hale Communication, Inc., last year, the company had more than 40 percent of the cable market. Hale, a multimillionaire, has donated thousands of dollars to the development of educational television at both major universities in the state. In addition, he built a camp for physically handicapped adults on his mountain estate and sends more than 300 individuals there each spring and summer for an extensive recreation training program. Hale lives in Birmingham with his wife of thirty years, Elizabeth. They are the adoptive parents to two Korean children: Lee, twenty-one, and Ben, eighteen.

Rachel Cabanis, forty-four, an Alabama native and 1956 graduate of Goucher College, completed law school at Harvard after a twenty-year career as a legal secretary with her husband's law firm in Montgomery. Her famous book about her decision to go to law school and her experiences there, *Breaking Through,* has been lauded as "the greatest statement of one woman's choices written in this decade." It won her a Pulitzer Prize (and at least a year's worth of speaking engagements). Mrs. Cabanis, now separated from her husband, Roy Cabanis, will return to Montgomery as a full partner in another law firm. She is being honored by the university for her "honesty and integrity in making difficult choices in a complex world and succeeding despite numerous obstacles."

New plant

You work for the Holesome Donut Company of Wilmington, Delaware. Your company wants to open as many plants as possible in the Sunbelt, and company officials have decided to establish a new doughnut factory in Repton, Alabama.

Write a press release announcing plans for the complex. Include as much of the following as you feel is significant.

Repton city officials had been bargaining for the new plant for two years. At least twelve small towns in Tennessee, Georgia, and Mississippi also wanted to be the site of the new plant. Repton was chosen because of its desirable location, the low interest rates local banks offered for development, and the willingness of city officials to help build roads and sidewalks, waste disposal facilities, and recreation areas near the plant.

Repton currently has a 14 percent unemployment rate, slightly below the state average. However, its main industry, a shoe factory, is reducing its payroll by half at the beginning of next year.

Construction on the $3 million doughnut factory is slated to begin on March 31. A tentative completion date of November 15 is set, and the factory should be in full operation by the beginning of next year.

The plant will provide 700 jobs for local people, and more than 100 families are expected to be brought in to work for the company.

The plant will make and package doughnuts for shipping to all parts of Alabama.

Company president Lonny Joe Underwood, an Alabama native who once owned a grocery store in Repton, made the following comment: "We believe that the future of America, like its past, lies in small towns like this. We want to be an integral part of this community and make it just as prosperous as it should be."

Tuition decrease

You are working in the public relations department of your university. The board of trustees is about to meet to consider tuition costs for next year. One of the proposals before the board is that tuition be lowered by 10 percent for all students, in-state, out-of-state, graduate students, and undergraduates. The president of the university has already polled most of the board on this issue and has general agreement from the board on this action. Your first assignment is to prepare a news release on this action with an embargo time of 11:45 a.m. Friday, which is when the board meeting will be finished.

You can use the following information to prepare your news release:

The president's statement: "I am extremely pleased that the board has seen fit to follow our recommendations on lowering tuition costs. During the past several years we have had to raise tuition a number of times for all of our students. Out-of-state students have been particularly hard hit. For some time we have been afraid that we have been pricing ourselves out of the market, even with in-state students. With more and more people attending junior colleges and other universities in the state, we have recognized that those who want to come to this university must have some relief.

"Unfortunately, of course, the board's actions will have some negative effects on some parts of the university. Cutting tuition means a reduction in our income, and that reduction will have to be made up in other areas. No faculty or staff member will lose his or her job because of these cuts, but we will not be able to offer as many of the programs as we have in the past. The faculty and staff members whose programs will be eliminated will be absorbed into other areas of the university. I am very pleased about that. The students attending these programs, of course, must find alternatives."

Programs to be cut: Women's Studies, Ornithology Department, Arts and Sciences Honors Program, Women's Golf Team, Men's Golf Team, Human Resources Management Institute, University Hosts and Hostesses Program, and the Department of Eastern Languages; the Geology Department will be merged with the Geography Department.

Tuition costs during the last five years:
Tuition per semester

Undergrad (in-state)	$500	$550	$650	$800	$1050
Undergrad (out-of-state)	$800	$800	$100	$1200	$1400
Graduates (in-state)	$600	$650	$750	$900	$1200
Graduates (out-of-state)	$850	$1000	$1100	$1200	$1700

Each of the final figures in the table above will be reduced 10 percent for the next term.

Overall enrollment increased at the university in the last five years from 14,500 students five years ago to 16,275 this year; however, last year the total enrollment was 16,700. Applications for next semester are down, and if they continue at the current rate, a 10 percent drop in enrollment from this year's figure is anticipated.

After the news release, you are to prepare two advertisements to run in the state's major newspapers telling about the new tuition rates at the university.

Press Association

You are the public relations officer for your state's Press Association. This association counts as its members all of the state's daily and weekly newspapers, and it performs a number of services, such as a statewide advertising bureau (if an advertiser wants to advertise in all of the state's newspapers, he or she can come to the Press Association and place the ad rather than going to the individual newspapers), information about the state's newspapers, a professional training program with a local university for people who work with the state's newspapers, and a lobbying service in the state legislature on bills that affect the press.

Recently, the Press Association board of directors decided that your office should do some special promotion for National Newspaper Week. Also, the press association has recently hired some university professors to conduct a survey about newspaper leadership in your state. That survey has been completed, and the board has decided to release the results and have them serve as the basis for this promotion.

Consequently, the Press Association has called a press conference for next Monday, the first day of National Newspaper Week. The press conference is scheduled for 10 a.m. The executive director of the Press Association, Ken Billiard, and this year's president of the Press Association, Slade Luketon, editor of the *Rogersville Register*, will be there to announce the results of the survey and to talk about newspapers.

Here are some facts about the survey: The survey was conducted during a two-week period in the fall by a polling organization at the state university. The number of people surveyed was 500, randomly selected from all across the state. The margin of error for the results is plus or minus 4 percent. The survey showed the following things: Newspaper readers are a "quality audience" (they tend to be married, more highly educated than the average person, have more annual income, own their own home, and vote regularly); newspaper readership is positively linked with income (only 43 percent of those with incomes of less than $30,000 read a newspaper regularly while 96 percent of those with incomes of more than $30,000 read a newspaper regularly); and 80 percent of everyone in the state reads a newspaper regularly; on the average, two newspapers are read in each home; more than half the people in the state read a newspaper every day; newspapers were named by 70 percent of the people as the most "thorough" medium (that is, giving the most complete reports), by 65 percent as the "most trustworthy" media (as opposed to television, 25 percent, and radio, 10 percent); and about 85 percent of the people in the survey said they regularly made decisions based on newspaper advertising.

Luketon's statement, to be released at the time of the press conference: "The results of this survey show that newspapers are a trusted and useful medium. We believe that a newspaper is the best buy that an advertiser or a consumer can make in today's market. Newspapers have been hiding their lights under a bushel for a long time. We haven't bothered to tell people how good we are and what we can do for them. We hope that our attention to National Newspaper Week will help us tell this story."

Billiard's statement: "These results clearly show that newspapers are here to stay. While a few have gone out of business elsewhere, the newspapers in this state have a strong following among many people. Those newspapers plan to continue to provide the excellent service to advertisers and readers that we have provided in the past."

You are to prepare a 250-word press release incorporating these statements and summarizing the results of the survey. The press release will be handed out to other media in the state.

You are also assigned to prepare two advertisements based on the survey results. At least one should be for print and will run in the state's newspapers. The other may be for print, radio, or television.

9–2 Speeches and statements

The following situations require that you draft speeches or statements. Follow the instructions below or those given to you by your instructor.

Commencement speech

You are writing in the public relations department of a local company which manufactures computers, computer parts, and computer-related equipment. The president of your company has been asked to be the commencement speaker for this year's high school graduation ceremony. The president asks you to draft a speech for him which should be about five to ten minutes long. He says he wants to bring a hopeful message — one that says that despite a period of locally high unemployment, the future looks bright for today's high school graduates.

Kiwanis speech

Look at the press release on page 324. The president of American Southern has been invited to make a short speech to the Midville Kiwanis Club after this announcement has been made. He wants to tell them a little more about why his company chose Midville for the location of the plant. Here are some of the reasons:

• the educational system; Midville has one of the best in the state; a high percentage of students graduate from high school and go on to college (85 percent and 62 percent, respectively; the company feels that this is the kind of community that it can ask its managers and their families to live in.

• the waterways; the manufacturing process used in the new plant will require abundant sources of water; it will also require rivers that can be navigated to major shipping areas; the Blount River in Midville is such a river.

• a generally favorable business climate; the state has some of the lowest business taxes in the region and that's what prompted American Southern to look at the state for a location here in the first place.

You may also use information found in the press release.

The Kiwanis Club is a service organization. The members get involved in a lot of community projects. They will want to know about American Southern's planned involvement in the community. The president wants to tell them that community involvement is important to the company; they offer to contribute money and people to causes such as the United Way; they generally sponsor YMCA soccer, basketball, and baseball teams in the youth leagues. He wants to tell them that once American Southern is located there, they will see what the needs of the community are and try to help out.

The speech should be 750 to 1,000 words long.

College day

The Chamber of Commerce in your hometown is sponsoring "College Day," and the president has asked you to come back and tell them about your experiences in college. You'll be one of three people who have been asked to speak at the meeting that day on this subject. The president tells you that he wants you to talk purely from your own experiences. Try to give the listeners a flavor of what it was like to go to the college you attend; how you felt about going to your first class; when and how you made friends; how much money it costs; what some of the things are that they could tell their high school-age children about college.

The speech should be 500 to 750 words long.

9–3 Letters

Write letters based on the following information. Follow the directions given by your instructor.

Letter of apology

Just after Christmas, a large department store receives a letter from a woman complaining about the rudeness of the sales people in the women's ready-to-wear department. The woman is not specific about her complaints but says that she was in the store twice before Christmas and she was ignored completely once and spoken to rudely by a young sales girl the other. The department head, on seeing the letter, says that Christmas was a very busy season, the store always seemed to be crowded, and the department had to hire some temporary and untrained people to work during that time. She says she doubts that the woman would feel slighted by the regular employees. Draft a letter of at least 150 words for the store manager's signature responding to the woman's complaint.

Employee dinner

You are working in the public relations department of the home office of an insurance company. The company is planning an employee appreciation dinner for home office employees. This is the fifth year the company has had such a dinner. One of them will be named Outstanding Home Office Employee for the year. Another will receive the Community Service Award, which is given to the home office employee who has contributed the most to the community. A string quartet from the local university will provide the entertainment for the dinner, and Paul Harvey, the radio commentator and newspaper columnist, will give a speech. You should draft a letter to all the employees to encourage them to attend. The dinner will begin at 6:00 p.m. at the Hilton Hotel on April 5. Employees who plan to attend should inform their supervisors by April 1.

Fund-raising letter: Consolidated Giving fund drive

The president of your university wants to send out a letter to all employees encouraging them to support the annual community Consolidated Giving fund drive. As a member of the PR department, you have been assigned to draft the letter. The letter should make the following points (but not necessarily in this order):

- contributing to the Consolidated Giving fund is easy and convenient; employees can sign up for a monthly payroll deduction; the card to do this with will accompany the letter;
- the university has always been a major contributor to the community's Consolidated Giving fund; last year, more than $200,000 was raised from university employees also; this year's goal is $250,000;
- Consolidated Giving supports more than fifty community projects; more than 95 percent of the contributions will stay within the community;
- each department within the university has been given a goal; it is important for every individual employee to respond.

The letter should be between 150 and 200 words.

Fund-raising letter: Public radio

The manager of the local public radio station (for which you are a volunteer) has asked you to draft a letter announcing an on-air fund-raising campaign for the station. The campaign is to begin in two weeks and will run for five days. The goal is $50,000 from the listeners. The letter that you are drafting will go to people who contributed last year. These people already have supported public radio, and they know the kind of programming that public radio has: the news shows "Morning Edition" and "All Things Considered" from National Public Radio; the classical music during the weekdays and the jazz and bluegrass on the weekends; the special broadcasts of musical events in the community.

This year's fund-raising campaign is particularly important, and it's important that the station get off to a good start with early contributions from previous supporters. It's important for the following reasons:

- the station needs a new emergency generator; bad weather had knocked the station off the air a number of times;
- the station needs to purchase a new compact disk player so it can play many of the new releases, some of which are available only on compact disks;
- the cost of many of the programs that the station has to buy has gone up during the past year—some by as much as 25 to 30 percent; some of these programs may have to be dropped if the station doesn't get more money.

The letter should be between 150 and 200 words.

9–4 Pamphlets and brochures

Swimming

Below is the design for a pamphlet that the local YMCA wants to publish and distribute about the benefits of a regular swimming program. The purpose of the pamphlet is to get people to join the Y and begin swimming or doing some form of exercise. The pamphlet will be distributed to local businesses, especially those close to the Y.

The pool at the YMCA is open during the following hours: 7–9 a.m., 11 a.m.–1:30 p.m., and 4:30–7:30 p.m. on Mondays through Fridays; 3–6 p.m. on Saturdays. People who want to join the Y should come by or call, 876-0987. A year's membership costs thirty-five dollars.

Here are some of the benefits of swimming:

• it's aerobic exercise, meaning that it conditions the heart and lungs; this exercise can help prevent heart disease, the nation's number-one killer;

• it can help control body weight;

• it can help to build up stamina in a person;

• it can relieve tension; many doctors believe that exercise is a good antidote for depression and other emotional stress;

• swimming is a particularly good exercise because it is not hard on your joints; this is important especially for elderly people who are more likely to suffer from arthritis; swimming often offers a lot of relief for arthritis;

• swimming exercises almost all the major muscles of the body;

• regular exercise is good for the self-image; you just feel better about yourself.

YMCA officials also caution that people may need to consult their doctors or physicians before beginning an exercise program.

You need to write about 300 words of copy for this brochure.

Travel brochure

The Chamber of Commerce for the county next to the one you live in wants your public relations agency to design and write a short travel pamphlet about the sights in the county. This pamphlet will be distributed by the State Department of Tourism and will be found in hotels, travel bureaus, and agencies and interstate rest stops.

Write about 300 words that would persuade a traveler to visit that county. You may also want to suggest a general design for the pamphlet. Here are some facts that you can use:

Probably the major scenic attraction of the county is the four covered bridges; all have been well preserved and date back to the 1800s; they are (1) the Morton Mill Bridge, the highest covered bridge above water (about seventy-five feet), located five miles east of Smithville on Highway 6; it's 220 feet long; built in 1877 and restored in 1976; located next to the bridge was Morton Mill, where farmers brought their corn and wheat to be ground from about the time the bridge was built until the 1930s; (2) the Ensley Bridge, the oldest one in the county, built in 1821; legend has it that there was a skirmish between companies of Confederate and Union soldiers during the Civil War; several were killed, and locals say you can hear the ghosts rustling through the grass and trees at dusk; it's located on

Highway 42 west of Springtown; (3) the Swann Bridge, built in 1921, is the newest of the four bridges; it is on the Old Barterville Highway, just south of Masontown; there was also a mill located next to it, and part of that mill building has been restored and is open to tourists; (4) the Nactor Bridge was built in 1900 and is to be found in the western part of the county on Highway 69 west of Smithville; the reason it was built is unclear, although some say a mill was located next to it for a while; if that's the case, it wasn't there very long because there are no records of it. Just why covered bridges were built is not exactly clear, although the ones that were located next to mills were probably built so that farmers would have some protection from the weather while waiting to get their wheat and corn ground. Since this is a small and still mostly rural county, the covered bridges are a big part of the heritage of the people.

The county offers some other attractions. It has several lakes and recreation areas, plus Rickwill Caverns, a 280-acre state park that is open all year around. The park features a restaurant that is actually located inside the cavern; you can also explore the caverns for a small admissions fee.

Finally, every October, there is the "Old Times Festival," a week-long fair that features everything from a tennis tournament to a quilt show; special tours of the covered bridges are conducted then.

9–5 Writing for the Web

Organizing a website

Pick an organization that you are familiar with. It could be a church, fraternity, sorority, your academic department, a high school, a civic or service organization, a club — or even your family. You assignment is to develop a website for that organization.

First, ask yourself these questions: what would I want a person surfing the Internet to know about this organization? How would I want that person to feel about the organization once he or she saw the website? What would I want that person to know about the organization?

Second, re-read pages 9 to 12 in Chapter 1 of this book. Many websites are organized in a tree-like structure. That is, there are a few major organizational units, and those units are broken down into smaller and small blocks.

As you are considering the organization and textual content of the website, you must also consider what pictures and graphics that you want to use. Does the organization have a logo or symbol of some type? Are there pictures of people that are relevant?

What textual materials already exist that should be included on your website? An organization might already have a constitution, set of rules or code of ethics that you should include. If so, you won't necessarily have to retype this material (particularly if it already exists in as electronic files), but you will have to write a short introduction for it.

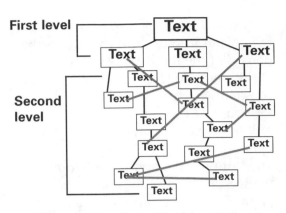

Many websites have this type of organization. The gray lines show where links can occur. Linking allows readers to move from point to point without observing the hierarchy of the text.

One organizational scheme that applies to many organizations is the following: structure, people, activities, calendar. That, however, is just one approach. Every organization is different, and each needs to be organized differently.

As a way of preparing for this assignment, you should examine closely several websites that are of interest to you or that have been set up for organizations similar to yours.

Here is what you should have to complete your assignment:

1. A statement of what you want to accomplish with the website—what you want surfers to know about your organization.

2. A structure or outline to show how the website will be organized.

3. Introductions for all of the first level and some of the second level parts of the website. (See the illustration above.)

4. A list of graphics and pictures that could be used for the website.

5. An explanation of some of the links that web surfers could use in getting to different parts of the material that you are show on the website.

10

Writers & the law

By Matthew D. Bunker

For better or worse, law is an important part of mass communication. The law is not always a threat to writers, of course. It can even be a positive force. For example, the law can help writers by enabling them to protect their work against theft by obtaining a copyright. On the other side of the coin, the law places limitations on what writers may say by allowing civil lawsuits against writers for defamation and invasion of privacy. The federal government also limits writers' freedoms when it regulates such activities as broadcasting and false advertising.

The following chapter is a brief sketch of some legal areas that might affect mass media writers. It is, of necessity, somewhat simplified. Legal matters are rarely black and white — in fact, legal doctrine is often enormously complex. Moreover, law is not stable; it is always changing and evolving, both "on the books" and through the interpretations of courts. For these reasons, writers who encounter possible legal difficulties should consult with editors, producers, and other superiors who can determine whether it is time to call the lawyers.

The First Amendment

Writers in the United States have a great deal of freedom in their work, much of which derives from the First Amendment to the United States Constitution. The First Amendment, which was ratified in 1791, provides significant protection for spoken and written communication. While the First Amendment also protects other rights, such as religious liberties, this chapter will focus on the "free speech" aspects of the amendment.

The relevant portion of the First Amendment states: "Congress shall make no law . . . abridging the freedom of speech, or of the press ... " This broad, general language leaves much to the imagination. What exactly is "the freedom of speech?" What sort of law or regulation would constitute "abridging" that freedom? Perhaps not surprisingly, these issues are still being argued about in the courts as our understanding of free speech evolves. Some would argue that the malleability of the First Amendment — the ability of the free speech principle to adapt to changed circumstances — is one of its greatest strengths. Others suggest that when the out-

Matthew D. Bunker is a former practicing attorney and teaches mass media law at the University of Alabama.

Figure 10-1

James Madison on freedom of the press

Congress shall make no law respecting an establishment of religion, or prohibiting the free
exercise thereof; or abridging freedom of speech, or of
the press; or the right of the people to peaceably
assemble, and to petition the Government for a
redress of grievances.

— First Amendment to the U.S. Constitution

Whatever facilitates a general intercourse of senti-
ments, as good roads, domestic commerce, a free
press, and particularly a circulation of newspapers
through the entire body of the people ... is favorable
to liberty.

— National Gazette, 1791

It is to the press mankind are indebted for having
dispelled the clouds which long encompassed religion, for disclosing her genuine lustre, and dissemi-
nating her salutary doctrines.

— Speech in the Virginia Assembly, 1799

lines of constitutional rights are uncertain, government may sub-
vert basic liberties.

One point worth noting immediately is that the First
Amendment states that "Congress" cannot abridge free speech. At
a first reading, that might suggest that only the federal government is limited by the First Amendment, because "Congress" is
the federal legislature. That is not the case, however. The U. S.
Supreme Court has ruled that the First Amendment applies to all
governmental authorities in the United States, including federal,
state, and local authorities. Thus, the First Amendment applies
not only to Congress, but to state legislatures, local city councils,
and even to state-funded institutions such as universities. None
of these institutions can trample on the right of free speech.

The First Amendment offers the strongest protection for speech
about politics, religion, and culture. Government can rarely stop
such speech ahead of time, called "prior restraint," or punish its
dissemination after the fact. Fully protected speech, such as
political, religious, and cultural speech, can only be restrained or
punished by government in dire circumstances. Other forms of
speech, such as advertising and indecent speech, receive less
protection, although there are still many circumstances in which
such speech is protected by the First Amendment. Finally, certain types of speech, such as obscenity, criminal threats, and the
like, are completely unprotected by the First Amendment. This
means government can regulate such "low value" speech as much
as it likes.

While the basics of free speech protection seem reasonably clear, in recent years writers and media organizations have faced novel legal assaults that have left their rights in question. A number of individuals and companies, unable to attack the media directly because of First Amendment rights, have launched peripheral or "end run" legal attacks that try to evade free speech protections. For example, companies unhappy with media coverage have sued the media based not on the information presented, but on how that information was gathered.

In a famous case, supermarket chain Food Lion sued ABC for an undercover news story that purported to show questionable food handling by Food Lion employees. Food Lion chose not to sue for defamation — that is, to challenge the truth of the story — but instead to bring claims for "fraud" and "trespass" based on the methods ABC used to get its hidden cameras into Food Lion stores. For instance, ABC producers used false resumés to gain employment in the stores.

In another widely reported case, CBS made a controversial decision not to air a story critical of the tobacco industry because of possible legal action. Once again, the potential legal claim was not based on the truth or falsity of the story, but how the information was acquired. In this case, tobacco company lawyers could have sued claiming CBS had acted improperly by persuading a former tobacco company employee to break his "confidentiality agreement" with his former employer and talk to CBS about the company. In other cases, companies have brought trademark suits against media organizations that used company symbols to parody a company's actions or provide social commentary.

The central theme of these cases is that companies that feel mistreated by the media are finding ingenious ways to punish or deter the press using legal actions that do not bring free speech protections into play. It is a disturbing trend to many who value free speech and a free press.

Defamation

Defamation is the legal term for harming someone's reputation. It is a great concern for those who work in media industries, because defaming someone can result in large damage awards against media companies, as well as the possibility of lost employment for the writers and editors who are involved. U. S. defamation law, which has evolved from English law, regards a person's reputation as a piece of his or her property, just like a house or car that person might own. If you harm an individual's reputation by stating something false about him or her, you may be required to pay that person damages, in the same way that you would have to pay to repair the person's car if you dented the fender. It is important to note that reputation refers to how others see us, not how we feel about ourselves. Not only that, but our reputations die with us. One cannot defame the dead.

Defamation consists of libel, which is written defamation, and slander, which is spoken defamation. Libel is the more serious of the two, because more people may come across a written statement over a longer period of time, causing greater harm to reputation. Many state laws treat defamation on radio or television as libel, even though it is not written. The remainder of this chapter will address only libel, rather than slander, since libel is the chief concern of writers.

Libel in the United States is generally not treated as a crime. It is, instead, often the subject of a civil suit, which is a lawsuit brought by one private person or corporation against another. Civil suits seek monetary damages rather than determinations of

---

Figure 10-2

Libelous words

Libel actions usually develop out of lack of thought or temporary mental lapses on the part of the communicator. No list of problem words and phrases is ever quite complete; but this is a beginning. Use these words and phrases with caution.

adulterer	gangster	peeping Tom
AIDS victim	gay	perjurer
alcoholic	grafter	pervert
ambulance chaser	herpes	pimp
atheist	hit-man	plagiarist
attempted suicide	homosexual	price cutter
bad morals	hypocrite	profiteer
bankrupt	illegitimate	pockets public funds
bigamist	illicit relations	prostitute
blackmail	incest	rapist
bordello	incompetent	recidivist
briber	infidelity	rogue
brothel	influence peddler	sadist
cheat	informer	scam-artist
collusion	insane	scandal monger
communist	intemperate	scoundrel
con man	intimate	seducer
convict	Jekyll-Hyde personality	short in accounts
corrupt		shyster
coward	junkie	skunk
drunk	kept woman	sneak
death-merchant	Ku Klux Klan	stuffed ballot boxes
divorced (when not)	lewd	underworld connections
drug addict or druggie	lascivious	
embezzler	liar	unethical
ex-convict	mental disease	unmarried mother
fascist	mental incompetent	unprofessional
fink	molester	unsound mind
fixed game	moral degenerate	vice den
fool	murderer	villain
fornicator	nazi	viper
fraud	paramour	
gambling house	paranoid	

guilt or prison sentences. In a civil suit, the plaintiff is the person bringing the suit, while the defendant is the person being sued. Anyone can be sued for libel, but media companies are frequent libel defendants.

The plaintiff's case

In order to succeed in a libel suit, a plaintiff must prove five points, or elements:

Publication. The plaintiff must prove that the libelous statement was published. This can be shown, for example, by proving that a libelous statement appeared in a newspaper, on a television news broadcast, in an advertisement, or as part of a public relations press release. Publication of libel can also occur when a statement is not transmitted to the general public, but to a small audience, such as the recipient of a letter.

Identification. The plaintiff in a libel suit must prove that he or she has been identified. This is relatively simple if the story contains the plaintiff's name, but there are many other ways to identify someone. For example, a photograph that is accidentally juxtaposed with a libelous story can create problems. Likewise, a detailed description of a person (age, lifestyle, occupation, and the like) can tip others off to the person's identity even if the individual's name is not mentioned in the story. Finally, writers may accidentally identify someone they do not intend to identify in a libelous story by getting a name wrong or by failing to separate the person they intend to identify from others with the same name. Remember, there are many people named Joseph Smith who are not criminals, even if one Joe Smith happens to run afoul of the law. For this reason, it is often wise to include identifying information to narrow the range of possible misidentification: middle initial, age, address, and other specifics are helpful.

Keep in mind that one can libel a corporation, which has its own legal identity and reputation. It is also possible to libel individuals by writing defamatory statements about groups, although the courts have held that the groups must be rather small in order for the individual members to bring suit successfully. For example, individual members of a five-member city commission could be libeled by a story describing how most of the commissioners took bribes, even if no names were mentioned. When groups get very large, the danger of a libel suit diminishes. For example, the statement that "all lawyers are corrupt" is about such a large group that no individual attorney could succeed in a libel suit based on the statement.

Defamation. The plaintiff must prove that the story has harmed his or her reputation. It could be that the story has made others hate the plaintiff, or perhaps simply shun him or her. Classic danger areas include false statements about: (1) political beliefs (calling someone a Nazi is not recommended); (2) illnesses, particularly mental illnesses or other diseases that might lead people to avoid the plaintiff; (3) business practices or professional competence (damage awards can be particularly large when a story affects an individual's livelihood); and, (4) criminal activity. Moreover, the use of the word "allegedly" will not shield a writer from liability. "Allegedly" simply implies that someone other than the writer is making the claim. It has no legal effect because someone who repeats a libelous statement is just as responsible for damages as the person who originated the statement.

Fault. The plaintiff must show that the writer was at fault in some way. The strength of this claim varies depending on the identity of the plaintiff, as we will see in the next section. Ordinary libel plaintiffs must prove that the writer was "negligent," or careless. A simple typographical error might warrant a finding of negligence. Plaintiffs who hold public offices or are "public figures" have a more stringent burden of proof, called actual malice. Actual malice, as will be discussed more fully later, means roughly that the writer was aware that a statement was false and published it anyway.

Damages. The plaintiff must prove that he or she was harmed in some way. Damages can be shown, for example, by a professional person whose revenues decreased after a libelous story appeared. Plaintiffs can also prove damages by demonstrating that their standing in the community was diminished by a libelous statement, even though it may be hard to place a precise dollar figure on the loss. Courts and juries can also award punitive damages to punish the defendant if the libel was particularly egregious.

Affirmative defenses

To defend against a libel suit, the defendant can try to prove that some element of the plaintiff's case is lacking. For example, the defendant might try to show that the plaintiff was not identified by the news story in question, or that no damages had accrued because of the story. In addition, libel defendants have a number of affirmative defenses that they can assert. Affirmative defenses include the following:

Truth. Truth can be an excellent defense against a libel claim, although procedurally defendants are not always required to prove truth. If a defendant can establish that a story was true, the defendant will almost certainly win the case. Libel, by definition, is a false statement about someone. It is worth keeping in mind, however, that truth is often a slippery subject. Even though a writer may be convinced a story is true, judges and juries often will not be convinced simply by a sincere statement from the witness stand. Ideally, the writer should have documents, credible eyewitnesses, or other concrete evidence that establishes the truth of claims made in a story.

Qualified privilege. Writers are generally entitled to quote from government officials acting in an official capacity, even if those officials make libelous statements. Thus, for example, a writer has a qualified privilege to quote from a police report stating that Joe Smith has been arrested for armed robbery, even if it later turns out that Smith is cleared of the charge. Similarly, statements made by judges during a trial, or by legislators while debating a bill on the floor of the legislature, are privileged. Writers asserting a qualified privilege must be able to show their reports were fair and accurate. Also, informal statements made by officials are not always protected.

Statute of limitations. Libel plaintiffs must bring suit within a specified period of time, often one or two years, depending on the state. If the plaintiff files suit after this time period, the limitations period has run out and the suit is dismissed.

Constitutional privilege. As discussed earlier, when public officials and public figures bring libel suits, their burden of proof is higher than when ordinary citizens sue for libel. In a series of cases, beginning with the landmark 1964 case of New York Times Co. v. Sullivan, the U. S. Supreme Court has ruled that public officials and public figures must prove actual malice in order to win libel damages. By using the term actual malice, the Court intends a special meaning that is not related to ill will or hatred. Instead, actual malice means that when the writer published the libelous statement, the writer either (1) knew the statement was false, or (2) had reckless disregard for the truth or falsity of the statement. As you might imagine, imposing an actual malice burden of proof on the plaintiff in a libel suit makes it very difficult to win the case. A public official or public figure plaintiff must show, in essence, that the writer knew the libelous statement was false and yet chose to publish it anyway. Or, if the writer was not sure the statement was false, at least he or she had serious doubts about it. Very few reputable news organizations operate this way, and in fact, very few plaintiffs have won libel suits when faced with having to prove actual malice on the part of the defendant.

Given this extraordinarily difficult burden of proof, it is not surprising that plaintiffs fight hard not be classified as public officials or public figures. Defendants fight equally hard to have the court declare that the plaintiff does fit into one of those categories. Often, the determination of whether the plaintiff is or is not a public official or public figure is the key to the lawsuit.

What criteria do courts use to decide if plaintiffs are public officials or public figures, and thus subject to the actual malice burden? "Public officials" are generally people who hold an elected office, or else hold a non-elective public office that gives them significant power of some sort. A good example of this second type of public official would be a public school principal. "Public figures" are famous people who have become household names (Michael Jordan is a good example). A second type of "public figure" is a person who, although not famous, nonetheless thrusts him- or herself into the public eye in order to affect some public

Figure 10-3

Chief Justice William Rehnquist on criticism of public figures

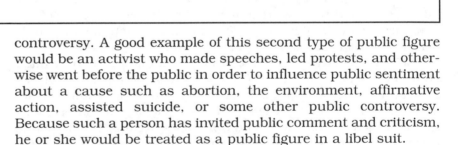

The sort of robust political debate encouraged by the First Amendment is bound to produce speech that is critical of those who hold public office or ... public figures. Such criticism, inevitably, will not always be reasoned or moderate; public figures as well as public officials will be subject to vehement, caustic, and sometimes unpleasantly sharp attacks.

– *Hustler Magazine v. Falwell, 1988*

controversy. A good example of this second type of public figure would be an activist who made speeches, led protests, and otherwise went before the public in order to influence public sentiment about a cause such as abortion, the environment, affirmative action, assisted suicide, or some other public controversy. Because such a person has invited public comment and criticism, he or she would be treated as a public figure in a libel suit.

To summarize, if a plaintiff is labeled a public official or public figure, the Supreme Court has said that he or she must prove actual malice in order to win a libel suit. In practice, this means that journalists have wider latitude to write critically about people who have achieved fame and power than about the average citizen. Such latitude clearly should not encourage irresponsible or sloppy writing or reporting, but it does provide some degree of legal protection to writers, particularly when criticizing government officials.

There are other affirmative defenses available to libel defendants, but those discussed above should give you some idea of how libel defenses work. The best way to avoid libel is not to rely on defenses, however. Instead, writers should strive for accuracy and fairness so that the possibility of a libel suit is diminished. Writers should also consult with a lawyer when it appears that a story has significant legal risks.

Privacy

In addition to libel, writers can be sued when their stories invade someone's privacy. Privacy is defined in many different ways, but most states recognize four different ways the media can invade privacy. These four methods of privacy invasion are called "torts" of privacy, which simply means that such conduct may result in a civil action. The four torts of privacy are as follows:

Publication of private facts. Writers may commit this tort when they publish some intensely personal fact or facts about an individual. Note that, unlike libel, publication of private facts consists of true information that nonetheless may result in damages against the writer. The legal harm in private facts cases is not to the reputation of the plaintiff, but instead results from shame or humiliation. The kinds of cases that have led to claims of publication of private facts have included stories about rape, sexual orientation, illnesses, and other topics that most people would prefer to keep private. Writers would do well to pause when they consider writing about this kind of information, even if they know that the information is accurate.

Fortunately for the media, suits involving publication of private facts fail. This is because courts generally protect defendants who publish personal information, as long as it is "newsworthy." Since many courts regard almost anything in which the public is interested as "newsworthy," plaintiffs who bring publication of private facts suits generally lose. Nonetheless, writers should be careful when venturing into very personal aspects of others' lives. Not only is legal liability still possible, but journalistic ethics often counsel against such revelations. For example, almost no reputable news media publish the names of rape victims, even though the Supreme Court has held that the First Amendment protects such publication.

Intrusion into seclusion. This privacy tort is committed when a writer trespasses into someone's "personal space," whether physically or by using technology. For example, using a telephoto lens to take pictures of an individual in his or her bedroom would be intrusion. Similarly, sneaking into someone's office file drawer to gather information would be legally risky. The crucial issue, courts have said, is whether the plaintiff has a reasonable expectation of privacy. That means, for example, that photographing someone in a public place would generally not be intrusion, because when people are in public they know that others can see them and that it is possible they may be photographed.

Intrusion is different from other torts we have examined so far in that it does not depend on publication of the information. If a television news crew gathers information by barging into someone's home, intrusion has taken place whether or not the footage is ever televised.

False light. False light is a privacy tort that looks very much like libel, although there are also some important differences. A writer commits false light by presenting someone as being something he or she is not — that is, portraying someone in a "false light." In a famous case that went before the U. S. Supreme Court, a reporter presented a woman in a false light by writing a story that portrayed her as "stoic" after the death of her husband. In fact, the woman was not stoic. Even worse, the reporter had never interviewed the woman, but had simply invented the interview after he went to speak with her and found she was not home.

Notice that in the example discussed above, the reporter probably did not commit libel. There is nothing defamatory about being "stoic" after a personal loss. The story would not diminish the woman's reputation. Some people might even applaud the woman's strength in the face of tragedy. Nonetheless, because the presentation is inaccurate and would be offensive to its subject, it constitutes false light. Although false light is conceptually distinct from libel, some states have refused to recognize false light as an independent tort. Even where it is recognized, it is often appended as a secondary claim to a plaintiff's libel suit. In any event, it is one more reason for writers to concentrate on accuracy and avoid statements or presentations that would tend to present someone in a false manner.

Appropriation. Appropriation is a tort that arises most frequently in the context of advertising and public relations. This tort is sometimes referred to as an individual's right of publicity. It is defined as the unauthorized use of a person's name, likeness, or other integral part of the individual's persona for commercial purposes. For example, one could not use movie star Brad Pitt's face or name in an advertisement for a product without his consent (and that would almost certainly be accompanied by a hefty endorsement fee, if he consented at all). Generally, the harm from appropriation is not so much a loss of privacy, but the loss of income celebrities suffer when an advertiser uses their persona in a campaign without their consent. It is not appropriation to use someone's name or likeness for legitimate news purposes. Thus, for example, Brad Pitt could not succeed in an appropriation suit against a newspaper or a television station that used his image in an entertainment report.

Sometimes the line is not completely clear between "commercial" uses of someone's name or likeness and other uses. In a lawsuit that involved golf sensation Tiger Woods, a company representing Woods filed an appropriation suit against a company that marketed an art print called "The Masters of Augusta." The print, created after Woods won golf's Masters Tournament in 1997, featured Woods' image. An Ohio federal court ruled against Woods' appropriation claim, holding that the print was not primarily commercial in nature and was an artistic creation protected by the First Amendment.

Aside from a celebrity's name or picture, appropriation can occur with other attributes associated with the him or her. For example, singer Bette Midler won a famous case in which a song in an automobile commercial was sung by a "sound-alike" singer who was able to mimic Midler's vocal style. Although neither Midler's name nor her likeness appeared in the commercial, her

Figure 10-4

The image of Tiger Woods

Tiger Woods sued Alabama artist Rick Rush because of the print shown here. The young golfer was seeking to retain as much commercial value for his image as possible, but a federal court in Ohio ruled that the artist had a First Amendment right to produce such a print. The artist argued that his position was the same as that of a newspaper photographer who would put a picture of Woods in a newspaper and then sell copies of the paper

distinctive singing voice was also a legally protected part of her persona that could not be taken without her consent. Thus, any time writers seek to associate an individual's persona with a product for commercial purposes, they should be certain they have that individual's permission.

Copyright

Copyright law in the United States originated as a way to protect those who produce creative works by giving them the right to a kind of commercial monopoly on their works. If creators are rewarded, the theory goes, they will work hard and create great artistic works, thus benefiting everyone. In essence, copyright law acts as an incentive for creators. Copyright protection extends not only to writers, but to composers, graphic artists, sculptors, and many other people who create original works. Copyright law is but one part of a larger area of law called "intellectual property" law, which also encompasses trademarks and patents. It is important for writers to have some basic knowledge of copyright law, not only to protect their own works, but to make certain that they are using others' works appropriately.

In order to copyright a work, the law says that the work must be "fixed in a tangible medium." This means that it must exist in some relatively permanent form. It could be a written work stored on paper or on a computer disk, a song recorded on audio tape, a painting on canvas, a motion picture on film, or a variety of other forms of expression.

An important result of the "fixed in a tangible medium" requirement is that ideas or events cannot be copyrighted. Thus, if a writer has an general idea for an advertising layout, the general idea cannot be copyrighted. Rather, only its particular expression in an individual ad could receive a copyright. The same goes for general ideas in fiction. A screenwriter could not copyright the general formula "boy meets girl, boy loses girl, boy finds girl." However, the screenwriter could protect her particular expression of that idea in a romantic comedy movie script. Moreover, events cannot be copyrighted. Anyone can write an account of the tragic explosion of the space shuttle Challenger, for example. What can be copyrighted is an individual writer's particular expression of that event — the way that writer tells the story, not the story itself.

Merely fixing words in a tangible medium does not guarantee that the result is copyrightable. Courts have held that in order to copyright a work, the work must have some minimal degree of creativity. For example, the U. S. Supreme Court held that telephone company white pages, which simply list customers' names alphabetically, were not sufficiently creative to warrant copyright protection. Nevertheless, although works must be minimally creative to be copyrighted, there is no requirement that they be good. A horrible novel is just as entitled to protection as a great work of art.

Copyright protection does not last forever. At some point, works cease to be legally protected and enter "the public domain," which means that anyone can use them. For example, filmmakers who have recently made popular movies based on works by William Shakespeare and Jane Austin are certainly not paying any royalties to the estates of those two literary geniuses. Under current U. S. law, copyright protection remains in effect for the author's life plus 70 years. When a copyright belongs to a corporation rather than to a human being, the term is either 120 years from the date of creation, or 95 years from the date of publication, whichever is shorter.

Corporate copyright ownership brings up an important point for writers: Who owns the copyright when a writer creates a work as an employee? The general answer is that the employer owns the work. Thus, for example, when a journalist writes a news story while in the employ of a newspaper, the newspaper owns the copyright to the resulting story. The same goes for a copywriter working for an advertising agency. The question of ownership becomes murkier when work is created by a "freelancer" who is not a full-time employee, but instead does individual projects, sometimes on the freelancer's own premises and equipment. The law gets complicated here, but the simplest way to avoid problems is to draw up a clear contract ahead of time specifying to whom the resulting copyrighted work will belong. Recently, freelancers have been battling major newspapers in court over the right to take free-lance contributions and place them into electronic databases such as LEXIS/NEXIS. The publishers have claimed that the electronic database versions were simply revisions of the original publication, while the freelancers have argued that use of their work in a database is a new publication that must be compensated. Again, a clear contractual agreement is the best means of assuring that writers can maintain control of their works.

The mere fact that a work is copyrighted does not someone else from using a part of the work. Clearly, wholesale theft of someone else's work would almost certainly result in a finding of copyright infringement by a court. However, the copyright law has created some breathing room for at least some uses by others that the copyright owner need not consent to. This breathing room is the idea of fair use. Fair use essentially says that although granting a copyright owner a type of monopoly serves society by encouraging creativity, the monopoly is not absolute. Society also has an interest in the wide dissemination of important works. Recently, copyright infringement cases involving on-line music services such as Napster and MP3.com have been testing the scope of fair use protection on the Internet.

How does one know whether the use of someone else's copyrighted material is a fair use? This question is not easily answered, because courts decide the matter on a case-by-case basis. In making fair use decisions, courts use four factors that they weigh to determine whether a use is fair. No single factor dictates the result. The four factors are as follows:

Nature of the copyrighted material. Courts look at the length of the original, how much effort went into creating it, and how widely available it is. Less creative works may receive less protection under this factor than those works that exhibit great creativity.

Nature of the use. Courts look with more favor on a use (borrowing) if it is for educational purposes than if it is solely to make money. For example, it's one thing for a teacher to photocopy a magazine article for classroom use, and quite another for someone to photocopy the same article and offer it for sale. A court might well grant fair use in the former case, but almost certainly would not in the latter.

Extent of the use. Courts look both at the quantity and the quality of the borrowed material. Quantity, of course, is relative to the total length of the work — it's one thing to borrow a single line from a lengthy book, and quite another if a line is borrowed from a haiku. Even if the quantity borrowed is relatively small, courts still may find that a use is not fair if the borrowed portion is the most valuable part of the work. For example, the "hook line" of a hit song may be a relatively small portion of the entire song, but it is nonetheless the heart of the work.

Commercial infringement. The final fair use factor looks at the extent to which the borrowing damages the market for the

Figure 10-5

Commonly misused trademarks

• The following are some commonly misused trademarks. These words are the names of products, but writers often use them to refer to the generic product. Each trademark is followed by a term that might be used in its place.

Autoharp, zither instrument
Baggies, plastic bag
Band-Aid, adhesive bandages
Bon Bons, ice cream
Breathalyzer, instrument to measure alcoholic content
Brillo, scouring pads
Chap Stick, lip balm
Clorox, bleach
Cool Whip, dessert topping
Dictaphone, recorder
Disposall, food waste disposer

Drano, drain opener
Ektachrome, photographic film
Fed Ex, overnight delivery service
Fig Newtons, cookies
Frisbee, flying disc
Handi-Wrap, plastic wrap
Hi-Liter, color markers
Hush Puppies, shoes
Jacuzzi, whirlpool baths
Jell-O, gelatin pudding
Kitty Litter, cat box filler
Kleenex, tissues
Kool-Aid, drinks
Krazy Glue, strong adhesives
Levi's, jeans
Lysol, disinfectant
Mace, tear gas
Naugahyde, plastic fabrics
Nautilus, weight training equipment

Pampers, diapers
Ping-Pong, table tennis
Plexiglas, see-through plastic glass
Pyrex, glassware
Reynolds Wrap, aluminum foil
Rollerblade, in-line skates
Sanforized, preshrunk fabrics
Seeing Eye, guide dogs
Sterno, cooking fuel
Tabasco, pepper sauce
Teflon, non-stick coatings
Vaseline, petroleum jelly
Vise-Grip, clamp
Windex, glass cleaner
Winnebago, motor home
Wite-Out, correction fluid
X-Acto, knife
Xerox, photocopier
Ziploc, resealable bags
Zippo, cigarette lighter

original work. Would the later work somehow serve as a substitute for the original, thus discouraging people from buying the original? If so, courts are less likely to declare the use a fair one.

Trademark

Unlike copyright law, trademark law operates to prevent consumer confusion and protect the business relationship between a company and its customers. A good trademark is worth a fortune to the company that owns it: think what would happen if all sports manufacturers were free to use the word "Nike" on their athletic gear. Consumers could not be certain they were getting the quality products they wanted, and the original trademark owner would lose a great deal of money because of the copy-cat products. Trademarks can include not only the names of products or services, but also logos, symbols, advertising catch-phrases, and other items that denote a product or service.

Because trademarks are so valuable, companies go to great lengths to protect their trademarks. One way that companies can lose their exclusive right to a trademark is by allowing its use as a generic term. For example, if the Coca-Cola Company allowed its trademark "Coke" to be used to mean any soft drink (as sometimes happens informally), the company might eventually lose the right to the trademark. The word "Coke" would have "gone generic," which means that any manufacturer could use it. The same thing would apply if the Xerox Corporation allowed its trademark "Xerox" to be used to refer to any photocopier machine. Or, perhaps even worse, if the company allowed others to use "Xerox" as a verb to denote the process of photocopying.

All of this means that writers must be careful in their use of trademark names. To maintain their trademarks and prevent generic use, companies often write sharp letters to mass media writers who misuse trademarks. Legal action by the trademark owner is possible. Companies also take out advertisements in media trade magazines, such as Columbia Journalism Review and the Quill, in order to alert writers to the proper use of their trademarks.

In order to use trademarks properly, writers must be certain to use the mark only to apply to a specific product by a specific company, not a broad class of products. The trademark should generally be used as a proper adjective followed by a generic noun, and never as a verb. For example, the word "Rollerblade" is the trademark of Rollerblade, Inc., a company that manufactures the skates. Writers should not refer to in-line skates in general as "rollerblades." Nor should writers use the verb form "rollerblading." The terms "in-line skates" or "in-line skating" would have to be used. It would be appropriate to write about "Rollerblade skates" only if the writer was referring specifically to that brand.

The International Trademark Association issues a "Trademark Checklist" that helps writers avoid such problems. The "Trademark Checklist" advises writers to use "lip balm" rather than "Chap Stik," "drain opener" rather than "Drano," "gelatin" rather than "Jell-O," and "insect traps" rather than "Roach Motel." All of the capitalized items are trademarks, as are many other common words that writers may accidentally misuse.

Advertising

Up until fairly recently, advertising was not protected by the First Amendment. The Supreme Court apparently felt that advertising (which the Court calls "commercial speech") was beneath the notice of the Constitution, which is concerned with weightier issues than ads for products and services. During the last three decades, however, the Supreme Court has gradually created greater protection for advertising. This protection is still not equal to the protection granted to political speech, for example, but it is nonetheless significant.

How can one tell whether an individual advertisement is entitled to protection under the First Amendment? First, the Supreme Court requires that the ad be truthful and in no way misleading. If the advertiser promises that its product will do something it can't do, the ad will not be protected. Second, the advertisement must relate to a legal product or service. For example, an advertisement for illegal drugs would not be protected speech.

If these two conditions are met — the ad is not misleading and concerns a legal activity — the Court requires that the advertisement be subjected to a complicated legal analysis. The gist of this analysis is that the government can regulate an advertisement if it has a very good reason for doing so — for example, protecting public health or well-being. If there is no such good reason, the ad is entitled to First Amendment protection and cannot be regulated by the government. Thus, for example, some legal limitations on alcohol advertising aimed at children have been approved because there is a sound reason for doing so. Alcohol use by minors is a serious social problem with numerous harmful consequences. On the other hand, a law that limited the distribution of advertising handbills on the street solely because they cause litter probably would not be constitutional. Litter, while unsightly, is not a serious enough problem to justify such a law.

Although First Amendment protection for advertising seems to be expanding, there is still a considerable amount of government regulation. This is particularly true for advertising that may mislead consumers, which you will recall is not protected by the First Amendment. The primary federal agency that enforces laws against misleading advertising is the Federal Trade Commission (FTC). Although other agencies at the state and federal level also enforce advertising laws, this section will concentrate on the FTC as perhaps the most important agency in this area.

The FTC is an independent federal agency with five commissioners and a large staff that polices advertisers. Because the FTC cannot look at every advertisement produced in the United States, the agency generally works by responding to complaints about ads.

To determine if an advertisement is misleading, the FTC examines three criteria. A deceptive ad is one that is (1) likely to mislead (2) a reasonable consumer (3) with a material statement or omission. This definition means, first, that a mere "likelihood" of deception is all that is required. The FTC need not prove that anyone was actually deceived, only that the ad created that likelihood. Second, the FTC looks at ads that might be deceptive from the vantage point of the "reasonable" consumer — sort of the average "Joe or Joan Sixpack." How particularly bright or naive consumers would react to the ad is irrelevant. Finally, a "material" statement or omission is something of consequence — a statement or omission that would actually cause consumers to buy the product based on the misrepresentation.

From the standpoint of those who write advertising copy, all of this means that the writer must be extraordinarily careful to describe products accurately in ad copy. Mere "puffery" (subjective claims about a product) is generally not regulated by the FTC. So, for example, claiming that a cookie is the "the most fudge-a-licious snack around," or that a sports car is "the ultimate high" would not lead to FTC action. However, inaccurate factual claims about actual performance that can be verified ("our ice cream is 100 percent fat free") could generate an FTC response.

Not only can the FTC act against misleading advertising, but competitors of companies employing misleading advertising can also bring legal actions. Recently, for example, makers of over-the-counter heartburn medications have been battling each other in court over the accuracy of various advertising claims. Competitor lawsuits are one more reason that advertisers must strive for a high degree of accuracy in their ads.

Broadcast regulation

Broadcasting is different from other media. In particular, the government has much wider latitude to regulate broadcasting than most other forms of mass media. Most broadcasting regulation is done by the Federal Communications Commission (FCC), a government agency that also regulates telephone, cable, and other communication technologies.

Broadcasting, which includes both radio and television broadcasting, is unique in that it uses the public airwaves for transmission of its messages. Because broadcasters use this scarce public resource, and because broadcasting is easily accessible to children, the United States Supreme Court has ruled that the content of broadcast media can be regulated much more intensely than the content of other media, such as newspapers or magazines. To understand what broadcasting is, it is important to understand what it is not. For example, a local television station that uses the airwaves is a broadcaster, while a cable service such as HBO, MTV, or ESPN is not. These cable services are delivered to cable companies by satellite, and then to subscribers' homes via coaxial cable. Because the cable services do not use the public airwaves, their content is less regulated than is that of the broadcasters.

Writers need to be aware that radio and television broadcasters are limited in their use of "indecent" material, and can be subject to fines or other FCC punishment if indecent matter is broadcast. For example, sexual or excretory expletives (the classic "dirty words") are considered indecent by the FCC. So are vulgar humor and sexual double entendres that hint at sexual activity without necessarily using expletives. Controversial radio personality Howard Stern has been subject to numerous FCC proceedings based on just such humor. Although such language would almost certainly be protected on cable, its broadcast over the airwaves can result in severe fines or other punishment for the broadcasting station. Under current law, 10 p.m. until 6 a.m. is considered a "safe harbor" for broadcast indecency because of the reduced likelihood that children will be in the audience during those hours.

Broadcasters are under other content limitations as well. For example, "payola," payments by record companies to programmers to play particular songs, is illegal. So is "plugola," which is a payment to broadcasters to promote particular products during their regular programming. Broadcasters are also prohibited from airing hoaxes or other programming that might frighten listeners. In addition, federal law contains a number of important provisions that ensure access to the airwaves by political candidates.

Conclusion

This chapter has touched upon a number of areas that can cause legal concerns for writers. Writers have a wonderful ally in the First Amendment. Nonetheless, legal minefields are plentiful. This need not result in abject fear for writers, but a healthy awareness of, and respect for, legal limitations is essential. Being involved in a legal proceeding can be a traumatic experience. Moreover, it can be detrimental to one's career. With care and thoughtfulness, writers can reduce the possibility that they will ever have an unpleasant encounter with the law.

Further reading

Kent R. Middleton et al., The Law of Public Communication, 5th ed., New York: Longman 2000.

Don R. Pember, Mass Media Law, New York: McGraw-Hill 2001.

Student Press Law Center, Law of the Student Press, 2nd ed. 1994.

John D. Zelezny, Communications Law, 3rd ed., Belmont, Calif.: Wadsworth 2001.

On the Web: The Reporters Committee for Freedom of the Press, www.rcfp.org, has excellent information about media law, including libel, privacy and newsgathering issues. The Freedom Forum First Amendment Center Web site, www.freedomforum.org, is devoted to First Amendment issues.

Appendix A

• The following is a standard listing of editing symbols that you should learn as quickly as possible.

Copy-editing symbols

Indent paragraph	⊐ The president said
Take out letter	occa**s**sionally
Take out word	the ~~red~~ hat
Close up words	week⌢end
Insert word	take it ^and^ run
Insert letter	encyclop^e^dia
Capitalize	<u>p</u>resident <u>w</u>ashington (cap)
Lowercase letter	the /President's cabinet (lc)
Insert hyphen	up ^-^ to ^-^ date =//
Insert period	end of the sentence⊙ ⊙
Insert quotation marks	the "orphan^"^ quote
Abbreviate	the U̶n̶i̶t̶e̶d̶ S̶t̶a̶t̶e̶s̶ U.S.
Spell out	(Gov.) Sam Smith (SP)
Use figure	(one hundred fifty-seven) 157
Spell out figure	the ③ horses (SP)
Transpose letters	pejo⁀ative (tr)
Transpose words	many|problems|difficult| (tr)
Circle any typesetting commands	(bfc) (clc)
Connect lines	the car wreck ✗✗✗✗✗✗
	injured two people

Writing for the Mass Media – Exams

Appendix B

• The exams in this section are meant to help students discover various writing, editing, and grammar problems. The key to these exams may be found in the Instructor's Manual to the book. That manual may be obtained from Allyn and Bacon or from the author of this text.

Grammar Exam

A Note to Instructors: This exam has been designed to test a student's ability to recognize correct grammatical formations. Students should be given about fifty minutes to complete the exam.

1. There_____many possible candidates. (a) is (b) are (c) was (d) none of the above

2. None_____ so blind as he who will not see. (a) is (b) are (c) either of the above (d) none of the above

3. Both of your excuses_____ plausible. (a) sound (b) sounds (c) either of the above (d) none of the above

4. Several of the members _____ absent (a) was (b) were (c) either of the above (d) none of the above

5. Few of my family really_____ me. (a) understand (b) understands (c) either of the above (d) none of the above

6. Many_____ surprised at the final score. (a) was (b) were (c) either of the above (d) none of the above

7. Some of the money_____ missing. (a) is (b) are (c) either of the above (d) none of the above

8. All of the cherries_____ ripe. (a) look (b) looks (c) either of the above (d) none of the above

9. _____ any of this evidence been presented? (a) Has (b) Have (c) either of the above (d) none of the above

10. Mary Sloan, one of the brightest girls, _____to represent the school in the contest. (a) were chosen (b) was chosen (c) have been chosen (d) none of the above

11. Baker took the handoff,_____ his way within one foot of the goal line. (a) bulldozes (b) bulldozing (c) bulldozed (d) none of the above

12. I will_____ you to swim. (a) learn (b) teach (c) either of the above (d) none of the above

13. Fans cheered as the touchdown _____(a) had been made (b) was made (c) either of the above (d) none of the above

14. The team plans_____ tomorrow. (a) to celebrate (b) to have celebrated (c) either of the above (d) none of the above

15. _____ the tickets, Mr. Selby took the children to the circus. (a) buying (b) having bought (c) either of the above (d) none of the above

16. It is customary for ranchers_____ their cattle. (a) to have branded (b) to brand (c) either of the above (d) none of the above

17. The pond has begun freezing because the temperature_____ (a) has dropped (b) dropped (c) either of the above (d) none of the above

18. They_____ Mary from the invitation. (a) accepted (b) excepted (c) either of the above (d) none of the above

19. The citizens_____ many reforms. (a) affected (b) effected (c) either of the above (d) none of the above

20. A large_____ of disgruntled men barred the entrance. (a) amount (b) number (c) either of the above (d) none of the above

21. What honor is there_____ the forty thieves? (a) among (b) between (c) either of the above (d) none of the above

22. You have_____ friends than she. (a) fewer (b) less (c) either of the above (d) none of the above

23. Is an author to blame for what the public_____ from his work? (a) infers (b) implies (c) either of the above (d) none of the above

24. My house is_____ his. (a) different from (b) different than (c) either of the above (d) none of the above

25. It is handy for everyone to know how to cook for _____. (a) hisself (b) himself (c) theirselves (d) themselves

26. The old man fascinated_____ children with stories of his adventures. (a) them
(b) us (c) we (d) none of the above

27. Between you and_____, the food could have been much better than it was. (a) I (b) me (c) she (d) none of the above

28. Why don't you get_____ some lunch? (a) your selves (b) yourselves (c) yourselfs (d) none of the above

29. Judy has just as much time to wash the dishes as_____.(a) I
(b) me (c) them (d) none of the above

30. _____ and_____ dad have the same hobbies. (a) She, her (b) Him, his
(c) Them, their (d) none of the above

31. The reforms_____ many citizens. (a) affected (b) effected (c) either of the
above (d) nonc of the above

32. The construction of fallout shelters_____ being considered. (a) was (b) were
(c) are (d) were not

33. Your contribution, in addition to other funds,_____ the success of our campaign. (a) have been assuring (b) assures (c) assure (d) were assuring

34. A combination of these methods_____ sure to succeed. (a) were (b) are
(c) is (d) none of the above

35. Each of their children_____ a different instrument. (a) have (b) play (c)
plays (d) either a or b

36. Val_____ me the very record I would have _____. (a) give,
choosed (b) gave, choosed (c) give, chosen (d) gave, chosen

37. By the time the sun_____, we had_____ nearly a hundred miles.
(a) rised, drove (b) raised, driven (c) rose, driven (d) had raised, driven

38. As I _____ there, my hat was_____ into the river. (a) sit,
blowed (b) sit, blown (c) sat, blown

39. Mr. Greenfield's lost eyeglasses_____ the object of everyone's search at
the church picnic. (a) were (b) was (c) is (d) be

40. He is one_____ broke it. (a) who (b) that (c) either of the above (d) none of
the above

41. _____ of class standing, everyone will take the test. (a) Regardless (b)
Irregardless (c) either of the above (d) none of the above

42. I must_____ find a job. (a) try and (b) try to (c) either of the above (d)
none of the above

43. The theater was_____ full by seven o'clock. (a) already
(b) all ready (c) either of the above (d) none of the above

44. The cast was_____ for the curtain call. (a) already (b) all ready (c) either
of the above (d) none of the above

45. Everything will be_____.(a) alright (b) all right (c) either of the above
(d) none of the above

46. Don't pay the bill_____ you received the goods. (a) unless (b) without
(c) but (d) whether

47. Both the doctor and his nurse_____to work on foot. (a) come (b) comes (c) has come (d) has came

48. If you_____, you would have passed easily. (a) would have took my advice (b) had taken my advice (c) had taken my advise (d) would have took my advise

49. If you will_____ me your radio, I'll fix it for you. (a) bring (b) take (c) either of the above (d) none of the above

50. Why don't you_____ someone else have a turn? (a) let (b) leave (c) either of the above (d) none of the above

51. Phil_____ and waited for his turn. (a) sit (b) set (c) sat (d) none of the above

52. Will they let_____ fellows use the pool? (a) us (b) we (c) either of the above (d) none of the above

53. Andy shot two more baskets than_____ .(a) he (b) him (c) her (d) either b or c

54. I_____ back in my chair and relaxed. (a) lie (b) laid (c) layed (d) lay

55. Dick_____ his books on a vacant seat. (a) layed (b) laid (c) lay (d) lie

56. I_____ down and waited for the dentist to call me in. (a) set (b) sat (c) sit (d) sitted

57. I lay awake, wondering where I had_____ the receipt. (a) lay (b) laid (c) lain (d) layed

58. The meat was still frozen, though I had_____ it on the stove to thaw. (a) set (b) sat (c) sit (d) layed

59. Glen_____ me the pictures he had taken at the game. (a) brung (b) bringed (c) bring (d) brought

60. I_____ past a house on which a tree had fallen. (a) drived (b) drive (c) driven (d) drove

61. The new teacher,_____ I met today, came from the South. (a) who (b) whom (c) whose (d) who's

62. The new teacher,_____ has taken Mr. Breen's position, came from the South. (a) who (b) whom (c) in formal usage, either would be correct (d) none of the above

63. Leroy feels quite_____ about getting a scholarship. (a) hopeful (b) hopefully (c) either of the above (d) none of the above

64. The detective's solution to the crime was_____ right. (a) altogether (b) all together (c) all to gather (d) all too gather

65. Henry is the_____ of the two. (a) more strong (b) strongest (c) stronger (d) most strong

66. You cannot vote_____ you are eighteen. (a) unless (b) without (c) unless being (d) without being

67. Ann_____ three lessons. (a) taking (b) taken (c) has taken (d) has took

68. Cross the streets_____.(a) careful (b) carefully (c) most careful (d) carefuller

69. There is no use feeling sorry_____ the vase is shattered on the floor. (a) for (b) as (c) besides (d) because

70. The weather looks_____ it is about to change for the better. (a) like (b) as (c) like as (d) as if

71. The girl waved goodbye,_____ her mother did not see her. (a) because (b) whether (c) but (d) since

72. It was_____ paid the bill. (a) her who (b) she who (c) her whom (d) her who

73. The two students assigned to this project are you and me. (a) Correct as is (b) you and I (c) I and you (d) me and you

74. Will you please tell me_____ I can solve this problem? (a) in as much as (b) whenever (c) with that which (d) so that

75. He walked right_____ the trap we set for him. (a) up on (b) in (c) into (d) in upon

76. She gets a larger allowance_____ she is older. (a) being that (b) because (c) being because of (d) none of the above

77. Too much food and rest_____ circus animals lazy. (a) make (b) makes (c) either of the above (d) none of the above

78. The footprints under the window_____ burglary. (a) suggests (b) suggest (c) either of the above (d) none of the above

79. Tracy Avenue is the only one of our streets that_____ from one end of the city to the other. (a) run (b) runs (c) either of the above (d) none of the above

80. The man acts as though he_____ the owner. (a) is (b) was (c) were (d) none of the above.

81. If he_____ registered later, he would have had the right classes. (a) would have (b) had (c) either of the above (d) none of the above

82. Each one of the ladies_____ splashed by the passing car. (a) was (b) were (c) are (d) a and c above are correct

83. The natives believe that noise, smoke, and dancing_____ away the evil spirits. (a) drives (b) drive (c) drived (d) none of the above

84. Please tell me_____ you_____ during the winter. (a) at where, live (b) where, live at (c) where, live (d) where at, live

85. _____ he _____ yet? (a) Have, ate (b) Has, ate (c) Have, eaten (d) Has, eaten

86. The New York Times still_____ a wide circulation. (a) has (b) have (c) either of the above (d) none of the above

87. Athletics_____ required of every student. (a) are (b) is (c) either of the above (d) none of the above

88. On the wall_____several posters. (a) was (b) were (c) is (d) either a or b

89. He failed _____ not studying. (a) due to (b) because of (c) owing to (d) because

90. She _____ her new clothes as if they made her superior to the rest of us. (a) flouted (b) flaunted (c) had flouted (d) flautened

91. He misspelled _____ words on this exam. (a) less (b) fewer (c) lesser (d) more fewer

92. Sue had_____ the cake on a kitchen chair. (a) sat (b) set (c) sitted (d) sit

93. The police will not_____ you park there. (a) leave (b) let (c) either of the above (d) none of the above

94. The gift from_____ and Bert came on Christmas Eve. (a) she (b) her (c) either of the above (d) none of the above

95. Norm and_____ share the same locker. (a) he (b) him (c) either of the above (d) none of the above

96. Ron doesn't live as far from the school as_____.(a) us (b) we (c) they (d) either b or c

97. The children amused_____ by asking riddles. (a) theirselves (b) themselves (c) either of the above (d) none of the above

98. I was sitting all by_____ in that last row. (a) my self (b) myself (c) either of the above (d) none of the above

99. Four of the committee members_____ married. (a) were (b) is (c) are (d) either a or c

100._____ and_____are good friends. (a) Her, me (b) He, she (c) She, I (d) either b or c

Diagnostic Exam

A Note to Instructors: This test has been designed to help you determine levels of understanding about knowledge and use of the language. The final ten questions on copy-editing symbols may or may not be relevant to your instruction.

1. Robert_____ from his bike.
(a) had fell (b) had fallen (c) fallen (d) falling

2. The plane with its crew_____ trying to take off now.
(a) is (b) be (c) are (d) been

3. Is the atmosphere on the moon_____ the atmosphere here on earth?
(a) different from (b) liken to (c) different than (d) as different as

4. Why is the referee so_____ the players?
(a) angry at (b) angry with (c) angry in (d) angry over

5. Why_____ allowed to join?
(a) was Ann and he (b) was Ann and him (c) were Ann and he (d) were Ann and him

6. Someone_____ turned on the automatic sprinkler.
(a) must of (b) might of (c) must to (d) must have

7. I noticed the dog as he_____ on the porch.
(a) laid (b) lay (c) lain (d) lied

8. Share the work_____ all the workers.
(a) between (b) amongst (c) betweens (d) among

9. The trunk was_____ heavy_____carry.
(a) to, to (b) too, too (c) too, to (d) to, too

10. Will you_____ come?
(a) try and (b) try to (c) be trying and (d) trying to

11. It was Ann who_____ the book on the table.
(a) layed (b) laid (c) lain (d) lay

12. The committee_____ holding an open meeting on Thursday.
(a) are (b) is (c) been (d) be

13. The new suit is_____.
(a) alright (b) al right (c) allright (d) all right

14. I am happy to_____ your offer to go to the games.
(a) accept (b) except (c) have excepted (d) having accepted

15. He spoke very_____.
(a) strange (b) stranger (c) strangest (d) strangely

16. He speaks_____.
(a) good (b) goodly (c) well (d) more better

17. She_____ finished the job in half the time.
(a) could of (b) can't of (c) could have (d) could had

18. Please_____ here.
(a) set (b) sit (c) to be set (d) to be sitted

19. He_____ a pint of milk.
(a) has drank (b) have drank (c) has drunk (d) have drunk

20. Either you or your friends_____ to blame for the accident.
(a) is (b) are (c) been (d) was

21. Neither Barbara nor Sara_____ homework on Saturdays.
(a) do (b) does (c) are doing (d) were doing

22. None of the programs_____ free from station breaks.
(a) is (b) are (c) be (d) being

23. Why are you still angry_____ me?
(a) at (b) with (c) by (d) against

24. If everyone does_____ share, we shall certainly finish on time.
(a) their (b) his or her (c) there (d) they're

25. _____, the majority of the board members promises to support
him.
(a) Regardless of who is chosen (b) Regardless of whom is chosen
(c) Irregardless of who is chosen (d) Irregardless of whom is chosen

Choose the correct style in exercise 26 through 35:
26. (a) in a baptist church
     (b) in a Baptist Church
     (c) in a baptist Church
     (d) in a Baptist church

27. (a) a Mother's Day gift
     (b) a Mother's day gift
     (c) a mother's day gift
     (d) a Mother's Day Gift

28. (a) the new Fall colors
     (b) the new fall colors
     (c) the New Fall Colors
     (d) the New fall colors

29. (a) the Brother of mayor Bates
     (b) the brother of Mayor Bates
     (c) the Brother of Mayor Bates
     (d) the brother of mayor Bates

30. (a) a brazilian pianist
    (b) a Brazilian Pianist
    (c) a Brazilian pianist
    (d) a brazilian Pianist

31. (a) at Eaton High School
    (b) at Eaton high school
    (c) at Eaton high School
    (d) at eaton high school

32. (a) on the North Side of Pine Lake
    (b) on the north Side of Pine Lake
    (c) on the North side of Pine lake
    (d) on the north side of Pine Lake

33. (a) Dodd tool company
    (b) Dodd Tool company
    (c) Dodd tool Company
    (d) Dodd Tool Company

34. (a) any Sunday in July
    (b) any sunday in july
    (c) any Sunday in july
    (d) any sunday in July

35. (a) a College Football star
    (b) a college football star
    (c) a college Football star
    (d) a College Football Star

36. Mabel asked, "To which colleges has Joan_____
    (a) applied."
    (b) applied"?
    (c) applied".
    (d) applied?"

37. _____ should be free of loose dirt and paint.
    (a) Before you paint the surface, of course,
    (b) Before you paint the surface of course,
    (c) Before you paint, the surface, of course,
    (d) Before you paint, the surface, of course

38. All the _____
    (a) students, whose reports were not handed in, failed.
    (b) students, who's reports were not handed in, failed.
    (c) students who's reports were not handed in failed.
    (d) students whose reports were not handed in failed.

39. "Before starting to write your _____ Miss Wright advised.
    (a) composition plan what you are going to say,"
    (b) composition plan what you are going to say"
    (c) composition, plan what you are going to say,"
    (d) composition, plan what you are going to say",

40. Choose the correct possessive case:
   (a) everyones friend
   (b) childrens' toys
   (c) the school's reputation
   (d) Is this your's?

41. Built in 1832,_____ is now a museum of early American life.
   (a) Dunham Tavern at 6709 Euclid Avenue in Cleveland, Ohio,
   (b) Dunham Tavern, at 6709 Euclid Avenue in Cleveland, Ohio,
   (c) Dunham Tavern, at 6709 Euclid Avenue in Cleveland Ohio
   (d) Dunahm Tavern, at 6709 Euclid Avenue in Cleveland, Ohio

42. "When you come to the stop_____"make a full stop."
   (a) sign", Dad repeated,
   (b) sign: Dad repeated,
   (c) sign," Dad repeated
   (d) sign," Dad repeated,

43. Every_____ lose his license.
   (a) motorist, who is caught speeding, should
   (b) motorist who is caught speeding should
   (c) motorist who is caught speeding; should
   (d) motorist, who is caught speeding should

44. _____ stimulates the heart and raises blood pressure.
   (a) Caffeine which is present, in both tea and coffee,
   (b) Caffeine, which is present in both tea and coffee,
   (c) Caffeine, which is present in both tea, and coffee
   (d) Caffeine, which is present in both tea and coffee

45. Choose the correct possessive case:
   (a) Barton's and McLean's store
   (b) Jack and Tom's responsibility
   (c) moons rays
   (d) editor-in-chiefs' opinion

Choose the correct spelling in exercises 46 through 65.

46. (a) fullfil (b) fulfil (c) fullfill (d) fulfill

47. (a) seperate (b) sepurate (c) separate (d) saperate

48. (a) defenitley (b) defientely (c) definitely (d) definitly

49. (a) calander (b) calandar (c) calendar (d) calender

50. (a) acomodat (b) accomadate (c) accommodate (d) accomodate

51. (a) amatur (b) ameteur (c) amateur (d) amater

52. (a) defisite (b) deficit (c) deficite (d) defecite
53. (a) auxelary (b) auxilary (c) auxiliary (d) auxilairy

54. (a) conceintous (b) consientius (c) conscientious (d) consentious

55. (a) presedent (b) presedant (c) precedent (d) precedant

56. (a) superentendent (b) superintindent (c) superintendint (d) superintendent

57. (a) recieve (b) riceive (c) ricieve (d) receive

58. (a) adaptability (b) adaptabilaty (c) adaptibility (d) adaptibilaty

59. (a) alegance (b) allegance (c) alegiance (d) allegiance

60. (a) privilege (b) priviledge (c) previledge (d) preveledge

61. (a) concede (b) conceed (c) consede (d) conceede

62. (a) elegible (b) eligible (c) elegeble (d) eligeble

63. (a) camoflauge (b) camouglauge (c) camouflage (d) camalage

64. (a) athleet (b) athlete (c) athelete (d) athilete

65. (a) genarosity (b) generosity (c) genatousity (d) generousity

66. Copy-editing symbol for "new paragraph": (a) The (b) The (c) The (d) The

67. Copy-editing symbol for "deletion":

    (a) paineted (b) paineted (c) paineted (d) paineted

68. Copy-editing symbol for "spell out a number": (a) 6 (b) 6 (c) 6 (d) 6

69. Copy-editing symbol for "use numerals": (a) forty (b) forty (c) forty (d) forty

70. Copy-editing symbol for "eliminate space":

    (a) ques tion (b) ques tion (c) ques tion (d) ques tion

71. Copy-editing symbol for "insert comma":

    (a) however (b) however (c) however (d) however

72. Copy-editing symbol for "retain copy":

    (a) never (b) never (c) never (d) never

73. Copy-editing symbol for "center copy":

    (a) John Doe (b) John Doe (c) John Doe (d) John Doe

74. Proper mark to indicate that the story does not end on this page:

   (a) More, (b) add, (c) continued, (d) ——

75. Proper mark to indicate the end of the story:

   (a) end, (b) —— (c) —30— (d) —

Appendix C

• This section contains a variety of words and phrases that often give writers difficulty. Much of this section is about words that have similar sounds but that have different meanings.

Mark Twain on using the right word

The difference between the right word and the almost right word is the difference between lightning and the lightning bug.

accede, concede
To *accede* is to agree, and is often used with the preposition *to*. To *concede* is to yield without necessarily agreeing.

access, excess
Access is a noun meaning "a way in"; *excess* is a noun meaning "too much."

adjured, abjured
To *abjure* is to renounce; to *adjure* is to entreat or to appeal.

opponent, adversary
While an *opponent* is simply on the opposite side, an *adversary* is openly hostile.

effect, affect
Effect is a change or result; *affect* is always a verb that means to pretend to feel or be, to like and display, or to produce an effect.

afterward, afterwards
Use *afterward*. The dictionary allows use of *afterwards* only as a second form.

aisle, isle
Aisle is a noun referring to a passageway; *isle*, also a noun, is a shortened form of island.

all right
That's the way to spell it. The dictionary may list *alright* as a legitimate word, but it is not acceptable in standard usage.

altar, alter
An *altar* is a tablelike platform used in a church service; to *alter* is to change something.

annual
Don't use *first* with it. If it's the first time, it's not *annual* yet.

anyone, any one
Anyone means any person as in "Did anyone come?"; *any one* refers to any member of a group as in, "Any one of you is welcome to come."

apprised, appraised
Apprise means to inform; *appraise* means to give or place a value on something.

arbitrator, mediator
An *arbitrator* is one who hears evidence from all persons concerned, then hands down a decision. A *mediator* is one who listens to arguments of both parties and tries by the exercise of reason to bring them to an agreement.

as, like
As is used to introduce clauses; *like* is a preposition and requires an object.

atheist, agnostic
An *atheist* is a person who believes there is no God. *Agnostic* is a person who believes it is impossible to know whether there is a God.

auger, augur
Auger, a noun, is a tool used for boring into wood or the ground. *Augur,* a verb, is used to imply foretelling.

adverse, averse
Adverse means unfavorable or hostile. One who is *averse* is reluctant.

biennial, biannual
Biennial means every two years. *Biannual* means twice a year and is a synonym for *semiannual.*

bloc, block
A *bloc* is a coalition of persons or a group with the same purpose or goal. Don't call it a *block,* which has some forty dictionary definitions.

bored, board
Bored is an adjective that means lacking interest; *board* is a noun that may refer to lumber or food or a group of people.

bullion, bouillon
Bullion is gold or silver in the form of bars, while *bouillon* is a clear broth for cooking or drinking.

cannon, canon
A *cannon* is a weapon; a *canon* is a law or rule. The books that are in the Bible are referred to as the canon.

Capitol, capital
Capital refers to a seat of government, generally a city. A *Capitol* is the building in which a legislature sits. It should be capitalized.

carats, karats
Carats are used to measure the weight of precious stones. *Karats* measure the ratio of gold to the mixed alloy.

censor, censer
Censor, the verb, means to prohibit or restrict; as a noun it means prohibitor. A *censer* is an incense burner or container.

chairwoman, chairperson
Under *AP Style, chairwoman* is used for a female; *chairman* is used for a man. *Chairperson* is used only when it is the organization's formal title.

cite, site
Cite is a verb that means to acknowledge; *site* is either a noun meaning location or a verb meaning to place.

complement, compliment
Complement is a noun and verb denoting completeness or the process of supplementing something. *Compliment* is a noun or verb that denotes praise or the expression of courtesy.

comprises, composes
Comprise means to contain, to include all or to embrace. It is best used in active voice, followed by an object. *Compose* means to create or put together.

conscience, conscious
Conscience is a noun which means a sense of right and wrong; *conscious* is an adjective meaning "aware."

consul, counsel
A *consul* is a diplomatic emissary residing in a foreign country, overseeing his or her country's interests there. A *counsel* is an attorney.

continuous, continual
Continuous means unbroken. *Continual* means repeated or intermittent.

couple of
You need the "of." It's never "a couple tomatoes."

demolish, destroy
They both mean "to do away with completely." You can't partially *demolish* or *destroy* something; nor is there any need to say "totally destroyed."

denotes, connotes
Denotes implies a specific meaning; *connotes* means to suggest or imply.

dietitian, dietician
Dietitian is the correct spelling for someone trained in the field of nutrition planning, not *dietician*.

different from
Things and people are *different from* each other. Don't write that they are different than each other.

difference, differential
Difference is a noun that refers to the amount by which two things are dissimilar. *Differential* is an adjective that means distinctive or making use of a difference. The two words are not interchangeable.

discomfiture, discomfort
Discomfiture is uneasiness or embarrassment, while *discomfort* is inconvenience or a physical lack of comfort.

disinterested, uninterested
Disinterested means impartial; *uninterested* refers to someone who lacks interest or doesn't care.

dissent, descent
Dissent is disagreement; it can be a verb or noun. *Descent* is the past tense of "to descend," or "to go down."

drown
Don't say someone was *drowned* unless an assailant held the victim's head under water. Just say the victim *drowned*.

due to, owing to, because of
Prefer the last. Wrong: The game was canceled *due* to rain. Stilted: *Owing* to rain, the game was canceled. Right: The game was canceled *because of* rain.

dyeing, dying
Dyeing refers to changing colors. *Dying* refers to death.

ecology, environment
They are not synonymous. *Ecology* is the study of the relationship between organisms and their environment. Right: The laboratory is studying the ecology of man and the desert. Right: There is much interest in animal ecology these days. Wrong: Even so simple an undertaking as maintaining a lawn affects ecology. Right: Even so simple an undertaking as maintaining a lawn affects our *environment*.

effective, efficient
Effective means producing an effect with emphasis on the process of doing so; *efficient* means producing results with minimum effort or time.

either
It means one or the other, not both. Wrong: There were lions on *either* side of the door. Right: There were lions on each side of the door.

elude, allude
Elude means to escape from. *Allude* means to refer to or mention.

eminent, imminent
Eminent is an adjective meaning prominent, important; *imminent* is an adjective that refers to something about to happen.

enervate, energize
To *enervate* is to drain or weaken, while to *energize* is to invigorate.

equal, equitable
Equal is an adjective that has no comparatives; that is, you cannot say that something is "more equal" or "less equal." The adjective *equitable* does have comparatives.

exaltation, exultation
Exaltation is high praise or to have raised in honor. *Exultation* is celebration or the act of rejoicing.

feign, fain
To *feign* is to pretend; *fain*, an adjective or adverb, means glad or willing.

flare, flair
Flare is a verb meaning to blaze with sudden, bright light or to burst out in anger; it is also a noun meaning a bright burst of light. *Flair* is conspicuous talent.

flout, flaunt
Flout means to mock, to scoff, or to show disdain for. *Flaunt* means to display ostentatiously.

fliers, flyers
Flier is the preferred term for both an aviator and a handbill.

Funeral service
A redundant expression. A *funeral* is a service.

gibe, jibe
To *gibe* means to taunt or sneer. *Jibe* means to shift in direction or, colloquially, to agree.

goodbye, goodby
It's *goodbye*, not *goodby*.

gourmet, gourmand
A *gourmet* is a person who is a judge of fine food; a *gourmand* is a person who eats to excess, a glutton.

grizzly, grisly
Grisly means horrifying; *grizzly* means bearish.

head up
People don't *head up* committees. They *head* them.

half-mast, half-staff
On ships and at naval stations ashore, flags are flown at *half-mast*. Elsewhere ashore, flags are flown at *half-staff*.

hopefully
One of the most commonly misused words, in spite of what the dictionary may say. *Hopefully* should be used to describe the way the subject feels— for instance, "Hopefully, I shall present the plan to the president." This means that I will be hopeful when I do it, not that I hope I will do it. And it is something else again when you attribute hope to a nonperson. You may write, "Hopefully, the war will end soon." What you mean is that you hope the war will end soon, but this is not what you are writing. What you should write is, "I hope the war will end soon."

human, humane
Human means referring to people; *humane* is an adjective meaning kindly.

hanged, hung
Hanged is used for people; *hung* refers to objects. One exception is the term "hung jury."

illicit, elicit
An *illicit* activity is illegal or unseemly. To *elicit* is to invoke.

imply, infer
Imply means to suggest or indicate; *infer* means to draw a conclusion from.

in advance of, prior to
Use "before"; it sounds more natural than either of the above.

indiscreet, indiscrete
Indiscreet means lacking prudence. *Indiscrete* means not separated into distinct parts.

it's, its
It's is the contraction of it is. *Its* is the possessive form of the word it.

leave, let
Leave alone means to depart from or cause to be in solitude. *Let alone* means to allow to be undisturbed. Wrong: The man had pulled a gun on her, but Mr. Jones intervened and talked him into leaving her alone. Right: The man had pulled a gun on her but Mr. Jones intervened and talked him into letting her alone. Right: When I entered the room, I saw that Jim and Mary were sleeping, so I decided to leave them alone.

lectern, podium, pulpit
A speaker stands behind a *lectern,* on a *podium* or *rostrum,* or in the *pulpit.*

fewer, less
Use *fewer* with countable items; use *less* with amounts or things not countable.

lie, lay
Lie is a state of being (John chose to lie in the sun), while *lay* is the action or work (He started to lay down the books). Lay needs an object to be used correctly.

like, as
Don't use *like* for *as* or *as if.* In general, use *like* to compare nouns and pronouns; use as when comparing phrases and clauses that contain a verb. Wrong: Jim blocks the linebacker like he should. Right: Jim blocks the linebacker as he should. Right: Jim blocks like a pro.

lineage, linage
Lineage means descent or ancestry. *Linage* means number of lines; newspapers often refer to the amount of advertising they have as "ad linage."

mantel, mantle
A *mantel* is a shelf, and a *mantle* is a cloak. *Mantle* also refers to a symbol of preeminence or authority.

marshall, marshal
Generally, the first form is correct only when the word is a proper noun: John Marshall. The second form is the verb form: Marilyn will marshal for forces. And the second form is the one to use for a title: fire marshal Stan Anderson, field marshal Erwin Rommel.

Mean, average, median
Use *mean* as synonymous with *average.* Both words refer to the sum of all components divided by the number of components. *Median* is the number that has as many components above it as below it.

noisome, noisy
Noisome means offensive or noxious. *Noisy* means loud or clamorous.

off, off of
When using *off,* the word *of* is not necessary. *Off* is an adequate preposition to carry the phrase.

official, officious
Something that is *official* is formally

authorized; one who is *officious* is impertinent or meddlesome.

over, more than
Over and *under* are best used for spatial relationships. When using figures, *more than* and *less than* are better choices.

palate, palette
Palate is the roof of the mouth. A *palette* is an artist's paint board.

parallel construction
Thoughts in series in the same sentence require *parallel construction.* Wrong: The union delivered demands for an increase of 10 percent in wages and to cut the work week to thirty hours. Right: The union delivered demands for an increase of thirty percent in wages and for a reduction in the work week to 30 hours.

parole, probation
Parole is the release of a prisoner before the sentence has expired, on condition of good behavior. *Probation* is the suspension of a sentence for a convicted person.

passed, enacted
Bills are *passed;* laws are *enacted.*

peacock, peahen, peafowl
Peacocks are male, *peahens* are female, and *peafowl* are both.

peddle, pedal
When selling something, you *peddle* it. When riding a bicycle or similar means of locomotion, you *pedal* it.

pour, pore
Pour means to flow in a continuous stream; *pore* means to gaze intently.

prescribe, proscribe
To *prescribe* is to order or recommend the use of. To *proscribe* is to forbid, denounce, or prohibit.

pretext, pretense
They're different, but it's a tough distinction. A *pretext* is that which is put forward to conceal a truth. Right: He was discharged for tardiness, but this was only a pretext for general incompetence. A *pretense* is a "false show," a more overt act intended to conceal personal feelings. Right: My profuse compliments were all pretense.

principal, principle
Principal means someone or something first in rank, authority, or importance. *Principle* means a fundamental truth, law, or doctrine.

prone, supine
Prone means lying face-down; *supine* means lying face-up. Prone can also mean inclined toward while supine can mean passive.

prophesy, prophecy
Prophesy is the verb; *prophecy* is the noun form.

survey, questionnaire
A *survey* is another word for a public opinion poll. A *questionnaire* is the set of questions that the respondents in the poll answer. Survey is not a synonym for questionnaire.

ravaged, ravished
To *ravage* is to wreak great destruction; to *ravish* is to abduct, rape, or carry away with emotion. Buildings and towns cannot be ravished.

raze, raise
To *raze* is to destroy or to demolish. To *raise* is to lift up or to increase.

reeked, wreaked
To *reek* is to permeate with an offensive or strong odor. To *wreak* means to punish or to avenge; it connotes destructive activity.

refute
The word connotes success in argument and almost always implies an editorial judgment. Wrong: Father Bury *refuted* the arguments of the proabortion faction.

rein, reign
The leather strap for a horse is a *rein*. *Reign* is the period a ruler is on the throne.

reluctant, reticent
If she doesn't want to act, she is *reluctant*. If she doesn't want to speak, she is *reticent*.

shut off, shut-off
Shut off is the verb form. The noun form, *shut-off*, is hyphenated.

stanch, staunch
Stanch is a verb that means to stop. *Staunch* is a adjective meaning strong.

stationary, stationery
Stationary means to stand still; *stationery* is writing paper.

suite, suit
Suite refers to a set of rooms and furniture; a *suit* refers to clothes, cards, or a law suit.

temperatures
They may get higher or lower, but they don't get warmer or cooler. Wrong: *Temperatures* are expected to warm up on Friday. Right: *Temperatures* are expected to rise on Friday.

their, there
Their is a possessive pronoun; *there* is an adverb indicating place or direction.

that, which
That tends to restrict the reader's thought and direct it in the way you want it to go; *which* is nonrestrictive, introducing a bit of subsidiary information. For instance: The lawnmower that is in the garage needs sharpening. (Meaning: We have more than one lawnmower. The one in the garage needs sharpening.) The statue that graces our entry hall is on loan from the museum. (Meaning: Of all the statues around here, the one in the entry hall is on loan.) The statue, which was in the hallway, survived the fire. (Meaning: The one statue survived the fire. It happened to be in the hallway.) Note that *which* clauses take commas, signaling that they are not essential to the meaning of the sentence.

troop, troupe
A *troop* is a group of people or animals. A *troupe* is an ensemble of actors, singers, dancers, etc.

under way,
Not underway. But don't say something got *under way*. Say it started, or began.

unique
Something that is *unique* is the only one of its kind. It can't be very unique or quite unique or somewhat unique or rather unique. Don't use it unless you really mean unique.

up
Don't use it as a verb. Wrong: The manager said he would *up* the price next week. Right: The manager said he would raise the price next week.

venerable, vulnerable
Venerable means respected because of age or attainments; *vulnerable* means open to attack or damage.

oral, verbal
Oral is used when the mouth is central to the idea, as in "He made an oral presentation." That means he spoke. *Verbal* may refer to spoken or written words.

versus, verses
Versus means to go against or abberate; *verses* are lines of poetry.

whom, who
A tough one, but generally you're safe to use *whom to* refer to someone who has been the object of an action: A 19-year-old woman, to whom the room was rented, left the window

open. *Who* is the word when the somebody has been the actor: A 19-year-old woman, who rented the room, left the window open.

whose, who's
Whose is the possessive form of who. *Who's* is the contraction of who is.

would
Be careful about using *would* when constructing a conditional past tense. Wrong: If Smith would not have had an injured foot, Thompson wouldn't have been in the lineup. Right: If Soderhelm had not had an injured foot, Thompson wouldn't have been in the lineup.

your, you're
Your is a pronoun that means "belonging to you"; *you're* is a contraction of "you are."

Appendix D

Advertising Copy Sheets

Advertising layout sheets

Copy platform sheets

Copy sheets

Radio script sheets

Television script sheets

Television storyboard sheets

The sheets in this section may be photocopied for classroom use.

Headline
Headline
Headline
Headline

SubheadSubheadSubheadSu

Body copyBody copyBody copyBody copyBody copyBody
copyBody copyBody copyBody copyBody copyBody
copyBody copyBody copyBody copyBody copyBody
copyBody copyBody copyBody copyBody copyBody
copyBody copyBody copyBody copyBody copyBody
copyBody copyBody copyBody copyBody copyBody
copyBody copyBody copyBody copyBody copyBody
copyBody copyBody copyBody copyBody copyBody
copyBody copyBody copyBody copyBody copyBody
copyBody copyBody copyBody copyBody copyBody
copyBody copyBody copyBody
copyBody copyBody copyBody
copyBody copyBody copyBody
copyBody copy

sloganslogansloganslogansloganslo-

Wright's Auto Repair, 126 Wesley Street, 555-6666

Suggested layout sheet for exercise 6-4, page 302

Pearsall Florist Shop, 222 Main Street, 643-ROSE

Suggested layout sheet for exercise 6-8, page 306

Sunshine Daycare Center, 1212 Wiltshire Blvd., 555-6666

Suggested layout sheet for exercise 6-13, page 310

COPY PLATFORM

Ad subject:

Ad problem:

Product characteristics:

Advertising objective:

Target market:

Competition:

Statement of benefit and appeal:

Creative theme:

Supportive selling points:

COPY SHEET

Product:
Medium:
Client:
Writer:

Headline:

Subhead:

Body copy:

Subhead or slogan:

Signature:

RADIO SCRIPT SHEET

Product:
Client:
Title:
Writer:
Length:

Source   Audio

TELEVISION SCRIPT SHEET

Product:
Client:
Title:
Writer:
Length:

Video   Audio

TELEVISION STORYBOARD

Product:
Client:
Title:
Writer:
Length:

Video   Audio

Frame time

Frame time

Frame time

Frame time

Frame time

Frame time

Frame time

Index

L

labels, on the web, 235
leads, 160-8
letters
    in PR, 348-353
    parts of, 350
    purposes and intents, 352

libel, affirmative defenses to, 382-4,
    proofs of 381-382
libelous words, 380
lexicon, 34
links, 241
lists, on the web, 234-5
live shots, 267
logos, 308

M

Madison, James, 378
mandatories, in ads 308
maps as graphics, 187
micro-macro story structure, 176
mini-documentary, 266
music, in ads 311

N

narrative story structure, 174
needs and appeals, 291-3, 301
news culture, 112
news releases, 343-8
news story
    characteristics of, 151-163
    organizing, 167
news values, 113
newscast, 265-6
newsletters, 353-4

O

observations, 123-4
Official Congressional Directory, 125
open-ended questions, 119-120
oral presentations, 359364
organizing a news story, 167
outdoor ads, 318

P

package stories, 267
pamphlets, 354-5
paraphrase, 118
participles 25
parts of speech, 23-4
passive voice, 25

permanency, 227
personal questions, 121
point-of-purchase ads, 318
press release,
    sample, 347
    characteristics of, 343-8
print ad, elements of 305-8
privacy, 385-387
probes, 20-1
problem-resolution, 312
product description, 296-9
prominence, 113
provoking action with ads, 313
proximity, 114
public relations, 337-364
punctuation, 26

Q

qualified privilege, 383
question and answer feature, 179
questions, types of, 119-122
quotes, 70-1
    direct,
    indirect,
    proper use of, 171-3

R

radio script sheet, 315
Reader's Guide to Periodical Literature,
    125
references, 125
Rehnquist, Chief Justice William,
    384
rewriting, 162

S

semantics, 34
sentence,
    fragment, 23
    run-on, 28, 29
    structure, 22-3
signatures, in ads 308
slice of life, 312
slogans, 308
sound bite, 266
sources, 70, 116-17
sources of information, 124-7
sound effects, 311
splash pages, 230
spelling, 29-32
spokesperson, 316-17
*Statistical Abstract of the United
    States*, 125
statute of limitations, 383

Stengel, Casey, 124-5
story boards, 316
story development, 163-173
story structure, 258-9
style, 61, 71-3, 260-4
subheads, 238-9
    in ads 307
subject-verb agreement, 24
summaries, 236-7
suspended interest features, 179

T

television script sheets, 314
testimonial, 317
that, uses of, 26
third person, use of 156
timeliness, 113, 254
trademark, 387-390
transitions, 65, 152-4
type-based graphics, 185

U

United States Government Manual,
    125

V

verbs of attribution, 154
video clips, 241
visual effects, 311-12
visual journalism, 183
voice-over, 266-7

W

5 Ws, 115-6
which, uses of, 26
Whitman, Walt, 160
Who's Who, 125
wordiness, 178
Web sites,
    expectations of, 229-231
    navigation within, 357, 376
    uses in PR, 356-9
Woods, Tiger 387
World Almanac and Book of Facts, 125
World Wide Web, see also Internet
    and Cyberspace, 225-252
wrap-around, 266
writing,
    ad copy, 302-4
    characteristics of, 2

NOTES

NOTES

NOTES

NOTES

NOTES

NOTES

NOTES

NOTES

NOTES

NOTES

NOTES

NOTES